John Skirving Ewart

The Manitoba School Question

John Skirving Ewart

The Manitoba School Question

ISBN/EAN: 9783744731805

Printed in Europe, USA, Canada, Australia, Japan

Cover: Foto ©Andreas Hilbeck / pixelio.de

More available books at **www.hansebooks.com**

THE MANITOBA SCHOOL QUESTION

BEING A COMPILATION OF

THE LEGISLATION, THE LEGAL PROCEEDINGS, THE
PROCEEDINGS BEFORE THE GOVERNOR-
GENERAL-IN-COUNCIL.

AN HISTORICAL ACCOUNT

OF THE

RED RIVER OUTBREAK IN 1869 AND 1870

ITS CAUSES, AND ITS SUCCESS

AS SHEWN IN

THE TREATY—THE MANITOBA ACT

AND A SHORT SUMMARY OF

PROTESTANT PROMISES.

JOHN S. EWART.

TORONTO:
THE COPP, CLARK COMPANY (LIMITED), PUBLISHERS.
1894.

TO

THE MEMORY OF

Alex., Archbishop of St. Boniface,

O. M. I.

MY CLIENT AND FRIEND.

THIS WORK IS INSCRIBED

In the hope that it may be of some avail in that struggle for liberty, to which was arduously given so much of his failing strength.

JOHN S. EWART.

CONTENTS.

PART I.

CHAPTER I.

	PAGE.
British North America Act	1
Manitoba Act	1
Manitoba School Acts prior to 1890	2
Manitoba School Acts, 1890	3
Act regulating the reference to the Supreme Court	5

CHAPTER II.

Barrett vs. The City of Winnipeg—

Affidavit of Dr. Barrett	6
" Archbishop Taché	7
" Dr. Bryce	8
" Mr. Hespeler	10
" Mr. Polson	10
" Mr. Sutherland	10
Judgments of Canadian Courts	11

CHAPTER III.

Logan vs. The City of Winnipeg—

Affidavit of Mr. Logan	11
" Bishop Machray	12
Letter of Mr. Howell	16
Affidavit of Mr. Hayward	16
" Mr. Polson	17
" Dr. Bryce	18
" Mr. Wood	19
" Mr. Cumberland	20
" Mr. Howell	20

CHAPTER IV.

Privy Council Judgments in both cases	21

CHAPTER V.

Petitions to Dominion Government and Actions of Government thereon—

	PAGE
Petition of members of R. C. Church, August, 1890	28
Order-in-Council 4th April, 1891	31
Petition of members of R. C. Church, 20th September, 1892	34
" Archbishop Taché, 22nd September, 1892	38
" Members of R. C. Church, November, 1892	38
Presentation of the Petitions	42
Order-in-Council, 29th December, 1892	42
Argument upon the appeal to the Governor-in-Council	51
Mr. Ewart's address	52
Manitoba not represented	67
Order-in-Council, 22nd February, 1893	68
" " 22nd April, 1893	68
" " 8th July, 1893	69
" " 31st July, 1893	70
Case submitted to Supreme Court	70
Judgments of the Supreme Court	72
Petition of R. C. Hierarchy	112
Order-in-Council, 26th July, 1894	118

PART II.

LETTERS, LECTURES AND ARTICLES ON THE SCHOOL QUESTION.

Arch. Taché—Thinks his ideas with regard to religious instruction in schools fully corroborated in England	123
" —Are the Public Schools of Manitoba the Continuation of the Protestant Schools of the same Province ?	139
Bishop Machray, Address before Anglican Synod, 1889	160
" " " " 1893	170
Rev. Dr. King, Lecture, Manitoba College	179
Rev. Principal Grant, Letter	196
Rev. Dr. Duval, Sermon	198
Mr. James Fisher, Speech in Legislative Assembly	206
Rev. Dr. Laing, Letter to Mr. Ewart	214
Mr. Ewart, Reply to Rev. Dr. Laing	217
" Open Letter to Mr. Greenway	220
" Reply to Criticisms	231
" The Week," Leading Article	241
Mr. Ewart's Reply	243
Leading Article	247
Leading Article	251
Mr. Ewart's Reply	252
Leading Article	254

	PAGE
Mr. D'Alton McCarthy, Article	256
Mr. Ewart, Isms in the Schools	263
Dr. Bryce, The Manitoba School Question	277
Mr. Le Sueur, State Education and "Isms"	284
Mr. Ewart, The Manitoba School Question	290
Mr. Joseph Martin, Extract from Address	304
Hon. Mr. Laurier, Extract from Speech	306
Mr. D'Alton McCarthy, Extract from Speech	307

PART III.

THE MANITOBA ACT AS A TREATY.—PROTESTANT PROMISES.

CAP.		
"	I.—Introductory	311
"	II.—The Red River Settlers	314
"	III.—Causes of the Outbreak—Proceed with the Surveys	316
"	IV.—Hon. Wm. McDougall at Pembina	326
"	V.—November and early December at Red River	329
"	VI.—Mr. McDougall, still at Pembina	339
"	VII.—"Call to Arms," and what came of it	341
"	VIII.—Mr. McDougall still at Pembina	345
"	IX.—Canadian Commissioners — Delegates to Ottawa — Provisional Government	347
"	X.—The Portage Escapade	355
"	XI.—The Prisoners—Thomas Scott	360
"	XII.—The Legislative Assembly	364
"	XIII.—The Red River Delegates and the List of Rights—The Manitoba Act	366
"	XIV.—Red River during the absence of Delegates	378
"	XV.—Return of one of the Delegates	382
"	XVI.—Col. Wolseley—Outrages against the Metis—Fenian Invasion	384
"	XVII.—"Rebellion" and Success	389
"	XVIII.—Protestant Promises	394

PART I.

CHAPTER I.

THE STATUTES.

The first requisite for a proper understanding of the Manitoba School Case is familiarity with the Statutes.

These are: (1) The British North America Act, (Canada's Constitutional Act); (2) The Manitoba Act, (Manitoba's Constitutional Act); (3) The Manitoba School Acts; and (4) The Act authorizing the Governor-General in Council to obtain the opinion of the Supreme Court.

The provisions of the B. N. A. Act, and the Manitoba Act, may best be understood, and appreciated, by being placed in parallel columns, the differences being indicated by italics:

BRITISH NORTH AMERICA ACT.	MANITOBA ACT.
In and for the Province the Legislature may exclusively make laws in relation to education, subject and according to the following provisions:	In and for the Province the said Legislature may exclusively make laws in relation to education, subject and according to the following provisions:
(1) Nothing in any such law shall prejudicially affect any right or privilege with respect to denominational schools which any class of persons have by law in the Province at the Union.	(1) Nothing in any such law shall prejudicially affect any right or privilege with respect to denominational schools which any class of persons have by law *or practice* in the Province at the Union.
(2) All powers, privileges and duties at the Union, by law conferred and imposed in Upper Canada on the separate schools and school trustees of the Queen's Roman Catholic subjects, shall be and the same are hereby extended to the dissentient schools of the Queen's Protestant and Roman Catholic subjects in Quebec.	
(3) *Where in any Province a system of separate or dissentient schools exists by law at the Union, or is thereafter established by the Legislature of the Province,* an appeal shall lie to the Governor-General in Council from any act or decision of any Provincial authority affecting any right or privi-	(2) An appeal shall lie to the Governor-General in Council from any Act or decision *of the Legislature of the Province*, or of any Provincial

lege of the Protestant or Roman Catholic minority of the Queen's subjects in relation to education.

authority, affecting any right or privilege of the Protestant or Roman Catholic minority of the Queen's subjects in relation to education.

(4) In case any such Provincial law as from time to time seems to the Governor-General in Council requisite for the due execution of the provisions of this section is not made, or in case any decision of the Governor-General in Council, on any appeal under this section, is not duly executed by the proper Provincial authority in that behalf, then, and in every such case, and as far only as the circumstances of each case require, the Parliament of Canada may make remedial laws for the due execution of the provisions of this section, and of any decision of the Governor-General in Council under this section.

(3) In case any such Provincial law as from time to time seems to the Governor-General in Council requisite for the due execution of the provisions of this section is not made, or in case any decision of the Governor-General in Council on any appeal under this section is not duly executed by the proper Provincial authority in that behalf then, and in every such case, and as far only as the circumstances of each case may require, the Parliament of Canada may make remedial laws for the due execution of the provisions of this section, and of any decision of the Governor-General in Council under this section.

APPLICATION OF B. N. A. ACT.

Do the provisions of the B.N.A. Act just quoted apply to Manitoba, or is Manitoba governed solely by the corresponding provisions in its own Act? This question depends upon the construction of section two of the Manitoba Act, which is as follows:

"The provisions of the B.N.A. Act, 1867, shall, except those parts thereof which are in terms made, or, by reasonable intendment, may be held to be specially applicable to, or only to affect one or more, but not the whole of the Provinces now composing the Dominion, and *except in so far as the same may be varied by this Act*, be applicable to the Province of Manitoba in the same way, and to the like extent, as they apply to the several Provinces of Canada, and as if the Province of Manitoba had been one of the Provinces originally united by the said Act."

MANITOBA SCHOOL ACTS PRIOR TO 1890.

The following is a summary of the Provincial legislation prior to the passing of the statutes of 1890—those which gave rise to the controversy. It is taken from the judgment of Mr. Justice Dubuc in the case of Barrett vs. Winnipeg.

"Under the said provisions of our constitution, the Provincial Legislature, at its first session, in 1871, passed an 'Act to establish a system of Education in this Province.' By the said Act, the Lieutenant-Governor in Council was empowered to appoint not less than ten, nor more than fourteen persons, to be a Board of Education for the province, of whom one-half were to be Protestants, and the other half Catholics; also one superintendent of Protestant schools and one superintendent of Catholic schools, who were joint secretaries of the board.

"The duties of the Board were described as follows : '1st. To make from time to time such regulations as they may think fit for the general organization of the common schools ; 2nd. To select books, maps and globes to be used in the common schools, due regard being had in such selection to the choice of English books, maps and globes for the English schools, and French for the French schools, but the authority hereby given is not to extend to the selection of books having reference to religion or morals, the selection of such being regulated by a subsequent clause of this Act ; 3rd. To alter and subdivide, with the sanction of the Lieutenant-Governor in Council, any school district established by this Act.'

"The general board was divided into two sections, and among the duties of each section we find the following : 'Each section shall have under its control and management the discipline of the schools of the section ; it shall make rules and regulations for the examination, grading and licensing of teachers, and for the withdrawal of licenses on sufficient cause ; it shall prescribe such of the books to be used in the schools of the section as have reference to religion or morals.'

"By section 13, the moneys appropriated to education by the Legislature were to be divided equally, one moiety thereof to the support of Protestant schools, the other moiety to the support of Catholic schools.

"The first board appointed by the Lieutenant-Governor in Council was composed of the Bishop of St. Boniface, the Bishop of Rupert's Land, several Catholic priests, several Protestant clergymen of various denominations, and a couple of laymen for each section.

"The said statute was amended from time to time, as the country was becoming more settled, and new exigencies arose. But the same system prevailed until the Act of last session ; the only substantial amendments were that, in 1875, the board was increased to twenty-one, twelve Protestants and nine Roman Catholics, and the moneys voted by the legislature were to be divided between Protestants and Catholics in proportion to the number of children of school age in the respective Protestant and Catholic districts.

"The more noticeable change in the system was that the denominational distinction between the Catholics and Protestants, and the independent working of the two sections became more and more pronounced under the different statutes afterwards passed. Section 27 of the Act of 1875, c. 27, says, that the establishment of a school district of one denomination shall not prevent the establishment of a school district of the other denomination in the same place.

"The same principle is carried out and somewhat extended by sections 39, 40, and 41 of the Act of 1876, c. 1.

"In 1877, by c. 12, s. 10, it was enacted that in 'no case a Protestant ratepayer shall be obliged to pay for a Catholic school, and a Catholic ratepayer for a Protestant school.'

"So it is manifest that, until the Act of last session, the school system created by the Provincial Legislature, under the provisions of the constitutional Act, was entirely based and carried on, on denominational principles as divided between Protestant and Roman Catholic schools."

Manitoba Statutes of 1890.

The following is a summary of the Statutes of 1890, taken from the same judgment :

At the last session of the legislature, two Acts were passed in respect to education. The first one, c. 37, abolished the Board of Education heretofore existing, and the office of Superintendent of Education, and creates a Department of Education which is to consist of the Executive Council or a committee thereof, appointed by the Lieutenant-Governor in Council, and also an advisory board composed of seven members, four of whom are to be appointed by the Department of Education, two by the teachers of the province, and one by the University Council. Among the duties of the advisory board is the power "To examine and authorize text books and books of reference for the use of the pupils and school libraries ; to determine the qualifications of teachers and inspectors for high and public schools ; to appoint examiners for the purpose of preparing examination papers ; to prescribe the form of religious exercises to be used in schools."

The next Act is, the Public Schools Act, c. 38. It repeals all former statutes relating to education. It enacts, amongst other things, as follows : Section 3, "All Protestant and Catholic school districts, together with all selections and appointments to office, all agreements, contracts, assessments and rate bills heretofore duly made in relation to Protestant or Catholic schools, and existing when this Act comes into force, shall be subject to the provisions of this Act." Section 4, "The term for which each school trustee holds office at the time his Act takes effect shall continue as if such term had been created by virtue of an election under this Act." Section 5, "All public schools shall be free schools, and every person in rural municipalities between the age of five and sixteen years, and in cities, towns and villages between the age of six and sixteen shall have the right to attend some school." Section 6, "Religious exercises in public schools shall be conducted according to the regulations of the advisory board. The time for such religious exercises shall be just before the closing hour in the afternoon. In case the parent or guardian of any pupil notifies the teacher that he does not wish such pupil to attend such religious exercises, then such pupil shall be dismissed before such religious exercises take place." Section 7, "Religious exercises shall be held in a public school entirely at the option of the school trustees for the district, and upon receiving written authority from the trustees, it shall be the duty of the teacher to hold such religious exercises." Section 8, "The public schools shall be entirely non-sectarian, and no religious exercises shall be allowed therein except as above provided."

It provides for the formation, alteration and union of school districts in rural municipalities and in cities, towns and villages, the election of school trustees and for levying a rate on the taxable property in each school district for school purposes.

Section 92 enacts that "the municipal council of every city, town and village shall levy and collect upon the taxable property within the municipality in the manner provided in this Act and in the Municipal and Assessment Acts, such sums as may be required by the public school trustees for school purposes."

Section 108, which provides for the legislative grant to schools, has the following sub-section : "(3) Any school not conducted according to all the provisions of this or any Act in force for the time being, or the regulations of the Department of Education, or the advisory board, shall not be deemed a public school within the meaning of the law, and shall not participate in the legislative grant." By section 143, "No teacher shall use or permit to be used as text books, any books in a model or public school, except such as are authorized by the advisory board, and no portion of the legislative grant shall be paid to any school in which unauthorized books are used." By section 179, "In cases where, before the coming into force of this Act, Catholic school districts have been established as in the next preceding section mentioned (*that is, covering the same territory as any Protestant district*), such Catholic school district shall, upon the coming into force of this Act, cease to exist, and all the assets of such Catholic school district shall belong to, and all the liabilities thereof be paid by the public school district."

ACT REGULATING REFERENCE TO SUPREME COURT.

The Act under which the reference was made by the Governor-General in Council (*infra*) is 54, 55 Vic., Cap. 25, sec. 4.

Section 37 of the said Act is hereby repealed and the following substituted therefor :

37. Important questions of law, or fact, touching provincial legislation, or the appellate jurisdiction as to Educational matters vested in the Governor-in-Council by "The British North America Act, 1867," or by any other Act or law, or touching the constitutionality of any legislation of the Parliament of Canada, or touching any other matter with reference to which he sees fit to exercise this power, may be referred by the Governor-in-Council to the Supreme Court for hearing or consideration ; and the Court shall thereupon hear and consider the same.

2. The Court shall certify to the Governor-in-Council for his information, its opinion on questions so referred, with the reasons therefor, which shall be given in like manner as in the case of a judgment upon an appeal to the said Court, and any judge who differs from the opinion of the majority shall in like manner certify his opinion and his reasons.

3. In case any such question relates to the constitutional validity of any Act which has heretofore been, or shall hereafter be passed by the legislature of any Province, or of any provision in any such Act, or in case for any reason the Government of any Province has any special interest in any such question, the Attorney-General of such Province, or in the case of the North-West Territories, the Lieutenant-Governor thereof, shall be notified of the hearing, in order that he may be heard if he thinks fit.

4. The Court shall have power to direct that any person interested, or where there is a class of persons interested, any one or more persons as representatives of such class, shall be notified of the hearing upon any reference under this section, and such persons shall be entitled to be heard thereon.

5. The Court may in its discretion request any counsel to argue the case as to any interest which is affected, and as to which counsel does not appear ; and the reasonable expenses thereby occasioned may be paid by the Minister of Finance and Receiver General out of the moneys appropriated by Parliament for expenses of litigation.

6. The opinion of the Court upon any such reference although advisory only, shall, for all purposes of appeal to Her Majesty in Council, be treated as a final judgment of the said Court between parties.

7. General rules and orders with respect to matters coming within the jurisdiction of the Court under this section may be made in the same manner, and to the same extent, as is provided by this Act with respect to other matters within its jurisdiction ; and, in particular, such rules and orders as to the judges making them seem best for the investigation of questions of fact involved in any reference thereunder.

CHAPTER. II.

BARRETT v. THE CITY OF WINNIPEG.

In November, 1890, proceedings were taken to test the validity of the Provincial Statutes above summarized. The form which the proceedings assumed was an application by Dr. Barrett (a Catholic ratepayer) to quash a by-law of the City of Winnipeg passed under the authority of the statutes. The following affidavits were filed upon that application.

Dr. Barrett's Affidavit.

I, John Kelly Barrett, of the city of Winnipeg, in the county of Selkirk and province of Manitoba, make oath and say :

1. That I am a ratepayer and resident of the city of Winnipeg aforesaid and have resided in the said city continuously for the past five years, and am a member of the Roman Catholic Church.

2. On and prior to the thirtieth day of April last a school district (having some years before been established) existed in the city of Winnipeg, and such school district was under the direction and management of the corporation known as "The School Trustees for the Catholic School District for Winnipeg, No. 1, in he province of Manitoba."

3. The said corporation has established and in operation a number of schools in Winnipeg, under the provisions of the various provincial statutes relating to schools, to one of which, namely, St. Mary's school, situate on Hargrave street, I have for three years past sent my children for instruction, which children are aged respectively ten, eight and five years.

4. That the said St. Mary's school is still in existence and the same teaching and religious exercises are continued as before the passing of the said Act, and my children still attend said school.

5. The paper writing now shown to me marked with the letter " A " is a true copy of By-law No. 480, passed by the Council of the city of Winnipeg, on the fourteenth day of July last, and the same is certified under the hand of the clerk of the said city and under the corporate seal thereof.

6. The said paper writing so certified as aforesaid was recieved by me from said clerk.

7. The paper writing now shown to me marked with the letter " B " is a true copy of By-law No. 483, passed by the Council of the City of Winnipeg on the twenty-eighth day of July last, and certified under the hand of the Clerk of the City and under the corporate seal thereof, and such paper writing was received by me from the said Clerk.

8. I am interested in the said By-law by virtue of being a resident and ratepayer of said city.

9. The paper writing now shown to me marked with the letter " C " is a true copy of a requisition sent to the Clerk of the said city by the School Trustees for the Protestant school district of Winnipeg, No. 1, on the twenty-eighth day of April last.

10. The paper writing now shown to me marked with the letter " D " is a true copy of the requisition sent to the Clerk of the said City by the School Trustees for the Catholic School district of Winnipeg, No. 1, in the Province of Manitoba, on the twenty-ninth day of April last.

11. That the estimate of all sums for the lawful purposes of the City of Winnipeg for the present year, as required to be made by section 283 of the

Municipal Act, passed in the fifty-third year of the reign of Her Majesty Queen Victoria, chapter 31, were based upon the two requisitions above referred to, copies of which are marked with the letters "C" and "D," as aforesaid, which requisitions were presented to the Council of said city on the fifth day of May last.

12. That the amounts of $75,000 and $2,550, mentioned in the said exhibits "C" and "D," respectively, form part of the sum $377,744.43 mentioned in said exhibit "A."

13. The effect of the said by-laws is that one rate is levied upon all Protestants and Roman Catholic ratepayers in order to raise the amount mentioned in said exhibits "C" and "D," and the result to individual ratepayers is that each Protestant will have to pay less than if he were assessed for Protestant schools alone, and each Roman Catholic will have to pay more than if he were assessed for Roman Catholic schools alone.

14. I have read the affidavit sworn to in this matter on the third day of October instant, by the Most Reverend Alexander Taché, and I say that so far as the same lies within my personal knowledge the same is true; as to the rest, I believe the same to be true.

ARCHBISHOP TACHE'S AFFIDAVIT.

I, Alexander Taché, of the town of St. Boniface, in the County of Selkirk, and Province of Manitoba, Archbishop of the Roman Catholic ecclesiastical Province of St. Boniface, make oath and say:

1. That I have been a resident continuously of this country since eighteen hundred and forty-five as a priest in the Roman Catholic Church, and as Bishop thereof since the year eighteen hundred and fifty, and now am the Archbishop and Metropolitan of the said Church, and I am personally aware of the truth of the matters herein alleged.

2. Prior to the passage of the Act of the Dominion of Canada, passed in the thirty-third year of the reign of Her Majesty Queen Victoria, chapter three, known as the Manitoba Act, and prior to the Order in Council issued in pursuance thereof there existed in the territory now constituting the Province of Manitoba, a number of effective schools for children.

3. These schools were denominational schools, some of them being regulated and controlled by the Roman Catholic Church, and others by various Protestant denominations.

4. The means necessary for the support of the Roman Catholic schools were supplied to some extent by school fees paid by some of the parents of the children who attended the schools and the rest was paid out of the funds of the Church, contributed by its members.

5. During the period referred to, Roman Catholics had no interest in or control over the schools of the Protestant denominations, and the members of the Protestant denominations had no interest in or control over the schools of Roman Catholics. There were no public schools in the sense of State schools. The members of the Roman Catholic Church supported the schools of their own Church for the benefit of Roman Catholic children and were not under obligation to, and did not contribute to the support of any other schools.

6. In the matter of education, therefore, during the period referred to, Roman Catholics were, as a matter of custom and practice, separate from the rest of the community, and their schools were all conducted according to the distinctive views and beliefs of Roman Catholics as herein set forth.

7. Roman Catholic schools have always formed an integral part of the work of the Roman Catholic Church. That Church has always considered the education of the children of Roman Catholic parents as coming peculiarly within its jurisdiction. The school, in the view of the Roman Catholics, is in a large measure the "children's church," and wholly incomplete and largely abortive if religious exercises be excluded from it. The church has always

insisted upon its children receiving their education in schools conducted under the supervision of the church, and upon them being trained in the doctrines and faith of the church. In education the Roman Catholic Church attaches very great importance to the spiritual culture of the child, and regards all education unaccompanied by instruction in its religious aspects as possibly detrimental and not beneficial to children. With this regard the church requires that all teachers of children shall not only be members of the church, but shall be thoroughly imbued with its principles and faith; shall recognize its spiritual authority and conform to its directions. It also requires that such books be used in the schools, with regard to certain subjects, as shall combine religious instruction with those subjects, and this applies peculiarly to all history and philosophy.

8. The Church regards the schools provided for by "The Public Schools Act," and being chapter 38 of the Statutes passed in the reign of Her Majesty Queen Victoria, in the fifty-third year of her reign, as unfit for the purpose of educating their children, and the children of Roman Catholic parents will not attend such schools. Rather than countenance such schools, Roman Catholics will revert to the system of operation previous to the Manitoba Act, and will establish, support and maintain schools in accordance with their principles and faith as aforementioned.

9. Protestants are satisfied with the system of education provided for by the said Act, "The Public Schools Act," and are perfectly willing to send their children to the schools established and provided for by the said Act. Such schools are, in fact, similar in all respects to the schools maintained by the Protestants under the legislation in force immediately prior to the passage of the said Act. The main and fundamental difference between Protestants and Catholics, with reference to education, is that while many Protestants would like education to be of a more distinctly religious character than that provided for by the said Act, yet they are content with that which is so provided and have no conscientious scruples against such a system; the Catholics, on the other hand, insist and have always insisted upon education being thoroughly permeated with religion and religious aspects; that causes and effects in science, history, philosophy and aught else should be constantly attributed to the Deity and not taught merely as causes and effects.

10. The effect of "The Public Schools Act" will be to establish public schools in every part of Manitoba where the population is sufficient for the purpose of a school, and to supply in this manner education to children free of charge to them or their parents further than their share, in common with other members of the community, of the amounts levied under and by virtue of the provisions contained in the Act.

11. In case Roman Catholics revert to the system in operation previous to the Manitoba Act, they will be brought in direct competition with the said public schools. Owing to the fact that the public schools will be maintained at public expense, and the Roman Catholic schools by school fees and private subscription, the latter will labor under serious disadvantage. They will be unable to afford inducements and benefits to children to attend such schools equal to those afforded by public schools, although they would be perfectly able to compete with any or all schools unaided by law-enforced support.

12. When in the foregoing paragraphs I speak of the faith or belief of the Roman Catholic Church, I speak not only for myself and the church in its corporate capacity, but for its members.

Rev. Dr. Bryce's Affidavit.

I, George Bryce, of the City of Winnipeg, in the County of Selkirk, in the Province of Manitoba, Professor in Manitoba College, make oath and say:

1. That I have been a resident of the Province of Manitoba since the year 1871; that I am the minister of the Presbyterian Church, longest resident in

the province; that I have been in constant communication with the officers and councils of the church, having been the first Moderator of the Synod of Manitoba and the North-west Territories of the Presbyterian Church in Canada, and I am personally aware of the truth of the matters herein alleged.

2. That I am familiar with opinions of the Presbyterians of the province in the years immediately succeeding the entrance of Manitoba into Confederation in 1870, and am aware that the Presbyterians of this province did not claim to have the church schools, which had been previously voluntarily maintained by them or by the church for them, continued to them at cost to the general public.

3. That in founding Manitoba College, in November 1881, I took over the highest class of Kildonan school as the beginning of the college, which had thus far continued a purely church institution, and for which I never heard the claim advanced that we were entitled to any consideration under the Manitoba Act; indeed, I have always considered the Government schools as entirely different and, up to 1871, unknown in the country, and for several years we did take younger students into our church college who might have been educated in the Government schools alongside.

4. That about the year 1876 a strong agitation took place in the province to have one public school system established, but this agitation failed to obtain effect in legislation.

5. The Presbyterian synod of Manitoba and the North-west Territories, which represented the largest religious body in Manitoba, passed in May, 1890, a resolution heartily approving of the Public School Act of this year, and I believe that it is approved of by the great majority of the Presbyterians of Manitoba.

6. That the Presbyterian Church is most solicitous for the religious education of all its children. It takes great care in the vows required of parents at the baptism of their children, and in urging its ministers to teach from the pulpit the duty of giving moral and religious training in the family. It is most energetic in maintaining efficient Sunday schools, which have been called the "children's church," and in requiring the attendance of the children at the church services, which is made a great means of instruction. I think it is our firm belief that this system joined with the public school system has produced, and will produce, a moral, religious and intelligent people.

7. That the Presbyterians are thus able to unite with their fellow Christians of other churches in having taught in the public schools (which they desire to be taught by Christian teachers) the subjects of a secular education, and I cannot see that there should be any conscientious objection on the part of the Roman Catholics to attend such schools, provided adequate means be provided of giving elsewhere such moral and religious training as may be desired; but on the other hand there should be many social and national advantages.

8. I believe all Presbyterians are anxious to have science, history and philosophy taught in such a manner as will intelligently recognize the divine purpose and influence in human affairs, but certainly I cannot desire to teach, as would be covered by the plea sometimes advanced that the instrumentality of evil and the deeds of bad men should be "constantly attributed to the Deity," nor do I believe the tendency of the public school as established in Manitoba at present to be toward any atheistic or irreligious goal, but that it will follow the current opinions of the settlers of Manitoba, a remarkably large number of whom are religious and intelligent.

9. That instead of it being a detriment that public schools will be "established in every part of Manitoba where the population is sufficient for the purpose of a school," it will be a benefit, as up to the present time large numbers of Roman Catholic children scattered through the general population have been able to get no education, and are in danger of growing up an illiterate class.

10. That when in the foregoing paragraphs I speak of the belief of Presbyterians, I speak simply of what I consider their belief to be, and I speak only for myself, as it is a privilege for every Presbyterian to think for himself, and to be directly responsible to God, and in my opinion the general feeling of what are known as the Protestant denominations is as I have indicated above.

Mr. Hespeler's Affidavit.

I, Wm. Hespeler, of the County of Selkirk, in the Province of Manitoba, financial agent, make oath and say:

1. That for the last seventeen years I have been a resident in the Province of Manitoba.

2. That for upwards of seven years I was a member of the Board of Education for the said province.

3. To my knowledge, His Grace Archbishop Taché, Archbishop of the Roman Catholic ecclesiastical province of Manitoba, has been a member and chairman of the Catholic section of the late Board of Education for four years, and I believe for a great deal longer.

4. That priests and leading laymen of the Roman Catholic Church were members of the Catholic section of said board, and a number of priests of said Roman Catholic Church were inspectors of schools under said board.

5. I am satisfied that the School Acts in force in this province prior to the first day of May last, were acceptable to the Roman Catholic Church.

Mr. Polson's Affidavit.

I, Alexander Polson, of the City of Winnipeg, in the County of Selkirk, in the Province of Manitoba, health inspector, make oath and say:

1. That for a period of fifty years I have been a resident in the Province of Manitoba.

2. That schools which existed prior to the Province of Manitoba entering Confederation were purely private schools and were not in any way subject to public control nor did they in any way receive public support.

3. No school taxes were collected by any authority prior to the Province of Manitoba entering Confederation, and there were no means by which any person could be forced by law to support any of said private schools. I think the only public revenue of any kind then collected was the customs duty, usually four per cent.

Mr. Sutherland's Affidavit.

I, John Sutherland, of the parish of Kildonan, in the County of Selkirk, in the Province of Manitoba, farmer, make oath and say:

1. That for the period of fifty-three years I have been a resident in the Province of Manitoba.

2. That schools which existed prior to the Province of Manitoba entering Confederation were purely private schools, and were not in any way subject to public control, nor did they in any way receive public support.

3. No school taxes were collected by any authority prior to the Province of Manitoba entering Confederation, and there were no means by which any person could be forced by law to support any of said private schools. I think the only public revenue of any kind then collected was the customs duty, usually four per cent.

JUDGMENTS IN BARRETT v. WINNIPEG.

The application to quash the By-laws was made to Mr. Justice Killam, who, on the 24th November, 1890, dismissed the application—in effect deciding that the Manitoba Statutes were valid.

An appeal was taken to the full Court, but without success. On the 2nd February, 1891, the appeal was dismissed, the Chief Justice and Mr. Justice Bain holding that the legislation was valid. Mr. Justice Dubuc, however, dissented, his opinion being that the Statutes were *ultra vires*.

A further appeal was taken to the Supreme Court of Canada, and on the 28th October, 1891, the Court (comprising five judges) unanimously held the Acts to be *ultra vires*.

A further appeal was taken to the Privy Council, and on the 30th day of July, 1892, judgment was given reversing the decision of the Supreme Court, and holding that the legislation was valid. Six judges heard the appeal, viz.: Lord Watson, Lord MacNaghten, Lord Morris, Lord Hannen, Lord Couch and Lord Shand. (The judgment is given in full below, just after the statement of the Logan v. Winnipeg case.)

CHAPTER III.

LOGAN v. THE CITY OF WINNIPEG.

In December, 1891, proceedings similar to those instituted by Dr. Barrett were taken by Mr. Alex. Logan, an Episcopalian. Upon this application the following affidavits were read:

AFFIDAVIT OF MR. LOGAN.

1. I was born in the year eighteen hundred and forty-one, at Point Douglass, in the Red River settlement in Rupert's Land, and I have always resided at the said Point Douglass, and still reside there.

2. The said Point Douglass is in the parish of St. John, in the Province of Manitoba, and is within the territorial limits of the City of Winnipeg, and I am a resident of the said city of Winnipeg and a ratepayer thereof to a large amount.

3. I am, and always have been, a member of the Church of England.

4. At the time of the union of the Province of Manitoba with Canada I was married and had two children.

5. At and for many years prior to the said union, there was a parochial denominational school of the Church of England within the said parish of St. John, and within the territory now comprised in the City of Winnipeg, and the said school was a day school conducted by teachers appointed by the Church of England Bishop of Rupert's Land, in which, and in addition to the

ordinary subjects taught in schools, the catechism of the Church of England was taught, and the pupils in said school were instructed in religious subjects according to the tenets of the Church of England.

6. The said school was continued up to, and for some time after, the union of the said Province with Canada, and the same school still exists in a modified form, and I attended said school as a pupil before said union and received my primary education therein.

7. I was well acquainted with the said Red River settlement before and after said union, and I say that at the time of said union there was established in each parish of the Church of England throughout said settlement a parochial denominational school, and in some parishes more than one of such schools, and in all such schools teachings in religions subjects according to the Church of England faith were conducted in a manner similar to the said school in the parish of St. John, and the children of English church parents attended said schools and no other schools.

8. Save and except the said English church parochial school of the parish of St. John and St. John's College, which also belonged to the Church of England, and except a private school kept by the Nuns on the property of the late William Drever, there was not at the time of said union any school or educational institution in existence within said territory now included in the city of Winnipeg.

9. The territory comprised in the City of Winnipeg covers an area of about twenty square miles.

10. The paper writing hereunto annexed and marked with the letter "A" is a certified copy of the above-mentioned by-law of the City of Winnipeg, No. 514, and said copy was received from the City clerk of the City of Winnipeg.

11. In and by said by-law a rate is levied for school purposes of four and two-tenths mills in the dollar upon all ratepayers alike, and upon persons of all religious denominations alike, and the moneys so raised are intended to be used in the support of public non-sectarian schools pursuant to the provisions of the Public Schools Act.

12. I have not yet paid my taxes for the year one thousand eight hundred and ninety-one imposed under said by-law.

13. I have at the present time three children of school age, namely, one of the age of fourteen years, one of the age of eleven years, and one of the age of five years, and I claim the right to have my children taught religious exercises in school according to the tenets of the Church of England, and I claim that such right was secured to me and other members of the Church of England, at the time of said union, by the provisions of the Manitoba Act.

14. I do not approve of the manner in which religious exercises are taught in schools where they are so taught under the provisions of the Public Schools Act, and I claim that the tax for the support of schools imposed upon me by said by-law, and pursuant to said Public Schools Act or by any other Act of the Legislature by which I am compelled to contribute for the support of schools not under the control of the Church of England, prejudicially affects my rights as a member of the Church of England, and if compelled to pay such tax I and other members of the Church of England are less able to support schools in which religious exercises and teachings in accordance with our form of worship could be conducted.

AFFIDAVIT OF BISHOP MACHRAY.

I, the Most Reverend Robert Machray, Doctor of Divinity, of the City of Winnipeg, in the Province of Manitoba, the Bishop of Rupert's Land, make oath and say:

1. In the year 1865 I was appointed by the Crown, on the recommendation of the Archbishop of Canterbury, under the sign manual of the Queen, Bishop of Rupert's Land.

2. The diocese of Rupert's Land, in 1865, covered the whole of the North-West Territories of Canada, the district of Keewatin, the present Province of Manitoba, and that portion of the westerly part of the Province of Ontario lying westerly of the height of land and running between Rat Portage and Port Arthur.

3. Subsequently the diocese was subdivided into eight bishoprics, one of which, still known as Rupert's Land, consists of the Province of Manitoba and that portion of the Province of Ontario referred to above. The whole of the said original diocese of Rupert's Land is now called the ecclesiastical province of Rupert's Land, of which I am the Metropolitan, and I am also Bishop of the smaller diocese of Rupert's Land last above described.

4. I have continued to be Bishop of the old diocese of Rupert's Land first above described, and of the smaller diocese last above described, ever since my appointment in 1865.

5. Upon my arrival in the diocese in 1865 I found there existed a great want of schools for the education of the youth, and I at once set about reorganizing St. John's College, and in 1866 I opened it for higher education, and it has so continued ever since, and I commenced as soon as I could the reorganization of the system of primary schools, of which I found most vacant.

6. I endeavored to start at least one parochial school in each parish where there was a missionary of the Church of England, and I so far succeeded in this work that with the assistance of the Church Missionary Society of the Church of England there were under my care in 1867 fourteen common parochial schools within the Red River settlement, as well as schools at the missions in Manitoba outside the settlement and missions in the interior.

7. In the year 1869 there were sixteen schools regularly organized for the teaching of boys and girls in the different parishes in the said Red River settlement, inclusive of Westbourne and Scanterbury.

8. I find that in my address to the synod of Rupert's Land, delivered on the 29th day of May, 1867, I used the following language with reference to the schools, viz. : "Passing now from the college to the common schools, I rejoice to say that there has been, during the past half year, a full opportunity for learning the elements of education—reading, writing and arithmetic—from the extreme end of the Indian settlement up to Westbourne, with the single exception of the small parish of St. Margaret's at the High Bluff, and in that parish a very creditable subscription was promised towards the salary of a master, so that I trust by another year even that blank may be supplied. And I believe the distances to be travelled to these schools are not greater than are frequently performed in our home parishes in England and Scotland. Excluding the school at Westbourne, which remains on the Church Missionary list, being about thirty-five miles beyond the settlement, we must look to the maintenance of fourteen schools. Of these, eight have hitherto been supported by the Church Missionary Society at a cost of £285 a year. The society said some time ago that this help must at once cease."

And in my charge to the synod of Rupert's Land on the 24th day of February, 1869, I used the following language : "Schools have been established in every parish, but the effort to maintain them has been a difficult one, from the larger amount now required to obtain the services of a schoolmaster and from frequent resignations. The whole question must, however, soon be grappled with. There must be some distinct regulations laid down defining the conditions under which grants from the diocesan fund are to be given, and some plan of diocesan inspection will be necessary. But before we can obtain all we could wish with our schools, I feel we must be able to provide still larger salaries and have trained teachers. How to secure such a training has been a good deal in my mind, but I do not yet see the way to the accomplishment of what I wish." And the statements therein made by me on those two occasions are, I believe, true in substance and in fact, and are given in the reports of the synod published at the time.

9. The schools which were established as above set forth continued until the establishment of public schools by the laws of Manitoba hereinafter referred to.

10. The teacher in each of these schools was under the control of the vestry and the clergyman of each parish, and in some cases there were two and even three parochial schools in one parish. The schools were opened and closed with forms of prayer, and the teacher of each of these schools was required to instruct the school every day in the Holy Scriptures, and he was required to teach the children the English Church catechism. The missionary in each parish was expected to look after such religious training and to teach the children or see that the children were taught according to the tenets of the Church of England, and the said schools were denominational schools belonging to and supported by the religious denomination of the Church of England.

11. The teachers were paid a salary, part of which was paid through me to the parish clergyman, as I was treasurer of the synod, and specially looked after the funds for the support and maintenance of these various schools.

12. The money for the payment of the school teachers and for the maintenance of the schools was procured partly from the funds of the church, partly from voluntary subscriptions and partly from fees charged the parents of the children attending the parochial schools; but as far as my knowledge goes, no child of any English Church parents was prevented from attending these schools by reason of poverty.

13. The schools above described were purely denominational schools; the teachers were members of the Church of England. I do not remember in my time any instance of a teacher who was not a member of our church, with one exception.

14. At the time of the union of this Province with Canada there were estimated to be, and I believe there were, about 12,000 Christians residing in this Province. Of these over 6,000 were Roman Catholic and nearly 5,000 were members of the Church of England, the rest were chiefly Presbyterians, with a few of other denominations.

15. The Christians residing in this Province, as above set forth, resided in what was known as the Red River settlement, and would practically be included in an area not exceeding sixty miles from the city of Winnipeg.

16. In the year 1871, when the first Public School Act of Manitoba was passed, I joined heartily with the Provincial Executive in endeavouring to carry into effect the school law then enacted, believing that under that Act public schools could be carried on giving such religious instruction as would be satisfactory to the members of the Church of England and to myself.

17. But many of the members of the Protestant section of the Board of Education did not hold the same views as myself as regards, for example, the necessity of not only reading but teaching the Bible, so that the religious instruction given in the schools was never satisfactory to me; but there was nothing in the Act preventing a more satisfactory amount of religious teaching when the members of the section became favorable to this, so I always looked forward to securing some day more satisfactory provision. With the great majority of the bishops and clergy of the Church of England, I believe that the education of the young is incomplete, and may even be hurtful if religious instruction is excluded from it.

18. The Public Schools Act passed by this Province in the year 1890 has so limited religious exercises that it is doubtful if under it there can be any religious teaching given in the schools, so that the public schools to-day are not, as regards religious teaching, as I hoped and expected they would be when the first Act was passed.

19. The religious and moral training given to children in the public schools of this Province, under sanction of the laws of this Province, is not in accordance with my views or wishes, and is not in accordance with the views of the Church of England; and consequently the present law, in taxing all

members of the Church of England, and giving no aid from the state to denominational schools, prejudicially affects the rights and privileges of the people belonging to the Church of England with respect to the denominational schools which they had by practice, and were lawfully exercising, before and at the union of this Province with Canada.

20. Before the union I, with the advice of my synod, controlled the religious training of children of persons belonging to the Church of England, in their education in the parochial schools.

21. When the first School Act was passed above mentioned, and when the first schools under that Act were established, the various parish vestries, with my sanction, permitted schools to be established and to be carried on under that Act in most, if not all, the school-houses in which the Church of England parish schools had previously been carried on, and my sanction was given in the hope and belief that at least those public schools would still give a religious and moral training such as I thought it necessary for children to receive; but if I had known then that the public schools law would permit and allow schools under that Act to be carried on without, or with as little, religious training as is now given in the public schools of this Province, I should have done what I could to resist it, and, if unable in our peculiar circumstances to continue those parochial schools, I should have encouraged the opening of such schools and the increasing of them as soon as it was permitted; and I have no doubt that if religious training is excluded from the public schools, as is threatened, this will be the policy in future of the Church of England and of myself. The re-establishment of our parish schools is merely a question of means and time.

22. If separate schools are granted to any body of Christians because of rights secured owing to practice existing prior to the union, then I claim that the Church of England is peculiarly entitled to such separate schools.

23. As far as I have had any influence, I have always endeavoured to influence public opinion and the Legislature as much as I could to have provision made for the religious training of youth, and by the Public Schools Act of 1890 I was deeply disappointed; and I believe that by that Act, if separate schools do not receive state aid as well as the schools under the Act, the children of parents of the Church of England have been prejudicially affected.

24. Before the Act of 1890 was passed, I expressed my views on the schools question, and on the rights of the people of the Church of England, under the Manitoba Act, in my charge to the synod, given on the 29th day of October, 1889, in which I used the following language: "Though we have not now any primary schools, it is not because, in view of the church, such schools are of small importance. The day was when we had a church primary school wherever we had a clergyman. That was our position when this Province was transferred to Canada, and it seems probable that the Dominion intended to recognize such efforts in the past and to protect the school interests that then existed. But our church saw such advantages in a national system of schools, and such reason to have confidence in the administration of it, that it went heartily into it, trusting that the schools would be worthy of a Christian people and give an education in which the first, namely, the religious interests of the children, would not be lost sight of. And I may say that the only reason which has led me for so many years to give up time that I could ill spare to be a member of the Board of Education has been the hope that, by conciliatory action, I might help in securing a measure of religious instruction reasonably satisfactory at once to ourselves and the other religious bodies."

25. One of the schools conducted by the Church of England as hereinbefore mentioned, was situate in the parish of St. John's, which parish now forms a part of the City of Winnipeg, and said school was situate at the time of the union of this Province with Canada in a territory which now forms part of the territory of the City of Winnipeg.

26. Said schools of the Church of England were supported in part by funds of the church, in part by voluntary subscriptions, and in part by fees voluntarily paid by members of the Church of England and by the parents and guardians of children attending such schools, and were in no way supported or aided by funds raised by general rates or taxation.

The above affidavit was made on the 3rd of December, 1891. On the 18th of the same month the following letter appeared in a Winnipeg newspaper, written by the gentleman who usually acted for the Bishop, and who was engaged upon the Logan application :

To the Editor of The Tribune.

Sir,— A good deal of controversy has been going on in reference to the attitude of the Bishop of Rupert's Land on the motion to quash the city by-law. That application was not made by or on behalf of the Church of England. It was not promoted or fostered in any way by the Bishop, and the affidavit made by him was merely a voluntary statement of facts and views which could have been forced from him under a supœna.

The judgments by the Supreme court judges in Barrett *vs.* Winnipeg point to the probable conclusion that the other denominations having schools here at the time of the transfer have equal rights with the Roman Catholics to denominational schools. If this is a good law, then at any time hereafter any member of the Church of England or any Presbyterian might quash any by-law hereafter passed, which imposed rates upon all Protestants in support of one system of schools in which religious teachings were carried on, materially different from the religious teachings carried on in the schools of the denomination at the time of the transfer.

Should this be held to be the law, then any act passed by the Local Legislature interfering with these rights would be *ultra vires*.

When our constitution makers gave the Local Legislature power to legislate as to schools, was that power made (1) subject to the rights of each of the above named three denominations to teach their peculiar religious doctrines in the schools, or was it simply limited (2) to Protestant as distinguished from Roman Catholic or (3) were there really no rights reserved to religious teachings in the public state-aided schools ?

It is certainly important to settle these principles at as early a date as possible. Only a portion can be settled by Barrett *vs.* Winnipeg, but all can be settled by the two cases being at once carried to the Privy Council.

If rights were reserved in the Manitoba act to denominations these rights are the rights of each individual ratepayer belonging to that denomination rather than the rights of the denomination, and it is as difficult to understand how a denomination or a church could set the law in motion as it is to understand how a denomination or the head of a church by any acts or omissions could deprive a ratepayer of a right conferred upon him by a statute.

Yours truly,
H. M. HOWELL.

AFFIDAVIT OF MR. HAYWARD.

I, Robert Henry Hayward, of the City of Winnipeg, in the Province of Manitoba, accountant, make oath and say :

1. I am now and have been for the past ten years a resident of the City of Winnipeg.

2. I am and have been for a number of years past a ratepayer of said city.

3. I am a member of the Church of England.

4. The religious exercises conducted in the public schools of the City of Winnipeg at the present time are those prescribed by the advisory board of the

Department of Education, pursuant to the provisions of the Public Schools Act, and such exercises consist of reading, without note or comment, of certain selections from the authorized English version of the Bible, or the Douay version of the Bible, and the use of a form of prayer.

5. The said selections from the Scriptures are not taught, but are simply read without comment, and neither the catechism of the Church of England nor any other catechism is taught in said schools, nor is any religious instruction given in said schools beyond the reading of said selections from the Bible, and the reading of said prayer.

6. The printed pamphlet now produced and shown to me and marked as exhibit "B" to this my affidavit, is a printed copy of the regulations of the said advisory board regarding religious exercises in public schools, and the said pamphlet was received from the Department of Education for the province of Manitoba.

7. I have read over the certified copy of the above mentioned by-law, which is annexed to the affidavit of Alexander Logan, sworn to herein on the 3rd day of this present month of December, and which certified copy is now produced and shown to me at the time of making this affidavit, and is marked as exhibit "A" to this affidavit.

8. In and by the said by-law a rate is levied for school purposes of $4\frac{13}{25}$ mills in the dollar upon all ratepayers of the City of Winnipeg alike, and upon members of the Church of England as well as upon members of all other religious denominations, no distinction being made in respect of religious denominations, and the moneys so raised are intended to be used in the support of public non-sectarian schools established pursuant to the provisions of the Public Schools Act.

9. The effect of said by-law is that members of the Church of England are compelled to pay a tax for the support of public non-sectarian schools in which there is not religious teaching according to the tenets of the Church of England.

10. I have one boy of school age, namely, the age of 13 years, and although I am compelled by the said by-law and by the Public Schools Act to contribute to the support of said public schools established under said Public Schools Act, I send him to a school established by the rector of the English church parish of All Saints, in the said City of Winnipeg, and under control and management of the said rector, where he receives religious instruction according to the tenets of the said Church of England in addition to ordinary school instruction, and I voluntarily pay fees for his tuition at said school, and I do not send him to any of the said public schools.

11. There are many other boys in the said City of Winnipeg sent by their parents, who are resident ratepayers of the City of Winnipeg and members of the Church of England, to the said All Saints' School, for reasons which I verily believe are similar to my own.

AFFIDAVIT OF MR. POLSON.

I, Alexander Polson, of the City of Winnipeg, in the County of Selkirk, in the Province of Manitoba, License Inspector, make oath and say :

1. That for a period of fifty years I have been a resident of the Province of Manitoba.

2. That schools which existed prior to the Province of Manitoba entering Confederation were, so far as the people were concerned, purely private schools, and were not in any way subject to public control, nor did they in any way receive public support. Attendance at such schools was voluntary, and only the parents or guardians who had children attending school paid any fees. There was no law or statute as to schools. The schools were under the direction of the clergy or the governing bodies of one of the three churches, the Roman Catholic, the Church of England and the Presbyterian.

3. No school taxes or rates were collected by any authority prior to the Province of Manitoba entering Confederation, and there were no means by which any person could be forced by law to support any of said private schools.

4. I think the only public revenue of any kind then collected was the customs duty of four per cent., but none of this was for schools. There were no municipal or school rates, and no direct taxes of any kind levied, whether by assessment on property, income tax, or otherwise.

AFFIDAVIT OF REV. DR. BRYCE.

I, George Bryce, of the City of Winnipeg, in the County of Selkirk, in the Province of Manitoba, Professor in Manitoba College, make oath and say:

1. That I have been a resident of the Province of Manitoba since the year 1871. That I am the minister of the Presbyterian Church longest resident in the Province; that I have been in constant communication with the officers and councils of the church, having been the first Moderator of the Synod of Manitoba and the North-west Territories of the Presbyterian Church in Canada, and I am personally aware of the truth of the matters herein alleged.

2. That I am familiar with the opinions of the Presbyterians of the Province in the years immediately succeeding the entrance of Manitoba into Confederation in 1870, and am aware that the Presbyterians of this Province did not claim to have the church schools, which had been previously voluntarily maintained by them or by the church for them, continued to them at cost to the general public, but were willing to support a public school system.

3. That in founding Manitoba College, in November, 1871, I took over the highest class of Kildonan school as the beginning of the college, which had thus far continued a purely church institution, and for which I never heard the claim advanced that we were entitled to any consideration under the Manitoba Act; indeed, I always considered the Government schools as entirely different, and, up to 1871, unknown in the country, and for several years we did take younger students into our church college, who might have been educated in the Government schools alongside.

4. That about the year 1876 a strong agitation took place in the Province to have one public school system established, but this agitation failed to obtain effect in legislation.

5. The Presbyterian Synod of Manitoba and the North-west Territories, which represents the largest religious body in Manitoba, passed in May, 1890, a resolution heartily approving of the Public School Act of this year, and I believe it is approved of by the great majority of the Presbyterians of Manitoba.

6. That the Presbyterian Church is most solicitous for the religious education of all its children. It takes great care in the vows required of parents at the baptism of their children, and in urging its ministers to teach from the pulpit the duty of giving moral and religious training in the family. It is most energetic in maintaining efficient Sunday schools, which have been called the "children's church," and in requiring the attendance of the children at the church services, which are made a great means of instruction. I think it is our firm belief that this system, joined with the public school system, has produced and will produce a moral, religious and intelligent people.

7. I believe that the views of a large number of the Presbyterians in this Province are represented by the following extracts from a public address delivered by the Rev. J. M. King, D.D., Principal of Manitoba College, on the 31st day of October, 1889. After giving reasons in opposition to purely secular schools, Dr. King proceeds:—"At the opposite extreme there is a system of separate or denominational schools, such as to some extent now obtains in this Province, a system under which not only is religious instruction given, but the distinctive doctrines and practices of individual churches are

taught. Does the continuance and extension of this system promise a solution of the educational difficulty? By no means. Less injurious probably in its operation, it is even more indefensible in principle than the one which has been so freely criticised. First, it is in direct violation of the principle of the separation of church and state. It is unnecessary, indeed it would be quite irrelevant to argue this principle here. It is that on which, rightly or wrongly, the state with us is constituted. I do not understand it to mean that the state may not have regard to religious considerations, such as it shows when it enforces the observance of the Sabbath rest, or that it may not employ religious sanctions, as it does when in its courts of law it administers an oath in the name of God; but I do not understand it to mean that the state is neither to give material aid to the operations of the church in any of its branches, nor to interfere with its liberties. Each, while necessarily influencing the other, has its own distinctive sphere, and must bear all the responsibilities of action within that sphere . . . . Second, the system of separate or sectarian schools operates injuriously on the well-being of the state. However useful it may be to the church or churches adopting it, enabling them to keep their youth well in hand and to preserve them from any danger to faith and morals which might result from daily contact with those of a different creed, it is in that measure hurtful to the unity and therefore to the strength of the state. It occasions a line of cleavage in society, the highest interests of which demand that it should as far as possible be one. It perpetuates distinctions, and almost necessarily gives rise to distinctions which are at once a reproach and a peril . . . . Surely the state should not, unless compelled to do so, lend the law and the authority support of public moneys to a system of education which so injuriously affects its unity and therefore its stability and well-being . . . . But if a purely secular system of education is deemed in the highest degree objectionable, and a denominational or sectarian system only less objectionable, what is it proposed to establish in their place? I answer, a system of public, unsectarian, but not non-religious schools. It is admitted on all hands that the main work of the school ought to be instruction in the various secular branches. Its primary aim is to fit those in attendance for the active duties of life. But as not inconsistent with this aim, rather as in a higher degree subservient to its attainment, it is desired that the religious element should have a definite place assigned to it in the life of the school; that it should be recognized to this extent at least, that the school should be opened and closed with prayer; that the Bible, or selections from it, should be read daily, either in common, or in the Douay version as the trustees may direct; that the morality inculated should be Christian morality, and that the teacher should be at liberty to enforce it, and should be encouraged to enforce it by those considerations, at once solemn and tender, which are embraced in the common belief of Christendom. A system of public education of this kind, in which religion has a definite but at the same time strictly guarded place assigned to it, ought to be acceptable to the great majority of the people of this Province. It has certainly much to recommend it. It has no sectarian features, and yet it is not godless. Religion is recognized in it in such form and degree as to make it possible to give a high tone to the life of the school, as to secure more or less familiarity with the contents of scripture on the part of every child, and as to make available for the teacher those lofty and sacred sanctions which have in all ages been found the most effective instruments in the enforcement of morality."

Affidavit of Mr. Wood.

I, Edmund M. Wood, of the City of Winnipeg, in the Province of Manitoba, Esquire, make oath and say:

1. I am an officer employed by the Government of Manitoba, and occupy

the position of chief clerk in the Department of Municipal Commissioner, and am also employed in the Public Works Department, and know the facts herein deposed to be true.

2. Pursuant to chapter 25 of the statutes passed in this Province in the fifty-second year of Her Majesty's reign, the Government of the Province of Manitoba erected a building to be used as the Manitoba Deaf and Dumb Institution, the erection and completion of which building with its furniture cost over $18,000.

3. The Government of the Province of Manitoba have for several years past carried on at public expense a school for the teaching of the deaf and dumb, and that school is now being carried on at an annual cost of about $7,500.00.

4. This money is paid out of the general funds of the Province, and the school is open to all classes of people of every creed and belief.

5. The school is purely non-sectarian, and is for the education in a purely secular way of all classes of children.

Affidavit of Mr. Cumberland.

I, Thomas Dickey Cumberland, of the City of Winnipeg, in the Province of Manitoba, Barrister, make oath and say:

1. I have examined the Dominion Government census returns of the census of the Province of Manitoba taken during the year 1886, and I find that the population of the said Province shown by said census was 108,640.

2. From the said returns I find that the five leading religious denominations in the said Province were according to the said census in number as follows, namely:—Roman Catholic, 14,651; Church of England, 23,206; Presbyterian, 28,406; Methodist, 18,648; and Baptist, 3,296.

3. I have been a resident of the Province of Manitoba since the year 1881.

4. I believe no material change has taken place in the relative numbers of the different denominations aforesaid since the year 1886 in Manitoba.

Affidavit of Mr. Howell.

I, Hector Mansfield Howell, of the City of Winnipeg, in the Province of Manitoba, Esquire, make oath and say:

1. I have resided in this province continuously for the last twelve years. I have travelled over large portions of this province, and am familiar with the general state of its settlement and the distribution of its population.

2. The chief city of the province is the City of Winnipeg, with a present population of about 25,000 people. There are two other towns with population of about 4,000 each, and there is a large number of villages with population ranging from 200 or 300 to 1,000 people.

3. According to the last census taken in this year, there is reported to be about 155,000 residents in the whole province, and in my opinion at least 50,000 of these reside in villages and in the towns and in the City of Winnipeg. The remainder of the population reside upon farms pretty evenly distributed over an area of country exceeding 23,000 square miles.

4. From my knowledge of the sparse settlement of this country, I verily believe that if separate schools are granted to the English Church people and to the Roman Catholics it will be very difficult to support any system of public schools except in the centres of population like towns and cities, and I verily believe that if three systems of schools were established, each system would be very defective and would be of little use towards general education.

JUDGMENT IN LOGAN V. WINNIPEG.

On 19th December, 1891, judgment was given by the Court of Queen's Bench of Manitoba. Prior to that time the Supreme Court of Canada had held that the Provincial Statutes were *ultra vires*. The Court of the Queen's Bench held itself bound by that decision. It declared that the Acts were invalid; and further that not only were Catholics a "class of persons" whose rights were, by the Manitoba Act, conserved; but that Episcopalians were also a "class of persons."

CHAPTER IV.

PRIVY COUNCIL JUDGMENTS—BOTH CASES.

Both cases (Barrett v. Winnipeg, and Logan v. Winnipeg) were carried to the Imperial Privy Council. On the 30th day of July, 1892, judgment was given reversing the order of the Supreme Court in Barrett v. Winnipeg, and of the Manitoba Court in Logan v. Winnipeg.

Lord Macnaghten delivered the judgment as follows:—These two appeals were heard together. In the one case the City of Winnipeg appeals from a judgment of the Supreme Court of Canada reversing a judgment of the Court of Queen's Bench for Manitoba; in the other from a subsequent judgment of the Court of Queen's Bench for Manitoba, following the judgment of the Supreme Court. The judgments under appeal quashed certain by-laws of the City of Winnipeg, which authorized assessments for school purposes in pursuance of the Public Schools Act, 1890, a statute of Manitoba to which Roman Catholics and members of the Church of England alike take exception. The views of the Roman Catholic Church were maintained by Mr. Barrett; the case of the Church of England was put forward by Mr. Logan. Mr. Logan was content to rely on the arguments advanced on behalf of Mr. Barrett, while Mr. Barrett's advisers were not prepared to make common cause with Mr. Logan, and naturally would have been better pleased to stand alone. The controversy which has given rise to the present litigation is, no doubt, beset with difficulties. The result of the controversy is of serious moment to the Province of Manitoba, and a matter apparently of deep interest throughout the Dominion. But in its legal aspect the question lies in a very narrow compass. The duty of this board is simply to determine as a matter of law whether, according to the true construction of the Manitoba Act, 1870, having regard to the state of things which existed in Manitoba at the time of the union, the Provincial Legislature has or has not exceeded its powers in passing the Public Schools Act, 1890. Manitoba became one of the provinces of the Dominion of Canada under the Manitoba Act, 1870, which was afterwards confirmed by an Imperial statute known as the British North America Act, 1871. Before the union it was not an independent Province, with a constitution and a legislature of its own. It formed part of the vast territories which belonged to the Hudson's Bay Company, and were administered by their officers or agents. The Manitoba Act, 1870, declared that the provisions of the British North America Act, 1867, with certain exceptions not material to the present question, should be applicable to the Province of Manitoba, as if Manitoba had been one of the provinces originally united by the Act. It established a legislature for Manitoba, consisting of a Legislative Council and a Legislative Assembly, and proceeded, in section 22, to re-enact with some modifications the provisions with regard to education which are to be found in section 93 of the British North America Act, 1867. Section 22 of the Manitoba Act, so far as it is material, is in the following terms:—" In and for the Province the said Legislature may exclusively make laws in relation to education, subject and according to the following provisions :—(1) Nothing in any such law shall prejudicially affect any right or privilege with respect to denominational schools which any class of persons have by law or practice in the Province at the union." Then follow two other sub-sections. Sub-section 2 gives an "appeal," as it is termed in the Act, to the Governor-General in Council from any Act or decision of the Legislature of the Province, or of any provincial authority "affecting any right or privilege of the Protestant or Roman Catholic minority of the Queen's subjects in relation to education." Sub-section 3 reserves certain limited powers to the Dominion Parliament in the event of the Provincial Legislature failing to comply with the requirements of the section or the decision of the Governor-General in Council. At the commencement of the argument a doubt was suggested as to the competency of the present appeal in consequence of the so-called appeal to the Governor-General in Council provided by the Act. But their Lordships are satisfied that the provisions of sub-sections 2 and 3 do not operate to withdraw such a question as that involved in the present case from the jurisdiction of the ordinary tribunals of the country. Sub-sections 1, 2 and 3 of section 22 of the Manitoba Act, 1870, differ but slightly from the corresponding sub-sections of section 93 of the British North America Act, 1867. The only important difference is that in the Manitoba Act, in sub-section 1, the words "by law" are followed by the words "or practice," which do not occur in the corresponding passage in the British North America Act. These words were no doubt introduced to meet the special case of a country which had not as yet enjoyed the security of laws properly so called. It is not perhaps very easy to define precisely the meaning of such an expression as "having a right or privilege by practice." But the object of the enactment is tolerably clear. Evidently the word "practice" is not to be construed as equivalent to "custom having the force of law." Their Lordships are convinced that it must have been the intention of the Legislature to preserve every legal right or privilege, and every benefit or advantage in the nature of a right or privilege, with respect to denominational schools which any class of persons practically enjoyed at the time of the union. What, then, was the state of things when Manitoba was admitted to the union? On this point their is no dispute. It is agreed that there was no law, or regulation, or ordinance with respect to education in force at that time. There were, therefore, no rights or privileges with respect to denominational schools existing by law. The practice which prevailed in Manitoba before the union is also a matter on which all parties are agreed. The statement on the subject by Archbishop Taché, the Roman Catholic Archbishop of St. Boniface, who has given evidence in Barrett's case, has been accepted as accurate and complete. "There existed," he says, "in the territory now constituting the Province of Manitoba a number of effective schools for children. These schools were denominational schools, some of them being regulated and controlled by the Roman Catholic Church, and others by various Protestant denominations. The means necessary for the support of Roman Catholic schools were supplied, to some extent, by school fees, paid by some of the parents of the children who attended the schools, and the rest were paid out of the funds of the church, contributed by its members. During the period referred to, Roman Catholics had no interest in, or control over, the schools of the Protestant denominations, and the members of the Protestant denominations had no interest in, or control over, the schools of the Roman Catholics. There were no public schools in the sense of state schools. The members of the Roman Catholic Church supported the schools of their own church for the benefit of the Roman Catholic children, and were not under obligation to and did not contribute to the support of any other schools. Now, if the state of things which the Archbishop describes as existing before the union had been a system established by law, what would have been the rights and privileges of the Roman Catholics with respect to denominational schools? They would have had by law the right to establish schools at their own expense, to maintain their schools by school fees or voluntary contributions, and to conduct them in accordance with their own religious tenets. Every other religious body which was engaged in a similar work at the time of the union would have had precisely the same right with respect to their denominational schools. Possibly this right, if it had been defined or recognized by positive enactment, might have had attached to it, as a necessary or appropriate incident, the right of exemption from any contribution under any circumstances to schools of a different denomination. But, in their Lordships' opinion, it would be going much too far to hold that the establishment of a national system of education upon an unsectarian basis is so inconsistent with the right to set up and maintain denominational schools that the two things cannot exist together, or that the existence of one necessarily implies or involves immunity from taxation for the purpose of the other. It has been objected that if the rights of Roman Catholics, and of other religious bodies, in respect of their denominational schools, are to be so strictly measured and limited by the practice which actually prevailed at the time of the union, they will be reduced to the condition of a "natural right" "which does not want any legislation to protect it." Such a right, it was said, cannot be called a privilege in any proper sense of the word. If that be so, the only result is that the protection which the Act purports to extend to rights and privileges existing "by practice" has no more operation than the protection which it purports to afford to rights and privileges existing "by law." It can hardly be contended that, in order to give a substantial operation and effect to a saving clause expressed in general terms, it is incumbent upon the court to discover privileges which are not apparent of themselves, or to ascribe distinctive and peculiar features to rights which seem to be of such a common type as not to deserve special notice or require special protection. Manitoba having been constituted a province of the Dominion in 1870, the Provincial Legislature lost no time in dealing with the question of education. In 1871 a law was passed which established a system of denominational education in the common schools, as they were then called. A Board of Education was formed, which was to be divided into two sections, Protestant and Roman Catholic. Each section was to have under its control and management the discipline of the schools of the section. Under the Manitoba Act the province had been divided into 24 electoral divisions, for the purpose of electing members to serve in the Legislative Assembly. By the Act of 1871 each electoral division was constituted a school district, in the first instance. Twelve electoral divisions, "comprising mainly a Protestant population," were to be considered Protestant school districts; twelve, "comprising mainly a Roman Catholic population," were to be considered Roman Catholic school districts. Without the special sanction of the section there was not to be more than one school in any school district. The male inhabitants of each school district, assembled at an annual meeting, were to decide in what manner they should raise their contributions towards the support of the school, in addition to what was derived from public funds. It is perhaps not out of place to observe that one of the modes prescribed was "assessment on the property of the school district," which must have involved, in some cases at any rate, an assessment on Roman Catholics for the support of a Protestant school, and an assessment on Protestants for the support of a Roman Catholic school. In the event of an assessment there was no provision for exemption, except in the case of a father or guardian of a school child, a Protestant in a Roman Catholic school district, or a Roman Catholic in a Protestant school district—who might escape by sending the child to the school of the nearest district of the other section and contributing to it an amount equal to what he would have paid if he had belonged to that district. The laws relating to education were modified from time to time, but the system of denominational education was maintained in full vigor until 1890. An Act passed in 1881, following an Act of 1875, provided among other things that the establishment of a school district of one denomination should not prevent the establishment of a school district of the other denomination in the same place, and that a Protestant and a Roman Catholic district might include the same territory in whole or in part. From the year 1876 until 1890 enactments were in force declaring that in no case should a Protestant ratepayer be obliged to pay for a Roman Catholic school, or a Roman Catholic ratepayer for a Protestant school. In 1890 the policy of the past nineteen years was reversed; the denominational system of public education was entirely swept away. Two Acts in relation to education were passed. The first (53 Vic., c. 37) established a Department of Education and a board consisting of seven members known as the "Advisory Board." Four members of the board were to be appointed by the Department of Education, two were to be elected by the public and high school teachers, and the seventh member was to be appointed by the University Council. One of the powers of the Advisory Board was to prescribe the forms of religious exercises to be used in the schools. The Public Schools Act, 1890 (53 Vic., c. 38), enacted that all Protestant and Roman Catholic school districts should be subject to the provisions of the Act, and that all public schools should be free schools. The provisions of the Act with regard to religious exercises are as follows:—"6. Religious exercises in the public schools shall be conducted according to the regulations of the Advisory Board. The time for such religious exercises shall be just before the closing hour in the afternoon. In case the parent or guardian of any pupil notifies the teacher that he does not wish such pupil to attend such religious exercises, then such pupil shall be dismissed before such religious exercises take place. 7. Religious exercises shall be held in a public school entirely at the option of the school trustees for the district, and upon receiving written authority from the trustees, it shall be the duty of the teachers to hold such religious exercises. 8. The public schools shall be entirely non-sectarian, and no religious exercises shall be allowed therein except as above provided." The Act then provides for the formation, alteration and union of school districts, for the election of school trustees, and for levying a rate on the taxable property in each school district for school purposes. In cities the municipal council is required to levy and collect upon the taxable property within the municipality such sums as the school trustees may require for school purposes. A portion of the legislative grant for educational purposes is allotted to public schools; but it is provided that any school not conducted according to all the provisions of the Act, or any Act in force for the time being, or the regulations of the Department of Education, or the Advisory Board, shall not be deemed a public school within the meaning of the law and shall not participate in the legislative grant. Section 141 provides that no teacher shall use or permit to be used as text books any books except such as are authorized by the Advisory Board, and that no portion of the legislative grant shall be paid to any school in which unauthorized books are used. Then there are two sections (178 and 179) which call for a passing notice, because, owing apparently to some misapprehension, they are spoken of in one of the judgments under appeal as if their effect was to confiscate Roman Catholic property. They apply to cases where the same territory was covered by a Protestant school district and by a Roman Catholic school district. In such a case Roman Catholics were really placed in a better position than Protestants. Certain exemptions were to be made in their favour if the assets of their district exceeded its liabilities, or if the liabilities of the Protestant school district exceeded its assets. But no corresponding exemptions were to be made in the case of Protestants. Such being the main provisions of the Public Schools Act, 1890, their Lordships have to determine whether that Act prejudicially affects any right or privilege with respect to denominational schools which any class of persons had by law or practice in the province at the union. Notwithstanding the Public Schools Act, 1890, Roman Catholics and members of every other religious body in Manitoba are free to establish schools throughout the province; they are free to maintain their schools by school fees or voluntary subscriptions; they are free to conduct their schools according to their own religious tenets without molestation or interference. No child is compelled to attend a public school. No special advantage other than the advantage of a free education in schools conducted under public management is held out to those who do attend. But then it is said that it is impossible for Roman Catholics, or for members of the Church of England (if their views are correctly represented by the Bishop of Rupert's Land, who has given evidence in Logan's case), to send their children to public schools where the education is not superintended and directed by the authorities of their church, and that, therefore, Roman Catholics and members of the Church of England who are taxed for public schools, and at the same time feel themselves compelled to support their own schools, are in a less favorable position than those who can take advantage of the free education provided by the Act of 1890. That may be so. But what right or privilege is violated or prejudicially affected by the law? It is not the law that is in fault; it is owing to religious convictions, which everybody must respect, and to the teaching of their church, that Roman Catholics and the members of the Church of England find themselves unable to partake of advantages which the law offers to all alike. Their Lordships are sensible of the weight which must attach to the unanimous decision of the Supreme Court. They have anxiously considered the able and elaborate judgments by which that decision has been supported. But they are unable to agree with the opinion which the learned judges of the Supreme Court have expressed as to the rights and privileges of Roman Catholics in Manitoba at the time of the union. They doubt whether it is permissible to refer to the course of legislation between 1871 and 1890, as a means of throwing light on the previous practice or on the construction of the saving clause in the Manitoba Act. They cannot assent to the view, which seems to be indicated by one of the members of the Supreme Court, that public schools under the Act of 1890 are in reality Protestant schools. The legislature has declared in so many words that the public schools shall be entirely unsectarian, and that principle is carried out throughout the Act. With the policy of the Act of 1890 their Lordships are not concerned. But they cannot help observing that, if the views of the respondents were to prevail, it would be extremely difficult for the Provincial Legislature, which has been entrusted with the exclusive power of making laws relating to education, to provide for the educational wants of the more sparsely inhabited districts of a country almost as large as Great Britain, and that the powers of the legislature, which on the face of the Act appear so large, would be limited to the useful but somewhat humble office of making regulations for the sanitary conditions of school-houses, imposing rates for the support of denominational schools, enforcing the compulsory attendance of scholars, and matters of that sort. In the result their Lordships will humbly advise Her Majesty that these appeals ought to be allowed, with costs. In the City of Winnipeg v. Barrett, it will be proper to reverse the order of the Supreme Court with costs and to restore the judgment of the Court of Queen's Bench for Manitoba. In the City of Winnipeg v. Logan, the order will be to reverse the judgment of the Court of Queen's Bench and to dismiss Mr. Logan's application and dischage the rule *nisi* and the rule absolute, with costs.

CHAPTER V.

PETITIONS TO DOMINION GOVERNMENT; AND ACTIONS OF GOVERNMENT THEREON.

Reference to the provisions of the B. N. A. Act and the Manitoba Act (see page 1) will show that under certain circumstances a religious minority has a right to appeal to the Governor-General in Council from certain Acts or decisions. In pursuance of these provisions the following petitions, amongst others, were presented, and the following proceedings were thereon taken:

PETITION OF AUGUST, 1890.

To His Excellency the Governor-General in Council:

The humble petition of the undersigned members of the Roman Catholic Church, in the Province of Manitoba, presented on behalf of themselves and their co-religionists in the said province, sheweth as follows:

1. Prior to the passage of the Act of the Dominion of Canada, passed in the thirty-third year of the reign of Her Majesty Queen Victoria, chapter three, known as "The Manitoba Act," and prior to the Order in Council issued in pursuance thereof, there existed in the territory now constituting the Province of Manitoba a number of effective schools for children.

2. These schools were denominational schools, some of them being regulated and controlled by the Roman Catholic Church, and others by various Protestant denominations.

3. The means necessary for the support of the Roman Catholic schools were supplied to some extent by school fees paid by some of the parents of the children who attended the schools and the rest was paid out of the funds of the church contributed by its members.

4. During the period referred to Roman Catholics had no interest in or control over the schools of the Protestant denominations, and the Protestant denominations had no interest in or control over the schools of the Roman Catholics. There were no public schools in the sense of State schools. The members of the Roman Catholic Church supported the schools of their own church for the benefit of the Roman Catholic children and were not under obligation to and did not contribute to the support of any other schools.

5. In the matter of education, therefore, during the period referred to, Roman Catholics were, as a matter of custom and practice, separate from the rest of the community.

6. Under the provisions of the Manitoba Act it was provided that the Legislative Assembly of the province should have the exclusive right to make laws in regard to education, subject to the following provisions:

(1) Nothing in any such law shall prejudicially affect any right or privilege with respect to denominational schools which any class of persons have by law or practice in the province at the union.

(2) An appeal shall lie to the Governor-General in Council from any Act or decision of the Legislature of the province, or of any provincial authority affecting any right or privilege of the Protestant or Roman Catholic minority of the Queen's subjects in relation to education.

(3) In case any such provincial law as from time to time seems to the Governor-General in Council requisite for the due execution of the provisions of this section is not made, or in case any decision of the Governor-General in Council, on any appeal under this section is not duly executed by the proper provincial authority in that behalf, then, and in every such case, and as far only as the circumstances of each case require, the Parliament of Canada may make remedial laws for the due execution of the provisions of this section, and of any decision of the Governor-General under this section.

7. During the first session of the Legislative Assembly of the Province of Manitoba, an Act was passed relating to education, the effect of which was to continue to the Roman Catholics that separate condition with reference to education which they had enjoyed previous to the erection of the province.

8. The effect of the statute, so far as the Roman Catholics were concerned, was merely to organize the efforts which the Roman Catholics had previously voluntarily made for the education of their own children. It provided for the continuance of schools under the sole control and management of Roman Catholics, and of the education of their children according to the methods by which alone they believe children should be instructed.

9. Ever since the said legislation, and until the last session of the Legislative Assembly, no attempt was made to encroach upon the rights of the Roman Catholics so confirmed to them as above mentioned, but during said session statutes were passed (53 Vic., chaps. 37 and 38) the effect of which was to deprive the Roman Catholics altogether of their separate condition in regard to education; to merge their schools with those of the Protestant denominations; and to require all members of the community, whether Roman Catholic or Protestant, to contribute, through taxation, to the support of what are therein called Public schools, but which are in reality a continuation of the Protestant schools.

10. There is a provision in the said Act for the appointment and election of an advisory board, and also for the election in each municipality of school trustees. There is also a provision that the said advisory board may prescribe religious exercises for use in schools, and that the said school trustees may, if they think fit, direct such religious exercises to be adopted in the schools in their respective

districts. No further or other provision is made with reference to religious exercises, and there is none with reference to religious training.

11. Roman Catholics regard such schools as unfit for the purposes of education, and the children of Roman Catholic parents cannot and will not attend any such schools. Rather than countenance such schools, Roman Catholics will revert to the voluntary system in operation previous to the Manitoba Act, and will at their own private expense establish, support and maintain schools in accordance with their principles and their faith, although by so doing they will have in addition thereto to contribute to the expense of the so-called Public Schools.

12. Your petitioners submit that the said Act of the Legislative Assembly of Manitoba is subversive of the rights of Roman Catholics guaranteed and confirmed to them by the statute erecting the Province of Manitoba, and prejudicially affects the rights and privileges with respect to Roman Catholic Schools which Roman Catholics had in the Province at the time of its union with the Dominion of Canada.

13. The Roman Catholics are in the minority in said Province.

14. The Roman Catholics of the Province of Manitoba therefore appeal from the said Act of the Legislative Assembly of Manitoba.

YOUR PETITIONERS THEREFORE PRAY—

1. That your Excellency the Governor-General in Council may entertain the said appeal, and may consider the same, and may make such provisions and give such directions for the hearing and consideration of the said appeal as may be thought proper.

2. That it may be declared that such Provincial law does prejudicially affect the rights and privileges with regard to denominational schools which Roman Catholics had by law or practice in the Province at the union.

3. That such directions may be given and provisions made for the relief of the Roman Catholics of the Province of Manitoba as to Your Excellency in Council may seem fit.

And your petitioners will ever pray.

†ALEX., Arch. of St. Boniface.
HENRI F., Ev. d'Anemour.
JOSEPH MESSIER, P.P. of St. Boniface.
T. A. BERNIER.
J. DUBUC.
L. A. PRUD'HOMME.
M. A. GIRARD.
A. A. LaRIVIÈRE, M.P.
JAMES E. PRENDERGAST, M.P.P.
ROGER MARION, M.P.P., and 4,257 more names.

ORDER IN COUNCIL, 4TH APRIL, 1891.

That on the consideration of the Privy Council of Canada of the two Acts aforesaid, the following report of the Honourable the Minister of Justice, dated 21st March, 1891, was approved by His Excellency the Governor-General in Council on the 4th day of April, 1891, viz.:—

DEPARTMENT OF JUSTICE, CANADA, 21st March, 1891.

To His Excellency the Governor-General in Council:

The undersigned has the honour to report upon the two Acts of the following titles passed by the Legislature of the Province of Manitoba at its session held in the year 1890, which Acts were received by the Honourable the Secretary of State on the 11th April, 1890 :—

Chapter 37, "An Act respecting the Department of Education," and Chapter 38, "An Act respecting the Public Schools."

The first of these Acts creates a Department of Education, consisting of the Executive Council or a committee thereof appointed by the Lieutenant-Governor in Council, and defines its powers. It also creates an Advisory Board, partly appointed by the Department of Education and partly elected by teachers, and defines its powers.

The "Act respecting Public Schools" is a consolidation and amendment of all previous legislation in respect to Public schools. It repeals all legislation which created and authorized a system of separate schools for Protestants and Roman Catholics. By the Acts previously in force either Protestants or Roman Catholics could establish a school in any school district, and Protestant ratepayers were exempted from contribution for the Catholic schools, and Catholic ratepayers were exempted from contribution for Protestant schools.

The two Acts now under review purport to abolish these distinctions as to the schools, and these exemptions as to ratepayers, and to establish instead a system under which Public Schools are to be organized in all the school districts, without regard to the religious views of the ratepayers.

The right of the Province of Manitoba to legislate on the subject of education is conferred by the Act which created the Province, viz., 32-35 Vic., chap. 3 (The Manitoba Act), section 22, which is as follows :—

"22. In and for the Province of Manitoba the said Legislature may exclusively make laws in relation to education, subject to the following provisions :—

"(1.) Nothing in any such law shall prejudicially affect any right or privilege with respect to denominational schools which any class of persons have by law or practice in the Province at the union.

"(2.) An appeal shall lie to the Governor-General in Council from any Act or decision of the Legislature of the Province, or of any Provincial authority affecting any right or privilege of the Protestant or Roman Catholic minority of the Queen's subjects in relation to education.

"(3.) In case any such Provincial law as from time to time seems to the Governor-General in Council requisite for the due execution of the provisions of this section is not made, or in case any decision of the Governor in Council, on any appeal under this section, is not duly executed by the proper Provincial authority in that behalf, then, and in every such case, and as far only as the circumstances of each case require, the Parliament may make remedial laws for the due execution of the provisions of this section, and of any decision of the Governor-General in Council under this section."

In the year 1870, when the "Manitoba Act" was passed, there existed no system of education established or authorized by law, but at the first session of the Provincial Legislature in 1871 an "Act to establish a system of education in the Province" was passed. By that Act the Lieutenant-Governor in Council was empowered to appoint not less than ten nor more than fourteen to be a Board of Education for the Province, of whom one-half were to be Protestants and the other half Catholics, with one Superintendent of Protestant, and one Superintendent of Catholic schools. The Board was divided into two sections, Protestant and Catholic, each section to have under its control and management the discipline of the schools of its faith, and to prescribe the books to be used in the schools under its care which had reference to religion or morals.

The moneys appropriated for education by the Legislature were to be divided equally, one moiety thereof to the support of Protestant schools, and the other moiety to the support of Catholic schools.

By an Act passed in 1875, the Board was increased to twenty-one, twelve Protestant and nine Roman Catholics; the moneys voted by the Legislature were to be divided between the Protestant and Catholic schools in proportion to the number of children of school age in the schools under the care of Protestant and Catholic sections of the Board respectively.

The Act of 1875 also provided that the establishment in a school district of a school of one denomination should not prevent the establishment of a school of another denomination in the same district.

Several questions have arisen as to the validity and effect of the two statutes now under review; among these are the following:—

It being admitted that "no class of persons" (to use the expression of the Manitoba Act), had "by law," at the time the province was established, "any right or privilege with respect to denominational (or any other) school," had "any class of persons" any such right or privilege with respect to denominational schools "by practice" at that time? Did the existence of separate schools for Roman

Catholic children, supported by Roman Catholic voluntary contributions, in which their religion might be taught and in which text books suitable for Roman Catholic schools were used, and the non-existence of any system by which Roman Catholics or any other, could be compelled to contribute for the support of schools, constitute a "right or privilege" for Roman Catholics "by practice" within the meaning of the Manitoba Act? The former of these, as will at once be seen, was a question of fact, and the latter a question of law, based on the assumption which has since been proved to be well founded, that the existence of separate schools at the time of the "union" was the fact on which the Catholic population of Manitoba must rely as establishing their "right or privilege" "by practice." The remaining question was whether, assuming the foregoing questions, or either of them, to require an affirmative answer, the enactments now under review, or either of them, affected any such "right or privilege?"

It becomes apparent at the outset that these questions required the decision of the judicial tribunals, more especially as an investigation of facts was necessary to their determination. Proceedings were instituted with a view to obtaining such a decision in the Court of Queen's Bench of Manitoba several months ago, and in course of these proceedings the facts have been easily ascertained, and the two latter of the three questions above stated were presented for the judgment of that court with the arguments of counsel for the Roman Catholics of Manitoba on the one side, and of counsel for the Provincial Government on the other.

The court has practically decided, with one dissentient opinion, that the Acts now under review do not "prejudicially affect any right or privilege with respect to denominational schools" which Roman Catholics had by "practice at the time of the Union," or, in brief, that the non-existence, at that time, of a system of public schools and the consequent exemption from taxation for the support of public schools and the consequent freedom to establish and support separate or "denominational" schools did not constitute a "right or privilege" "by practice" which these Acts took away.

An appeal has been asserted, and the case is now before the Supreme Court of Canada, where it will in all probability, be heard in the course of next month.

If the appeal should be successful, these Acts will be annulled by judicial decision; the Roman Catholic minority of Manitoba will receive protection and redress. The Acts purporting to be repealed will remain in operation, and those whose views have been represented by a majority of the Legislature cannot but recognize that the matter has been disposed of with due regard to the constitutional rights of the province.

If the legal controversy should result in the decision of the Court of Queen's Bench being sustained, the time will come for Your Excellency to consider the petitions which have been presented by and on behalf of the Roman Catholics of Manitoba for redress under sub-sections 2 and 3 of section 22 of the "Manitoba Act," quoted in the early part of this report, and which are analogous to the provisions made by the British North America Act, in relation to the other provinces.

These sub-sections contain, in effect, the provisions which have been made as to all the provinces, and are obviously those under which the constitution intended that the Government of the Dominion should proceed, if it should at any time become necessary that the Federal powers should be resorted to for the protection of a Protestant or Roman Catholic minority, against any Act or decision of the Legislature of the province, or of any provincial authority, affecting any "right or privilege" of any such minority "in relation to education."

      Respectfully submitted,
         JOHN S. D. THOMPSON,
           Minister of Justice.

PETITION 20TH SEPTEMBER, 1892.

Prior to the date of the following petition judgment had been given in the Privy Council in the cases of Barrett v. Winnipeg and Logan v. Winnipeg, as set out at page 21 :

To His Excellency the Governor-General in Council :

The humble petition of the undersigned members of the Roman Catholic Church, in the Province of Manitoba, and dutiful subjects of Her Most Gracious Majesty, doth hereby respectfully represent that :

The seventh Legislature of the Province of Manitoba, in its third session assembled, did pass in the year eighteen hundred and ninety an Act intituled "An Act respecting the Department of Education," and also an Act respecting public schools, which deprive the Roman Catholic minority in the said Province of Manitoba of the rights and privileges they enjoyed with regard to education previous to and at the time of the union, and since that time up to the passing of the Acts aforesaid.

That subsequent to the passing of said Acts, and on behalf of the members of said Roman Catholic Church, the following petition has been laid before Your Excellency in Council (Set out at page 28) :

That on the consideration of the Privy Council of Canada of the two Acts aforesaid, the following report of the Honorable the Minister of Justice, dated 21st March, 1891, was approved by His Excellency the Governor-General in Council on the 4th April, 1891, viz : (Set out at page 31.)

That a recent decision of the Judicial Committee of the Privy Council in England having sustained the judgment of the Court of Queen's Bench of Manitoba, upholding the validity of the Acts aforesaid, your petitioners most respectfully represent that, as intimated in said report of the Honorable the Minister of Justice, *the time has now come for Your Excellency to consider the petitions which have been presented by and on behalf of the Roman Catholics of Manitoba for redress under sub-sections 2 and 3 of section 22 of the "Manitoba Act."*

That your petitioners, notwithstanding such decision of the Judicial Committee of the Privy Council in England, still believe that their rights and privileges in relation to education have been prejudicially affected by said Acts of the Provincial Legislature.

Therefore, your petitioners most respectfully and most earnestly pray that it may please Your Excellency in Council to take into consideration the petitions above referred to, and to grant the conclusions of said petitions and the relief and protection sought for by the same.

And your petitioners will ever pray.

SAINT BONIFACE, 20th September, 1892.

Members of the Executive Committee of the National Congress.

T. A. BERNIER, Acting President. H. F. DESPARS.
A. A. C. LARIVIÈRE. M. A. KERVALK.
JOSEPH LECOMTE. TÉLESPHORE PELLETIER.
JAMES E. P. PRENDERGAST. DR. J. H. OCT. LAMBERT.
J. ERNEST CYR. JOSEPH Z. C. AUGER.
THEO. BERTRAND. A. F. MARTIN.

Secretaries. { A. E. VERSAILLES.
{ R. GOULET, JR.

PETITION 22ND SEPTEMBER, 1892.

To His Excellency the Governor-General in Council:

The humble petition of the undersigned, Archbishop of the Roman Catholic Church in the Province of Manitoba, respectfully sheweth:—

1. That two statutes, 53 Vic., chap. 37 and 38, were passed in the Legislative Assembly of Manitoba to merge the Roman Catholic Schools with those of the Protestant denominations, and to require all members of the community, whether Roman Catholic or Protestant, to contribute, through taxation, to the support of what are therein called Public Schools, but which are in reality a continuation of the Protestant Schools.

2. That on the 4th of April, 1890, James E. P. Pendergast, M.P.P. for Woodlands, transmitted to the Honourable the Secretary of State for Canada a petition, signed by eight members of the Legislative Assembly of Manitoba, to make known to His Excellency the Governor-General the grievances under which Her Majesty's Roman Catholic subjects of the Province of Manitoba were suffering by the passation of the two said Acts, respectively intituled: "An Act respecting the Department of Education," and "An Act respecting Public Schools," (53 Vic., chap. 37 and 38). The said petition ended by the following words: Your petitioners, therefore, humbly pray that Your Excellency may be pleased to take such action "and grant such relief and remedy as to Your Excellency may seem meet and just."

3. That on the 7th of April, the same year, 1890, the Catholic section of the Board of Education in a petition signed by its President, the Archbishop of St. Boniface, and its Secretary, T.A. Bernier, "most respectfully and earnestly prayed His Excellency the Governor-General in Council that said last mentioned Acts (53 Vic., chap. 37 and 38) be disallowed to all intents and purposes."

4. That on the 12th of April, 1890, the undersigned brought before His Excellency some of the facts concerning the outbreak which occurred at Red River during the winter of 1869-70; the part that the undersigned was invited, by Imperial and Federal authorities, to take in the pacification of the country; the promise intrusted to the undersigned in an autograph letter from the then Governor-General that the people of Red River "may rely that respect and attention will be extended to the different religious persuasions;" the furnishing the undersigned with a proclamation to be made known to the dissatisfied population, in which proclamation the then Governor-General declared: "Her Majesty commands me to state to you that she will be always ready, through me as Her representative, to redress all well-founded grievances." By Her Majesty's authority I do therefore assure you that on your union with Canada "all your civil and religious rights and privileges will be respected." In the strength of such assurance, the people of Red River consented to their union with Canada and the Act of Manitoba was passed, giving guarantees to the minority that their rights and privileges, acquired by law or practice, with regard to education, would be protected. The cited Acts, 53 Vic., chap. 37 and 38, being a violation of the assurances given to the Red River population, through the Manitoba Act, the undersigned ended his petition of the 12th April, 1890, by the following words:—

"I therefore most respectfully and most earnestly pray that Your Excellency, as the representative of our most beloved Queen, should take such steps that in your wisdom would seem the best remedy against the evils that the above mentioned and recently enacted laws are preparing in this part of Her Majesty's domain."

5. That later on, working under the above mentioned disadvantage and wishing for a remedy against laws which affected their rights and privileges in the matter of education, 4,267 members of the Roman Catholic Church, in the Province of Manitoba, on behalf of themselves and their co-religionists, appealed to the Governor-General in Council from the said Acts of the Legislature of the Province of Manitoba, the prayer of their petition being as follows:—

"(1) That Your Excellency the Governor-General in Council may entertain the said appeal, and may consider the same, and may make such provisions and give such directions for the hearing and consideration of the said appeal as may be thought proper.

"(2) That it may be declared that such Provincial law does prejudicially affect the rights and privileges with regard to denominational schools which Roman Catholics had by law or practice in the province at the union.

"(3) That such directions may be given and provisions made for the relief of the Roman Catholics of the Province of Manitoba as to Your Excellency in Council may seem fit."

6. That in the month of March, 1891, the Cardinal Archbishop of Quebec and the Archbishops and Bishops of the Roman Catholic Church in Canada, in a petition to His Excellency the Governor-General in Council, sheweth that the 7th Legislature of the Province of Manitoba, in its third session assembled, had passed an Act intituled, "An Act respecting the Department of Education," and another Act to be cited, "The Public School Act," which deprived the Catholic minority of the province of the rights and privileges they enjoyed with regard to education, and the venerable prelates added : "Therefore, your petitioners humbly pray Your Excellency in Council to afford a remedy to the pernicious legislation above mentioned, and that in the most efficacious and just way."

7. That on the 21st March, 1891, the Honorable the Minister of Justice reported on the two Acts alluded to above, chap. 37, "An Act respecting the Department of Education," and chap. 38, "An Act respecting Public Schools," and here are the conclusions of his report : "If the legal controversy should result in the decision of the Court of Queen's Bench (adverse to Catholic views) being sustained, the time will come for Your Excellency to consider the petitions which have been presented by and on behalf of the Roman Catholics of Manitoba for redress under sub-sections 2 and 3 of section 22 of the Manitoba Act, quoted in the early part of this report, and which are analogous to the provisions made by the British North America Act in relation to the other provinces. Those sub-sections contain in effect the provisions which have been made as to all the provinces, and are obviously those under which the constitution intended that the Government of the Dominion should proceed if it should at any time become necessary that the Federal

powers should be resorted to for the protection of a Protestant or Roman Catholic minority against any Act or decision of the Legislature of the province, or of any provincial authority, affecting any 'right or privilege' of any such minority 'in relation to education.'" A committee of the Honorable the Privy Council having had under consideration the above report, submitted the same for approval, and it was approved by His Excellency the Governor-General in Council on the 4th of April, 1891.

8. That the Judicial Committee of Her Majesty's Privy Council has sustained the decision of the Court of Queen's Bench.

9. That your petitioner believes that the time has now "come for Your Excellency to consider the petitions which have been presented by and on behalf of the Roman Catholics of Manitoba for redress, under sub-sections 2 and 3 of section 22 of the Manitoba Act," as it has "become necessary that the Federal power should be resorted to for the protection of the Roman Catholic minority."

Your petitioner therefore prays—

1. That Your Excellency the Governor-General in Council may entertain the appeal of the Roman Catholics of Manitoba, and may consider the same, and may make such provisions and give such directions for the hearing and consideration of the said appeal as may be thought proper.

2. That such directions may be given and provisions made for the relief of the Roman Catholics of the Province of Manitoba as to Your Excellency in Council may seem fit.

And your petitioner will ever pray.

† ALEX. TACHÉ,
Arch. of St. Boniface.

St. Boniface, 22nd September, 1892.

PETITION, NOVEMBER, 1892.

To His Excellency the Governor-General in Council.

The humble petition of the members of the Roman Catholic Church residing in the Province of Manitoba sheweth as follows:—

1. Prior to the passage of the Act of the Dominion of Canada, passed in the 33rd year of the reign of Her Majesty Queen Victoria, chap. 3, known as the Manitoba Act, and prior to the Order in Council issued in pursuance thereof, there existed in the territory now constituting the Province of Manitoba, a number of effective schools for children.

2. These schools were denominational schools, some of them being regulated and controlled by the Roman Catholic Church, and others by various Protestant denominations.

3. The means necessary for the support of the Roman Catholic schools were supplied to some extent by school fees paid by some of the parents of the children who attended the schools, and the rest was paid out of the funds of the church contributed by its members.

4. During the period referred to, Roman Catholics had no interest in or control over the schools of the Protestant denominations, and the members of the Protestant denominations had no interest in or control over the schools of the Roman Catholics. There were no Public schools in the sense of State schools. The members of the Roman Catholic Church supported the schools of their own church for the benefit of Roman Catholic children and were not under obligation to, and did not contribute to the support of, any other schools.

5. In the matter of education, therefore, during the period referred to, Roman Catholics were as a matter of custom and practice separate from the rest of the community.

6. Under the provisions of the Manitoba Act, it was provided that the Legislative Assembly of the Province should have the exclusive right to make laws in regard to education, subject, however, and according to the following provisions :—

"(1.) Nothing in any such law shall prejudicially affect any right or privilege with respect to denominational schools, which any class of persons have by law or practice in the Province at the union.

"(2.) An appeal shall lie to the Governor-General in Council from any Act or decision of the Legislature of the Province, or of any Provincial authority affecting any right or privilege of the Protestant or Roman Catholic minority of the Queen's subjects in relation to education.

"(3.) In case any such Provincial law as from time to time seems to the Governor-General in Council requisite for the due execution of the provisions of this section is not made, or in case any decision of the Governor-General in Council, or any appeal under this section is not duly executed by the proper Provincial authority in that behalf, then, and in every such case, and as far only as the circumstances of each case require, the Parliament of Canada may make remedial laws for the due execution of the provisions of this section, and of any decision of the Governor-General under this section."

7. During the first session of the Legislative Assembly of the Province of Manitoba an Act was passed relating to education, the effect of which was to continue to the Roman Catholics that separate condition with reference to education which they had enjoyed previous to the erection of the province.

8. The effect of this statute, so far as the Roman Catholics were concerned, was merely to organize the efforts which Roman Catholics

had previously voluntarily made for the education of their own children. It provided for the continuance of schools under the sole control and management of Roman Catholics, and of the education of their children according to the methods by which alone they believe children should be instructed. Between the time of the passage of the said Act and prior to the statute next hereinafter referred to, various Acts were passed amending and consolidating the said Act, but in and by all such later Acts the rights and privileges of the Roman Catholics were acknowledged and conserved and their separate condition in respect to education continued.

9. Until the session of the Legislative Assembly held in the year 1890, no attempt was made to encroach upon the rights of the Roman Catholics so confirmed to them as above mentioned, but during said session statutes were passed (53 Vic., chaps. 37 and 38) the effect of which was to repeal all the previous Acts; to deprive the Roman Catholics altogether of their separate condition in regard to education; to merge their schools with those of the Protestant denominations; and to require all members of the community, whether Roman Catholic or Protestant, to contribute, through taxation, to the support of what are therein called public schools, but which are in reality a continuation of Protestant schools.

10. There is a provision in the said Act for the appointment and election of an advisory board, and also for the election in each district of school trustees. There is also a provision that the said advisory board may prescribe religious exercises for use in schools, and that the said school trustees may, if they think fit, direct such religious exercises to be adopted in the schools in their respective districts. No further or other provision is made with reference to religious training.

11. Roman Catholics regard such schools as unfit for the purposes of education, and the children of Roman Catholic parents cannot and will not attend any such schools. Rather than countenance such schools, Roman Catholics will revert to the voluntary system in operation previous to the Manitoba Act, and will at their own private expense establish, support and maintain schools in accordance with their principles and their faith, although by so doing they will have in addition thereto to contribute to the expense of the so-called public schools.

12. Your petitioners submit that the said Acts of the Legislative Assembly of Manitoba are subversive of the rights of Roman Catholics guaranteed and confirmed to them by the statute erecting the Province of Manitoba, and prejudicially affect the rights and privileges with respect to Roman Catholic schools which Roman Catholics had in the province at the time of its union with the Dominion of Canada.

13. Your petitioners further submit that the said Acts of the

Legislative Assembly of Manitoba are subversive of the rights and privileges of Roman Catholics provided for by the various statutes of the said Legislative Assembly prior to the passing of the said Acts, and affect the rights and privileges of the Roman Catholic minority of the Queen's subjects in the said province in relation to education, so provided for as aforesaid, thereby offending both against the British North America Act and the Manitoba Act.

14. Roman Catholics are in a minority in the said province, and have been so for the last fifteen years.

15. The Roman Catholics of the Province of Manitoba, therefore, appeal from the said Acts of the Legislative Assembly of the Province of Manitoba.

Your petitioners therefore pray —

1. That Your Excellency the Governor-General in Council may entertain the said appeal and may consider the same, and may make such provisions and give such directions for the hearing and consideration of the said appeal as may be thought proper.

2. That it may be declared that the said Acts (53 Vic., chaps. 37 and 38) do prejudicially affect the rights and privileges with regard to denominational schools which Roman Catholics had by law or practice in the province at the union.

3. That it may be declared that the said last mentioned Acts do affect the rights and privileges of the Roman Catholic minority of the Queen's subjects in relation to education.

4. That it may be declared that to Your Excellency the Governor-General in Council, it seems requisite that the provisions of the statutes in force in the Province of Manitoba prior to the passage of the said Acts, should be re-enacted in so far at least as may be necessary to secure to the Roman Catholics in the said province the right to build, maintain, equip, manage, conduct and support these schools in the manner provided for by the said statutes, to secure to them their proportionate share of any grant made out of the public funds for the purposes of education, and to relieve such members of the Roman Catholic Church as contribute to such Roman Catholic schools from all payment or contribution to the support of any other schools; or that the said Acts of 1890 should be so modified or amended as to effect such purposes.

5. And that such further or other declaration or order may be made as to Your Excellency the Governor-General in Council shall, under the circumstances, seem proper, and that such directions may be given, provisions made and all things done in the premises for the purpose of affording relief to the said Roman Catholic minority in the said province as to Your Excellency in Council may seem meet.

And your petitioners will ever pray.

†ALEX., Arch. of St. Boniface, O.M.I.
T. A. BERNIER, President of the National Congress.
JAMES E. P. PRENDERGAST, Marie de la Ville de St. Boniface
J. ALLARD, O.M.I., V.G., and about 137 others.

JOHN S. EWART,

Counsel for the Roman Catholic minority in the Province of Manitoba.

PRESENTATION OF THE PETITIONS.

The petitions were referred by the Governor-General in Council to a sub-committee of the Council. The sub committee sat on the 26th November, 1892, when Mr. Ewart, Q.C., on behalf of the petitioners, orally presented the petitions. The members of the sub-committee present were: The Hon. Sir John Thompson (presiding), the Hon. Mr. Bowell, and the Hon. Mr. Chapleau. The Hon. Mr. Ouimet was also present by invitation to hear the argument. As Mr. Ewart's address was repeated in more extended form when he appeared before the full Council it is not thought proper to insert it here.

ORDER IN COUNCIL, 29TH DECEMBER, 1892.

The Committee of the Privy Council have had under consideration a report, hereto annexed, from a sub-committee of Council, to whom were referred certain memorials to Your Excellency, complaining of two statutes of the Legislature of Manitoba, relating to education, passed in the session of 1890.

The Committee, concurring in the report of the sub-committee, submit the same for Your Excellency's approval, and recommend that Saturday, the 21st day of January, 1893, at the chamber of the Privy Council, at Ottawa, be fixed as the day on which the parties concerned shall be heard with regard to the appeal in the matter of the said statutes.

The Committee further advise that a copy of this minute, if approved, together with a copy of the report of the sub-committee of Council, be transmitted to the Lieutenant-Governor of Manitoba.

JOHN J. MCGEE,
Clerk of the Privy Council.

REPORT OF SUB-COMMITTEE.

To His Excellency the Governor-General in Council :

The sub-committee to whom were referred certain memorials, addressed to Your Excellency in Council, complaining of two statutes of the Legislature of Manitoba, relating to education, passed in the session of 1890, have the honour to make the following report :—

The first of these memorials is from the officers and executive committee of the "National Congress," an organization which seems to have been established in June, 1890, in Manitoba.

This memorial sets forth that two Acts of the Legislature of Manitoba, passed in 1890, intituled respectively, "An Act respecting the Department of Education" and "An Act respecting Public Schools," deprive the Roman Catholic minority in Manitoba of rights and privileges which they enjoyed with regard to education previous to the establishment of the province, and since that time down to the passage of the Acts aforesaid, of 1890.

The memorial calls attention to the fact that soon after the passing of those Acts, (and in the year 1891) a petition was presented to Your Excellency, signed by a large number of the Roman Catholic inhabitants of Manitoba, praying that Your Excellency might entertain an appeal on behalf of the Roman Catholic minority against the said Acts, and that it might be declared "that such Acts had a prejudicial effect on the rights and privileges, with regard to denominational schools, which the Roman Catholics had, by law or practice, in the province, at the union ;" also that directions might be given and provision made in the premises for the relief of the Roman Catholics of the province of Manitoba.

The memorial of the "National Congress" recites, at length, the allegations of the petition last hereinbefore referred to, as having been laid before Your Excellency in 1891. The substance of those allegations seem to be the following : That, before the passage of the Act constituting the province of Manitoba, known as the "Manitoba Act," there existed, in the territory now constituting the province, a number of effective schools for children, which schools were denominational, some of them being erected and controlled by the authorities of the Roman Catholic Church, and others by the authorities of various Protestant denominations ; that those schools were supported, to some extent by fees, and also by assistance from the funds contributed by the members of the church or denomination under whose care the school was established ; that at that period the Roman Catholics had no interest in or control over the schools of Protestant denominations, nor had Protestants any interest in or control over the schools of Roman Catholics ; that there were no public schools in the province, in the sense of State schools; that members of the Roman Catholic Church supported schools for their own children and for the benefit of Roman Catholic children, and were not under obligations to contribute to the support of any other schools.

The petition then asserted that, in consequence of this state of affairs, the Roman Catholics were separate from the rest of the community, in the matter of education, at the time of the passage of the Manitoba Act.

Reference is then made to the provisions of the Manitoba Act by which the legislature was restricted from making any law on the subject of education which should have a prejudicial effect on the rights and privileges, with respect to denominational schools, "which any class of persons had, by law or practice, in the province at the 'union.'"

The petition then set forth that, during the first session of the Legislative Assembly of the province of Manitoba, an Act was passed relating to education, the effect of which was to continue to the Roman Catholics the separate condition, with reference to education, which they had enjoyed previous to the union; and that ever since that time, until the session of 1890, no attempt was made to encroach upon the rights of the Roman Catholics in that regard; but that the two statutes referred to, passed in the session of 1890, had the effect of depriving the Roman Catholics altogether of their separate condition with regard to education, and merged their schools with those of the Protestant denominations, as they required all members of the community, whether Roman Catholic or Protestant, to contribute to the support of what was therein called "Public Schools," but what would be, the petitioners alleged, in reality a continuation of the Protestant schools.

After setting forth the objections which Roman Catholics entertain to such a system of education as was established by the acts of 1890, the petitioners declared that they appealed from the Acts complained of and they presented the prayer for redress which is hereinbefore recited.

The petition of the "Congress" then sets forth the minute of Council, approved by Your Excellency on the 14th April, 1891, adopting a report of the Minister of Justice, which sets out the scope and effect of the legislation complained of, and also the provisions of the Manitoba Act with reference to education. That report stated that a question had arisen as to the validity and effect of the two statutes of 1890, referred to as the subject of the appeal, and intimated that those statutes would probably be held to be *ultra vires* of the Legislature of Manitoba if they were found to have prejudicially affected "any right or privilege with respect to denominational schools which any class of persons had, by law or practice, in the province, at the union." The report suggested that questions of fact seemed to be raised by the petitions, which were then under consideration, as to the practice in Manitoba with regard to schools, at the time of the union, and also questions of law as to whether the state of facts then existing constituted a "right or privilege" of the Roman Catholics, within the meaning of the saving clauses in the Manitoba Act, and as to whether the Acts complained of (of 1890) had "prejudicially affected" such "right or privilege." The report sets forth that these were obviously questions to be decided by a legal tribunal, before the appeal asserted by the petitioners could be taken up and dealt with, and that if the allegations of the petitioners and their contentions as to the law, were well founded, there would be no occasion for Your Excellency to entertain or act upon the appeal, as the courts would decide the Acts to be *ultra vires.* The report and the minute adopting it, were clearly based on the view that consideration of the complaints and appeal of the Roman Catholic minority, as set forth in the petitions, should be deferred until the legal controversy should be determined, as it would then be ascertained whether the appellants should find it necessary to press for consideration of their application for redress under the saving clauses of the British North America Act and the Manitoba Act, which seemed, by their view of the law, to provide for protection of the rights of a minority against legislation (within the competence of the legislature), which might interfere with rights which had been conferred on the minority, *after the union.*

The memorial of the "Congress" goes on to state that the Judicial Committee of the Privy Council, in England, has upheld the validity of the Acts complained of and the "memorial" asserts that the time has now come for Your Excellency to consider the petitions which have been presented by and on behalf of the Roman Catholics of Manitoba for redress under sub-sections 2 and 3 of section 22 of the Manitoba Act.

There was also referred to the sub-committee a memorial from the Archbishop of Saint Boniface, complaining of the two Acts of 1890, before mentioned, and calling attention to former petitions on the same subject, from members of the Roman Catholic minority in the province. His Grace made reference, in this memorial, to assurances which were given by one of Your Excellency's predecessors before the passage of the Manitoba Act, to redress all well founded grievances and to respect the civil and religious rights and privileges of the people of the Red River Territory. His Grace then prayed that Your Excellency should entertain the appeal of the Roman Catholics of Manitoba and might consider the same, and might make such directions for the hearing and consideration of the appeal as might be thought proper and also give directions for the relief of the Roman Catholics in Manitoba.

The sub-committee also had before them a memorandum made by the "Conservative League" of Montreal remonstrating against the (alleged) unfairness of the Acts of 1890, before referred to.

Soon after the reference was made to the sub-committee of the memorial of the "National Congress" and of the other memorials just referred to, intimation was conveyed to the sub-committee, by Mr. John S. Ewart, Counsel for the Roman Catholic minority in Manitoba, that, in his opinion, it was desirable that a further memorial, on behalf of that minority, should be presented, before the pending application should be dealt with, and action on the part of the sub-committee was therefore delayed until the further petition should come in.

Late in November this supplementary memorial was received and referred to the sub-committee. It is signed by the Archbishop of Saint Boniface, and by the President of the "National Congress," the Mayor of Saint Boniface, and about 137 others, and is presented in the name of the "Members of the Roman Catholic Church resident in the Province of Manitoba."

Its allegations are very similar to those hereinbefore recited, as being contained in the memorial of the Congress, but there is a further contention that the two Acts of the Legislative Assembly of Manitoba, passed in 1890, on the subject of education, were "subversive of the rights and privileges of the Roman Catholic minority provided for by the statutes of Manitoba prior to the passing of the said Acts of 1890, thereby violating both the British North America Act and the Manitoba Act."

This last mentioned memorial urged :—

(1.) That Your Excellency might entertain the appeal and give directions for its proper consideration.

(2.) That Your Excellency should declare that the two Acts of 1890 (chapters 37 and 38), do prejudicially affect the rights and privileges of the minority, with regard to denominational schools, which they had by law or practice, in the province, at the union.

(3.) That it may be declared that the said Acts affect the rights and privileges of Roman Catholics in relation to education.

(4.) That a re-enactment may be ordered by Your Excellency, of the statutes in force in Manitoba, prior to these Acts of 1890, in so far, at least, as may be necessary to secure for Roman Catholics in the province the right to build, maintain, &c., their schools, in the manner provided by such statutes, and to secure to them their proportionate share of any grant made out of public funds of the province for education, or to relieve such members of the Roman Catholic Church as contribute to such Roman Catholic schools from payment or contribution to the support of any other schools ; or that these Acts of 1890 should be so amended as to effect that purpose.

Then follows a general prayer for relief.

In making their report the sub-committee will comment only upon the last memorial presented, as it seems to contain, in effect, all the allegations embraced in the former petitions which call for their consideration and is more specific as to the relief which is sought.

As to the request which the petitioners make in the second paragraph of their prayer, viz : "That it may be declared that the said Acts (53 Vic., 37 and 38) do prejudicially affect the rights and privileges with regard to denominational schools which the Roman Catholics had by law or practice in the province of Manitoba at the time of the union." the sub-committee are of opinion that the judgment of the Judicial Committee of the Privy Council is conclusive as to the rights with regard to denominational schools which the Roman Catholics had at the time of the union, and as to the bearing thereon of the statutes complained of, and Your Excellency is not, therefore, in the opinion of the sub-committee, properly called upon to hear an appeal based on those grounds. That judgment is as binding on Your Excellency as it is on any of the parties to the litigation, and, therefore, if redress is sought on account of the state of affairs existing in the province at the time of the union, it must be sought elsewhere and by other means than by way of appeal under the sections of the British North America Act and of the Manitoba Act, which are relied on by the petitioners as sustaining this appeal.

The two Acts of 1890, which are complained of, must, according to the opinion of the sub-committee, be regarded as within the powers of the Legislature of Manitoba, but it remains to be considered whether the appeal should be entertained and heard as an appeal against statutes which are alleged to have encroached on rights and privileges with regard to denominational schools which were acquired by any class of persons in Manitoba, not *at the time of the union* but *after the union.*

The sub-committee were addressed by counsel for the petitioners as to the right to have the appeal heard, and from his argument, as well as from the documents, it would seem that the following are the grounds of the appeal :—

A complete system of separate and denominational schools. *i.e.,* a system providing for Public Schools and for Separate Catholic Schools, was, it is alleged, established by Statute of Manitoba in 1871 and by a series of subsequent Acts. This system was in operation until the two Acts of 1890 (chapters 37 and 38) were passed.

The 93rd section of the British North America Act, in conferring power on the provincial legislatures, exclusively, to make laws in relation to education, imposed on that power certain restrictions, one of which was (sub-section 1) to preserve the right with respect to denominational schools which any class of persons had in the province at the union. As to this restriction it seems to impose a condition on the validity of any Act relating to education, and the sub-committee have already observed that no question, it seems to them, can arise, since the decision of the Judicial Committee of the Privy Council.

The third sub-section, however, is as follows:—

"Where in any province a system of separate or dissentient schools exists by law at the union, or is thereafter established by the legislature of the province, an appeal shall lie to the Governor-General in Council, from any Act or decision of any provincial authority, affecting any right or privilege of the Protestant or Roman Catholic minority of the Queen's subjects in relation to education."

The Manitoba Act passed in 1870, by which the Province of Manitoba was constituted, contains the following provisions, as regards that province:—

By section 22 the power is conferred on the legislature, exclusively, to make laws in relation to education, but subject to the following restrictions:

(1.) "Nothing in any law shall prejudicially affect any right or privilege with respect to denominational schools which any class of persons have, by law or practice, in the province, at the union."

This restriction, the sub-committee again observe, has been dealt with by the judgment of the Judicial Committee of the Privy Council.

Then follows:

(2.) "An appeal shall lie to the Governor-General in Council from any Act or decision of the Legislature of the province, or of any provincial authority, affecting any right or privilege of the Protestant or Roman Catholic minority of the Queen's subjects in relation to education."

It will be observed that the restriction contained in sub-section 2 is not identical with the restriction of sub-section 3 of the 93rd section of the British North America Act, and questions are suggested, in view of this difference, as to whether sub-section 3 of section 93 of the British North America Act applies to Manitoba, and, if not, whether sub-section 2 of section 22 of the Manitoba Act is sufficient to sustain the case of the appellants; or, in other words, whether, in regard to Manitoba, the minority has the same protection against laws which the legislature of the province has power to pass, as the minorities in other provinces have, under the sub-section before quoted from the British North America Act, as to separate or denominational schools established after the union.

The argument presented by counsel on behalf of the petitioners was, that the present appeal comes before Your Excellency in Canada, not as a request to review the decision of the Judicial Committee of the Privy Council, but as a logical consequence and result of that decision, inasmuch as the remedy now sought is provided by the British North America Act, and the Manitoba Act, not as a remedy to the minority against statutes which interfere with the rights which the minority had at the time of the union, but as a remedy against statutes which interfere with rights acquired by the minority after the union. The remedy, therefore, which is sought, is against Acts which are *intra vires* of the Provincial Legislature. His argument is also that the appeal does not ask Your Excellency to interfere with any rights or powers of the Legislature of Manitoba, inasmuch as the power to legislate on the subject of education has only been conferred on that legislature with the distinct reservation that Your Excellency in Council shall have power to make remedial orders against any such legislation which infringes on rights acquired after the union by any Protestant or Roman Catholic minority in relation to separate or dissentient schools.

Upon the various questions which arise on these petitions the sub-committee do not feel called upon to express an opinion, and so far as they are aware, no opinion has been expressed on any previous occasion in this case or any other of a like kind, by Your Excellency's Government or any other Government of Canada. Indeed, no application of a parallel character has been made since the establishment of the Dominion.

The application comes before Your Excellency in a manner differing from applications which are ordinarily made, under the constitution, to Your Excellency in Council. In the opinion of the sub-committee, the application is not to be dealt with at present as a matter of a political character or involving political action on the part of Your Excellency's advisers. It is to be dealt with by Your Excellency in Council, regardless of the personal views which Your Excellency's advisers may hold with regard to denominational schools and without the political action of any of the members of Your Excellency's Council being considered as pledged by the fact of the appeal being entertained and heard. If the contention of the petitioners be correct, that such an appeal can be sustained, the inquiry will be rather of a judicial than a political character. The sub-committee have so treated it in hearing counsel, and in permitting their only meeting to be open to the public. It is apparent that several other questions will arise, in addition to those which were discussed by counsel at that meeting, and the sub-committee advises that a date be fixed, at which the petitioners, or their counsel, may be heard with regard to the appeal, according to their first request.

The sub-committee think it proper that the Government of Manitoba should have an opportunity to be represented at the hearing, and they further recommend, with that view, that if this report should be approved, a copy of any minute approving it, and of any minute fixing the date of the hearing with regard to the appeal, be forwarded, together with copies of all the petitions referred to, to

His Honour the Lieutenant-Governor of Manitoba, for the information of His Honour's advisers.

In the opinion of the sub-committee, the attention of any person who may attend on behalf of the petitioners, or on behalf of the Provincial Government, should be called to certain preliminary questions which seem to arise with regard to the appeal.

Among the questions which the sub-committee regard as preliminary are the following :—

(1). Whether this appeal is such an appeal as is contemplated by sub-section 3 of section 93 of the British North America Act, or by sub-section 2 of section 22 of the Manitoba Act.

(2). Whether the ground set forth in the petitions are such as may be the subject of appeal under either of the sub-sections above referred to.

(3). Whether the decision of the Judicial Committee of the Privy Council in any way bears on the application for redress based on the contention that the rights of the Roman Catholic minority which accrued to them after the union have been interfered with by the two statutes of 1890 before referred to.

(4). Whether sub-committee 3 of section 93 of the British North America Act applies to Manitoba.

(5). Whether Your Excellency in Council has power to grant such orders as are asked for by the petitioner, assuming the material facts to be as stated in the petition.

(6). Whether the Acts of Manitoba, passed before the session of 1890, conferred on the minority a "right or privilege with respect to education," within the meaning of sub-section 2 of section 22 of the Manitoba Act, or established "a system of separate or dissentient schools," within the meaning of sub-section 3 of section 93 of the British North America Act, and if so, whether the two Acts of 1890, complained of, affect "the right or privilege" of the minority in such a manner as to warrant the present appeal.

Other questions of like character may be suggested at the hearing, and it may be desirable that arguments should be heard upon such preliminary points before any hearing shall take place on the merits of the appeal

Respectfully submitted,

Jno. S. D. Thompson.
M. Bowell.
J. A. Chapleau.
T. Mayne Daly.

ARGUMENT UPON APPEAL TO THE GOVERNOR-GENERAL IN COUNCIL.

Notice having been given to the Province and to the representatives of the Roman Catholics, the Governor-General in Council sat to hear argument on the 21st day of January, 1893. The following is a very accurate account of the proceedings taken from *The Empire*:—

Ottawa, Jan. 22.—It was an historic scene which was enacted yesterday in the Privy Council chamber here—historic because for the first time in the history of the Dominion an appeal was being heard by the Governor in Council under the provisions of section 93 of the Confederation Act. Following the precedent set by the subcommittee of the Privy Council, which heard the preliminary argument, the proceedings yesterday were open to the public. Every leading newspaper in the Dominion had its representative present, while about a dozen gentlemen represented the great Canadian public. Among the more notable outsiders present were Rev. Father Lacombe, the famous N.W. missionary ; Mr. Lariviere, M.P for Provencher; Mr. Bernier, the new Senator from Manitoba, and ex-Ald. John Heney, of Ottawa. Solicitor-General Curran also dropped in to hear what was going on.

Hon. Mr. Ives governed the meeting in his capacity as President of the Privy Council. Seated at his right hand was the first minister, Sir John Thompson, and on his left Hon Mr. Bowell, the senior Privy Councillor. Then ranged about the round table, commencing at Sir John Thompson's right according to seniority, were : Sir A. P. Caron, Hon. John Costigan, Hon. Mr. Foster, Hon. Mr. Haggart, Hon. Mr. Patterson and Hon. Mr. Daly. To the left of Hon. Mr. Bowell were Hon. Messrs. Tupper, Ouimet and Angers, the latter being the junior Privy Councillor. As previously intimated would be the case, there was no representative present on behalf of the Manitoba Government. Mr. J. S. Ewart, Q.C. of Winnipeg, appeared for Archbishop Taché and the Roman Catholic minority of Manitoba, and was accorded a position at the round table for his convenience, between Hon. Messrs. Bowell and Tupper.

The president, in opening the proceedings, stated that the object was to hear counsel on the points suggested by the sub-committee in their report to Council, based on the argument heard on November 26th last.

POINTS FOR CONSIDERATION.

The committee in its report recommended that in any future argument which took place on the schools question, the following

points might be considered, and they are quoted here in order that
the trend of Mr. Ewart's argument may be the better understood:

"1. Whether this appeal is such an appeal as is contemplated
by sub-section 3 of section 93 of the B.N.A. Act, or by sub-section 2
of section 22 of the Manitoba Act.

"2. Whether the grounds set forth in the petitions are such as
may be the subject of appeal under either of the sub-sections above
referred to.

"3. Whether the decision of the Judicial Committee of the
Privy Council in any way bears on the application for redress based
on the contention that the rights of the Roman Catholic minority
which accrued to them after the union have been interfered with by
the two statutes of 1890, before referred to.

"4. Whether sub-section 3 of section 93 of the B.N.A. Act
applies to Manitoba.

"5. Whether the Governor in Council has power to grant such
orders as are asked for by the petitioners, assuming the material
facts to be stated in the petition.

"6. Whether the Acts of Manitoba passed before the session of
1890, conferred on the minority a 'right or privilege with respect
to education' within the meaning of sub-section 2 of section 22 of
the Manitoba Act, or established 'a system of separate or dissentient
schools' within the meaning of sub-section 3 of section 93 of the
B.N.A. Act, and if so, whether the two Acts of 1890 complained of
affect the right or privilege of the minority in such a manner as to
warrant the present appeal."

MR. EWART'S ADDRESS.

Mr. Ewart addressed the Council as follows: Honorable
Gentlemen of the Privy Council,—It is suggested by the Order in
Council, in pursuance of which I have now the honour of addressing
you, that the argument should be confined to those questions which
may properly be termed preliminary or technical, and that all
argument upon the merits of the appeal should be postponed until
another occasion. In my address I shall, as far as possible,
conform to this suggestion, but I may find it necessary for the
clear statement of my argument, to exceed in some slight degree
the proposed limit. Although I shall base most strongly my case
upon the Manitoba Act, yet believing that that statute can best be
approached after a perfect understanding of the British North
America Act, I shall crave the indulgence of the Council while, for
a few moments, I discuss the Act of Confederation, and the
conditions existing in the various provinces which demanded the
peculiar provisions that it contained. Among all the questions
which have divided and distracted Canadian politics, I suppose there

has been none which has given rise to greater difference of opinion than the subject of education. That difference of opinion was not only natural, but inevitable. So long as accepted theories of government determined that the state had nothing to do with education, so long as each church educated or left uneducated its own people, there was no difficulty. But when the state finally and in recent years determined to educate its citizens, it was inevitable that the question of how to educate should give rise to conflicting opinion. And the question is an exceedingly difficult one. First of all we must determine whether there is to be one kind of school or more kinds than one. A great many assert that if the state is to teach it must have but one method of doing it—there can be only one right way, and therefore there should be only one way. In former days this was almost the universal belief with reference to religion. There must be a state church; there can only be one true church; therefore establish that kind and suppress all others. Acts of Uniformity, Test Acts and all other apparatus—the whole power of the state was employed, time and again, to compel people to think alike. But men were made dissimilar and will remain so until they cease to be men and become angels. All efforts to compel them to worship in one church failed. The advocates of uniformity in education have to face such difficulties as these: 1. Can the state teach morality? 2. If so, can morality be taught without revealing that upon which it is based? Can a teacher say, This is right, and be denied the power to answer the question, Why is it right? 3. If morality and its basis are to be taught, what is that basis? Is it religion? If so, is religion dogmatic theology? If so, whose dogmas constitute religion? Or is the basis an enlightened utility, evolved by experience, and hardened by practice into habit and reality? 4. In short, can education be separated from morality, and can morality be separated from religion? If a unanimous answer can be given to all these questions then a case is made for uniformity.

On the other hand a great many contend that the state, disregarding mere eccentric opinion, should provide schools upon different models, in order that in this way the solution, and the compulsory adoption of the solution, of all these questions may be obviated. This may be somewhat more expensive than the uniformity method, but it is urged more effective, because by it you can get the children to go to the schools, which after all seems to be of some importance.

In Canada prior to confederation these differences were accentuated by the fact that a very large proportion of the inhabitants were Roman Catholics, and that by the dogmas of their church it was impossible for them to approve of the only kind of schools that those of other denominations would attend. Prior to 1863 a large number of Protestants in Upper Canada belonged to the uniformity party; were determined that there should be only one kind of schools; that that kind should of course be their kind; and that Roman Catholics should either (1) abandon education altogether, or (2) abandon their religion, or (3) provide private schools for themselves besides providing public schools for others. A spirit of tolerance and of good sense, however, finally prevailed and the great leaders of the uniformity party, the Hon. George Brown and Hon. Alex. Mackenzie, lived to extend their sympathy and support to the Roman Catholics in their struggle for the right to educate their children as they thought proper. The result of this prolonged and better conflict made two things tolerably clear :—(1) That Protestants and Roman Catholics were wholly irreconcilable upon this question of education, and (2) that from time to time as one generation exceeded another, we might expect a recrudesence of attempts by religious majorities to coerce the minorities into their way of thinking.

It was under these circumstances, and with a Protestant minority in Lower Canada, and a Roman Catholic minority in all the other provinces, that the framers of the Confederation Act proceeded to deal with the question of education. They had to proportion legislative jurisdiction between the Federal and the Provincial Legislatures. What has to be done with education? Was it to be assigned to the Dominion or the provinces? It was a matter of local concern and would be most naturally assigned to the provinces; but that would be to leave the Protestant minority in Qubec, and the Roman Catholic minority in the other provinces at the mercy of opposing majorities. A compromise was adopted—a compromise so essential that without it confederation could never have taken place (as Sir Oliver Mowat tells us) and the compromise was this, that the provinces should have jurisdiction over education, but should in the exercise of that jurisdiction be subject to certain restrictions and limitations for the protection of minorities. These restrictions and limitations were of two kinds —first, the provinces were to have no power to prejudicially affect any right or privilege with respect to denominational schools which any class of persons had by law at the date of the union, and second an appeal should lie to the Governor-General in council whenever any right or privilege of the religious minority was affected in any province in which separate schools had been once established, whether before or after the union; and the Governor General could call upon the legislatures to pass laws for the purpose of carrying out his award. That was the compromise agreed upon; the province in the matter of education shall not be omnipotent : as to some matters they shall have no power at all—they must not prejudicially affect rights existing at the union : as to other matters their power shall be subject to appeal, and their work subject to revision, by the Governor-General in Council.

Now let me point out that the Confederation Act speaks of two classes of rights and privileges; first, those which existed at the union, and second, those which came into existence after the union. A province is absolutely powerless to prejudice the rights which existed at the union, but as to those which came into existence afterwards — those created by the province itself—the province gave, and the province can take away, subject only to supervision by the Governor-General in Council and by the Federal Parliament. The distinction between the two classes of cases is, in the Confederation Act, perfectly clear. The third sub-section in terms applies to cases in which there was no separate school system prior to the union; it applied only to cases where such a system was subsequently erected. The rights and privileges, therefore, to which it refers must include those created after the union. Such is the Confederation Act, and such was the system of checks and balances by which the framers of that statute endeavoured to safeguard the interests of the minorities in all the provinces, whether Protestant or Catholic; a system under which the provinces were not left to contend with one another, with reciprocity of intolerance; but one under which the central power, basing its authority not upon provincial majorities, but upon all the majorities, and therefore being more certain to be unaffected by local and evanescent passion, would exercise a controlling power over local legislation.

Manitoba entered the union in 1870. At that time Protestants and Roman Catholics were then in about equal numbers. The question of education was certain to be one of the first things dealt with by the Legislature which should there be erected, and it became the duty of the Dominion Parliament to formulate such a constitution as would best serve the interests of the future inhabitants. Again came the question, what power is to be given with reference to education? The people are at present about equally divided, but it is inevitable that one side or the other (we cannot now tell which) will in years to come be in the majority. Shall we leave them to fight it out, letting the more numerous win? Or shall we provide for the future minority? Following the precedent of the Confederation Act, and the dictates of all experience, the latter course was adopted. Power was given to the Legislature to make laws with regard to education, but no plenary power was accorded. There are again two limitations: first that the Legislature should have no power prejudicially to affect rights which existed at the union; and, second, that there should be an appeal to the Governor-General in Council whenever *any* right or privilege should be affected.

Now, I am well aware that it will be urged that there are not two limitations here, but there is a limitation and a remedy for its breach —that the limitation prohibits violation of rights at the union, and that the appeal is in case of the violation of such rights. I say that I am aware of this, because last July I heard it argued at great length before the Judicial Committee of the Privy Council in England. Sir Horace Davy and Mr. Dalton McCarthy did their best to get the

Committee to take that view of the matter. They argued that the proceedings in the action were wrongly taken; that the courts had no jurisdiction; that if the Act was *ultra vires* there was a remedy given by the statute, viz., an appeal to the Governor-General in Council; and that that being the remedy provided by statute, there could be no remedy by appeal to the courts. At first their Lordships were much taken with this view, and interrupted the argument upon the merits to hear what counsel for Mr. Barrett had to say upon the point. The result was the complete overthrow of the idea, and the argument upon the merits proceeded. In order that the point debated may clearly appear, perhaps I may be allowed to quote from the remarks of judges and counsel made during the argument:

The Attorney-General (counsel for Mr. Barrett)—"I contend that sub-sections 2 and 3 do not depend on *ultra vires* at all. Sub-sections 2 and 3 depend on the Protestant or Catholic minority being able to make a case, before the Governor-General on petition, that other legislation is required. It does not suggest that the Act which the Governor is going to consider is an *ultra vires* Act. It might be perfectly legitimate and lawful, passed by the Provincial Legislature within its narrowest powers."

Sir Horace Davey (counsel for Manitoba Government)—"My Lords, the difference between my learned friend the Attorney-General's view and the view which I presented to your Lordships appears to me to turn upon the construction and effect which he puts upon sub-sections 2 and 3. Now, there at once I must take issue with him. I do not agree that sub-section 2 does relate to anything but what is *ultra vires*. I cannot for myself frame the proposition which would lead to the inference that sub-section 2 was intended to deal with cases which were *ultra vires*."

Mr. McCarthy—"Now, the ordinary rule is that when in a matter of this kind a particular remedy is pointed out in the statute which confers the right, of course that special remedy must be followed.

Lord Watson—"Assuming that they have done what they have power to do—under the constitution of Manitoba, I mean—if they were establishing separate and dissentient schools, a system of separate or dissentient schools, then their acts with regard to these schools might come under section 3."

Mr. McCarthy—"That is what I was venturing to contend could not be done."

Lord Watson—"The right to determine whether the province has exceeded its powers or not is one thing, but undoubtedly what is contemplated here is not cases of excess of power by the Provincial Legislature, but cases where, acting within their power, they have not done what the minority thought justice. Sub-section 2 would suggest this: that the Dominion Legislature were under the impression that that there might be provisions within the power of the Provincial

Legislature which would affect the rights of these persons without affecting the minority prejudicially in the sense of sub-section 1 so as to make them *ultra vires*."

Mr. McCarthy at one place having intimated his intention of continuing the argument, Lord Shand said : "After the intimation you have heard it will not be a very hopeful argument, to say the least of it."

I refer to the proceedings of the Judicial Committee for two purposes : (1) to show that the Committee decided that these two subsections did not stand in the relation of limitation and remedy ; and (2) to show that, according to Lord Watson, "undoubtedly what is contemplated" in the second sub-section " is not cases of excess of power by the Provincial Legislature, but cases where, acting within their power, they have not done what the minority thought justice." And, indeed, the matter seems to me, with all deference to those who argued otherwise, to be not open to question. Of what possible utility is a power to appeal from an *ultra vires* statute, and what remedial legislation (it is that we seek) would be necessitated by an *ultra vires* Act ? An *ultra vires* statute, *ex vi termini*, is nothing at all. How can we appeal from nothing at all ? How can we ask for remedial legislation if there is nothing to remedy ? Surely the first requisite of a remedial action is a living subject. You don't apply remedies to dead people. On the contrary, you bury them, being as they are actually defunct and not properly amenable to medical skill. Suppose that the Manitoba School Act had been held to be *ultra vires*, and therefore dead, still-born, never any vitality in it, would we be here to-day appealing from it ? And, if we were, would we not be told that we were taking altogether too much trouble over a mere corpse ? And yet it is said that we cannot appeal because the Act is alive, because it is not mere dead lumber, in which case also we could not appeal. If it were *ultra vires*, it is admitted that we could appeal, but only to be laughed at. As it is not, we cannot appeal at all. In order to found an appeal there must be a good Act, and a good Act cannot be appealed from. Such are the absurdities which are finding some currency—even in the newspapers. Again, we can only appeal from a statute which affects rights or privileges. We must be able to show that we are hurt. But how can an *ultra vires* Act affect rights, privileges or anything else ? How could we possibly say that an *ultra vires* Act had injured us ? The statute gives an appeal in some case or another. Clearly it must be from a statute, a real, veritable statute, and not from a form, figure or simulacrum of a statute.

Allow me to answer this argument in another way. Let us suppose that the draftsman of the Manitoba Act desired to prohibit the Legislature from passing certain laws, and to provide a remedy in case the prohibition were disregarded, how would he have proceeded ?

The first sub-section would, no doubt, have been drawn as it appears, but the second would clearly have been in this fashion: An appeal shall lie to the Governor-General in Council from any Act of the Legislature prejudicially affecting *such* rights or privileges. But, instead, as I shall proceed to show, that sub-section is in no way connected with the preceding clause, but, on the contrary, provides for a totally different set of circumstances. In my address before a committee of your Honorable Council, on the 26th November last, I entered into a more minute comparison of the language of the two sub-sections for the purpose of showing their dissimilarity, of showing how impossible it is to contend that they stand in the relation of prohibition and remedy than I intend to undertake to-day. My remarks upon that occasion were very fully reported, and have been, thanks to the enterprise of the press, widely circulated. An official report also, I am informed, is in the possession of the Council. I shall, therefore, abstain from a repetition of the argument to be derived from such a comparison, contenting myself by pointing out in a few words that there is nothing in common between the two sub-sections:

1. Under sub-section 1 an Episcopalian or Presbyterian, as such, could complain (it was so held in the Logan case); while under sub-section 2 they could only complain, if at all, as belonging to the body of Protestants.

2. Under sub-section 1 any Protestant could complain; while under sub-section 2 no Protestant could complain unless Protestants were in a minority in the province. As a concrete example, Mr. Logan, as an Episcopalian, had a sufficient *locus standi* before the Judicial Committee of the Privy Council; but he never could appeal under sub-section 2, because the Roman Catholics, and not the Protestants, are in the minority in Manitoba.

3. Under sub-section 1 an Act is *ultra vires*, and there can be no appeal from it, there being nothing to appeal from; while under sub-section 2 an appeal is given from Legislative Acts, which must be *intra vires*, in order to be Legislative Acts.

4. Under sub-section 1 the rights preserved are those "with respect to denominational schools"; while under sub-section 2 those referred to are "in relation to education." The distinction between these expressions is the very ground-work of the decision of the Judicial Committee of the Council.

5. Under sub-section 1 there must be a prejudicial affecting of a right; while under sub-section 2 there need be no prejudice. Plainly, the two sub-sections have nothing in common between them. But it is argued that if my view of the statute be correct then the Act is wholly unprecedented, that there is nothing anywhere at all analogous to the position I assign to the Local Legislatures. Was there ever any such thing heard of as an appeal from a Legislative

Assembly? In the first place, I would not be disconcerted could I discover no precedent or analogy. Show me a precedent for the British North America Act. It recites that the intention is to model confederation upon the constitution of the United Kingdom. Prof. Bryce (now a member of the Imperial Cabinet) terms this a piece of "official mendacity," and books have been written to prove what it really is modelled upon. The truth of the matter is that it is an original production, and we might as well search for the prototype of the American, as for that of the Canadian constitution. In an original production we necessarily find some original things, but we never on that account refuse to give language its true meaning and insist that every original thing is in reality old and stale, arriving at this conclusion by eliminating all that is new, because there is no precedent for it.

But for those who insist upon precedent and analogy let me say this: What have we here? An Act of a Local Legislature with an appeal to the Governor in council? Yes, but that is not all; the Governor in council can do nothing without the Canadian Parliament. So that in reality it is an Act of the Local Legislature, with an appeal to the Federal Parliament. Some years ago Parliament, in one short paragraph, transferred jurisdiction over almost every local railway in Canada from the provinces to the Dominion. Railways that had been built largely by provincial subsidies were swept beyond provincial jurisdiction. How was that done? The answer is simple. Parliament has by the constitution power to transfer local works to its own jurisdiction. And what is the power of disallowance? A Local Legislature desires to build railways in certain directions, and so enacts. The Governor-General thinks otherwise and disallows the legislation. Here are two cases in which there is something very like an appeal, and in one of them an appeal, not to Parliament, but to the Governor-General in Council merely.

Other examples can easily be given in which provincial jurisdiction is subordinated to Dominion Acts of Parliament. The Assemblies may enact certain legislation with reference to insolvency and other matters, which will be valid in the absence of Dominion legislation, but the Dominion may at any time supersede the provincial statutes. This, although well known to lawyers, may not be easily accepted by laymen, and for those I offer a reference to section 95 of the British North America Act. There surely is something startling for those who declaim about provincial rights, as though there was no such thing as federal jurisdiction, as though the highest provincial patriotism consisted in the repudiation of those parts of our constitution which assign to the federal authorities those powers which seem for the moment to stand in their way. This is the section:

"In each province the Legislature may make laws in relation to agriculture in the province, and to immigration into the province; and it is hereby declared that the Parliament of Canada may from time to time make laws in relation to agriculture in all or any of the provinces, and to immigration into all or any of the provinces: and any law of the legislature of a province relative to agriculture, or to immigration, shall have effect, in and for the province, as long and as far only as it is not repugnant to any act of the Parliament of Canada."

This seems also to be something very like an appeal. Manitoba declares that the matter of cutting thistles shall be attended to by each individual owner of land, with a penalty merely for neglect. The Dominion chooses to ordain that some public official is to see that thistles are cut and that the owner shall pay for the work. Even in the matter of cutting thistles the Local Legislature must bow to the Dominion Parliament; and are we surprised that with reference to education—perhaps the most important subject in the whole field of legislative action, an appeal should, under well defined circumstances, be vested in the Federal Parliament? Let no one hereafter say that the present appeal is without precedent or analogy.

And let me say, in passing from this part of my argument, that it is as idle to talk of interference with provincial rights, should the appeal in this case be allowed, as it would be to complain of the interference of the Supreme Court with a decision of the Manitoba Court of the Queen's Bench. We have our own court, why cannot we make its decisions final and conclusive? Shall not a province be permitted to regulate its own affairs? No, under our constitution it cannot do so. The province cannot evade the appeal which the Dominion Parliament has provided shall lie from all final judgments of the Manitoba Court, nor should the province complain if any other kind of appeal provided for by the constitution be prosecuted.

Another question must be answered. Assuming that an appeal lies from some *intra vires* Acts, does an appeal lie from this particular Act? The answer to this question depends upon whether or not the Act affects any right or privilege of Roman Catholics in relation to education. Two points are usually urged against the present appeal. (1) That the Privy Council having held the Act to be *intra vires* there can be no appeal, and (2) that the Privy Council having held that no right or privilege has been affected, therefore there can be no appeal. The former of these arguments I have already answered. Let me reply to the latter.

Rights of Roman Catholics: How can Roman Catholics or anybody else acquire rights in relation to education? There is only one way so far as sub-section 2 is concerned, and that is by statute. The Act, therefore, means that if any right or privilege which has been acquired under any statute has been affected an appeal shall lie. The Act means this or nothing, for no right or privilege could otherwise be acquired. No appeal is given in respect of rights acquired by practice. If this be conceded, as it probably will, the only point for debate is, whether the statutes giving the rights and privileges must have been passed prior to the union; or, is there an appeal from a statute passed after the union? Clearly, I say, the latter, and for several reasons :

Firstly—There was no statute relating to education in Manitoba prior to the union ; and to confine the appeal to the violation of such statutes is again to argue that we must appeal from nothing at all ; and even worse this time, that we must not have a word to say for ourselves when we do appeal.

Secondly—There is nothing in the statute which limits the appeal to the case of rights acquired before the union. The difference in the language in the sub-sections cannot fail to be observed. One speaks of rights existing at the time of the union —violation of these is *ultra vires*; the other speaks of rights and privileges in relation to education, without any limit as to date. Violation of these gives a right of appeal.

Thirdly—But even had we not this difference in the language of the sub-sections to aid us in their interpretation, yet under the ordinary rules for the construction of statutes there could be no difficulty in assigning the meaning for which I contend. Suppose a statute provided that if one man destroyed another man's property he should be imprisoned, would any one argue that the Act only referred to property which was owned at the time of the passing of the Act? Suppose a statute provided that if one man interferes with another man's right to any of his property he should be fined, would any judge limit the Act to rights which existed when the statute was passed? And suppose a statute provides that if a Legislature (instead of an individual) interferes with the rights of certain people, there shall be an appeal, is there, in the change from individual to Legislature, to be found any good reason for changing the scope of the word "rights"?

Fourthly—As I have already shown, there can be no doubt that under the third section of the British North America Act there may be an appeal when rights acquired after the union have been affected. Whatever else may be put forward, it can never be pretended that the minority in Manitoba is in worse plight than are the minorities in the other provinces. It would be a strange interpretation that would except Manitoba from the principle which applies to the other provinces, viz., that whenever there are separate schools there is a right of appeal in respect of rights acquired after the union.

It really seems to be wasting breath to argue against such possible pretensions, but let me, in addition to the reasons which I have given, refer to one or two authorities illustrative of the rule which I have invoked. (1) The statute 8 Anne, c. 7, provided that "if any prohibited goods whatsoever shall be imported into any part of Great Britain then" the goods shall be forfeited. A subsequent statute prohibited the importation of foreign leather gloves. Chief Baron Thompson said: "Then the question arises whether this statute (of Anne) applies to goods subsequently prohibited by other Acts; and we are of opinion that the statute is not so confined in its operation, but that whenever a subsequent Act prohibits the importation of goods the provisions of the 8th Anne immediately attach, as much as if they had been prohibited at the time of making the statute." (Attorney-General v. Saggers, I. Price 182). (2) Lord Holt lays it down as a general rule that "when an Act of Parliament creates a new interest, it shall be governed by the same law that like interests have been governed before." (Lane v. Cotton, 12 Mod. 486). (3) Our own Supreme Court Act provides that "an appeal shall lie to the Supreme Court from all final judgments of the highest" Provincial Court. Is that provision limited to judgments theretofore rendered, or to judgments rendered under statutes which then existed? Clearly not. It would apply to all judgments affecting the rights of any person, whether the judgments or the rights of the persons existed at the time of passing the Supreme Court Act, or whether they came into existence 15 years afterwards.

And the broad good sense of the matter is abundantly apparent. The Legislature is constitutionally prohibited from diminishing rights which existed prior to its own existence. It may, however, accord further and other rights if it sees fit so to do, and having done so, and the people having accepted and lived and worked in the enjoyment of these rights and privileges, the rights become, as it were, vested rights, which may not be affected, should the Governor-General in Council think the proceedings inequitable or unfair.

My argument is not complete without showing that some rights or privileges conferred by Manitoba legislation have been affected; and yet the facts necessary to prove that are so well known that I shall but lightly refer to them. Prior to the union, Roman Catholics had established and were supporting schools for the children of their own faith. The Episcopalians and Presbyterians were similarly engaged. During the first session of the Manitoba Legislature a School Act was passed. It provided for Protestant schools and Roman Catholic schools. The former were handed over to the Protestants for management and the latter to the Roman Catholics. Each body had complete control over their own schools, could teach what they liked and how they liked. Each proceeded in the way we should have anticipated; the Protestants made their schools secular, or nearly so, and the Roman Catholics pursued their accustomed policy. With some alterations this law continued for twenty years. Under it the Roman Catholics built and equipped a very large number of schools, and there never was any well founded complaint as to the method they employed, save only that the schools were too Catholic.

The Act of 1890 professed to abolish both the Protestant and and the Roman Catholic schools and to erect public schools. In effect, it abolished the Roman Catholic schools, left the Protestant ones standing, and handed over all the Roman Catholic schools and property to the Protestants. The name "Protestant" was changed to "Public." In other respects the schools to-day are the same as when they were called Protestant and were shaped and fashioned by Protestants, many of whom were Protestant divines. It is one of the errors which (with all due respect to them) the Judicial Committee of the Privy Council fell into, to suppose that the statute did not work any confiscation of Roman Catholic property. Special provision is made by the statute for the relief of Roman Catholics in Districts where there were schools of both kinds, and to this the Privy Council makes special allusion, but of these districts there were very few. No similar provision is made for their protection in the great majority of cases. In over 70 districts the Roman Catholic schools are by the statute to become public schools, which means that Roman Catholics are to walk out of them and that education is to be carried on there upon an almost purely secular footing. That the Roman Catholics have not been so far compelled to hand over their school apparatus and materials in those districts is on this account alone—there are no Protestants in these districts to use them.

And this leads me to point out not only the injury inflicted by the statute, but the utterly wanton character of the injury. At the time of the passing of the School Act of 1890 there were 86 Roman Catholic School districts in the province. In 68 of these it may be said that there was, comparatively, hardly a single Protestant. The residents were almost entirely Roman Catholic. In eight of the remainder—those principally within the limits of cities or towns— there were both Protestant and Roman Catholic schools, and population enough for each. In only four districts could it be said that the population was not only mixed, but so sparse that the separate school system created the slightest difficulty. Now, what reason can be urged for attempting to close the schools in the 68 districts? The people there are homogeneous, all desire one sort of school and are anxious to tax themselves to support that kind of school. What kind of statesmanship is it that would deny that simple right to so large a section of the people? And what more can be said for interference with the schools in the cities and towns? In Nova Scotia and New Brunswick, where there is no separate school system by law, the people are so tolerant, and I shall add so sensible, in the administration of the statutes, that for all practical purposes Roman Catholics are, in cities, really in the enjoyment of almost all they can desire. Their schools are called public schools, and are supported as the others, but a judicious eye is tightly closed as to the religious portion of the education there imparted. In Manitoba it is different. Roman Catholics have to pay their taxes to support the Protestant schools, and have to support their own out of their private purses. Were there any disposition on the part of the Manitoba Government to act fairly with the Roman Catholics, I say that their schools in the 68 districts and in the eight would never in any way have been interfered with; and as to the other four the resources of civilization need not be largely drawn upon in order to find some easy solution of the circumstances there existing. The absence of four good men from a city might afford ground for the destruction of the whole population, but surely the presence of four bad ones would not be thought to supply satisfactory reason for the same comprehensive action.

So far I have been endeavoring to prove that power to deal with the present appeal exists. Before closing, however, I desire, with all deference and respect, to contend that not only has His Excellency in council this power, but that it is his bounden duty to hear the appeal, and to adjudicate thereon as its merits may require; that the constitution has given to the Catholic minority of the Queen's subjects in Manitoba, as a right, an appeal from Acts of the Legislative Assembly; that His Excellency in Council cannot decline to hear such an appeal, and cannot refuse, whether out of regard for the Legislature, or for any other reason, to deliver a judgment upon the merits of the case when brought before him. It is a well-known rule for the construction of statutes that where functions of a public nature are bestowed upon individuals, such persons have no right to refuse to exercise their powers. The rule includes cases in which jurisdiction of a judicial character is given. Even when the language of a statute is permissive—the judge *may* do so and so— yet that is always held to mean that if a proper case is made out he *shall* do so and so. Allow me to quote a passage from Maxwell on Statutes (pages 295-6): "It is a legal, or rather a constitutional principle, that powers given to public functionaries or others, for public purposes or the public benefit, were always to be exercised when the occasion arises." And again: "But as regards the imperative character of the duty, it was laid down by the King's Bench (R. v. Hastings, 1 D. and R., 48), that words of permission in an Act of Parliament when tending to promote the general benefit, are always held to be compulsory; and as regards courts and judicial functionaries, who act only when appealed to, the same rule was in substance re-stated by the Common Pleas in laying down that whenever a statute confers an authority to do a judicial act (the word "judicial" being used evidently in its widest sense), in a certain case, it is imperative on those so authorized to exercise the authority when the case arises, and its exercise is duly applied for by a party interested and having a right to make the application; and that the exercise depends, not on the discretion of the courts or judges, but upon proof of the particular case out of which the power arises."

Our Supreme Court Act (as I have said) provides that "An appeal shall lie to the Supreme Court from all final judgments" of provincial courts. The Manitoba Act, in similar terms, provides that "An appeal shall lie to the Governor-General in Council from any Act or decision of the Legislature of the province." What would we say of the Supreme Court, did it refuse to hear an appeal, or to deal with it as justice required, merely because the case involved some political or otherwise troublesome question? With all proper respect, and for identical reasons, I say that His Excellency in Council cannot decline to exercise the important powers by the Manitoba Act conferred upon him for the protection of the Roman Catholic minority in that province; and I humbly claim as a right that the petitions shall be heard and adjudicated upon. The recent order in council is beyond doubt correct, if I may be permitted to say so, in asserting that if His Excellency has jurisdiction "the enquiry will be rather of a judicial than of a political character." If then I have shown that there is power to entertain the appeal, it appears to be indubitable that there is a constitutional duty to entertain it, and to dispose of it as justice and the right of the minority shall require.

Should it be thought that I am, in' this contention, putting my claim to a hearing on the merits upon too high ground, let me urge this further reason why such a hearing should be accorded us. Although His Excellency in Council can make a remedial order, that order has no binding effect upon anyone. It is the Parliament of Canada, and that body only, that has the right to interfere with the legislation of the provinces. It is, however, a necessary pre-requisite of parliamentary jurisdiction that the initiative should come from His Excellency in Council. This body is, as it were, a grand jury having power to put a matter in train for the trial, but having no final judicative function. The question which a grand jury has to answer is not, Is the prisoner guilty? but, Is there a fair prospect that a petit jury will find him so? And in much the same way, although I freely admit that the cases are far from being rigorously parallel, I contend, that if His Excellency in Council shall find that there is a fair case for the exercise of parliamentary jurisdiction, then the initiating order ought to be made, so that Parliament may debate and dispose of the matter.

And in considering whether there is a reasonable prospect of Parliament granting relief to the Roman Catholic minority in Manitoba, we must not forget, for it is an extremely important consideration, the action of Parliament in former years. Passing over other instances of its action, with the mere assertion that during the last thirty years there has been no break in the steadfast consistency with which both political parties have adhered to the

principle of separate schools, allow me for a moment to recall
in brief outline some of the salient features of the New Brunswick school case. In 1871 the Legislature of New Brunswick
passed a School Act. There had not been prior to that time, and
there never has been by law, a system of separate schools in that
province. There was, therefore, no right of appeal to His Excellency
in Council, and Parliament had no more jurisdiction in the matter
than it had with reference to home rule in Ireland. It could, if it
wished, express sympathy one way or another, but it had no legislative
power. In 1872 the Hon. Mr. Costigan moved an address to His
Excellency in Council praying that the statute should be disallowed.
The following amendment was moved on behalf of the Government:

"That this House regrets that the School Act recently passed in
New Brunswick is unsatisfactory to a portion of the inhabitants of
that province, and hopes that it may be so modified at the next
session of the Legislature of New Brunswick as to remove any just
grounds of discontent that now exist."

This amendment was carried by the large majority of 117 to 52,
which figures, however, do not adequately show the full significance
of the vote, because in the minority was a large number who desired
to vote for the main motion which was a very much stronger
declaration in favor of the Catholic minority. The Legislature of
New Brunswick, not having modified the Act, the Hon. Mr. Costigan
again (in 1875) brought the matter before Parliament. He then
proposed an amendment to the Confederation Act in order that in that
way the Roman Catholic minority in New Brunswick might obtain
relief. An amendment was moved as follows:

"That on the 29th May, 1872, the House of Commons adopted
the following resolution (as I have quoted it); that this House regrets
that the hope expressed in said resolution has not been realized; and
that a humble address be presented to Her Most Gracious Majesty the
Queen embodying this resolution, and praying that Her Majesty will
be graciously pleased to use her influence with the Legislature of
New Brunswick to secure such a modification of the said Act as shall
remove such grounds of discontent."

The amendment was carried by 114 to 73, but again in the
minority, for the same reason as before, was a large number who were
opposed to the amendment only because it did not go far enough in
favor of the Roman Catholics. Here is a case in which, although
Parliament had no jurisdiction whatever, yet by overwhelming votes,
and in unmistakable language, it indicated its adherence to the policy
of fair play to minorities. Can there be a shadow of a doubt as
to the action of Parliament in the present case, in which, by the action
of this Council, I trust it will have jurisdiction. If anyone has a
doubt I refer him to the vote of last session with reference to the
separate schools in the North West territories.

CHAP. V.]   MR. EWART'S ADDRESS.   67

I humbly submit, therefore, that for this reason, also, in order that Parliament may have power to deal with the matter, that the remedial order should be made.

Various questions are proposed in the recent order in council. I have thought it best to answer them altogether by the argument which I have now completed. I trust that in what I have said I have made it clear that the replies to those questions ought to be as follows :

1. This is an appeal contemplated by sub-section 3 of section 93 of the B.N.A. Act and sub-section 2 of section 22 of the Manitoba Act.

2. The grounds set forth in the petition are such as may be the subject of an appeal.

3. The decision of the Judicial Committee of the Privy Council has no bearing upon the appeal for redress so far as it is based upon rights acquired after the union, further than that decision finally disposes of the contention that the second sub-section of the Manitoba Act furnishes a remedy merely against *ultra vires* statutes.

4. Sub-section 3 of section 93 of the B.N.A. Act applies to Manitoba unless it is varied by the Manitoba Act. If it is not varied it applies, and if it is, the variation has widened and not narrowed its scope. It is immaterial to the petitioners which alternative is adopted.

5. His Excellency the Governor-General in Council has power to grant the orders asked for by the petitioners.

6. The Acts of Manitoba, passed prior to the session of 1890, conferred on the minority a right or privilege with respect to education within the meaning of sub-section 2 of section 22 of the Manitoba Act; and established a system of separate or dissentient schools within the meaning of sub-section 3 of section 93 of the B.N.A. Act; and the two Acts of 1890 affected, beyond question, such rights and privileges, in such manner as to warrant the present appeals. I have, therefore, to ask that your honourable body may be pleased to appoint some early day for the hearing of the appeal upon its merits. And I have to thank you for the kind attention with which you have listened to my argument upon this most important question.

MANITOBA NOT REPRESENTED.

On the conclusion of Mr. Ewart's argument, Hon. Mr. Ives announced that a communication had been received from the Leiutenant-Governor of Manitoba enclosing a copy of a letter from the Provincial Secretary in which he stated that the copies of petitions presented by the Governor-General in council complaining of the two statutes of Manitoba, relating to education, passed in the session of 1890, with accompanying documents, had been duly received from the Privy Council at Ottawa. The Provincial Secratary concludes his letter as follows: "I am instructed to say that Your Honor's Government has decided that it is not necessary to be represented at the hearing of the appeal on the 21st inst."

Hon. Mr. Ives then asked if anyone else desired to be heard. There was no response, whereupon the President of the Privy Council remarked "We will consult upon the subject if the public will kindly retire."

Whereupon the public retired and the proceedings terminated."

ORDER IN COUNCIL, 22ND FEBRUARY, 1893.

The Committee of the Privy Council, having considered the arguments advanced by Mr. Ewart on behalf of the petitioners in Manitoba who have requested redress from Your Excellency with respect to certain statutes of that province relating to education, are of opinion that the important questions of law which were suggested in the report of the sub-committee to whom said petitions were referred should be authoritatively settled before the appeal which has been asserted by said petitions be further proceeded with.

The committee, therefore, advise that a case be prepared on this subject, in accordance with the provisions of the Act, 54-55 Vict., chapter 25, and they recommend that if this report be approved a copy thereof be transmitted by telegraph to His Honor the Lieutenant-Governor of Manitoba and to John S. Ewart, counsel for the petitioners, in order that, if they be so disposed, the Government of Manitoba and the said counsel may offer suggestions as to the preparation of such a case, and as to the questions which should be embraced therein.

JOHN J. McGEE,
Clerk of the Privy Council.

ORDER IN COUNCIL, 22ND APRIL, 1893.

On a report dated 20th April, 1893, from the Acting Minister of Justice, submitting in conformity with the order of Your Excellency in Council, dated 22nd February, 1893, and under the provisions of the Act 54-55 Vict., cap. 25, a draft which he has had prepared of a case for reference to the Supreme Court of Canada for hearing and consideration touching certain statutes of the Province of Manitoba relating to education, and the memorials of certain petitioners in Manitoba complaining thereof.

The committee, on the recommendation of the Acting Minister of Justice, advise that certified copies of the draft be transmitted, respectively, to the Lieutenant-Governor of Manitoba and to Mr. John S. Ewart, counsel for the petitioners, in order that, if they be so disposed, the Government of Manitoba and the said counsel for the petitioners may offer any suggestions or observations which they may desire to make with respect to such case, and the questions which should be embraced therein.

All of which is respectfully submitted for Your Excellency's approval.

JOHN J. McGEE,
Clerk of the Privy Council.

ORDER IN COUNCIL, 8TH JULY, 1893.

On a report dated 7th July, 1893, from the Acting Minister of Justice, submitting that in conformity with an order of Your Excellency in Council, dated 22nd April, 1893, a draft case prepared for reference to the Supreme Court of Canada, touching certain statutes of the Province of Manitoba relating to education, and the memorials of certain petitioners in Manitoba complaining thereof, was communicated to the Lieutenant-Governor of Manitoba, and to Mr. John S. Ewart, Q.C., counsel for the petitioners, for such suggestions and observations as they might respectively desire to make in relation to such case, and the questions which should be embraced therein. No reply has been received from the Lieutenant-Governor of Manitoba. Mr. Ewart, under date, 4th May, 1893, has made certain observations and suggestions which he (the Minister) has had under consideration. The Minister upon such consideration has made some amendments to the draft case which he submits for your Excellency's approval.

The Minister recommends that the case as amended, copy of which is herewith submitted, be approved by Your Excellency, and that copies thereof be submitted to the Lieutenant-Governor of Manitoba and to Mr. Ewart, with the information that the same is the case which it is proposed to refer to the Supreme Court of Canada touching the statutes and memorials above referred to.

The committee submit the same for Your Excellency's approval.

JOHN J. McGEE,
Clerk of the Privy Council.

ORDER IN COUNCIL, 31st JULY, 1893.

On a report dated 20th of July, 1893, from the Acting Minister of Justice, submitting with reference to his report of the 7th July, inst., which was approved on the 8th July, 1893, submitting a case for reference to the Supreme Court of Canada touching certain statutes of the Province of Manitoba relating to education, and the memorials of certain persons complaining thereof,

The Minister recommends that the case, a copy of which is appended to the above-mentioned Order in Council, be referred to the Supreme Court of Canada for hearing and consideration, pursuant to the provisions of an Act respecting the Supreme and Exchequer Courts, Revised Statutes, Canada, chapter 135, as amended by 54 and 55 Victoria, chapter 25, section 4.

The committee submit the same for Your Excellency's approval.

JOHN J. McGEE,
Clerk of the Privy Council.

CASE.

OTTAWA, 7th July, 1893.

Case submitted to the Supreme Court of Canada by His Excellency the Governor-General in Council, pursuant to the authority of the Revised Statutes of Canada, chapter 135, intituled: "An Act respecting the Supreme and Exchequer Courts," as amended by section 4 of chapter 25 of the Acts of the Parliament of Canada, passed in the 54th and 55th years of Her Majesty's reign, intituled: "An Act to amend chapter 135 of the Revised Statutes, intituled: 'An Act respecting the Supreme and Exchequer Courts.'"

Annexed hereto is an order of His Excellency the Governor-General in Council, made on the 29th December, 1892, (*a*) approving of a report of a sub-committee of Council thereto annexed (*b*) upon certain memorials complaining of two statutes of the Legislature of Manitoba relating to education, passed in the session of 1890. The memorials therein referred to, and all correspondence in connection therewith, are hereby made part of this case, together with all statutes, whether Provincial, Dominion, or Imperial, in any wise dealing with, or affecting, the subject of education in Manitoba, and all proceedings had or taken before the Court of Queen's Bench, Manitoba, the Supreme Court of Canada, and the Judicial Committee of the Privy Council, in the causes of Barrett *v.* The City of Winni-

---

(*a*) See page 42. (*b*) See page 43.

peg, and Logan v. The City of Winnipeg; and all decisions or judgments in such cases are to be considered as part of this case and are to be referred to accordingly.

The questions for hearing and consideration by the Supreme Court of Canada, being the same as those indicated in the report of the sub-committee of Council above referred to, are as follows:

1. Is the appeal referred to in the said memorials and petitions, and asserted thereby, such an appeal as is admissible by sub-section 3 of section 93 of the British North America Act, 1867, or by sub-section 2 of section 22 of the Manitoba Act, 33 Victoria (1870), chapter 3, Canada?

2. Are the grounds set forth in the petitions and memorials such as may be the subject of appeal under the authority of the sub-sections above referred to, or either of them?

3. Does the decision of the Judicial Committee of the Privy Council in the cases of Barrett v. the City of Winnipeg, and Logan v. the City of Winnipeg, dispose of, or conclude, the application for redress based on the contention that the rights of the Roman Catholic minority which accrued to them, after the union, under the statutes of the province, have been interfered with by the two statutes of 1890, complained of in the said petitions and memorials?

4. Does sub-section 3 of section 93 of the British North America Act, 1867, apply to Manitoba?

5. Has His Excellency the Governor-General in Council power to make the declarations or remedial orders which are asked for in the said memorials and petitions, assuming the material facts to be as stated therein, or has His Excellency the Governor-General in Council any other jurisdiction in the premises?

6. Did the Acts of Manitoba relating to education, passed prior to the session of 1890, confer on or continue, to the minority, a "right or privilege in relation to education," within the meaning of sub-section 2 of section 22 of the Manitoba Act, or establish a system of "separate or dissentient schools within the meaning of sub-section 3 of section 93 of the British North America Act, 1867, if said section 93 be found to be applicable to Manitoba; and, if so, did the two Acts of 1890 complained of, or either of them, affect any right or privilege of the minority in such a manner that an appeal will lie thereunder to the Governor-General in Council?

ORDER IN COUNCIL, 15TH AUGUST, 1893.

The committee on the recommendation of the acting Minister of Justice advise that pursuant to the provisions of the Act 54-55 Victoria, chapter 25, the Attorney-General of the Province of

Manitoba be notified that in accordance with an Order of His Excellency the Governor-General in Council dated the 31st day of July, 1893, a case touching certain statutes of the said province relating to education, and the memorials of certain petitioners complaining thereof, was referred to the Supreme Court of Canada for hearing and consideration, and that such case will be heard at the next ensuing sittings of the said court, to wit, on the third day of October next, or so soon thereafter as may be. The committee further advise that a like notice be sent to Mr. John S. Ewart, Q.C., of Winnipeg, counsel for the petitioners.

The committee advise that the Attorney-General for the Province of Manitoba and Mr. Ewart be requested to acknowledge the receipt of such notice respectively.

The committee submit the same for Your Excellency's approval.

JOHN J. MCGEE,
Clerk of the Privy Council.

JUDGMENTS OF THE SUPREME COURT.

THE CHIEF JUSTICE:—This case has been referred to the court for its opinion by His Excellency the Governor-General in Council, pursuant to the provisions of "An Act respecting the Supreme and Exchequer Courts," Revised Statutes of Canada, chapter 135 as amended by 54 and 55 Victoria, ch. 25, sec. 4.

Six questions are propounded which are as follows:

(Here follow the questions. See page 71).

To put it in a concise form, the questions which we are called upon to answer are whether an appeal lies to the Governor-General in Council either under the British North America Act, 1867, or under the Dominion Act establishing the Province of Manitoba, against an Act or Acts of the Legislature of Manitoba passed in 1890, whereby certain Acts or parts of Acts of the same Legislature, previously passed, which had conferred certain rights on the Roman Catholic minority in Manitoba in respect of separate or denominational schools, were repealed.

The matter was brought before the court by the Solicitor-General, on behalf of the crown, but was not argued by him. On behalf of the petitioners and memorialists who had sought the intervention of the Governor-General Mr. Ewart Q.C. appeared. Mr. Wade Q.C. appeared as Counsel on behalf of the Province of Manitoba when the matter first came on, but declined to argue the case, and the court then, in exercise of the powers conferred by 54 and 55 Vic., chapter 25, section 4 (substituted for the Revised Statutes of Canada, chapter 135, section 37), requested Mr. Christopher Robinson Q.C., the senior member of the bar practising before this court, to argue the case in the interest of the Province of Manitoba, and on a subsequent day the matter was fully and ably argued by Mr. Ewart and Mr. Robinson.

The proper answers to be given to the questions propounded depended principally on the meaning to be attached to the words "any right or privilege of the Protestant or Roman Catholic minority of the Queen's subjects in relation to education" in sub-section 2 of section 22 of the Manitoba Act. Do these words include rights and privileges in relation to education which did not exist at the union, but (in words of section 93, sub-section 3 of the British North America Act) have been "thereafter established by the legislature of the province," or is this right or privilege mentioned in sub-section 2 of section 22 of the Manitoba Act, the same right or privilege which is previously referred to in sub-section 1 of section 22 of the Manitoba Act, viz.: one which any class of persons had by law or practice in the province at the union, or a right or privilege other than one which the Legislature of Manitoba itself created?

(The learned Chief Justice here quoted sec. 93 of the B.N.A. Act, sub-secs. 1 and 3; and sec. 22 of the Manitoba Act, sub-secs. 1 and 2. See page 1.)

It is important to contrast these two clauses of the Acts in question, inasmuch as there is intrinsic evidence in the later Act that it was generally modelled on the Imperial statute, the original Confederation Act; and the divergence in the language of the two statutes is therefore significant of an intention to make some change as regards Manitoba by the provisions of the later Act.

It will be observed that the British North America Act, section 93, sub-section 3, contains the words, "or is thereafter established by the Legislature of the Province," which words are entirely omitted in the corresponding section (section 22, sub-section 2) of the Manitoba Act. Again, the same sub-section of the Manitoba Act gives a right of appeal to the Governor-General in Council from the Legislature of the province, as well as from any provincial authority, whilst by the British North America Act the right of appeal to the Governor-General is only to be from the Act or decision of a provincial authority. I can refer this difference of expression in the two Acts to nothing but to a deliberate intention to make some change in the operation of the respective clauses. I do not see why there should have been any departure in the Manitoba Act from the language of the British North America Act unless it was intended that the meaning should be different. On the other hand, it may well be urged that there was no reason why the provinces admitted to confederation should have been treated differently; why a different rule should prevail as regards Manitoba from that which, by express words, applied to the other provinces. On the other hand, there is, it seems to me, much force in the consideration, that whilst it was reasonable that the organic law should preserve vested rights existing at the union from spoliation and interference, yet every presumption must be made in favor of the constitutional right of a legislative body to repeal the laws which it has itself enacted. No doubt this right may be controlled by a written constitution which confers legislative powers, and which may restrict those powers and make them subject to any condition which the constituent legislators may think fit to impose. A notable instance of this is, as my brother King has pointed out, afforded by the constitution of the United States, according to the construction which the Supreme Court, in the well-known "Dartmouth College case," put upon the provision prohibiting the State Legislatures from passing laws impairing the obligation of contracts. It was there held, with a result that has been found most inconvenient, that a Legislature which had created a private corporation could not repeal its own enactment granting the franchise, the reason assigned being that the grant of a franchise of a corporation was a contract. This has in practice been got over by inserting in such Acts an express reservation of the right of the Legislature to repeal its own Act. But, as it is a *primâ facie* presumption that every legislative enactment is subject to repeal by the same body which enacts it, every statute may be said to contain an implied provision that it may be revoked by the authority which has passed it, unless the right of repeal is taken away by the fundamental law, the over-riding constitution which has created the Legislature itself. The point is a new one, but having regard to the strength and universality of the presumption that every legislative body has power to repeal its own laws, and that this power is almost indispensable to the useful exercise of legislative authority since a great deal of legislation is of necessity tentative and experimental, would it be arbitrary or unreasonable, or altogether unsupported by analogy, to hold, as a canon of constitutional construction, that such an inherent right to repeal its own Acts cannot be deemed to be withheld from a legislative body having its origin in a written constitution, unless the constitution itself, by express words, takes away the right? I am of opinion that in construing the Manitoba Act we ought to proceed upon this principle, and hold the Legislature of that province to have absolute powers over its own legislation, untrammelled by any appeal to federal authority, unless we find some restriction of its rights in this respect in express terms in the constitutional Act?

Then, keeping this rule of construction just adverted to in view, is there anything in the terms of sub-section 2 of section 22 of the Manitoba Act by which the right of appeal is enlarged, and an appeal from the Legislature is expressly added to that from any provincial authority, whilst in the British North America Act, section 93, sub-section 3, the appeal is confined to one from provincial authority only, which expressly or necessarily implies that it was the intention of those who framed the constitution of Manitoba to impose upon its Legislature any disability to exercise the ordinary powers of a Legislature to repeal its own enactments? I cannot see that it does, and I will endeavor to demonstrate the correctness of this opinion.

It might well have been considered by the Parliament of the Dominion in passing the Manitoba Act that the words "any provincial authority" did not include the Legislature. Then, assuming it to have been intended to conserve all vested rights—"rights or privileges existing by law, or practice, at the time of the union"—and to exclude, or subject to federal control, even legislative interference with such pre-existent rights or privileges, this prohibition or control would be provided for by making an Act or decision of the Legislature, so interfering, the subject of appeal to the Governor-General in Council.

If, however, the words of section 93, sub-section 3, "or is hereafter established by the Legislature" had been repeated in section 22, the Legislature would have been in express and unequivocal terms restrained from repealing laws of the kind in question, which they had themselves enacted, except upon the conditions of a right to appeal to the Governor-General. If it was intended not to do this, but only to restrain the Legislature of Manitoba from interfering with "rights and privileges" of the kind in question existing at the union, this end would have been attained by just omitting altogether from the clause the words "or shall have been thereafter established by the Legislature of the province." This was done.

Next, it is clear that in interpreting the Manitoba Act the words "any provincial authority" do not include the Legislature, for that expression is there used as an alternative to the "Legislature of the province."

It is not to be presumed that Manitoba was intended to be admitted to the union upon any different terms from the other provinces, or with rights of any greater or lesser degree than the other provinces. Some difference may have been inevitable owing to the difference in the pre-existing conditions of the several provinces. It would be reasonable to attribute any difference in the terms of union, and in the rights of the province, to this, and as far as possible, by interpretation, to confine any variation in legislative powers and other matters, to such requirements as were rendered necessary by the circumstances and conditions of Manitoba at the time of the union.

Now, let us see what would be the effect of the construction which I have suggested of both Acts—the British North America Act, section 93, and the Manitoba Act, section 22, in their practical application to the different provinces as regards the right of Provincial Legislatures to interfere with separate or denominational schools to the prejudice of a Roman Catholic or Protestant minority.

First, then, let us consider the cases of Ontario and Quebec, the two provinces which had by law denominational schools at the union. In these provinces any law passed by a Provincial Legislature impairing any right or privilege in respect of such denominational schools would, by force of the prohibition contained in sub-section 1 of section 93 of the British North America Act, be *ultra vires* of the Legislature and of no constitutional validity.

Should the Legislatures of these provinces (Ontario and Quebec) after confederation have conferred increased rights or privileges in relation to education or minorities, I see nothing to hinder them from repealing such Acts to the extent of doing away with the additional rights and privileges so conferred by their own legislation without being subject to any condition of appeal to federal authority.

What is meant by the term "provincial authority"? The Parliament of the Dominion, as shown by the Manitoba Act, hold that it does not include the Legislature, for in sub-section 2 of section 22 they use it as an alternative expression and so expressly distinguish it from the Legislature. It is true the British North America Act did not emanate from the Dominion Parliament, but nevertheless the construction which that Parliament has put on the British North America Act, if not binding on judicial interpreters, is at least entitled to the highest respect and consideration. Secondly, the words "provincial authority" are not apt words to describe the Legislature, and in order that a Provincial Legislature should be subjected to an appeal, when it merely attempts to recall its own Acts, the terms used should be apt, clear and unambiguous. To return, then, to the cases of Ontario and Quebec, should any "provincial authority," not including in these words the Legislature, but interpreting the expression as restricted to administrative authorities (without at present going so far as to say it included courts of justice), by any act or decision affect any right or privilege, whether derived under a law or practice existing at the time of confederation, or conferred by a provincial statute since the union, still remaining unrepealed and in force, that would be subject to an appeal to the Governor-General.

Secondly—As regards the provinces of Nova Scotia and New Brunswick, those provinces not having had any denominational schools at the time of the union, there is nothing in their case for sub-section 1 of section 93 to operate upon. Should either of these provinces by after-confederation legislation create rights and privileges in favor of Protestant or Catholic minorities in relation to education, then so long as these statutes remained unrepealed and in force an appeal would lie to the Governor-General from any Act or decision of a provincial administrative authority, affecting any of such rights or privileges of a minority, but there would be nothing to prevent the legislatures of the provinces now under consideration from repealing any law which they had themselves enacted conferring such rights and privileges, nor would any Act so repealing their own enactments be subject to appeal to the Governor-General in council.

Thirdly. We have the case of the Province of Manitoba. Here, applying the construction before mentioned, the provincial powers in relation to education would be not further restricted but somewhat enlarged in comparison with those of the other provinces. Acting upon the presumption that in the absence of express words in the Act of the Dominion Parliament, which embodies the constitution of the province, withholding from the Legislature of the province the nominal right of altering or repealing its own Acts, we must hold that it was not the intention of Parliament so to limit the Legislature by the organic law of the province. What, then, is the result of the legislation of the Dominion as regards Manitoba? What affect is to be given to section 22 of the Manitoba Act? By the first sub-section any law of the province prejudicing any right or privilege with respect to denominational schools in the province existing at the union is *ultra vires* and void. This clause was the subject, and the only subject, of interpretation in Barrett *v.* Winnipeg (1) and the point there decided was that there was no such right or privilege, as was claimed in that case, existing at the time of the admission of the province into the union. Had any such right or privilege been found to exist there is nothing in the judgment of the Privy Council against the inference that legislation imparting it would have been unconstitutional and void. That decision has, in my opinion, but a very remote application to the present case. The second sub-section of section 22 of the Manitoba Act is as follows:—

> An appeal shall lie to the Governor General in Council from any Act or decision of the Legislature of the province or any other Provincial authority affecting any right or privilege of the Protestant or Roman Catholic minority of the Queen's subjects in relation to education.

I put aside as entirely irrelevant here the question whether it was, or was not, intended by this sub-section 2 to confer on the Privy Council of the Dominion appellate jurisdiction from the provincial judiciary, a question the decision of which, I may say in passing, might well be influenced by the consideration that the power given to Parliament by the British North America Act to create Federal courts had not at the time of the passage of the Manitoba Act been exercised.

The first subject of appeal is, then, any Act or decision of the Legislature of the province affecting any right or privilege of the minority in respect of the matters in question. Now if we are to hold, as I am of opinion we must hold, that it was not the intention of Parliament by these words so to circumscribe the Legislative rights conferred by them on Manitoba as to incapacitate that Legislature from absolutely, and without any subjection to federal control, repealing its own enactments, and thus taking away rights which it had itself conferred, the right of appeal to the Governor-General against legislative Acts must be limited to a particular class of such Acts, viz.: to such as might prejudice rights and privileges not conferred by the Legislature itself, but rights and privileges which could only have arisen before confederation, being those described in the first sub-section of section 22. That we must assume, in the absence of express words that, it was not the intention of Parliament to impose upon the Manitoba Legislature a disability so anomalous as an incapacity to repeal its own enactments, except subject to an appeal to the Governor-General in Council, and possibly the intervention of the Dominion Parliament as a paramount Legislature, is a proposition I have before stated.

Therefore, the right of appeal to the Governor-General in Council must be confined to Acts of the Legislature affecting such rights and privileges as are mentioned in the first sub-section, viz.: those existing at the union when belonging to a minority, either Protestant or Catholic. Then there would also be the right of appeal from any provincial authority. I will assume that the description "provincial authority" does not apply to courts of justice. Then these words "provincial authority" could not, as used in this sub-section 2 of section 22 of the Manitoba Act, have been intended to include the Provincial Legislature, for it is expressly distinguished from it, being mentioned alternately with the Legislature. "An appeal shall lie from any Act or decision of the Legislature or of any "provincial authority," is the language of the section. It must then apply to the provincial executive or administrative authorities. No doubt an appeal would lie from their Acts or decisions, upon the ground that some right or privilege existing at the date of the admission of the province to the Federal Union was thereby prejudiced. In this respect Manitoba would be in the same position as Ontario and Quebec. Unlike the cases of those provinces, and also unlike the case of the two maritime provinces, Nova Scotia and New Brunswick, there would not, however, in the case of Manitoba, be an appeal to the Governor-General in Council from the Act or decision of any "provincial authority," upon the ground that some right or privilege not existent at the time of the union, but conferred subsequently by Legislation, had been violated. This construction must necessarily result from the right of appeal against Acts or decisions of provincial authorities, and against Acts or decisions of the Legislature, being limited to such as prejudiced the same class of rights or privileges. The wording of this sub-section 2 shows clearly that only one class of rights or privileges could have been meant, and that the right of appeal was therefore to arise upon an invasion of these, either by the Legislature or by a provincial authority. Then, as the impossibility of holding that it could have been intended to impose fetters on the Legislature and to incapacitate it from absolutely repealing its own Acts, requires us to limit the appeal against its enactments to Acts affecting rights and privileges existing at the union, it must follow that the right of appeal must be in like manner limited as regards Acts or decisions of provincial authorities. This, however, although it makes a difference between Manitoba and the other provinces, is not a very material one. The provincial authorities would of course be under the control of the courts; they could therefore be compelled, by the exercise of judicial authority, to conform themselves to the law. Much greater would have been the difference between Manitoba and the other provinces if we were to hold that whilst, as regards the provinces of Nova Scotia and New Brunswick, their Legislatures could enact a separate school law one session and repeal it the next, without having their repealing legislation called in question by appeal, and whilst, as regards Ontario and Quebec, although rights and privileges existing at confederation were made intangible by their Legislatures, yet any increase or addition to such rights and privileges which these Legislatures might grant could be withdrawn by them at their own pleasure, subject to no federal revision, yet that the Legislation of Manitoba, on the same subject, should be only revocable subject to the revisory power of the Governor-General in Council.

I have thus endeavored to show that the construction I adopt has the affect of placing all the provinces virtually in the same position, with an immaterial exception in favor of Manitoba, and it is for the purpose of demonstrating this that I have referred to appeals from the Acts and decisions of provincial authorities, which are not otherwise in question in the case before us.

That the words "any provincial authority" in the third sub-section of section 93 of the British North America Act do not include the Legislature is a conclusion which I have reached not without difficulty. In intrepreting the Manitoba Act, however, what we have to do is to ascertain in what sense the Dominion Parliament in adopting the same expression in the Manitoba Act understood it to have been used in the British North America Act.

That they understood these words not to include the Provincial Legislatures is apparent from section 22, sub-section 2 of the Manitoba Act, wherein the two expressions "provincial authority" and "Legislature of the province" are used in the alternative, thus indicating that in the intendment of Parliament they meant different subjects of appeal.

Again, why were the words contained in the third sub-section of section 93 of the British North America Act "or thereafter established by the Legislature of the Province" omitted, when that section was in other respects transcribed in the Manitoba Act? The reason it appears to me is plain. So long as these words stood with the context they had in the British North America Act they did not in any way tie the hands of the Provincial Legislatures as regards the undoing, alteration or amendment of their own work, for the words "any provincial authority" did not include the Legislature. But when in the Manitoba Act the Dominion Parliament thought it advisable for the better protection of vested rights—"rights and privileges" existing at the union—to give a right of appeal from the Legislature to the Governor-General in Council, it omitted the words "or is thereafter established by the Legislature of the province," with the intent to avoid placing the Provincial Legislature under any disability or subjecting it to any appeal as regards the repeal of its own legislation, which would have been the effect if the third sub-section of section 93 of the British North America Act had been literally re-enacted in the Manitoba Act with the words "of the Legislature of the province" interpolated as we now find them in sub-section 2 of the latter Act. This seems to me to show conclusively that the words "rights or privileges" in sub-section 2 of section 22 were not intended to include rights and privileges originating under Provincial Legislation since the union, and that the Legislature of Manitoba is not debarred from exercising the common legislative right of abrogating laws which it has itself passed relating to denominational or separate schools or educational privileges, nor is such repealing legislation made subject to any appeal to the Governor-General in Council.

In my opinion all the questions propounded for our opinion must be answered in the negative.

Fournier, J.—By the statute 33 Vic., ch. 3, sec. 2 (D), the Manitoba Act, the provisions of the British North America Act, except so far as the same may be varied by the said Act, are made applicable to the Province of Manitoba, in the same way, and to the like extent, as they apply to the several provinces of Canada, and as if the Province of Manitoba had been one of the provinces united by the British North America Act. This Act was imperialized, so to speak, by 34 Vic., ch. 38 (Imp.), which declares that 32 and 33 Vic., ch. 3 (D), shall be deemed to have been valid and effectual for all purposes whatsoever.

If we are now called upon to construe certain provisions of this statute, it seems to me that the same considerations will apply as if the provisions appeared in the British North America Act itself under the heading "Manitoba," and therefore as stated by the late Chief Justice of this court, Sir W. Richards, in the case of Severn v. The Queen (1), "in deciding important questions arising under the Act passed by the Imperial Parliament for federally uniting the provinces of Canada, Nova Scotia and New Brunswick, we must consider the circumstances under which that statute was passed, the condition of the different provinces, their relations to one another, as well as the system of government which prevailed in those provinces and countries." For convenience, therefore, I will place in parallel columns the sections of the Manitoba Act and the corresponding sections of the British North America Act, in relation to education, upon which we are required to give an answer.

(Here follow the sections arranged as at page 1.)

What was the existing state of things in the territory then being formed into the Province of Manitoba? Rebellion, as I have already stated in the case of Barrett v. Winnipeg, (2), had thrown the people into a strong and fierce agitation, inflamed religious and national passions and caused the greatest disorder, which rendered necessary the intervention of the Federal Government; and as matters then stood, on the 2nd March, 1870, the Government of Assiniboia, in order to pacify the inhabitants, appointed the Rev. Mr. Ritchot and Messrs. Black and Scott as joint delegates to confer with the Government of Ottawa, and negotiate the terms and conditions upon which the inhabitants of Assiniboia would consent to enter confederation with the provinces of Canada.

Mr. Ritchot was instructed to immediately leave with Messrs. Black and Scott for Ottawa, in view of opening negotiations on the subjects of their mission with the Government at Ottawa.

When they arrived at Ottawa, the three delegates, Messrs. Ritchot, Black and Scott, received on the 25th April, 1870, from the Hon. Mr. Howe, the then Secretary of State for the Dominion of Canada, a letter informing them that the Hon. Sir John A. Macdonald and Sir George Cartier had been authorized by the Government of Canada to confer with them on the subject of their mission, and that they were ready to meet them.

---

(1) 2 Can. S.C.R. 70   (2) 19 Can. S.C.R. 374.

The Rev. Mr. Ritchot was the bearer of the conditions upon which they were authorized to consent for the inhabitants of Assiniboia to enter confederation as a separate province.

These facts appear in exhibit L, Sessional Papers of Canada, 1893, 33 D., and in exhibit N of the same Sessional Papers we see that the following conditions, arts. 5 and 7, read as follows:

"(5.) That all properties, all rights and privileges possessed, be respected, and the establishing and settlement of the customs, usages and privileges be left for the sole decision of the local Legislature."

"(7.) That the schools shall be separate, and that the moneys for schools shall be divided between the several denominations *pro ratâ* of their respective populations."

Now, after negotiations had been going on, and despatches and instructions from the Imperial Government to the Government of Canada on the subject of the entrance of the Province of Manitoba into the confederation had been received, the Manitoba Constitutional Act was prepared, and section 22 inserted as a satisfactory guarantee for their rights and privileges in relation to matters of education, as claimed by the above articles 5 and 7. And until 1890 the inhabitants of the Province of Manitoba enjoyed these rights and privileges under the authority of this section and local statutes passed in conformity therewith.

However, it seems by the decision of the Judicial Committee of of the Privy Council in the case of Barrett *v.* Winnipeg (1) that the delegates of the North-west and the Parliament of Canada, although believing that the inhabitants of Assiniboia had before the union "by law or practice," certain rights and privileges with respect to denominational schools—for the words used in sub-section 1 of this section 32 are, "which any class have by law or practice in the province at the union"—had in point of fact no such right or privilege by law or practice with respect to denominational schools, and therefore that sub-section 1 is, so to speak, wiped out of the Manitoba Constitutional Act, having nothing to operate upon.

But if the parties agreeing to these terms of union, were in error in supposing they had by law or practice prior to the union certain rights or privileges, they certainly were not in error in trusting that the Provincial Legislature (as the Legislature of Quebec did after the union of the Protestant minority) which was being created would forthwith settle and establish their usages and privileges and secure by law, and in accordance with arts. 5 and 7 of the bill of rights, separate schools for the Catholics of Manitoba and would make provisions so that the moneys would be divided between the Protestant and Catholic denominations *pro ratâ* to their respective populations. These once established and secured by their own local Legislature in accordance with the terms of the union, is not the minority perfectly within the spirit, and the words, of the Constitutional Act, in contending that rights and privileges so secured by an Act of the Legislature are at least in the same position as rights secured to minorities in the Provinces of Quebec and Ontario under section 93 of the British North America Act, and that sub-sections 2 and 3 were inserted in the Act so that they might be protected by the Governor-General against any subsequent legislation, by either a Protestant or Catholic majority in after years?

In the present reference, being again called upon to construe this same section 22, but as if sub-section 1 was repealed or wiped out by judicial authority, we must, I think, take into consideration the historical fact that the Manitoba Act of 1870 was the result of the negotiations with parties who agreed to join and form part of the Confederation as if they were inhabitants of one of the provinces originally united by the British North America Act, and we must credit the Parliament of Canada with having intended that the words "an appeal shall lie to the Governor-General in Council from any act or decision of the Legislature of the province, or of any provincial authority, affecting any right or privilege of the Protestant or Roman Catholic minority of the Queen's subjects in relation to education," (which are also the words used in the 93 section of the British North America Act) should have some effect. The only meaning and effect I can give them is that they were intended as an additional guarantee or protection to the minority, either Protestant or Catholic, whichever it might happen to be, that the laws which they knew would be enacted immediately after the union by their own Legislature in reference to education, would be in accordance with the terms and conditions upon which they were entering the union; this guarantee was given so as to prevent, later on, interference with their rights and privileges by subsequent legislation without being subject to an appeal to the Governor-General in Council, should such subsequent Act of the Legislature affect any right or privilege thus secured to the Protestant or Catholic minority by their own Legislature.

In my opinion the words used in sub-section 2: "an appeal shall lie from any Act of the Legislature," necessarily mean an appeal from any statute which the Legislature has power to pass in relation to education if *at the time* of the passing of such statute there exists by law any right or privilege enjoyed by the minority. There is no necessity of appealing from statutes which are *ultra vires*, for the assumption of any unauthorized power by any local Legislature under our system of government is not remedied by appeal to the Governor-General in Council but by courts of justice.

Then, as to the words "right or privilege" in this sub-section, they refer to some right or privilege in relation to education to be created by the Legislature which was being brought into existence, and which, once established, might thereafter be interfered with at the hand of a local majority so as to affect the Protestant or Catholic minority in relation to education.

It is clear, therefore, that the Governor-General in Council has the right of entertaining an appeal by the British North America Act, as well as by sub-section 2 of section 22 of the Manitoba Act. He has also the power of considering the application upon its merits. When the application has been considered by him upon its merits, if the Local Legislature refuses to execute any decision to which the Governor-General in Council has arrived in the premises, the Dominion Government may then, under sub-section 3 of section 22 of the Manitoba Act, pass remedial legislation for the execution of his decision.

In construing, as I have done, the words of sub-section 2 of the 22nd section of the Manitoba Constitutional Act, which is, as regards an appeal to the Governor-General in Council, but a reproduction of sub-section 3 of section 93 of the British North America Act, except that the clear, unequivocal and comprehensive words "from any Act or decision of the Legislature of the province" are added, I am pleased to see that I am but concurring in the view expressed by Lord Carnarvon on the 19th February, 1867, when speaking of this right of appeal to be granted to minorities when a local Act might affect rights or privileges in matters of education, as the following extracts from Hansard's Parliamentary Debates, 3rd series, February 19th, 1867, show :

" Lord Carnarvon —" Lastly in the 93rd clause, which contains the exceptional provisions to which I referred, your Lordships will observe some rather complicated arrangements in reference to education. I need hardly say that this great question gives rise to nearly as much earnestness and division of opinion on that, as on this, side of the Atlantic. This clause has been framed after long and anxious controversy in which all parties have been represented, and on conditions to which all have given their consent. It is an understanding which, as it only concerns the local interests affected, is not one that Parliament would be willing to disturb, even if in the opinion of Parliament it were susceptible of amendment ; but I am bound to add, as the expresssion of my own opinion, that the terms of the agreement appear to me to be equitable and judicious. For the object of the clause is to secure to the religious minority of one province the same rights and privileges and protection which the religious minority of another province may enjoy. The Roman Catholic minority of Upper Canada, the Protestant minority of the Province of Quebec, and the Roman Catholic minority of the Maritime Provinces, will thus stand on a footing of entire equality. But in the event of any wrong at the hand of the local majority, the minority have a right to appeal to the Governor-General in Council, and may claim the application of any remedial laws that may be necessary from the central Parliament of the confederation."

This being so, the next point of inquiry is whether the Acts of 1890 of Manitoba affect any right or privilege secured to the Catholic minority in matters of education after the union, for we have now nothing to do with the inquiry whether the Catholic minority had at the time of the union any right by law or practice, that point, as I have already stated, having been decided adversely to their contention by the decision of the Privy Council in the case of Barrett *v.* Winnipeg (1). By referring to the legislation from the date of the union to 1890, it is evident that the Catholics enjoyed the immunity of being taxed for other schools than their own, the right of organization, the right of self-government in this school matter, the right of taxation of their own people, the right of sharing in Government grants for education, and many other rights under the statute of a most material kind. All these rights were swept away by the Acts of 1890, as well as the properties they had acquired under these Acts with their taxes and their share of the public grants for education. Could the prejudice caused by the Acts of 1890 be greater than it has been? The scheme that runs through the Acts of 1871 and 1881 up to 1890, as Lord Watson, of the Privy Council, is reported to have so concisely stated on the argument of the case of Barrett *v.* Winnipeg (which is printed in the Sessional Papers of Canada, 1893), appears to have been that "no ratepayers shall be taxed for contribution towards any school except one of his own denomination," and I will add that this scheme is clearly pointed out in arts. 5 and 7 of the conditions of union above already referred to, which were the basis of the Constitutional Act.

Now, is this a legal right or privilege enjoyed by a class of persons? In this case the immunity from contributing to any schools other than one of its own denomination was acquired by the Catholic minority *quâ* Catholics by statute, and Catholics certainly, at the time the legislation was passed, represented a class of persons comprising at least one-third of the inhabitants of the Province of Manitoba. It is unnecessary, I think, after reading the able judgments delivered in the case of Barrett *v.* Winnipeg (2) to show by authority that the right so acquired by the Catholic minority after the union by the Act of 1871 was a legal right, and that if it is shown by subsequent legislation, enacted by the Legislature of the Province of Manitoba, that there has been any interference with such right, then I am of the opinion that such interference would come within the very words of this section 22 of the Manitoba Constitutional Act, which gives a right of appeal to the Governor-General in Council from "any Act of the Legislature" (words which are not in section 93 of the British North America Act, but are in subsection 2 of section 22 of the Manitoba Act) affecting a right

(1) [1892] A. C. 445. (2) 19 S. C. R. 374; [1892] A. C. 445.

acquired by the Roman Catholic minority of the Queen's subjects in relation to education.

The only other question submitted to us I need refer to is the 4th question. Does sub-section 3 of section 93 of the British North America Act, 1867, apply to Manitoba? The answer to this question is to be found in the second section of the Manitoba Act (33 Vic.) which says "from and after the said date the provisions of the British North America Act shall apply, except those parts thereof which are in terms made, or by reasonable intendment, may be held to be, specially applicable to, or only to affect one or more, but not the whole of the provinces now comprising the Dominion, and except so far as the same may be varied by this Act, and be applicable to the province of Manitoba, in the same way, and to the like extent as they apply to the several provinces of Canada, and as if the province of Manitoba had been one of the provinces originally united by the said Act." The Manitoba Act has not varied the British North America Act, though sub-section 2 of section 22 has a somewhat more comprehensive working than the sub-section 3 of section 93 of the British North America Act, in relation to appeal in educational matters. A statute does not vary, or alter, if it merely makes further provision it is simply an addition to it. The second sub-section is wider but does not vary at all from the third sub-section of section 93 of the British North America Act, save in this that there is an addition to it, that it includes it, and goes beyond it by adding the words "and from any Act of the Legislature." The third sub-section of the British North America Act provides that in two cases there is to be an appeal. There is nothing inconsistent in the Manitoba Act which says that in all cases there shall be an appeal, it goes beyond the British North America Act, it does not vary it, but leaves it as it is and adds to it.

We see that by the opinion expressed by some of the Lords of the Privy Council, how far the right of appeal extends under section 2 of the Manitoba Act, for in the argument on that question before the Privy Council, Sessional Papers, No. 33a, 33b, 1893, we read, at p. 134, that when Mr. Ram (counsel) was arguing on behalf of Mr. Logan in the case of Winnipeg *v.* Logan he said:

"I venture to think that under sub-section 2 what was contemplated was this: that apart from any question, *ultra vires* or not, if a minority said, 'I am oppressed,' that was the who party had had to come under that section 3 and appeal to the Government."

Lord Hannen added:
"It has a right to appeal against any Act of the Legislature."
And Lord Shand:
"Even *intra vires.*"

This being also my opinion, I will only add that, having already stated that I think that we should read the Manitoba Constitutional Act in the light of the British North America Act, and that it was intended, as regards all civil rights in educational matters, to place the province of Manitoba on the same footing as the provinces of Quebec and Ontario, and that sub-section 1 of section 22 having been enacted for the purpose of protecting rights held by law or practice prior to the union, but which have been declared not to exist, I am of the opinion that sub-section 2 of section 22 of the Manitoba Constitutional Act provides for an appeal to the Governor-General in Council, by memorial or otherwise, on the part of the Roman Catholic minority contending that the two Acts of the Legislative Assembly of Manitoba, passed in 1890, on the subject of education, are subversive of the rights and privileges of the Roman Catholic ratepayers not to be taxed for contribution towards schools, except those of their own denomination, and that such right has been acquired by statute subsequent to the union.

For the above reasons, I answer the questions submitted by His Excellency the Governor-General in Council, as follows:

1. Yes.
2. Yes.
3. No.
4. Yes.
5. Yes.

Taschereau J.—I doubt our jurisdiction on this reference or consultation. Is section 4 of 54 and 55 Vic. ch. 25 which purports to authorize such a reference to this court for hearing "or" consideration *intra vires* of Parliament? By which section of the British North America Act is Parliament empowered to confer on this statutory court any other jurisdiction than that of a court of appeal under section 101 thereof? This court is evidently made, in the matter, a court of first instance, or rather, I should say, an advisory board of the Federal Executive, substituted, *pro hâc vice*, for the law officers of the Crown, and not performing any of the usual functions of a court of appeal, nay, of any court of justice whatever. However, I need not, at present, further investigate this point. It has not been raised, and a similar enactment to the same import has already been acted upon. This is not conclusive, it is true; but our answers to the questions submitted will bind no one, not even those who put them, nay, not even those who give them, no court of justice, not even this court. We give no judgment, we determine nothing, we end no controversy; and, whatever our answers may be, should it be deemed expedient, at any time, by the Manitoba Executive to impugn the constitutionality of any measure that might hereafter be taken by the federal authorities against the provincial legislation, whether such measure is in accordance with, or in opposition to, the answers to this consultation, the recourse, in the usual way, to the courts of the country remains open to them. That is, I presume the consideration, and a very legitimate one, I should say, upon which the Manitoba Executive acted by refraining to take part in the reference, a course that I would not have been surprised to see followed by the petitioners, unless indeed they are assured of the interference of the federal authorites should it eventually result from this reference that, constitutionally, the power to interfere with the provincial legislation as prayed for exists. For if, as a matter of policy, in the public interest, no action is to be taken upon the petitioners' application, even if the appeal lies, the futility of these proceedings is apparent.

Assuming, then, that we have jurisdiction, I will try to give, as concisely as possible, the reasons upon which I have based my answers to the questions submitted.

In the view I take of the application made to His Excellency the Governor-General in Council by the Catholics of Manitoba, I think it better to invert the order of the questions put to us, and to answer first the fourth of these questions, that is, whether sub-section 3 of section 93 of the British North America Act applies to Manitoba. To that question the answer, in my opinion, must be in the negative. That section of the British North America Act applies to every one of the provinces of the Dominion, with the exception, however, of Manitoba, for the reason that, for Manitoba, in its special charter, the subject is specifically provided for by section 22 thereof. The maxims *lex posterior derogat priori*, and *specialia generalibus derogant*, have both here, it seems to me, their application. If it had been intended to purely and simply extend the operation of that section 93 of the British North America Act to Manitoba, section 22 of its charter would not have been enacted. The course since pursued for British Columbia and Prince Edward Island would have been followed. But where we see a different course pursued we have to assume that the difference in the law was intended, I cannot see any other reason for it, and none has been suggested. True it is that the words "or practice" in sub-section 1 of section 22 are an addition in the Manitoba charter which the Dominion Parliament desired to specially make to the analogous provision of the British North America Act, but that was no reason to word sub-section 2 thereof so differently as it is from sub-section 3 of section 93 of the British North America Act. Then this difference may be easily explained, though its consequences may not have been foreseen; I speak cautiously and mindful that I am not here allowed to controvert or even doubt anything that has been said on the subject by the Privy Council. It is evident, to my mind, that it was simply because it was assumed by the Dominion Parliament that separate or denominational schools had previously been, in that region, and were then, at the union, the basis and principle of the educational system, and with the intention of adapting such system to the new province, or rather of continuing it as found to exist, that, in the Union Act of 1870, the words of sub-section 3 of section 93 of the British North America Act, "where in any province a system of separate or dissentient schools exists by law at the union, or is thereafter established by the Legislature of the province," were stricken out as unnecessary and inapplicable to the new province. And I do not understand that the Privy Council denies to the petitioners their right to separate schools.

However, the reason of this difference between the constitution of the province and the British North America Act cannot, in my view of the question, bring much assistance in the present investigation: the fact remains, whatever may have been the reason for it, that no appeal is given to the minority, in Manitoba, in relation to the rights and privileges conceded to them since the union as distinguished from those in existence at the union. They have no rights but what is left to them by the judgment in the Barrett case; and, if I do not misunderstand that judgment, the appeal they now lay claim to is not, as a logical inference, thereby left to them.

And in vain now, to support their appeal, would they urge that the statute so construed is unreasonable, unjust, inconsistent and contrary to the intentions of the lawgiver; uselessly would they contend that to force them to contribute pecuniarily to the maintenance of the public, non-Catholic, schools, is to so shackle the exercise of their rights as to render them illusory and fruitless, or that to tax, not only the property of each and every one of them individually, but even their school buildings, for the support of the public schools is almost ironical; uselessly would they demonstrate the utter impossibility for them to efficaciously provide for the organization, maintenance and management of separate schools, and the essential requirements of a separate school system without statutory powers and the necessary legal machinery; ineffectively would they argue that to concede their right to separate schools, and withal, deprive them of the means to exercise that right, is virtually to abolish it, or to leave them nothing of it but a barren theory. With all these, and kindred considerations, we, here, in answering this consultation, are not concerned. The law has authoritatively been declared to be so, and with its consequences, we have nothing to do. *Dura lex, sed lex. Judex non constituitur ad leges reformandas. Non licet judicibus de legibus judicare, sed secundum ipsas.* The Manitoba legislation is constitutional, therefore it has not affected any of the rights or privileges of the minority, therefore the minority has no appeal to the federal authority. The Manitoba Legislature had the right and power to pass that legislation; therefore any interference with that legislation by the federal authority would be *ultra vires* and unconstitutional.

By an express provision of the British North America Act of 1871, it must not be lost sight of, the Dominion Parliament has not the power to, in any way, alter the Manitoba Union Act of 1870.

For these reasons I would answer negatively the fourth of the questions submitted, and say that, in my opinion, sub-section 3 of section 93 of the British North America Act does not apply to Manitoba.

I take up now the first of these questions : Does the right of appeal claimed by the petitioners exist under section 22 of the Manitoba Act? And here again, in my opinion, the answer must be the negative, for the reason that it is conclusively determined, by the judgment of the Privy Council, that the Manitoba legislation does not prejudicially affect any right or privilege that the Catholics had by law or practice at the union, and if their rights and privileges are not affected there is no appeal. The rights or privileges mentioned in sub-section 2 of section 22 are the same rights and privileges that are mentioned in sub-section 1, that is to say, those existing at the union, upon which sub-section 3 provides for the interference, in certain cases, of His Excellency the Governor-General in Council, and it is as to such rights or privileges only that an appeal is given. The appeal given, in the other provinces, by section 93 of the British North America Act as to the rights or privileges conferred on a minority after the union, is, as I have remarked, left out of the Manitoba constitution. Assuming however, that the Manitoba constitution is wide enough to cover an appeal, by the minority, upon the infringement of any of their rights or privileges created since the union, or assuming that section 93 of the British North America Act, sub-section 3, applies to Manitoba, I would be inclined to think that, by the *ratio decidendi* of the Privy Council, there are no rights or privileges of the Catholic minority that are infringed by the Manitoba legislation so as to allow of the exercise of the powers of the Governor in Council in the matter, as the Manitoba statutes must now be taken not to prejudicially affect any right or privilege whatever enjoyed by the Catholic community. It would seem, no doubt, by the language of both section 93 of the British North America Act, and of section 22 of the Manitoba charter, that there may be Provincial legislation which, though *intra vires*, yet might affect the rights or privileges of the minority so as to give them the right to appeal to the Governor in Council. For it cannot be of *ultra vires*, legislation that an appeal is given. And the petitioners, properly disclaiming any intention to base their application on the unconstitutionality of the Manitoba statutes, even for infringement of rights conferred upon them since the union, urge that though the Privy Council has determined that the legislation in question does not affect the rights existing at the union so as to render it *ultra vires* yet that it does affect the rights conferred upon them by the Provincial Legislature since the union, so as to give them, though *intra vires*, an appeal to the Governor in Council. I fail to see, however, how this ingenious distinction, for which I am free to admit both the British North America Act, and the Manitoba special charter, give room, can help the petitioners. I assume here that the petitioners have an appeal upon rights or privileges conferred upon them since the union, as contra distinguished from the rights previously in existence. The case is precisely the same as if the present appeal was as to their rights existing at the union. They might argue that though the Privy Council has held this legislation to have been *intra vires* yet their right to appeal subsists, and, in fact, exists because it is *intra vires*. But what would be this ground of appeal? Because the legislation affects the rights and privileges they had at the union. And the answer would be one fatal to their appeal, as it was to their contentions in the Barrett case, that none of these rights and privileges have been illegally affected. Now, the rights and privileges they lay claim to under the Provincial legislation anterior to 1890 are, with the additions rendered necessary by the political organization of the country to enable them to exercise these rights, the same, in principle, that they had by practice at and before the union, and which were held by the Privy Council not to be illegally affected by the legislation of 1890.

And I am unable to see how, on the one hand, this legislation might be said to affect those rights so as to support an appeal and, on the other hand, not to affect the same rights so as to render it *ultra vires*.

The petitioners, it seems to me, would virtually renew their impeachment of the constitutionality of the Manitoba legislation of 1890 upon another ground than the one taken in the Barrett case, namely upon the rights conferred upon them since the union, whilst the controversy in the Barrett case was limited to their rights as they existed at the union. But that legislation, as I have said, is irrevocably held to have been *intra vires*, and it is not open to the petitioners to argue the contrary even upon a new ground. And if it is *intra vires*, it cannot be that it has illegally affected any of the rights or privileges of the Catholic minority though it may be prejudicial to such right. And if it has not illegally affected any of those rights or privileges, they have no appeal to the Governor in Council

It has been earnestly urged on the part of the petitioners, in their attempt to distinguish the two cases, that in the Barrett case it was only their liability to assessment for the public schools that was at issue, and, consequently, that the decision of the Privy Council, binding though it be, does not preclude them from now taking, on appeal from the provincial legislation of 1890, the ground

that this legislation sweeps away the statutory powers conceded to
them under the previous statutes, and without which their establishment and administration of a separate school system is impracticable.
But here, again, it must necessarily be on the ground that their rights
and privileges, or some of their rights and privileges, have been
prejudicially affected that they have to rest their case, and from that
ground they are irrevocably ousted by the judgment of the Privy
Council, where not only the assessment clauses thereof, more directly
in issue, but each and every one of the enactments of the statute
impugned, were, as I read that judgment, held to have been, and to
be, *intra vires*.

Were it otherwise, and could the question be treated as *res
integra*, it might have been possible for the petitioners to establish
that they are entitled to the appeal claimed on that ground, namely,
that the statutes of 1890, by taking away the rights and privileges
of a corporate body vested with the powers essential to the organization and maintenance of a school system that had been granted to
them by the previous statutes, are subversive of those rights and
privileges and prejudicially affect them.

They might cogently urge in support of that proposition, and
might, perhaps, have succeeded in convincing me, that to take away
a right, to cancel a grant, to repeal the grant of a right, to revoke a
privilege, prejudicially affects that grant, prejudicially, injuriously
affects that privilege. They might also perhaps have been able to
convince me that the license to own real estate, the authorization to
issue debentures, to levy assessments, the powers of a corporation, that
had been granted to them, constituted for them rights and privileges.

And to the objection that no appeal lies under section 22 of the
Manitoba charter but upon rights existing at the union they might
perhaps have successfully answered, either that section 93 of the
British North America Act extends to Manitoba, or, if not, that the
legislation of Manitoba in the matter, since the union, prior to 1890,
should be construed as declaratory of their right to separate
schools, or a legislative admission of it, a legislation required merely
to secure to them the means whereby to exercise that right, and
that, consequently, their appeal relates back to a right existing at
the union, so as to bring it, if necessary, under the terms of section
22 of the Manitoba Union Act.

However, from these reasons the petitioners are now precluded.
If any of their rights and privileges had been prejudicially affected
this legislation would be *ultra vires*; and it is settled that it is not
ultra vires.

And the argument against their contention is very strong, that
it being determined that it would have been in the power of the
Manitoba legislature to establish, in 1871, at the outset of the
political organization of the province, the system of schools that they

adopted in 1890, by the statutes which the petitioners now complain
of, it cannot be that by their adopting and regulating a system of
separate schools, though not obliged to do so, they, forever, bound
the future generations of the province to that policy, so that, as long
at least as there would be even only one Roman Catholic left in the
province, the legislature should be, for all time to come, deprived of
the power to alter it, though the constitution vests them with the
jurisdiction over education in the province. To deny to a legislative
body the right to repeal its own laws, it may be said, is so to curtail
its powers that an express article of its constitution must be shown
to support the propositions; it is not one that can be deductively
admitted.

If this legislation of 1890, it may be still further argued against
the petitioners' contentions, had been adopted in 1871, it would it
must now be conceded, have been constitutional, and that being so,
would the Catholic minority, then, in 1871, have had a right of
appeal to the Governor in Council? Certainly, that is partly the
same question in a different form. But it demonstrates, put in that
shape, that the petitioners have now no right of appeal. The answer
to their claim would then have been that they had no appeal because
none of their rights and privileges had been prejudicially affected.
Now in my opinion, they have no other rights and privileges, in the
construction that these words bear in the Manitoba charter, than
the rights and privileges they had in 1870. And if they would
have had no appeal then, on a legislation in 1871 similar to that of
1890, they have none now, if none of their rights and privileges have
been prejudicially affected.

I would answer the first question in the negative. This conclusion determines my answers to the other questions submitted to
the court, and, consequently, as at present advised, I would answer
the six of them as follows:

To No. 1, I would answer, No.
To No. 2, I would answer, No.
To No. 3, I would answer, Yes.
To No. 4, I would answer, No.
To No. 5, I would answer, No.
To No. 6, I would answer, No.

Gwynne, J.—The questions submitted in the case stated by the
order of His Excellency the Governor-General in Council for the
opinion of this court are as follows:

(Here follow the questions. See page 71.)

The memorials and petitions referred to in and made part of the
case were presented to His Excellency the Governor-General in
Council in April, 1890, and in September and October, 1892; that

of August, 1890, was signed by His Grace the Archbishop of St. Boniface and 4,266 others, members of the Roman Catholic Church.

(Here follows the petition. See page 28.)

A report of the Minister of Justice, dated 21st March, 1891, upon the two Acts of the Legislature of the Province of Manitoba, 53 Vic., caps. 37 and 38, has also been made part of the case submitted to us, in which reference is made to the cases of Barrett *v.* Winnipeg and Logan *v.* Winnipeg, then proceeding in appeal to the Supreme Court of Canada, and also to the said petition of His Grace the Archbishop of St. Boniface and others, in the following terms:

(Here follow extracts from the report. See page 31.)

The petitions of September, 1892, were two, the son of T. A. Bernier, representing himself to be acting president of the body called the National Congress, and of eleven others, members of the Executive Committee of the said body; and the other, dated 22nd September, 1892, was a petition of His Grace the Archbishop of St. Boniface.

In the former the petitioners set out at large the above petitions of August, 1890, and and the report of the Minister of Jusice from which the above extract is taken, and concluded as follows:

(Here follows part of the petition. See page 34.)

The petition of His Grace the Archbishop of St. Boniface sets forth the matter as alleged in the petition signed by him and others in the petition of April, 1890, and certain extracts from the said report of the Minister of Justice of March, 1891, including that above extracted, and concluded as follows:

(Here follow extracts from the petition. See page 35.)

And the petition prayed that His Excellency the Governor-General in Council might entertain the appeal of the Roman Catholics of Manitoba and might consider the same and might make such provisions and give such directions for the hearing and consideration of the said appeal as might be thought proper and that such directions might be given and provisions made for the relief of the Roman Catholics of the province of Manitoba as to His Excellency in Council might seem fit.

These petitions are framed upon the contention and assumption that the facts as stated in the petitions as to the rights and privileges of Roman Catholics in Manitoba in relation to education at the time of the creation of the province entitled them to procure, by appeals to His Excellency in Council under section 22 of the Manitoba Act, the annulment and repeal of provincial Acts, 53 Vic., ch. 37 and 38, notwithstanding that these Acts had been declared by the judgment of the Judicial Committee of the Privy Council in England to have been, and to be, Acts quite within the jurisdiction of the Legislature of Manitoba to enact. The petition of November, 1892, is however framed with a further contention. It is signed by His Grace the Archbishop of St. Boniface, T. A. Bernier as president of the body called the National Congress, James E. P. Prendergast as mayor of St. Boniface, J. Allard, O. M. I., V. G., John S. Ewart and 137 others. The petition sets out verbatim the matters alleged in the first twelve paragraphs of the above petition of August, 1890, and it then proceeds.

The pretension of the petitioners therefore appears to be that the 22nd section of the Manitoba Act entitled the petitioners, notwithstanding the judgment of the Privy Council in England in Barrett v. Winnipeg and Logan v. Winnipeg (1), to invoke, and to obtain, the interference of His Excellency the Governor-General in Council to compel, in effect, a repeal by the Provincial Legislature of the said Acts of 53rd Vic., and the re-enactment of the statutes in force in the province in relation to education at the time of the passing of the Acts 53rd Vic., upon the grounds following:

1. That the Acts of 53rd Vic. prejudicially affect the rights and privileges with regard to denominational schools which Roman Catholics had enjoyed previous to the erection of the province; and

2. That the said Acts 53rd Vic. prejudicially affect the rights and privileges of Roman Catholics in the province, provided for by various statutes of the Provincial Legislature enacted prior to the passing of the Acts of 53rd Vic.

Under these circumstances, the case which has been submitted to us has been framed in the shape in which it has been for the purpose of presenting to us purely abstract questions of law.

The learned members of the judicial committee of the Privy Council who advised Her Majesty upon the appeals in the cases of Barrett v. Winnipeg and Logan v. Winnipeg (2) adopting the evidence of the Archbishop of St. Boniface as to the rights and privileges in relation to denominational schools enjoyed by Roman Catholics before the passing of the Manitoba Act in the territory by that Act erected into the province of Manitoba, say in their report:

"Now, if the state of things which the Archbishop describes as existing before the union had been a system established by law,

(1) [1892] A.C. 1892.　(2) [1892] A.C. 445

what would have been the rights and privileges of the Roman Catholics with respect to denominational schools? They would have had by law the right to establish schools at their own expense, to maintain their schools by school fees or voluntary contributions, and to conduct them in accordance with their own religious tenets. Every other religious body which was engaged in a similar work at the time of the union would have had precisely the same right with respect to their denominational schools. Possibly the right, if it had been defined or recognized by positive enactment, might have had attached to it, as a necessary or appropriate incident, the right of exemption from any contribution, under any circumstance, to a school of a different denomination. But in their Lordships' opinion it would be going much too far to hold that the establishment of a national system of education upon a non-sectarian basis is so inconsistent with the right to set up and maintain denominational schools, that the two things cannot exist together, or that the existence of one necessarily implies or involves immunity from taxation for the purpose of the other."

They then minutely review the provisions of the provincial statutes enacted prior to the passing of the Acts of 1890, and of the Acts of 1890 themselves, and proceed as follows:

"Notwithstanding the Public School Acts, 1890, Roman Catholics and members of every other religious body in Manitoba are free to establish schools throughout the province; they are free to maintain their schools by school fees or voluntary contributions; they are free to conduct their schools according to their own religious tenets, without molestation or interference. No child is compelled to attend a public school, no special advantage, other than the advantage of a free education in schools conducted under public management, is held out to those who do attend."

To this it may be added, that Roman Catholics are not excluded from the advisory board erected by the Acts. They are equally eligible as Protestants to such board, and as members thereof can equally with Protestants exert their influence upon the board with regard to religious exercises in public schools, and in short, Roman Catholics and Protestants of every denomination are in every respect placed, by the Acts, in precisely the same position. The judgment of the Privy Council then proceeds as follows:

"But when it is said that it is impossible for Roman Catholics or for members of the Church of England (if their views are correctly represented by the Bishop of Rupert's Land, who has given evidence in Logan's case) to send their children to public schools where the education is not superintended and directed by the authorities of their church, and that therefore Roman Catholics and members of the Church of England who are taxed for public schools, and at the same time feel themselves compelled to support their own schools, are in a less favorable position than those who can take advantage of the free education provided by the Act of 1890; that may be so, but what right or privilege is violated or prejudicially affected by the law? It is not the law that is in fault, it is owing to religious convictions which everybody must respect, and to the teaching of their church that Roman Catholics and the members of the Church of England find themselves unable to partake of advantages which the law offers to all alike."

The judgment then summarily rejects the contention that the public schools created by the Acts of 1890 are in reality Protestant schools and concludes in declaring and adjudging that those Acts do not prejudicially affect the rights and privileges enjoyed by Roman Catholics in the territory now constituting the province of Manitoba, prior to the passing of the Manitoba Act, taking those rights and privileges to have been as represented by the Archbishop of St. Boniface, and even assuming them to have been secured or conferred by positive law, and so that they are not enacted in violation of section 22 of the Manitoba Act, but are within the exclusive jurisdiction of the Provincial Legislature to enact.

"Their Lordships of the Privy Council, in Barrett *v.* Winnipeg and Logan *v.* Winnipeg (1) put a construction upon this section 22 which, independently, is to my mind sufficiently apparent, but which I quote as a judicial enunciation of their Lordships' opinion. They say:

"Their Lordships are convinced that it must have been the intention of the Legislature to preserve every legal right of privilege with respect to denominational schools which any class or persons practically enjoyed at the time of the union."

The language of the section is, I think, sufficiently clear upon that point, and all its sub-sections are enacted for the purpose of securing the single object, namely, the preservation of existing rights. The section enacts:

(Here follows the section. See page 1).

If any law should be passed in violation of the qualification contained in the first sub-section under the general jurisdiction conferred by the section, to make laws in relation to education, that is to say, in case any Act should be passed by the Provincial Legislature prejudically affecting any right or privilege with respect to denominational schools which any class of persons had by law or practice in the province at the union, such an Act would be *ultra vires* of the Provincial Legislature to enact, and would therefore have no force; and as it was to preserve these rights and

---

(1) [1892] A.C. 445.

privileges with respect to denominational schools, whatsoever they
were, which existed at the time of the union, that the 22nd section
was enacted, it is obvious, I think, that it is against such an
Act of the legislature and against any decision of any provincial
authority, acting in an administrative capacity, prejudicially
affecting any such right, that the appeal is given by the 2nd sub-
section, and so likewise the remedies provided in the 3rd sub-section
relate to the same rights and privileges, and to the better securing
the enjoyment of them. The 2nd and 3rd sub-sections are designed
as means to redress any violation of the rights preserved by the
section. To subject any Act of the legislature to the appeal provided in the 2nd sub-section, and to the remedies provided in the
3rd sub-section, it is obvious that such an Act must be passed in
violation of the condition subject to which any jurisdiction is
conferred upon the Provincial Legislature to make laws in relation
to education, and must therefore be *ultra vires* of the Provincial
Legislature, for the language of the section expressly excludes from
the Provincial Legislature all jurisdiction to pass such an Act. The
jurisdiction, whatever its extent may be, which the Provincial
Legislature has over education being declared to be excessive, there
can be no appeal to any other authority against an Act passed by
the legislature under such jurisdiction, and any Act of the
legislature passed in violation of any of the provisions in section 22,
subject to which the jurisdiction of the legislature is restricted, is
not within their jurisdiction and is therefore *ultra vires*. The
appeal, therefore, which is given by the 2nd sub-section must be
only concurrent with the right of all persons injuriously affected by
such an Act to raise in the ordinary courts of justice the question of
its constitutionality. If any doubt could be entertained upon this
point it is concluded, in my opinion, by their Lordships of the
Privy Council in Barrett *v.* Winnipeg and Logan *v.* Winnipeg,
(1), in the following language :

"At the commencement of the argument a doubt was suggested
as to the competency of the present appeal, in consequence of the
so-called appeal to the Governor in Council provided by the Act,
but their Lordships are satisfied that the provisions of sub-sections 2
and 3 do not operate to withdraw such a question as that
involved in the present case from the jurisdiction of the ordinary
tribunals of the country."

If an Act of the Provincial Legislature which is impeached upon
the suggestion of its prejudicially affecting such rights and privileges
as aforesaid is not made by the 2nd section of the Manitoba Act
ultra vires of the Provincial Legislature it cannot be open to
appeal under sub-section 2 of that section. The section does not

---

(1) [1892] A.C. 445.

profess to confer upon the executive of the Dominion or the Dominion Parliament, any power of interference whatever with any Act in relation to education passed by the Provincial Legislature of Manitoba which is not open to the objection of prejudicially affecting some right or privilege with respect to denominational schools, which some class of persons had by law or practice in the province at the union: all Acts of the Provincial Legislature not open to such objection are declared by the section to be within the exclusive jurisdiction of the Provincial Legislature; and as the Acts of 1890 are declared by their Lordships not to be open to such objection, and to have therefore been within the jurisdiction of the Provincial Legislature to pass, those Acts cannot, nor can either of them, be be open to any appeal under the 2nd sub-section of this section.

It has been suggested however that the rights and privileges, whether conferred or recognized by the Acts of the Legislature of Manitoba in force prior to and at the time of the passing of the Acts of 1890 and which were thereby repealed, were within the protection of the 22nd section and that this was a matter not under consideration in Barrett v. Winnipeg and Logan v. Winnipeg (1); and that therefore the right of appeal under sub-section 2 of section 22 against such repeal does exist notwithstanding the decision of the Privy Council in Barrett v. Winnipeg and Logan v. Winnipeg (2). This contention appears to have been first raised expressly in the petition presented in October, 1892, although it is implicitly comprehended in the paragraphs of the petition of August, 1890, which is repeated verbatim in that of October, 1892, wherein the Act of the Provincial Legislature of 1871 is relied upon as having had "the effect to continue to the Roman Catholics that separate condition with reference to education which they had enjoyed previous to the creation of the province, and, in so far as Roman Catholics were concerned, merely to organize the efforts which the Roman Catholics had previously voluntarily made for the education of their own children and for the continuance of schools under the sole control and management of Roman Catholics, and of the education of their children according to the methods by which alone they believe children should be instructed."

But this statute of 1871, and all the statutes passed by the legislature of Manitoba in relation to education prior to 1890, were specially brought under the notice of their Lordships of the Privy Council, and were fully considered by them in their judgment as already pointed out, and if the repeal by the Act of 1890 of the Acts of the Provincial Legislature then in force in relation to education constituted a violation of the condition contained in section 22, subject to which alone the jurisdiction of the Provincial

(1) [1892] A.C. 445.   2) [1892] A.C. 445.

Legislature to make laws in relation to education was restricted, it is inconceivable to my mind that their Lordships, having all these statutes before them, could have pronounced the Acts of 1890 to be within the jurisdiction of the Provincial Legislature to pass. But however this may be there is nothing, in my opinion, in the Manitoba Act which imposed any obligation upon the legislature of Manitoba to pass the Acts, which are repealed by the Acts of 1890, or which placed those Acts when passed in any different position from that of all Acts of a legislature, which constitute the will of the legislature for the time being, and only until repealed,—and nothing which warrants the contention that the repeal of those Acts by the Acts of 1890 constitued a violation of the condition in the 22nd section subject to which the jurisdiction of the legislature was restricted; and nothing, therefore, which gives any appeal against such repeal.

Whether or not the 3rd sub-section of section 93 of the British North America Act of 1867, assuming that section to apply to the Province of Manitoba, would have the effect of restraining the powers of the Provincial Legislature in such manner as to deprive them of jurisdiction to repeal the said Acts, it is unnecessary to enquire, for that section does not, in my opinion, apply to the Province of Manitoba, special provision upon the subject of education being made by the 22nd section of the Manitoba Act. For the above reasons, therefore, the questions submitted in the case must, in my opinion be answered as follows :—

The 1st, 2nd, 4th and 5th in the negative; the 3rd in the affirmative, and the 6th, which is a complex question, as follows:

The Acts of 1890 do not, nor does either of them, affecit any right or privilege of a minority in relation to education within the meaning of sub-section 2 of section 22 of the Manitoba Act in such manner that an appeal will lie thereunder to the Governor-General in Council. The residue of the question is answered by the answer to question No. 4.

KING J.—It may be convenient first to regard the constitutional provisions respecting education as they affect the original provinces of the confederation. By section 93 of the British North America Act it is provided that in and for each province the Legislature may exclusively make laws in relation to education, subject and according to the provisions of four sub-sections. The first sub-section provides that nothing in any such law shall prejudicially affect any right or privilege with respect to denominational schools which any class of persons had by law in the province at the union.

The second sub-section extends to the dissentient schools of the Queen's Protestant and Roman Catholic subjects in Quebec all the powers, privileges and duties which were at the union conferred and imposed by law in Upper Canada (Ontario) on the separate school trustees of the Queen's Roman Catholic subjects there.

The third sub-section gives to the Governor-General in Council the right on appeal to decide whether or not an Act or decision of any provincial authority affects any right or privileges of the Protestant or Roman Catholic minority in relation to education enjoyed by them under a system of separate or dissentient schools in the province, whether such system of separate or dissentient schools shall have existed by law at the union, or shall have been thereafter established by the legislature of the province.

The fourth sub-section provides that if upon appeal the Governor-General in Council shall decide that the educational right or privilege of the Protestant or Roman Catholic minority has been so affected, and if the Provincial Legislature shall not pass such laws as from time to time seem to the Governor-General in Council requisite for the due execution of the provisions of the section, or if the proper provincial authority shall not duly execute the decision of the Governor-General in Council on the appeal, then in every such case, but only as far as the circumstances of each case require, the Parliament of Canada may make remedial laws for the due execution of the provisions of this section and of any decision of the Governor-General in Council under the section. In other words, if the requisite remedy, either by Act of the Legislature, or Act or decision of the proper provincial authority in that behalf, is not applied, then concurrent legislative authority to the requisite extent is given to the Dominion Parliament; and to this extent the legislative authority of the Provincial Legislature ceases to be exclusive.

The terms "separate" and "dissentient" schools used in the above sub-sections were derived from the school systems of Upper and Lower Canada. At the union the two larger confederating provinces, Upper Canada (Ontario) and Lower Canada (Quebec) had each a system of separate or dissentient schools, the Canadian method of dealing with the question of religion (as between Protestants and Roman Catholics) in the public school system.

In Upper Canada the Roman Catholics were in the minority, and in Lower Canada the Protestants were in a still smaller minority. In Upper Canada there was a non-denominational public system, with a right in the Roman Catholics to a separate denominational system. In Lower Canada the general public system was markedly Roman Catholic with a right to the Protestant minority to schools of their own. In Upper Canada the minority schools were called "separate" schools; in Lower Canada "dissentient" schools. It was because the powers and privileges of the Upper Canada minority in relation to their schools were greater than those of the Lower Canada minority that by the terms of union these were agreed to be assimilated by adopting for Quebec the more enlarged liberties of the Upper Canada law ; and this was given effect to by sub-section 2 of section 93 already cited.

In the case of the two other of the original confederating provinces, Nova Scotia and New Brunswick, there was not in either a system of separate or dissentient schools.

The bounds of the Dominion have been since enlarged ; in 1870, by the admission of the North West Territory and Rupert's Land ; in 1871, by the admission of British Columbia, and in 1872, by the admission of Prince Edward Island. In the case of British Columbia and Prince Edward Island (these being established and independent provinces) the terms of union were agreed upon by the Governments and Legislatures of Canada and the provinces respectively. In each case the above recited provisions of the British North America Act respecting education were adopted and made applicable without change. In neither of these newly added provinces was there a system of separate or dissentient schools.

With regard to the North-West Territories and Rupert's Land there was no established government and legislature representing the people, and after the acquisition of the North-West Territories and Rupert's Land, the Parliament of Canada, after listening to representations of representative bodies of people, passed an Act for the creation and establishment of the new Province of Manitoba out of, and over, a portion of the newly acquired territory ; and it is with regard to this Act, (33 Vict. c. 3) that the present questions arise.

By section 2 it is declared that :

(Here follows the section. See page 2.)

The Act then deals specially with a number of matters, as for instance the constitution of the executive and legislative authority, the use of both the English and French languages in legislative and judicial proceedings, financial arrangements and territorial revenue, etc., and by section 22 makes the following provisions respecting education :

(Here follows the section. See page 1.)

Sub-section 1 of section 22 of the Manitoba Act differs from sub-section 1 of section 93 of the British North America Act of 1867, in the addition of the words "or practice" after the words "which any class of persons had by law."

In Winnipeg v. Barrett (1) the Judicial Committee of the Privy Council held that the Manitoba Education Act of 1890 did not

(1) [1892] A.C. 445.

CHAP. V.]   JUDGMENTS OF THE SUPREME COURT.   103

prejudicially affect any right or privilege with respect to denominational schools which the Roman Catholics practically enjoyed at the time of the establishment of the province.

The 2nd sub-section of section 93, British North America Act, has of course, no counterpart in any of the sub-sections of section 22, Manitoba Act, because sub-section 2, section 93, British North America Act, is a clause specially applicable to, and affecting only, the Province of Quebec.

The 3rd sub-section of section 93, British North America Act, and the 2nd sub-section of section 22, Manitoba Act, deal with the like subject, viz.: the right of the religious minority to appeal to the Governor General in Council in case of their educational rights or privileges being affected; and here again there are differences.

One difference is, that whereas by the clause in the British North America Act the appeal lies from an "Act or decision of any provincial authority" affecting any right or privilege of the Protestant or Roman Catholic minority in relation to education; in the Manitoba Act the appeal lies from "any Act or decision of the Legislature of the province" as well as from that of any provincial authority. This was either an extension of the right of appeal or the getting rid of an ambiguity, according as the words "any provincial authority" as used in the British North America Act did not, or did, extend to cover "Acts of the Provincial Legislature."

The addition in the 1st sub-section of the Manitoba Act of the words "or practice"; and the addition in sub-section 2 of the words "of the Legislature of the province," would (so far as the context of these words is concerned) seem to show an intention on the part of Parliament to extend the constitutional protection accorded to minorities by the British North America Act, or at all events to make no abatement therein.

Then there is another difference between the language of the 3rd sub-section of the British North America Act and the 2nd sub-section of the Manitoba Act. The former begins as follows: "Where in any province a system of separate and dissentient schools exists by law at the union or is thereafter established by the Legislature of the province, an appeal shall lie," etc., while in the Manitoba Act the introductory part is omitted, and the clause begins with the words, "An appeal shall lie," etc., the two clauses being thereafter identical, with the exception that in the Manitoba Act (as already mentioned) the appeal in terms extends to complaints against the effect of Acts of the legislature as well as of acts or decisions of any provincial authority.

After this reference to points of distinction I cite subsection 2 of the Manitoba Act again in full, for sake of clearness:

"An appeal shall lie to the Governor General in Council from any Act or decision of the legislature of the province, or of any provincial authority, affecting any right or privilege of the Protestant or Roman Catholic minority of the Queen's subjects in relation to education."

On the one side it is contended that in order to give the appeal, the rights or privileges of the religious minority need to have been acquired and to have existed prior to and at the time of the passage of the Act. On the other side it is contended that it is sufficient if the rights and privileges exist at the time of their alleged violation irrespective of the time when they were acquired.

In the argument before the judicial committee of Winnipeg v. Barrett, a shorthand report of which was submitted to parliament last session (No. 11 Sessional Papers), Sir Horace Davey, counsel for the city of Winnipeg, argued that subsection 2 does not relate to anything but what is *ultra vires* under subsection 1. He says (p. 43).

"I cannot for myself frame the proposition which would lead to the inference that sub-section 2 was intended to deal with cases which were *intra vires*, and I beg leave to observe that it would be contrary to the whole scope and spirit of this legislation to provide for Parliament intervening, not where the Provincial Parliament has acted beyond its powers—that I could conceive—but to allow the Dominion Parliament to intervene, not to correct mistakes where the Provincial Legislature has gone wrong and exceeded their power."

In an interruption at this point by their lordships, Lord Macnaghten asks:

"Supposing some rights were created after the union, and then legislation had taken those rights away?"

This question is not directly answered, but afterwards (p. 44) Sir Horace thus continues:

"It all comes back to the same point, that the Protestant and Roman Catholic minority have a right to come with a grievance to the Governor General. What is that grievance? Why, that they are deprived of some right or privilege which they ought to have and are entitled to enjoy. If they are not entitled by law to enjoy it they are not deprived of anything, and it would be an extraordinary system of legislation, having regard to the nature of this Act, to say that the Dominion Parliament has in certain cases to sit by way of a court of appeal from the Provincial Parliament, not to correct mistakes where the Provincial Parliament has erroneously legislated on matters not within its jurisdiction, but on matters of policy. If that be the effect to be given to these sub-sections, I venture to submit to your lordships that it will have rather startling consequences, and it will for the first time make the Legislature of the Dominion Parliament a court of appeal, or give them an appeal, from the exercise of the discretion of the Provincial Parliament, or in other words, it will place the Provincial Parliament in the position that it will be liable to have its decisions overruled by the Dominion Parliament, and therefore in a position of inferiority."

I have quoted at great length because of the strong presentation by eminent counsel of that view, and to show that the attention of their lordships was powerfully drawn to the provisions of sub-section 2. The full report shows that all the sub-sections of the two sections of the two Acts were exhaustively discussed.

In the judgment their lordships say that:

"Subsections 1, 2, and 3 of section 22 of the Manitoba Act, 1870, differ but slightly from the corresponding sections of section 93 of the British North America Act, 1867. The only important difference is that the Manitoba Act in sub-section 1 the words "by law" are followed by the words "or practice" which do not occur in the corresponding passage in the British North America Act, 1867."

There would be a marked and very considerable difference between the corresponding clauses, if in the one case rights and privileges of the religious minority were recognized as subjects of protection whenever acquired, while in the other case they were not recognized as subjects of protection unless they existed at the time of the passing of the constitutional act.

Not wanting to put undue stress upon this, let us look at the clauses for ourselves. In sub-section 1, Manitoba Act, there is an express limitation as to time; the rights and privileges in denominational schools that are saved are such as existed, by law or practice, at the union. But in sub-section 2 nothing is said about time at all; and the natural conclusion upon a reading of the two clauses together is that, with regard to the rights and privileges referred to in the latter clause, the time of their origin is immaterial. Such also is the ordinary and natural meaning of sub-section 2, regarded by itself. Read by itself it extends to cover rights and privileges existent at at the time of the act or thing complained of. The existence of the right, and not the time of its creation, is the operative and material fact. And this agrees with the corresponding provisions of the British North America Act, where sub-section 1 refers to rights, etc., acquired before, or at, union, while sub-section 3, in terms, covers rights, etc., acquired at any time. In any other view there was clearly no necessity to add the words "or any Act of the Legislature" in the remedial provision of the Manitoba Act, for such Act would be wholly null and void under sub-section 1.

There is, indeed, an undeniable objection to treating as an appealable thing the repeal by a Legislature of an Act passed by itself. Ordinarily all rights and privileges given by Act of Parliament are to be enjoyed *sub modo*, and are subject to the implied right of the same Legislature to repeal or alter if it chooses to do so. But the fundamental law may make it otherwise. An illustration of this is afforded by the constitution of the United States, which prohibits the States, but not Congress, from passing any law impairing the obligation of contract, and this has been held to prevent the State Legislatures from repealing, or materially altering, their own Acts conferring private rights, when such rights have been accepted. It does not extend to Acts relating to Government, as, for instance, to public officers, municipal incorporations, etc., but it extends to private and other corporations, educational or otherwise, and also to Acts exempting incorporated bodies, by special Act, from rates or taxes. These are irrepealable, and the constitutional provision has been found onerous.

It is certainly anomalous under our system and theory of parliamentary power, that a Legislature may not repeal or alter in any way an Act passed by itself.

Still weighty as this consideration is, I can give no other reasonable interpretation to the Act in question than that, under the constitution of Manitoba, as under the constitution of the Dominion, the exercise by the Provincial Legislature of its undoubted powers in a way so as to give rights and privileges by law to the minority in respect of education, lets in the Dominion Parliament to concurrent legislative authority for the purpose of preserving and continuing such rights and privileges, if it sees fit to do so.

By the British North America Act it was not clear whether the words "act or decision of any provincial authority," covered the case of an Act of the Provincial Legislature, or was confined to Administrative Acts, but in the Manitoba Act the words explicitly extend to an Act of that Legislature.

Any ambiguity in sub-section 2 of the Manitoba Act is, I conceive, to be resolved in the light of the corresponding provisions of the British North America Act. As the provisions of the British North America Act are to be applicable, unless varied, I think it reasonable that ambiguous provisions in the special Act should be construed in conformity with the general Act.

Passing, however, from it as a matter of construction, it does not seem reasonable that Parliament, in forming, in 1870, a constitution for Manitoba, intended to disregard entirely constitutional limitations such as were three years before established as binding upon the original members of the confederation. On the contrary, by the addition of the words "or by practice" in 1st sub-section, and of the words "or any Act of the Legislature" in 2nd sub-section, and by the provision of section 23 providing for the use of French and English languages in the courts and Legislature, there is manifested a greater tenderness for racial and denominational differences. Further, unless sub-section 2 has the meaning suggested, the entire series of limitations imposed by sub-sections 1, 2 and 3 are entirely inoperative. For the Judicial Committee has in effect declared that no right or privilege in respect of denominational schools existed prior to the union, either by law or practice, and therefore there was nothing on which sub-section 1 could practically operate; and as there was clearly no system of separate or dissentient schools established in Manitoba by law prior to the union, the provisions of sub-sections 2 and 3 are inoperative if the rights and privileges in relation to education are to be limited to rights and privileges before the union.

There is no doubt that this construction limits the powers of the Legislature and restrains the exercise of its discretion, but the same thing may be said of the effect of an appeal against "any act or decision of any provincial authority" in Nova Scotia or New Brunswick, in case either of such provinces were to adopt a system of separate schools. The Legislature might not choose to pass the remedial legislation necessary to execute the decision of the Governor General in Council, and the Dominion Parliament could then exercise its concurrent power of legislation in effect overriding the legislative determination of the Provincial Legislature. The provision may be weak, one-sided, as giving finality to a chance legislative vote in favour of separate schools, inconsistent with a proper autonomy, and without elements of permanence, but if it is in the constitutional system it must receive recognition in the court of law.

Assuming then that clause 2 covers rights and privileges whensoever acquired, the next question is as to the meaning of the words "rights and privileges of the Protestant or Roman Catholic minority in relation to education?" Here again, I think, we are to go to clause 3 of section 93, British North America Act. I think that the reference is to minority rights under a system of separate schools, and that it is essential that the complaining minority should have had rights or privileges under a system of separate or dissentient schools existing by law at the union or thereafter established by the legislature of the province. The generality of the words under clause 2 of the Manitoba Act is to be explained by clause 3, section 93, British North America Act, and to have the same meaning as the corresponding words in it.

The two remaining questions then, are: Was a system of separate or dissentient schools established in Manitoba prior to the passage of the Manitoba Education Act of 1890? And, have any rights or privileges of the Roman Catholic minority in relation thereto been prejudicially affected?

One of the learned judges of the Queen's Bench of Manitoba thus succinctly summarizes the school legislation of Manitoba in force at the time of the passing of the Act in 1890:

"Under the school Acts in force in the province previous to the passing of the Public School Act of 1890, there were two distinct sets of public or common schools, the one set Protestant and the other Roman Catholic. The board of education, which had the general management of the public schools, was divided into two sections, one composed of the Protestant members and one of the Roman Catholic members, and each section had its own superintendent. The school districts were designated Protestant or Roman Catholic, as the case might be. The Protestant schools were under the immediate control of trustees elected by the Protestant ratepayers of the district, and the Catholic schools in the same way were under the control of trustees elected by the Roman Catholic ratepayers; and it was provided that the ratepayers of a district should pay the assessments that were required to supplement the legislative grant to the schools of their own denomination, and that in no case should Protestant ratepayers be obliged to pay for a Roman Catholic school, or a Catholic ratepayer for a Protestant school."

I would only add that assessments were to be ordered by the ratepayers (Catholic or Protestant, as the case may be) of the school district, and that the trustees were empowered in many cases to collect the rates themselves, instead of making use of the public collectors. The trustees were empowered to employ teachers exclusively who should hold certificates from the section of the board of education of their own faith. By the act of 1871 the board of education was composed equally of Protestants and Roman Catholics, but by the Act of 1881 the proportion was 12 Protestants and 9 Roman Catholics.

Now, the system of education established by the Act of 1881 was not in terms, and, *eo nomine*, a system of separate or dissentient schools, and if the constitutional provision requires that they should be such in order to come within the Act, then the minority did not have the requisite rights and privileges in respect of education. As to this, I have had doubts arising from the opinion that, where rights and privileges have no other foundation than the legislative authority whose subsequent Acts in affecting them is impeached, the restraint upon the general grant of legislative authority should be applied only where the case is brought closely within the limitation. At the same time, we are to give a fair and reasonable construction to a remedial provision of the constitution, and are to regard the substance of the thing. Now the Roman Catholics were in the minority in 1881, and are still, and a system of schools was established by law, under which they had the right to their own schools—Catholic in name and fact—under the control of trustees selected by themselves, taught by teachers of their own faith, and supported, in part, by an assessment ordered by themselves upon the persons and property of Roman Catholics, and imposed, levied and collected as a portion of the public rates, the persons and property liable to such rate being at the same time exempt from contribution to the schools of the majority, *i.e.*, Protestant schools. This, although not such in name, seems to me to have been essentially a system of separate or dissentient schools, of the same general type as the separate school system of Ontario, and giving therefore to the minority rights and privileges in relation to education in the sense of sub-section 2, section 22, Manitoba Act, and sub-section 3, section 93, British North America Act.

It is true that the schools of the majority were Protestant schools, and that the majority had the same right as the minority, but I do not think that this renders the minority schools any the less essentially separate schools of the Roman Catholics. In Quebec the majority schools are distinctly denominational.

Then, was the right and privilege of the Roman Catholic minority in this system of separate schools prejudicially affected by the Act of 1890? And if so, to what extent?

In the judgment of the judicial committee in The city of Winnipeg v. Barrett (1), speaking of the right there claimed on behalf of the rights and privileges which they had by practice at the time of the union, their lordships say:

"Now if the state of things which the archbishop describes as existing before the union had been established by law, what would have been the rights and privileges of the Roman Catholics with respect to denominational schools? They would have had, by law, the right to establish schools at their own expense, to maintain their schools by school fees or voluntary contributions, and to conduct them in accordance with their own religious tenets. Every other religious body which was engaged in a similar work, at the time of the union, would have had precisely the same right with respect to their denominational schools. Possibly this right, if it had been defined or recognised by positive enactment, might have had attached to it, as a necessary or appropriate incident, the right of exemption from any contribution under any circumstances to schools of a different denomination. But, in their lordship's opinion, it would be going much too far to hold that the establishment of a national system of education, upon an unsectarian basis, is so inconsistent with the right to set up and maintain denominational schools, that the two things cannot exist together, or that the existence of one necessarily implies or involves immunity from taxation for the purpose of the other."

The rights and privileges of the denominational minority under the Act of 1881 and amending acts, were different from the assumed rights in denominational schools which the same class had by practice at the time of union. It could not be said to be merely "the right to establish schools at their own expense, to maintain their schools by school fees or voluntary contributions, and to conduct them in accordance with their own religious tenets"; it was a right as Roman Catholics by law to establish schools and to maintain them through the exercise by them of the state power of taxation, by the imposition,

---

(1) [1892] A.C. 445.

levying and collecting of rates upon the persons and property of all
Roman Catholics, such persons and property being at the same time
exempted from liability to be rated for the support of the public
schools of the majority, then denominated and being Protestant
schools. By the Act of 1890 the Protestant schools are abolished
equally with the Roman Catholic schools, and a system of public
schools set up, which is neither Protestant nor Roman Catholic, but
unsectarian. The question then is whether the language of their lordships is applicable to this state of things, and whether or not it can be
said (changing their lordship's language to suit the facts) that the
establishment of the national system of education upon an unsectarian
basis is so inconsistent with the right to set up and maintain by the
aid of public taxation upon the denominational minority, a system of
denominational schools, that the two cannot co-exist; or that the existence of the system of denominational minority schools (supposing it
still in existence) necessarily implies or involves immunity from taxation for the purpose of the other. It rather seems to me that no
reasonable system of legislation could consistently seek to embrace
these two things, viz: 1st, the support of a system of denominational
schools for the minority, maintainable through compulsory rating of
the persons and property of the minority; and 2nd, the support of a
general system of rating all persons and property, both of the majority and minority. The effect of such a scheme would be to impose a
double rate upon a part of the community for educational purposes.
The logical result of this view would be that by the establishment of
a general non-sectarian system (as well as by the abrogation of the
separate school system) the rights and privileges are previously given
by law to the denominational minority in respect of education were
necessarily affected. Of course the minority would obtain equality by
giving up their schools; but the present inquiry at this point is
whether a right acquired by law to maintain a system of separate
schools has been affected by an Act which takes away the legal organization and status of such schools, and their means of maintenance, by
the repeal of the law giving these things, and which subjects the
persons and property of the denominational minority to an educational
rate for general non-sectarian schools, instead of leaving them subjected
to an educational rate for the support of the separate and denominational schools. It is true that by the Act of 1881 and amending Acts,
the exemption was an exemption from contribution to the Protestant
schools, and the schools under the act of 1890 are not Protestant
schools; but the substantial thing involved in the exemption under
the Acts of 1881 and amending Acts was, that the ratepayer to the support of the Catholic schools should not have to pay rates for the
support of the schools established by the rest of the community, but
should have their educational rates appropriated solely to the support
of their own schools. This was an educational right or privilege

accorded to them, in relation to education, under a system of separate schools established by law, which the legislature, if possessing absolute or exclusive authority to legislate on the subject of education without limitation or restraint, might very well withdraw, abrogate or materially alter, but which, under the constitutional limitations of the Manitoba Act, can be done only subject to the rights of the minority to seek the intervention of the Dominion Parliament, through the exercise of the concurrent legislative authority, that thereupon becomes vested in such parliament, upon resort being first had to the tribunal of the Governor-General in Council. Although there are points of difference between this case and what would have been the case if the prior legislation of Manitoba had established a system of separate schools following precisely the Ontario system, I cannot regard the difference as other than nominal, and I treat this case as though the Act of 1881 and amending Acts distinctly established a system of separate schools, giving for the general public a system of undenominational public schools, and to the Catholic minority the right to a system of separate schools. In such case I do not see how the passing of such an Act as the Act of 1890 could fail to be said (by abolishing the separate schools) to affect the rights and privileges of the minority in respect of education. With some changes of phraseology, and some change of method, I think that what has been done in the case before us is essentially the same. If the clauses of the Manitoba Act are to have any meaning at all, they must apply to save rights and privileges which have no other foundation originally than a statute of the Manitoba Legislature. The constitutional provision protects the separate educational status given by an Act of the Legislature to the denominational minority. The view that the effect of this is to restrain the proper exercise by the Legislature, of its power to alter its own legislation, is met by the opposite view that there is no improper restraint if it is a constitutional provision, and that in establishing a system of separate schools the Legislature may well have borne in mind the possibly irrepealable character of its legislation in thereby creating rights and privileges in relation to education. I therefore answer the questions of the case as follows:

1. Yes.
2. Yes.
3. No.
4. Yes, to the extent as explained by the above reasons for my opinion.
5. Yes.
6. Yes.

PETITION OF THE CARDINAL, ARCHBISHOPS, AND BISHOPS OF THE
ROMAN CATHOLIC CHURCH IN CANADA, MAY, 1894.

To His Excellency the Governor-General of Canada in Council:

MAY IT PLEASE YOUR EXCELLENCY,—The petition of the undersigned, His Eminence the Cardinal Archbishop of Quebec, the Most Reverend Archbishops and the Right Reverend the Bishops of the Roman Catholic Church in the Dominion of Canada, devoted subjects of Her Most Gracious Majesty the Queen, humbly sheweth:

1. Since the establishment of the Province of Manitoba until 1890, the public schools of the province, as established by law, were either Protestant or Catholic schools. They all enjoyed the same rights and received respectively their legitimate share of legislative grants. They were independent one from another, being conducted, directed, and supported by the respective sections of the population for which they were established. The system gave such satisfaction that it was the cause of no complaint, and the two sections of the population with their respective schools lived in peace, concord, harmony, and mutual good-will.

2. In 1890 laws were passed changing the school system and replacing it with enactments which are, for a portion of the community, a source of grief, regret and hardship. Practically, and in spite of all assertions to the contrary, the result of the new system is purely and simply the legal suppression of all Catholic schools, and the maintenance of all Protestant schools, with all the rights and privileges they enjoyed previous to the school laws of 1890. Catholic schools are abolished by law, while Protestant schools have nothing to suffer from the new enactment; nay, they gain by it, as the Catholic ratepayers have now to help to the support of Protestant schools, which are exactly what they were, and to which, naturally, Catholic parents cannot conscientiously send their children.

3. The Public Schools Act of 1890, being 53 Vic., ch. 38 (now ch. 127 of Revised Statutes of 1891) decrees, in sections 241-242, that "in cases where, before the coming into force of this Act, Catholic school districts have been established, covering the same territory as any Protestant school district . . . such Catholic school districts shall cease to exist." The law has been put in force wheresoever it could be applied; for instance, in Winnipeg, Brandon, etc. There the Catholic trustees have ceased to be recognized since the 1st May, 1890, while the Protestant trustees remained in office and caused taxes to be levied on Catholic as well as Protestant parents, notwithstanding the fact that no Catholic children are attending the said Protestant schools.

4. Section 192 says: "Religious exercises in the public schools shall be conducted according to the regulations of the Advisory Board." It is, therefore, lawful to have prayers and religious exercises in the public school of Manitoba, provided the same are fixed and determined by the Advisory Board. Just now all the members of the said Board are Protestants, and, owing to the condition of the country, it is clear that Catholics will never have but very little influence, if any, in the said Board."

Therefore, Protestant children will be allowed to pray according to their parents' desire, while Catholic children are deprived of the same liberty, and this under the penalty of forfeiting their legitimate share of public money, because in order to secure to his or her school the government grant, the teacher must declare under oath that no prayer or religious exercise, except as prescribed by the Advisory Board, has been used in the school. Suppose a school attended exclusively by Catholic children, with a Catholic teacher, the said school would be deprived of the legislative grant, should the teacher or the pupils cross themselves or make use of the Hail Mary.

5. Religious instruction is not prohibited in the Public Schools of Manitoba; in that respect, and under the heading of morals the regulations framed under the old system by the Protestant section of the Board are retained under the new system; "Stories, memory gems, sentiments in the school lessons, examination of motives, didactic talks, teaching the ten Commandments, etc., are means to be employed." All this, of course, is to be used from a Protestant point of view, so much so that the actual chairman of the Advisory Board, who has always been the chairman of the Protestant section of the Board of Education, and who is no less a personage than the Archbishop of Rupert's Land, declared before the Synod, in 1893, that the above quoted privileges "are not small things in themselves, but they are doubly important because they carry with them for the teacher a degree of liberty in his teaching of what may come before the classes in their literature and otherwise," and His Grace adds: "The teachers who ignore these exercises can hardly be realizing their position as Christian men."

The liberty above mentioned is naturally for Protestants alone because it is enacted that those public schools are "non-sectarian," that is to say, that no Catholic teaching can be permitted while facilities are afforded to zealous and intelligent Protestant teachers to impress upon their pupils their own religious convictions.

See appendix A, pamphlet by Archbishop Taché, April, 1893, and appendix B, Dr. J. R. Morrison's paper read before the Junior Liberal Conservative Association, of St. John, N. B., February 13th, 1894.

6. For the last four years the Catholics of Manitoba have been subjected to unfair and unjust treatment resulting from the change in

the school laws in 1890. They asked in vain for relief. Instead of a remedy, they have been made the victims of a fresh injustice, the new Manitoba law, 57 Vic., ch. 28, assented to on March 2nd, 1894.

The clause 151 of the Public School Act of 1890 reads as follows: "Any school not conducted according to all the provisions of this or any Act in force for the time being, or the regulations of the department of education, or the Advisory Board, shall not be deemed a public school within the meaning of the law, and such school shall not participate in the legislative grant."

To this provision, in force since 1890, has been added this year the section 4 of the new law, which reads as follows: "Section 151 of chapter 127 is hereby amended by adding thereto the following words: Nor the municipal grant, nor shall any school assessment be levied or school taxes be collected for the benefit of such school."

The consequences of this new enactment is that no municipality, even one exclusively Catholic, without a single Protestant in its limits, has any power to levy a single dollar for Catholic schools, while a Catholic municipality where are ten Protestant children is obliged by law to levy on all the Catholics as well as on the parents of the ten Protestant children the money required for the education of the said ten Protestant children.

7. The same law of 1894 goes further and decrees the confiscation of all school property in all the districts which do not submit their schools to the new law, and it says in section 2, "In every case in which the organization of a school district fails to be continued—the council of the municipality in which such school district lies shall have full power and authority, and it shall be the duty of the said council to take charge of all the property of such school district, real and personal, and to administer the same for the benefit of the creditors of such school district, if any."

Such is the real position of the Catholics of Manitoba, though all their school property has been acquired with their own money, without any help from Protestant purse or public fund, and in Protestant municipalities the Catholic school property, real and personal, goes to the benefit of Protestants.

8. The example given in Manitoba has been partly followed in the North-west Territories. There the Catholic separate schools have been retained, but in virtue, of the Ordinance No. 22, A.D. 1892, they are deprived of their own liberty of action and of the character which distinguishes them from other schools. So that, in reality, the Catholics of the North-west are reduced, partly at least, to the hardship imposed upon their brethren of Manitoba. In both cases the result is very detrimental to the cause of education and really has in both cases created bad feelings, dissensions, and the most deplorable results.

See appendix C, memorial of Archbishop Taché, March, 1894.

9. The undersigned take the liberty to affirm that they deeply regret the condition of affairs above mentioned.

The painful experience of the Catholics of Manitoba and the North-west Territories is also resented by the Catholics of the Dominion. The undersigned have no hesitation in stating that a similar feeling certainly exists among many Protestants, who, though separated by faith, are united with the Catholics in a sentiment of justice, fair play, and desire for the prosperity of their common country.

The undersigned appreciate the political advantages enjoyed by Canada and have no desire for any other regime, satisfied that there is, in the institutions of the country and in the spirit of justice and conciliation which prevails among its inhabitants, a remedy against what, just now, is the subject of their complaints. The Canadian constitution acknowledges equal rights for all citizens, and for all classes of citizens. Therefore, Canadians should not be oppressed because they are Catholics.

10. The undersigned cannot shut their eyes to a fact closely connected with the history of their country: Catholic missionaries have not waited for the facilities and material advantages, now offered by Canada to bring thereto the light of Christian civilization. On the contrary, they were the first pioneers of the sacred cause and they sealed their missions with their blood. Without fear or hesitation they buried their existence among the most barbarous savages, whom they tamed and induced peaceably to hand over their own country to the Canadian authorities. The Catholic missionaries accompanied that noble task on the banks of the Saskatchewan and Red Rivers, as well as on those of the St. Lawrence and the Ottawa, and they did this, when alongside of the crosses they planted, they fondly rested their gavel on the *fleur de lis* flag.

Everyone knows that the same missionaries, while their eyes were yet moist with the tears they naturally shed, when they had to sever the ties by which their whole existence had hereto been bound up, were as faithful to British dominion as they had been to the banner of the land of their origin. It is well known that it is largely due to the fidelity of Canadian Catholic apostles that England owes the quiet possession of the noble colony which France had planted on the St. Lawrence and its tributaries. What then happened among the inhabitants of La Nouvelle France, was possible solely because its inhabitants were Catholics, and because England had respected their religious convictions. The knowledge of what they allude to, renders more incomprehensible to the undersigned the fact that the Catholics of Manitoba and the North-west are badly treated because they are Catholics.

11. Catholics believe in the necessity of religious instruction in schools. This conviction imposes upon them conscientious obligations,

and these obligations give them rights of which they connot be
deprived. They cannot be satisfied by the saying, others do not
believe as you do, therefore you must change your convictions; others
are satisfied and even wish that their children should be brought up
and educated in such a way, therefore, you Catholics, you cannot
stand aside, or, if you do, do so at your own expense. Such an
argument is neither fair nor just.

The undersigned, pastors of souls, are at one with their flocks, in
insisting on the rights they claim, and they are fully determined to
preserve them in their integrity. There is in this a question of
justice, of natural equity, of prudence and of social economy, closely
connected with the fundamental interests of the country.

The Catholics, being under the obligations of educating their
children, according to their faith, and the religious principles they
profess, have, in our free country, the right of establishing their
separate schools, and that right they must be allowed to exercise,
without being forced to the burden of double school taxes.

The undersigned also take the liberty to state, that the Federal
Parliament has endowed the schools of Manitoba and the North-west
with a large domain, in assigning to the support of such schools the
eighteenth part of all public lands. Those lands are Canadian
property, and how could the Federal Parliament consent to deprive
the Catholics of these countries of their legitimate share in the profit
derived from such lands, simply because this class of citizens adheres
to its religious convictions and wishes to comply with conscientious
obligations?

See appendix D. "A page of the history of the schools of Manitoba,"
by Archbishop Taché.

12. The undersigned petitioners are fully aware that Manitoba
and the North-west Territories were received into confederation, after
promises made to the first inhabitants of that vast country in the
name and by the authority of Her Majesty. The immediate
representatives of our beloved Queen assured them, that "respect
and attention would be extended to the different religious persuasions
and that, on their union with Canada, all their civil and religious
rights and privileges would be respected." In the estimation of
Catholics, their religious rights are not respected and their religious
persuasions are not treated with respect and attention, when there are
difficulties thrown, by law, in the way of securing to their children
an education, conducted in accordance with their religious convictions.

13. The undersigned, while petitioning as they do, repudiate the
idea of interference with political parties, or with the direction of
affairs, purely political or temporal. Their sole object is to secure for
the Catholics a protection, needed for the accomplishment of their
religious obligations, and it is in that view, and in that view only,

that they petition His Excellency the Governor-General in Council, and ask the honorable members of the Senate and the House of Commons of Canada, of whatsoever party they may be, to help in a fair settlement of the actual difficulties.

Therefore, your petitioners humbly pray His Excellency the Governor-General in Council :

1. To disallow the Act of Manitoba, 57 Vic., chap. 28, 1894, and intituled "An Act to amend the Public School Act."

2. To give such directions and make such provisions for the relief of the Roman Catholics of the province of Manitoba, as His Excellency in Council may seem fit, with regard to the Manitoba School laws of 1890.

3. To communicate with the Lieutenant-Governor of the Northwest Territories, in order that, by amending ordinances, redress should be given to meet the grievances of which the Catholics of the North-west complain on account of the Ordinance No. 22, assented to at Regina on the 31st of December, 1892.

And your petitioners, as in duty bound, will ever pray.

(Signed),

    E. A. TASCHEREAU, Cardinal, Archbishop of Quebec.
    ALEX. TACHÉ, Archbishop of St. Boniface, O.M.I.
    C. O'BRIEN, Archbishop of Halifax.
    EDWARD CHARLES FABRE, Archbishop of Montreal.
    JOSEPH THOMAS DUHAMEL, Archbishop of Ottawa.
    JOHN WALSH, Archbishop of Toronto.
    JAMES VINCENT CLEARY, Archbishop of Kingston.
    L. N. BEGIN, Archbishop of Cyrène, Coadjuteur of His Eminence Cardinal Taschereau.
    J. VITAL GRANDIN, Ev. de St. Albert.
    L. F. LAFLÈCHE, Ev. des Trois Rivieres, O.M.I.
    ISIDORE CLUT, O.M.I., Ev. D'Arindele.
    EMILE GROUARD, Ev. d'Ibara, O.M.I. Vic. Apost., Arthab., MacKenzie.
    ALBERT PASCHAL, O.M.I., Ev. de Mosinopolis, Vic. Apost.
    PAUL DURIEU, O.M.I., Ev. de New Westminister.
    L. Z. MOREAU, Bishop of St. Hyacinthe.
    JOHN CAMERON, Bishop of Antigonish.
    J. SWEENY, Bishop of St. John, N.B.
    JAMES ROGERS, Bishop of Chatham.
    JAMES CHARLES MCDONALD, Bishop of Charlottetown.
    J. N. LEMMENS, Bishop of Victoria and Vancouver.
    T. J. DOWLING, Bishop of Hamilton.
    DENIS O'CONNOR, Bishop of London.

R. A. O'Connor, Bishop of Peterborough.
Alexander MacDonell, Bishop of Alexandria.
Joseph Emard, Bishop of Valleyfield.
Paul S. Larocque, Bishop of Sherbrooke.
Maxime Decelles, Bishop of Druzipara.
Elphege Gravel, Bishop of Nicolet.
André Albert Blais, Ev. de St. Germain de Rimouski.
Narcisse Zephirin Lorrain, Ev. de Cythère et Vicaire Apostolique de Pontiac.
M. T. Labrecque, Ev. de Chicoutimi.

Order in Council, 26th July, 1894.

The Committee of the Privy Council have had under consideration a memorial addressed to your Excellency in Council by His Eminence Cardinal Taschereau, Archbishop of Quebec, and by the Roman Catholic archbishops and bishops in Canada, on the subject of the laws relating to education in the Province of Manitoba and in the Northwest territories. The memorial sets forth the condition of the public schools in the Province of Manitoba from the establishment of the province until 1890, and proceeds to state that "In 1890 laws were passed changing the school system and replacing it by other enactments which are, for a portion of the community, a source of grief, regret and hardship." The memorial asserts that "the result of the new system is purely and simply the legal suppression of all Catholic schools, and the maintenance of all Protestant schools, with all the rights and privileges enjoyed previous to the school laws of 1890," and that the "Catholic ratepayers have now to help to the support of Protestant schools, which are exactly what they were, and to which naturally Catholic parents cannot conscientiously send their children."

The memorial proceeds to state in detail some of the provisions of the enactments of Manitoba in 1890, which are claimed to have the effect previously stated. It further states that "for the last four years the Catholics of Manitoba have been subjected to unfair and unjust treatment resulting from the change of the school laws of 1890"; that "they asked in vain for relief; instead of a remedy they have been made the victims of a fresh injustice in the new Manitoba law, 57 Vic., chap. 28, assented to on March 2, 1894," one of the provisions of which forbids aid to be given by any municipality to any school not conducted according to the school system adopted in 1890. The effect of this enactment is stated by the memorialists to be "that no municipality, even one exclusively Catholic, without a single Protestant in its limits, has any power to levy a single dollar for Catholic schools, while a Catholic municipality, where there are 10 Protestant children, is obliged by law to levy on all the Catholics as well as on the parents of the 10 Protestant children, the money required for the education of the 10 Protestant children." The memorial complains also that the enactment of 1894 "decrees the confiscation of all school property in all the districts, which do not submit their schools to the new law," even though the school property may have been acquired by Catholics with their own money.

The memorial further states that in the North-west territories "the Catholic separate schools have been retained, but, in virtue of the ordinance number 22, of 1892, they are deprived of their liberty of action and of the character which distinguishes them from other schools," and that there, as well as in Manitoba, the result is very detrimental to the cause of education, and really has in both cases created bad feelings, dissensions and the most "deplorable results." It adds that "the painful experience of the Catholics of Manitoba and of the North-west territories is also resented by all Catholics of the Dominion, and has excited sympathy among many Protestants who, though separated by faith, are united with the Catholics in a sentiment of justice and fair play," and the desire of the prosperity of their common country. The memorialists make reference to the many claims to gratitude which Catholic missionaries have established by their work in times past, in connection with Christian missions and in spreading civilization as well as religion through what are now the British possessions in North America, and in encouraging sentiments of loyalty to British rule and British institutions when those possessions came under the British flag, and they seem (properly, in the view of the committee) to consider that these circumstances give a strong claim for generous recognition of the rights of Catholics in Manitoba and the North-west. They also refer to the fact "that the Federal Parliament has endowed the schools of Manitoba and the North-west with a large domain in assigning to the support of such schools the eighteenth part of all public lands." They cite the promise made to the inhabitants of Manitoba and the North-west, when Rupert's Land was acquired by Canada in the name and by the authority of Her Majesty that "respect and attention would be extended to the different religious persuasions, and that on their union with Canada all their civil and religious rights and privileges would be respected." The memorialists add that "in the estimation of Catholics" their religious rights are not respected, and their religious persuasions are not treated with respect and attention, when there are difficulties thrown, by law, in the way of securing to their children an education conducted in accordance with their religious conviction.

The memorialists "repudiate the idea of interference with political parties, or with the direction of affairs political or temporal."

They state that "their sole object is to secure for the Catholics a protection needed for the accomplishment of their religious obligations;" and that "it is in that view only, that they petition His Excellency the Governor-General in Council, and ask the honorable members of the Senate and of the Commons of Canada, of whatsoever party they may be, to help in a fair settlement of the actual difficulties;" and they pray, first, for the disallowance of the Manitoba School Act of 1894; second, to give such directions and make such provisions for the relief of the Roman Catholics of the Province of Manitoba as Your Excellency in Council may see fit with regard to the Manitoba school laws of 1890; third, to communicate with the Lieutenant-Governor of the North-west in order that by amending ordinances, redress should be given to meet the grievances of which the Catholics of the North-west complain on account of the ordinance No. 22, of 1892.

The committee, having taken all these matters into consideration, have the honor to recommend that a copy of the memorial above referred to, and also of this report, if approved, be transmitted to the Lieutenant-Governor of Manitoba, with a request that he will lay the same before his advisers and before the Legislature of that province; and that copies of the same be also sent to the Lieutenant-Governor of the North-west, with the request that he will lay them before the Executive Committee of the Territories and Legislature thereof.

The committee beg to observe to Your Excellency that the statements which are contained in this memorial are matters of deep concern and solicitude in the interests of the Dominion at large, and that it is a matter of utmost importance to the people of Canada that the laws which prevail in any portion of the Dominion should not be such as to occasion complaint of oppression or injustice to any class or portion of the people, but should be recognized as establishing perfect freedom of equality, especially in all matters relating to religion and religious belief and practice; and the committee therefore humbly advise that Your Excellency may join with them in expressing the most earnest hope that the Legislatures of Manitoba and of the North-west respectively may take into consideration at the earliest possible moment the complaints which are set forth in this petition, and which are said to create dissatisfaction among Roman Catholics, not only in Manitoba and the Northwest, but likewise throughout Canada, and may take speedy measures to give redress in all the matters in relation to which any well-founded complaint or grievance be ascertained.

The committee advise that a copy of this report be sent to each of the memorialists.

PART II.

LETTERS, LECTURES,

AND

ARTICLES

ON

THE SCHOOL QUESTION.

CHAPTER I.

ARCHBISHOP TACHÉ.

THINKS HIS IDEAS WITH REGARD TO RELIGIOUS INSTRUCTION IN SCHOOLS FULLY CORROBORATED IN ENGLAND.

(Letter to The Free Press—August, 1889.)

SIR,—In the beginning of the establishment of Canadian authority in this country, there was little difficulty in securing denominational schools. After they had been recognized by law, efforts were made to change their character, but since 1877 nothing was attempted publicly in that direction. During these last twelve years the cause of education has made great progress in Manitoba; the fact is, there are few new countries, if any, which have a larger development in that direction. Visitors of intelligence are in reality very much astonished at the harmonious and efficacious work of our system; as a rule, the population is satisfied with the management of the schools, by the respective Boards, and if we can judge this management by the result, surely there is not much reason for complaint. I am perfectly aware that the system in itself does not meet the views of everyone. There are men, earnest and honest, who would like that it had never been established, but these very men, precisely for the same reasons, are anxious to avoid rash measures or violation of the rights of others.

Since last week there has been a good deal of talking and writing about the question of schools. Without attaching too much weight to what might have been said under certain impulses, or to please certain parties, I am fully aware of the importance of the question, and feel confident that no government will attempt any measure violating the acquired rights of any important section of the people of Manitoba. I cherish the idea that our public men are not to be guided by the narrow ideas of bigoted individuals who think it is a glorious thing to attack others and a meritorious one to do harm to their neighbors.

Ignorance is so great among such narrow-minded men that they think, and they say, that our system of schools is to be changed because it admits of religious instruction in conformity to the wishes of the parents, and, to show more blindness, they say that the ideas which have been predominant in our system are "mediæval relics, fit for priestly-ridden people; that they are ideas behind the times, and not in accordance with the spirit of the age; anti-British, and unworthy of an English country."

These, and similar repeated attacks have suggested to me the thought of bringing before these men the knowledge of what has occurred in England at a very recent date, and to show thereby that the views, entertained by Catholics and many Protestants in Manitoba with regard to religious instruction in elementary schools, are not so adverse to English wishes and practice as the adversaries of our schools believe and say. Of course, I have not the presumption of furnishing information to educated men, who devote some attention and time to the cause of education, but I think I will say something new to many who had no chance to consider the facts I am about to recall.

The facts I am going to speak of are in connection, with:—

1. The Royal Commission appointed to inquire into the working of the elementary education Acts in England and Wales.
2. The work accomplished by that commission.
3. Conviction expressed by the commissioners.
4. Some of their conclusions and recommendations.

Of course, I can only touch on the subject in a very light and inadequate manner. The gigantic work of that commission is shewn by the reports, of which a copy lies on my table, and is contained in nine large quarto volumes, forming nearly five thousand pages and mostly in double columns. It may seem ridiculous to endeavor to bring within a small compass, adequate information with regard to such a labor, but as the work is inaccessible to most, I hope I may be pardoned in writing a few lines in reference to it.

1. ROYAL COMMISSION.

The 15th of January, 1886, a commission was appointed to enquire into the working of the Elementary Education Acts, England and Wales, and that by a royal proclamation which reads as follows:

"Victoria R.

"Victoria by the grace of God, of the United Kingdom of Great Britain and Ireland, Queen, defender of the faith. To our right trusty and well beloved councillor, Sir Richard Assheton Cross, Knight Grand Cross of our most honorable Order of the Bath, one of our principal secretaries."

Then are given the titles of nobility, of official or social position, of twenty-one other members of the commission, whose names are repeated below

. . . . . "and our trusty and well beloved George Shipton, Esq. Greeting.

" Whereas we have deemed it expedient that a commission should forthwith issue to enquire into the working of the Elementary Education Acts in England and Wales.

"Now, know ye, that we, reposing great trust and confidence in your knowledge and ability, have authorized and appoint, and do by these presents authorize and appoint you the said Sir Richard Asheton Cross, Henry Edward Manning, Cardinal Archbishop, Dudley Francis Stuart, Earl of Harrowby, Frederic Earl Beauchamp, Frederic Bishop of London, Charles Bowyer, Baron Norton, Anthony John Mundella, Sir Francis Richard Sandford, Sir John Lubbock, Sir Bernhard Samuelson, James Harrison Rigg, Robert William Dale, Robert Gregory, Benjamin Frederick Smith, Thomas Daniel Cox Morse, Charles Henry Alderson, John Gilbert Talbot, Sydney Charles Burton, Thomas Edmund Heller, Bernard Charles Molloy, Samuel Rathbone, Henry Richard and George Shipton, to be our commissioners for the purpose aforesaid. And for the better effecting the purpose of this our commission, we do, by these presents, give and grant unto you, or any six or more of you, full power to call before you such persons as you shall judge likely to afford you any information upon the subject of this our commission; and also to call for, have access to and examine all such books, documents, registers and records, as may afford you the fullest information on the subject, and to inquire of and concerning the premises by all other lawful ways and means whatsoever.

"And we do further, by these presents, authorize and empower you, or any six or more of you, to visit and personally inspect such places in our United Kingdom as you may deem expedient for the more effectual carrying out of the purpose aforesaid.

"And we do, by these presents, will and ordain that this our commission shall continue in full force and virtue, and that you, our said commissioners, or any six or more of you, may from time to time proceed in the execution thereof and of every matter and thing therein contained from time to time by adjournment.

"And we do further ordain that you, or any six or more of you, have liberty to report your proceedings under this our commission from time to time if you shall judge it expedient so to do.

"And our further will and pleasure is that you do, with as little delay as possible, report to us under your hands or seals, or under the hands and seals of any six or more of you your opinion upon the several matters herein submitted for your consideration.

"Given at our Court at Saint James, the fifteenth day of January, one thousand eight hundred and eighty-six, in the forty-ninth year of our reign.

By Her Majesty's command,

RICHARD ASHETON CROSS.

On the 10th of March, 1886, Her Majesty appointed the Honorable E. Lyulph Stanley as substitute to the Right Honorable H. J. Mundella, who had resigned his seat upon the commission.

At a later period Mr. Bernard C. Molloy withdrew from the commission. His place was filled by the Duke of Norfolk, who was appointed a commissioner on the 15th of June, 1887.

There is no doubt that the commission is purely English, it emanates from our beloved Queen, and is addressed to some of her most distinguished subjects, selected on account of their known ability, as well as their love for their country. These twenty-five commissioners have for the field of their labor, England and Wales; there is nothing of foreign proclivities in these men. Most of them are Protestants and belonging to different denominations; their social position identifies them with all that is honorable and fair; their loyalty to the Crown does not admit of doubt; the trust of their Sovereign imposes upon them the duty to meet her views as fully as possible; so we can be assured that such a commission commands respect and attention, not only in England and Wales, but through all the immense domains of Her Majesty.

Let us review what has been accomplished by this commission of Royal appointment, composed of men of distinction and ability, and entrusted with a sacred cause.

2. THE WORK OF THE COMMISSION.

The work of the commission is immense, and will give just cause of surprise to those who believe that the question of education can be fairly and sufficiently discussed in a political speech, or a careless letter to the press, or by a fanatic who thinks it is only necessary to appeal to passions.

I invite those who are not acquainted with the efforts of the said commission to pay some attention to the short analysis I take the liberty of publishing, and which suffices to give a striking proof of the conscientiousness with which a matter of such great moment as the cause of education is approached in the very heart of the British Empire.

The Royal Commissioners immediately after their appointment set to work with a zeal worthy of themselves and of the trust with which they had been honored by their beloved Sovereign. The inquiry began on the 20th of January, 1886, and lasted until July, 1888. The commissioners themselves state in their reports to Her Majesty, the sources from which they gather their information and say: " After considering the numerous applications received from persons desiring to give evidence before us, we determined to summon representatives of all public bodies who were in any way concerned with the administration and working of the elementary education Acts, and of all classes of persons whom these Acts, most immediately affect, in addition to such other witnesses as, either from their special knowledge, or from their experience, we thought likely to furnish valuable information. No representative witness, so far as we know, has been precluded from giving evidence before us."

"Mr. Patrick Cumin, Secretary to Your Majesty's Education Department, was the first witness called, whom we heard at great length. We next examined several of Your Majesty's Chief Inspectors of schools; and these witnesses were followed by representatives of the leading educational societies.

"Thirteen consecutive meetings were exclusively devoted to the evidence of the elementary teachers. In many instances, doubtless, they express the views of a large and influential organization of their professional brethren whose carefully formulated opinions had been, at an early state of our inquiry, placed in our hands."

"The management of Public Elementary schools was the subject which next occupied our attention; nine managers of different kinds of schools appeared before us, and gave us the benefit of their long and varied experiences."

"After these the representatives of school boards were called. Our next group of witnesses consisted of representatives of voluntary schools. These gentlemen were followed by an equal number of members of school attendance committees.

"The Welsh bi-lingual difficulty has received our attention.

"Full evidence has also been tendered to us on the subject of the religious instruction given in public elementary schools. Six of the leading advocates of the policy of separating religious from secular instruction in daily elementary schools, five of whom belong to different non-conformist bodies, also appeared before us."

The first report of the commissioners was presented to Her Majesty in 1886, the second in April, 1887, and the third in July 1887. The three are the minutes of the evidence gathered from the oral witnesses mentioned above. The three reports fill three large quarto volumes in double columns, with an aggregate number of 2,421 pages; to arrive at that result the Royal Commissioners sat for 95 long days; they called 151 witnesses; scrutinized their ideas and views on education by asking 59,809 questions, to which these witnesses gave as many replies. Besides the 95 days devoted to hearing oral testimony, the Commissioners sat 51 other days to complete their work.

They conducted "an important statistical inquiry on an extensive scale; having come to the conclusion that the opinion of the country as a whole on the working of the Education Acts ought to be ascertained, and that valuable documentary information might be obtained from managers and teachers of public elementary schools, both voluntary and board, as well as from school boards, we obtained permission to employ a staff for that purpose, under the superintendence of a statistical official. We accordingly issued circulars addressed to managers of voluntary schools, school boards and teachers. A circular was also addressed to the principals of all the existing training colleges."

The knowledge thus acquired was tabulated and was reported to both Houses of Parliament in 1888 and fills a quarto volume of 487 pages.

Not satisfied with such an accumulation of testimony, the Royal Commission published further information obtained in answer to inquiries made by another circular addressed to the principals of training colleges in England and Wales in receipt of a government grant ; the answers being published in a separate volume. To this may be added 95 papers furnished to the commission and published by their order. The commissioners, to facilitate the study of their wonderful work, caused an index to evidence and also a digest to this evidence to be prepared, the two covering no less than 580 pages, quarto.

Interesting reports, from outside of the mother country were obtained through Her Majesty's diplomatic agents, and are reported ay the commissioners in a separate volume of 335 pages. These accounts of the condition of elementary education in certain foreign countries were appreciated by Her Majesty's commission, and widely differ from certain foreign notions recently published. True, the German empire has been consolidated in such a way that, in some respects, it is foremost on the list of nations ; but it would be a great mistake to believe that this result has been obtained by the state divorcing from religion or banishing the teaching of religion from its schools. The Royal Commission proves otherwise :—

"In Prussia in all the elementary schools the religious instruction is compulsory as well as the other branches of instruction. The religious instruction is given by the teacher, excepticnally by clergymen and by special teachers of religion."

"The religious instruction is obligatory on all the scholars. Also for the religious instruction of the minority provisions are made, partially at the expense of the state: for this pupose means are regularly granted by the government."

"Saxony—Religious instruction is given in the schools of the state. In Protestant schools by the master ; in Catholic schools by priests."

"The religious instruction is obligatory on all the scholars. But a minority of Catholic scholars would be taught by a local Catholic priest."

"Wurtemburg—The schools of the state give religions as well as secular instruction ; the third part of the school time is devoted to religious instructions. The greatest part of the religious instruction is given by the teacher."

"The religious instruction is not obligatory on all the scholars ; the minority may take part in the religious instruction of the majority; but if the parents prefer that their children may not do so they may be excused."

"Bavaria.—In the schools of the state religious education forms part of the curriculum, and is given by the parish priest." "The religious instruction is obligatory on all the scholars."

Exhaustive other information is furnished by the Royal Commission; not only about the German Empire, but even many other countries, and no doubt it is desirable to see its interesting reports within reach of the men who wish to speak and write about religious instruction and moral training in schools, partly or wholly, supported by the state.

The above analysis, short as it is, suffices to prove that, very likely, there are few among those who talk about education laws, who have taken so much trouble as the Royal Commission of England to satisfy themselves what direction ought to be given in order to secure the good of individuals, the happiness of families, and the welfare of nations.

I invite my countrymen, whoever they may be, to weigh the conviction arrived at by the Royal Commissioners, after an investigation of such magnitude, that it could be considered as a waste of money, time and intelligence, were not the great cause of education at stake.

3. CONVICTION EXPRESSED.

The conscientious conviction of the Royal Commission is expressed in their final report in a volume of 500 pages, by itself a valuable source of information and a kind of synopsis of the whole inquiry conducted with such zeal, patient labor, and wonderful results.

The final report is divided into seven parts.

Part I. deals with the existing law.

Part II. relates to the existing state of facts.

Part III. treats of the machinery for carrying on elementary education.

Part IV. is confined to the education and instruction given in public elementary schools.

Part V. deals with the government examination, the parliamentary grant, etc.

Part VI. treats of local educational authorities.

Part VII. consists of a summary of leading conclusions and recommendations.

Only two of the seven parts have a general character, the five others being of more local application. I will quote largely from Part IV., that is to say, from chapter first of that part, on religious and moral training; and which covers from page 112 to 127. The divisions with letters prefixed are mine, and the quotation is taken *passim*, but continues through the chapter.

(*a*) Paramount Importance of Religious and Moral Training in Schools—" Having been commissioned by Your Majesty to inquire into the Working of the Elementary Education Acts, we should fail in our duty did we not review the religious moral effect of the present system, and of the provisions made by law for enabling and controlling religious as well as secular instruction. While the whole commission is animated by one and the same desire to secure for the children in the public elementary schools the best and most thorough instruction in secular subjects, suitable to their years, and in harmony with the requirements of their future life, it is also unanimously of opinion that their religious and moral training is a matter of still higher importance alike to the children, the parents and the nation, though the views of its members differ as to the method whereby this object of supreme moment should be attained."

(*b*) The parents insist upon Religious Instruction in schools— " Upon the importance of giving religious as well as moral intruction, as part of the teaching in day public elementary schools, much evidence was brought before us. . . . All the evidence is practically unanimous as to the desire of the parents for the religious and moral training of their children."

(*c*) Religious instruction given in English schools. "The answers we have received to circular A 3, testify that out of 385 school boards, 348 give daily religious instruction, and 123 have religious examinations; and out of 3,496 teachers of departments, who have sent in replies to circular D, 3,161 say that they give daily religious instruction, and 2,372 say examinations in religious knowledge are held annually.

(*d*) Sunday school and home religious instructions deficient.— " We must add that though we highly value the influence of Sunday schools, it is admitted that many scholars in elementary schools do not either attend them or any place of worship, and that their parents are often too ignorant or too indifferent to give their children any religious instruction. Such children, therefore, are entirely dependent upon instruction in the day schools for any knowledge of the scriptural truths which ought to be the common heritage of all the people in a Christian country. We hope that the religious and moral training in all board schools may be raised to the high standard which has been attained already in many of them, and that it will be made clear that the state, while scrupulously maintaining its provisions for safe-guarding the rights of conscience, does not wish to discourage any of the managers, teachers, and members of school boards, connected with any of the elementary schools of the country who are endeavoring to bring up their children in love and obedience to God."

(e) *Inspection of religious instruction recommended.*—"The need for annual inspection of religious instruction in board schools corresponding to that made by the diocesan inspector in church schools, in presence, especially of the strong competition to which religious instruction is exposed by the restriction of the government examination to secular subjects, has been recognized in evidence before us by the representatives of many important school boards; and we gather that a movement is extending itself for securing that an annual examination should be held with a view to test the efficiency of the scriptural instruction."

(f) *Grant to Christian schools not an endowment to religious education.*—"We cannot, therefore, concur in the view that the State may be constructively regarded as endowing religious education when under these conditions it pays annual grants for secular instruction in aid of voluntary local effort to schools in which religious instruction forms part of the programme."

(g) *Prohibition of religious teaching an injury to parents' conscientious feelings.*—"But while we are most anxious that conscientious objections of parents to religious teaching and observances, in the case of their children, should be most strictly respected, and that no child should, under any circumstances, receive any such training contrary to a parent's wishes, we feel bound to state that a parent's conscientious feeling may be equally injured, and should be equally respected and provided for, in the case where he is compelled by law to send his child, for all his school time, to a school where he can receive no religious teaching."

"This grave injury to conscience may easily now arise in the case where a single board or voluntary school suffices for the whole school supply of a district, or where only one school is within a reasonable distance of a man's home. In that school, as we have seen it at this moment the case, with a certain number of voluntary and board schools, the Bible may not be read or taught, and there may be no religious teaching."

(h) *Proposal to prohibit religious instructions in schools repudiated.*—"The views of those who would remove from day elementary schools all religious teaching and observance have received our attentive consideration."

"Those who hold this view in favor of purely secular schools did not shrink from urging before us, through the witnesses who represented them, that the State should take the extreme step of prohibiting religious instruction in public elementary schools."

"Even those witnesses, however, who strenuously advocated the secularization of public elementary education, most emphatically declared that they regarded religion as the true basis of education, and only contended for its exclusion from the day school in the belief that it could be provided in some other and better way."

"In questions of this character it is impossible to have negative provisions which have not also a positive side. Thus, for children to attend day schools in which no religious teaching was given would, in the opinion of those who think that the daily lessons should be accompanied with religious teaching, be practically leading them to undervalue the importance of religion. They would hold that the impression left upon the children's minds would be that religion was a matter of inferior moment, at all events, to that secular teaching which they were acquiring day by day."

"In support of the contention that religious instruction should be excluded from the day school, it was further urged by Dr. Crosskey that it makes an undesirable tax on the teacher's energies. But, on the other hand, we have had brought before us trustworthy testimony, some of it from teachers themselves, that, as a body, they would consider it a great loss if they were debarred from giving Bible lessons to their scholars. Moreover, the religious instruction given by teachers, we have been told by the Rev. J. Duncan, greatly increases the moral influence of the teacher. The moral character of teachers themselves, Archdeacon Norris, formerly Her Majesty's inspector of schools in various populous counties, thinks, would suffer if they were forbidden to impart religious instruction, and, finally, against the attempt, on this or any other ground, to prohibit teachers from giving moral and religious instruction in their schools, Mr. Cumin, secretary of the committee of Council on Education, emphatically protests. He believes that many excellent teachers would absolutely refuse to be restricted in their teaching to secular subjects."

"It was urged that religion was dishonored by being included in a programme consisting chiefly of secular subjects."

"But we have no evidence tending to show that these results actually occur, and it can scarcely be supposed that if such were found to be the result, religious bodies and school boards would still continue to make such great efforts as we find they now do in order to maintain an efficient system of religious instruction in the schools for which they are responsible. On the other hand, we have positive evidence that children who have received religious teaching in the day school are better prepared to profit by Sunday school teaching and to become themselves teachers in Sunday schools."

"But were there more weight due than we have been able to attach to these and other like reasons for prohibiting elementary teachers from giving religious instruction in the day school, there are positive arguments of great value in favor of the principle of religious instruction being given by the teachers. We have spoken of the evidence tending to show that teachers, as a body, would strongly oppose its removal out of their hands. Even more to be considered, in our judgment, are the wishes of the parents."

"A large body of witnesses, consisting among others of Her

Majesty's inspectors, teachers, and managers, speaking both for board and voluntary schools, deposed before us to the great value which the parents generally set on the religious instruction given to their children in the day school."

"We are convinced that, if the State were to secularize elementary education, it would be in violation of the wishes of the parents, whose views in such a matter are, we think, entitled to the first consideration. . . ."

"Many other children would have no other opportunity of being taught the elementary doctrines of Christianity, as they do not attend Sunday schools, and their parents, in the opinion of a number of witnesses, are quite unable to teach them."

(*i*) No efficient substitute for the system of utilizing school staff and the hours of school attendance for religious instruction.—"But those who contemplate this change and advocate the exclusion of religious teaching in all public elementary schools state that they look to supply the void thus created by other, and, as they think, by better means. It is not asserted by them with much confidence that the duty of educating children religiously can be wholly left to their parents. Abundant evidence from all classes of witnesses is before us tending to show that many parents are unable to undertake this branch of their children's education, even if they were willing, and that if it were left to them it would be omitted."

"We concur with those witnesses who gave it as their opinion that without the ordinary school staff it would be impossible to give efficient religious instruction, on any large scale, to large bodies of children. The clerk of the school board of Liverpool expressed his conviction that ministers of all denominations would be quite inadequate to deal with the instruction of that vast and growing population, and that to forbid religious instruction during the regular hours of school would be most disastrous. . . ."

"But after hearing all that could be said for it, we cannot recommend the plan thus suggested of religious instruction to be given by voluntary teachers, on the school premises, out of school hours, for the success of which even those most anxious to try the experiment will not be answerable. It would, in our opinion, be no efficient substitute for the existing system of utilizing the school staff and the hours of school attendance for this purpose, a system which has taken deep root in the country, and appears to give general satisfaction to parents."

(*j*) Greater support should be given by the State to the moral element of training in English schools.—"As to the moral training given in the schools, the opportunities permitted to Her Majesty's inspectors of enquiring into the efficiency of moral training have been under the existing arrangements necessarily limited."

"We are strongly of opinion that much greater support should be given by the State to the moral element of training in our schools. . . . We recommend, therefore, that general fundamental and fixed instructions should be laid down as to moral training, making it an essential condition of the efficiency of a public elementary school."

"And as we have found with regret that in recent years this branch of the inspector's duty has not received the attention it deserved, we, therefore, think it necessary to make it a distinct recommendation that it should be considered the first duty of Her Majesty's inspectors to inquire into and report upon the moral training."

"After hearing the arguments for a wholly secular education, we have come to the following conclusions:

"(1.) That it is of the highest importance that all children should receive religious and moral training. (2.) That the evidence does not warrant the conclusion that such religious and moral training can be amply provided otherwise than through the medium of elementary schools. (3.) That in schools of a denominational character, to which parents are compelled to send their children, the parents have a right to require an operative conscience clause, so that care be taken that the children shall not suffer in any way in consequence of their taking advantage of the conscience clause. (4.) That inasmuch as parents are compelled to send their children to school it is just and desirable that, as far as possible, they should be enabled to send them to a school suitable to their religious connections or preferences. (5.) We are also of opinion that it is of the highest importance that the teachers who are charged with the moral training of the scholars should continue to take part in the religious instruction. We should regard any separation of the teacher from the religious teaching of the school as injurious to the moral and secular training of the scholars."

May I respectfully ask those who might read the above quotations to pause over them, and say if really they could consider as unprogressive, or unreasonable, or adverse to the enlightenment of the growing generation, the men who conscientiously entertain the same views as the Royal Commission with regard to religious instruction in the elementary schools.

4.—Conclusion and Recommendation.

Part VII. of the final report consists exclusively of a summary of leading conclusions and recommendations. It seems that the convictions expressed and the conclusions arrived at, as quoted above from Part IV. of the report, could be considered as sufficient recommendation on the part of the commission. The distinguished commissioners judged otherwise, and, wishing to see their views carried into effect, they thought proper to have Part VII. of their report exclusively filled up with their conclusions and recommendations. Some are mere repetitions of what had been said before; nevertheless, the commissioners attached such importance to them that they did not shrink from repeating them again.

They brought the same conclusions and recommendations from number 1 to 198. I will select out of them thirty numbers which have a more direct relation with certain objections raised against our school laws and their application. The numbers, the reader will see, do not all follow one another, but each one is quoted fully. The whole of the 198 numbers can be found in the final report from page 208 to page 223. Here are my quotations:

"(24) That in framing regulations for fixing the qualifications required of teachers, it will be desirable to bear in mind that there are some with a natural aptitude and love for teaching, who have not received a college training, but who could not be excluded from the profession without a loss to our schools."

"(25) That the employment of women of superior social position and general culture as teachers has a refining and excellent effect upon schools."

"(33) That to encourage managers of voluntary schools as well as school boards to extend the advantages of central class teaching to their pupil-teachers, extra grants should be offered to those managers or boards who successfully adopt that course."

"(44) That whilst recommending that facilities should be afforded in one or other of the ways suggested for the establishment of day training colleges, we think that no portion of the cost of establishing or maintaining new day training colleges should fall upon the rates."

"(45) That, in their proposals, the following points will require serious attention of Parliament :"

"(1) The question of security for the religious and moral instruction of those who are to be trained as teachers."

"(57) That while we desire to secure for the children in the public elementary schools the best and most thorough instruction in secular subjects, suitable to their years and in harmony with the requirements of their future life, we are also unanimously of opinion that their religious and moral training is a matter of still higher importance, alike to the children, the parents and the nation."

"(58) That there can be no doubt, from the statement of the witnesses, whether favorable or hostile to teaching religion in schools, and from the testimony afforded by the action of both school boards and voluntary schools, as to the opinion of the country generally on the subject of religious and moral training in day schools, and that all the evidence is practically unanimous as to the desire of the parents for the religious and moral training of their children."

"(59) That to secularize elementary education would be a violation of the wishes of parents, whose views in such a matter are, we think, entitled to the first consideration."

"(60) That the only safe foundation on which to construct a theory of morals, or to secure high moral conduct, is the religion which our Lord Jesus Christ has taught the world. That as we look to the Bible for instruction concerning morals, and take its words for the declaration of what is morality, so we look to the same inspired source for the sanctions by which they may be enabled to do what they have learned to be right."

"(61) That the evidence does not warrant the conclusion that religious and moral training can be amply provided otherwise than through the medium of elementary schools.

"(62) That in the case of a considerable number of children, if they do not receive religious instruction and training from the teachers in the public elementary schools, they will receive none, and that this would be a matter of the gravest concern to the state."

"(63) That all registers should be marked before the religious teaching and observances begin, scrupulous care being taken, in accordance with the letter and spirit of the Education Act to provide for the case of children whose parents object to such teaching and observances."

"(64) That it is of the highest importance that the teachers who are charged with the moral training of the scholars should continue to take part in the religious instruction, and that any separation of the teacher from the religious teaching of the school would be very injurious to the moral and secular training of the scholars."

"(65) That we cannot recommend the plan which has been suggested of religious instruction to be given by voluntary teachers on the school premises out of school hours. That such a plan would be no efficient substitute for the existing system of utilizing the school staff and the house of school attendance for this purpose, a system which has taken deep root in the country, and appears to give general satisfaction to the parents."

"(66) That the state cannot be constructively regarded as endowing religious education, when, under the conditions of the Act of 1870, it pays annual grants in aid of voluntary local effort for secular instruction in schools, in which religious instruction forms part of the programme."

"(69) That inasmuch as parents are compelled to send their children to school, it is just and desirable that, as far as possible, they should be enabled to send them to a school suitable to their religious convictions or preferences."

"(70) That in schools of a denominational character to which parents are compelled to send their children, the parents have a right to require an operative conscience clause, and that care be taken that the children shall not suffer in any way in consequence of their taking advantage of the conscience clause."

"(71) That the absence of any substantiated case of complaint and the general drift of the evidence convince us that the conscience clause is carefully observed both by teachers and managers."

"(72) That we recognise, nevertheless, the importance of removing, if possible, any suspicion of unfair play or undue influence in the administration of the conscience clause from the minds of those who entertain such impressions. And any further precautions which might tend in that direction, without compromising still higher interests, are deserving of the most careful consideration."

"(73) That, greatly as the estimate of the value of the religious instruction given in board schools varies with the standpoint from which it is regarded, there is good ground for concluding that where care is bestowed on the organization of such instruction, and sufficient time is allowed for imparting it, it is of a nature to affect the conscience and influence the conduct of the children of whose daily training it forms a part. That it is much to be hoped that the religious and moral training in all elementary schools may be raised to the high standard which has been already reached in many of them."

"(74) That exactly the same facilities to hold annual examinations of their schools in religious knowledge should be given by law to school-boards as are now allowed under section 76 of the Act of 1870 to the managers of voluntary schools."

"(75) That increased support should be given by the state to the moral element of training in our schools, almost the only reference to the importance of such matters made by the state being that which is made in the Code under the head of discipline."

"(76) That general, fundamental and fixed instructions to Her Majesty's inspectors should be laid down as to moral training, making it an essential condition of the efficiency of a public elementary school, that its teachings should comprise such matters as instruction in duty and reverence to parents ; honor and truthfulness in word and act ; honesty, consideration and respect for others ; obedience, cleanliness, good manners, purity, temperance, duty to country, the discouragement of bad language, and the like."

"(77) That it should be the first duty of Her Majesty's inspectors to inquire into and report upon the moral training and condition of the schools, under the various heads set forth, and to impress upon the managers, teachers, and children the primary importance of this essential element of all education.

"(86) That we are opposed to the introduction of a set of official government text books ; but that, with the view of indicating to managers and teachers the range and study intended to be covered by the requirements of the code, a more or less extended programme should be published for each subject, similar to those adopted in the science and art directory, with a view of showing within what limits the official examinations should be confined ; and also, that in the syllabuses for pupil teachers' definitions, in programmes of studies, which leave no doubt as to their interpretation, are specially required."

"(80) That the provisions of the code, which requires that if only one class subject is taken, it must be 'English,' should be repealed."

"(108) "That in Wales permission should be given to take up the Welsh language as a specific subject ; to adopt an optional scheme to take the place of English as a class subject, founded on the principle of substituting a graduated system of translation from Welsh to English, for the present requirements in English grammar : to teach Welsh along with English as a class subject ; and to include Welsh among the languages in which candidates for Queen's scholarships and for certificates of merit may be examined."

"(109) "That the introduction of elaborate apparatus for gymnastic exercises into playgrounds is not to be recommended.

"(138) That the state should continue to recognize voluntary and board schools as together forming the national provision for elementary education ; and that both ought to continue to participate in equal conditions in the parliamentary grant."

I need not repeat that the commission, whose work I have so highly reviewed, is entirely English, and that its conclusions should not be treated lightly, at least by those who constantly make an appeal to their British origin or British proclivities. For my part, I will not hesitate to say that I felt a particular pleasure in ascertaining once more that my views on religious instruction in the schools, far from being adverse to those entertained in the mother country, are in perfect harmony with them.

In my estimation, the school is the church of the children, and there only, in many instances, could be realized the words of the best friend of children when He said : " Suffer little children to come unto Me." Yes, Christian parents, suffer your little ones to go to Christ through the religious and moral training they ought to receive in their respective elementary schools. For the " Lord is a God of all knowledge," and that which brings children nearer to God cannot be an impediment to the acquiring of true and useful knowledge. These are the cherished ideas of my life ; study, experience and observation, and the testimony of the most illustrious men of all ages and countries, have confirmed me in these ideas and, in reality, they are, as quoted above, the conclusion arrived at by the Royal Commission appointed by our beloved Queen to inquire into the working of the Elementary Education Acts of England and Wales.

Thanking you for granting me the space in your journal,

I remain, your obedient servant,

† ALEX., Archbishop of St. Boniface, O.M.I.

CHAPTER II.

PAMPHLET BY ARCHBISHOP TACHÉ.

ANSWERING THE QUESTION: "ARE THE PUBLIC SCHOOLS OF MANITOBA THE CONTINUATION OF THE PROTESTANT SCHOOLS OF THE SAME PROVINCE."

20th April, 1893.

Having learned that the Judicial Committee of the Privy Council had rendered a decision contrary to the interests of the Catholics of Manitoba on the school question, I thought it my duty to claim anew the intervention of the federal authorities, and I did so, in a petition addressed to His Excellency the Governor General in Council. A paragraph of that petition has attracted especial attention, both in the Commons and in the press. Here is the paragraph:

That two statutes, 53 Vic., chap. 37 and 38, were passed in the Legislative Assembly of Manitoba, to merge the Roman Catholic schools with those of Protestant denominations, and to require all members of the community, whether Roman Catholic or Protestant, to contribute through taxation to the support of what are therein called public schools, but which are in reality a continuation of the Protestant schools."

Certainly I should never have used that language if I had not felt convinced of its correctness; my assertions nevertheless have been denied by some and doubted by others. I owe to myself and and the sacred cause I endeavor to protect, to give the proofs, which have forced on my mind the conviction I have expressed. Those proofs I will adduce; especially from public documents.

Daily obversation convinces me that the question of the Catholic schools of Manitoba is far from having been studied in its entire aspect, and that, not only by the adversaries of those schools, but even by some of those who desire to protect them. The subject is very dry and in no way attractive; nevertheless, I pray those who feel some interest in the matter to examine carefully what follows, and I take the liberty to dedicate to them what I now write.

I can easily forsee that this new action on my part may provoke the repetition of the abuse which has been lavished on me in some newspapers. I may assure those so disposed that I will not answer them. I shall leave them in the enjoyment of such pastime, coupled with the trouble of finding out why I keep silent under such attacks.

To secure an easier understanding of what I am going to say, I will first give the meaning to be attached to some of my expressions. I will call "Old Regime" the laws of education passed by the

Legislature of Manitoba, and in force in the province until the 1st May, 1890. I will call "New Regime" the laws of education in force since that date.

"Public Protestant Schools" meant, under the old regime, schools established, controlled and supported by Protestants for the use of Protestant children; on the other hand, "Public Catholic Schools" meant schools established, controlled and supported by Catholics, for the use of Catholic children, and were recognized by the law; the public schools of to-day are those established by the new regime.

What I undertake to prove is this: The actual public schools of Manitoba are the continuation of the former Protestant public schools of the province, and to make my undertaking good, I must first show the condition of public schools, Protestant and Catholic, under the old regime and demonstrate afterwards that the new regime, while destroying the public Catholic schools, maintains the public Protestant schools, of which they are in reality but the continuation.

I. OLD REGIME.

The Province of Manitoba was admitted into Canadian Confederation on the 15th July, 1870. It began to organize in September. Its first parliament was summoned for and opened the 15th day of March, 1871. One of the first tasks of the new legislature was the question of public instruction, and on the 3rd May the Lieutenant Governor assented to a law, passed under the title "An Act to establish a System of Education in the Province."

While entering upon such a grave question, the Government, the Legislative Council, and the Legislative Assembly of the new province had to look, and in fact did look, into the constitution of Canada—the British North America Act, 1867, clause 93, and into the constitution of the Province of Manitoba—"Manitoba Act, 1870," clause 22, for guidance in their task. They easily found there two things: 1st. That the provincial authorities are not absolute in matters of education. 2nd. That, regarding the same matter, the constitution of the whole Dominion, and the constitution of Manitoba both recognized that the "Subjects of the Queen," formed two different sections, named respectively "Protestant" and "Roman Catholic," and that, even if one of the sections was in a minority in any province.

The two mentioned sections existed in the Province of Manitoba. A census taken by the government towards the end of 1870, had just ascertained the numerical relation between the two groups, as well as that of the whole population. 12,228 was the total population. The Catholics had registered more than all the others taken together; they were then the majority of the Queen's subjects, while the Protestants were the minority. It was decided, nevertheless, that no attention should be paid to the difference and that the two sections should be considered as equal in number. The equality of numbers, supported by equality of rights, dictated naturally the equality of privileges and obligations, hence the following dispositions made by the first law of our system of education.

1. The Lieutenant Governor in Council may appoint not less than ten and not more than fourteen persons to be a board of education for the Province of Manitoba, of whom one-half shall be Protestants and the other half Catholics.

2. The Lieutenant Governor in Council may appoint one of the Protestant members of the board to be superintendent of Protestant schools, and one of the Catholic members to be superintendent of the Catholic schools. . . . .

10. Each section shall have under its control and management the discipline of the schools of the section.

11. It shall make rules and regulations for the examination, grading and licensing of the teachers. . . . . . .

13. From the sum appropriated by the Legislature for common school education, there shall first be paid the incidental expenses of the board and of the sections, ... and the residue then remaining shall be appropriated to the support and maintainance of common schools, one moiety thereof to the support of Protestant schools, and the other moiety to the support of Catholic schools.

This legislation sanctioned the rights and privileges to denominational schools, enjoyed by the population, by practice, before the union with Canada. The law made the schools denominational between Roman Catholics and Protestants, according to the distinction expressed in the constitutional dispositions establishing the Canadian confederation and the Province of Manitoba.

The increase of the population and other circumstances required amendments to the first law, but, let it be remembered, those amendments did not alter the fundamental principle on which the school system rested; on the contrary they fortified and supported it more and more.

In 1875 the numerical equilibrium had ceased, the Protestants had increased in numbers more rapidly than the Catholics; hence certain dispositions of the Act 38 Vic., chap. 27. Its first clause fixed at twelve the number of Protestant members of the Board of Education, and at nine the number of Catholic members.

Clause 4 says: The sum voted by the Legislature for common school purposes shall be divided between the Protestant and Roman Catholic sections of the board in proportion to the number of children, aged from 5 to 16 years, and residing in the different districts in the province.

In order to avoid the confusion which would have been the result of certain expressions, the clause 28 enacted that the words "dissident or separate schools" should be replaced by the words "Protestant district or Catholic district as the case may be."

After ten years of experience all the school Acts till then enacted and the amendments thereto, were all repealed and the Act 44 Vic. chapter 4, was passed instead—1881.

What was to be the nature of this new law, resulting from experience, reflection and work? Had the population manifested any desire for any change in the principles and general direction determined by the first laws on education? Shall legislators, to answer their own aspiration, and those of their own constituents, enact radical modifications in the system already adopted? No, the principles remained as they were, their application had given general satisfaction, the interested parties were pleased; the characteristic aspect of the school laws of Manitoba not only remained what it was, but received a new impulse, in the law passed after ten years of experience. Let us examine it, and if it is necessary to understand its true spirit, to resort to long quotations, the reader will pardon them as they seem necessary to comprehend the situation.

The government being the first executive authority of the law, the latter indicates the duty of the former in the following clauses and sub-clauses.

1. The Lieutenant Governor in Council shall appoint, to form and constitute the board of education for the province of Manitoba, a certain number of persons not exceeding twenty-one, twelve of whom, shall be Protestants and nine Roman Catholics.

9. The Lieutenant-Governor in Council shall appoint one of the Protestant members of the board to be superintendent of the Protestant schools, and one of the Catholic members to be superintendent of the Catholic schools.

The government who has the custody of public monies must act as follows in dividing the amount voted by the Legislature for the school.

84. The sum appropriated by the Legislature for common school purposes shall be divided between the Protestant and Roman Catholic sections of the Board of Education, in the manner hereinafter provided, in proportion to the number of children between the ages of five and fifteen inclusive.

85. The provincial treasurer and one other member of the Executive Council, to be appointed by the Lieutenant-Governor, shall form a committee for the apportionment of education funds and legislative grant, between the Protestant and Roman Catholic sections of the Board of Education. . . .

The Board of Education mentioned in the law, and whose members are appointed by the Government, is to be renewed, and must act according to the following clauses:

3. It shall be the duty of the Board: (a) To make from time to time such regulations as they may think fit for the general organization of the common schools. (b) To make regulations for the registering and reporting of daily attendance at all the common schools in the province. . . . . (c) To make regulations for the calling of meetings. . . . .

5. The board shall resolve itself into two sections, the one consisting of the Protestant and the other of the Roman Catholic members thereof; and it shall be the duty of each section

(a) To have under its control and management the schools of the section. . . .

(b) To arrange for the proper examination, grading and licensing of the teachers. . . .

(c) To select all the books, maps and globes to be used in the schools under its control. . . .

(d) To appoint inspectors, who shall hold office during the pleasure of the section appointing them. . . .

The superintendents are the executive officers of their respective sections, and as such their duties are well defined in the Act.

The school districts had attracted the solicitude of the Legislature, which, on that important point as well as on the rest, was unwilling to disturb the basis on which rested the whole school system.

Here are the principal dispositions of the law on this point:

12. (a) The establishment of a school district of one denomination shall not prevent the establishment of a school district of the other denomination in the same place, and a Protestant and a Catholic district may include the same territory in whole or in part.

SUPPORT OF SCHOOLS.

It was not enough to establish a system of public and free schools, where all the children could be admitted and instructed; it was absolutely necessary to provide for the expenses and maintenance. The rules to be followed for the partition of the public moneys and the legislative grant, have been already quoted from the law. It may be mentioned now how to provide for the balance of funds required for the construction and support of the schools.

25. For the purpose of supplementing the legislative grant it shall be the duty of the boards of trustees of all school districts from time to time to prepare and lay before the municipal council an estimate of such sums as may be required for school purposes during the current school year. The said council, employing their own lawful authority, shall forthwith levy and collect the said sums by assessment on the real and personal property within the school district, and shall pay over the same to the said board of trustees as collected.

30. The ratepayers of a school district, including religious, benevolent and educational corporations, shall pay their respective assessments to the schools of their respective denominations, and in no case shall a Protestant ratepayer be obliged to pay for a Catholic school, or a Catholic ratepayer for a Protestant school.

NORMAL SCHOOLS.

The 30th May, 1882, the Lieutenant-Governor of Manitoba assented to an Act "To establish Normal Schools in connection with Public Schools." This Act, 45 Victoria, chap. 8, is a complement of the preceding, and does not in any way alter the main lines traced before. Here is its first clause:

1. The Protestant and Catholic sections of the Board of Education are hereby respectively empowered

(a) To establish in connection with the Protestant public schools of the City of Winnipeg, and with the Roman Catholic public schools of St. Boniface, normal school departments, with a view to the instruction and training of teachers of public schools in the science of education and the art of teaching.

The above mentioned Acts, 44 and 45 Vic., were amended during the following years, but no modification was made in the fundamental principle of the laws that I have named. The old regime—that code, one in its origin, became dual in its application to the whole province, in order to facilitate education, while safeguarding the just desires of the parents and removing the friction that is a natural consequence of the domination of a portion of the population over the other.

I have no intention of commencing a dissertation on the merit or shortcomings of the old school laws; I am looking after facts, and will not delay with praise or condemnation of theories and convictions, which have their opponents and supporters. My own views on the matter of education are not the object of this essay; I consider the facts as they existed under the old regime in order to fully establish the facts as they are under the new regime. For the sake of clearness I recapitulate.

The system of public schools of Manitoba was created by law. That law, entrusted to the Government, passed from it to the interested parties by the nomination of a school board. No one in the province was *ex-officio* member of the board; all its members were appointed by the Government; the choice was restricted only by the consideration that the law entertained for the religious convictions of the population. It was also the executive of the province which remitted to the board and its sections the public money voted by the Legislature for the maintenance of schools; the law equally protected all the religious beliefs; the faith of some parents did not deprive their children of the legitimate share of the public money to which they were entitled as citizens of Manitoba of school age.

The Government knew what was going on each year. Official reports were submitted and acquainted it with all that was interesting in the province regarding schools. The whole was laid before the representatives of the people, to whom the Government is responsible. Nothing was concealed, there were no privileges, no exclusion in the system : equal individual rights were equally protected. The Board of Education was a second factor in the system. In order that it could accomplish its duties with more ease and justice towards everyone, it was divided into two sections, or committees. These two sections were, as it were, benevolent currents running from the same spring and circulating through the country in all directions, conveying with them the satisfaction and fecundity of intellectual culture. The two currents could deepen their channels, increase the volume of their waters, become stronger or weaker; the course could be more or less rapid, more or less regular, according to circumstance, but they had always to run on parallel lines; the law, in maintaining them within those parallels, prevented encroachment or confusion, in order that they could continue their course, spreading everywhere the advantages of the instruction and the education agreeably to the convictions of the parents, permitting the conscience of everyone to breathe freely and to acknowledge in the law a protection and not a tyranny. Alongside of these parallel currents were planned the school districts; the law entrusted their creation and direction to citizens whose ideas harmonized with the feelings of the parents of the children using the schools. Then the teachers, the inspectors, the programme of studies, the disciplinary regulations, the religious and moral teaching; in a word, all that could secure the good management of the school, all that was according to the views of the parties interested and was entrusted respectively to the direction of each section of the board. The fact is, that during nineteen years the two sections have acted as mentioned above. Each section was perfectly independent, and consequently the action of one was in no way embarrassed by the actions or omissions of the other. If they exercised influence with one another in any way, it was merely through a generous emulation which contributed to the general welfare.

The existence of **Protestant** schools alongside of Catholic schools never interfered with the good relations between citizens and neighbors; the result was quite different, as affirmed by the following words of Mr. J. B. Somerset, superintendent of Protestant schools. His conviction is expressed in the following words, page 7 of the report he addressed to the Lieutenant-Governor on April 29th, 1886:

> It is gratifying to all lovers of good citizenship, as well as of educational progress, to note that from the organization of this system of management in 1871, at which period the Protestant schools numbered sixteen and the Catholic seventeen, to the present there has been an almost entire absence of the friction and disagreement that have marked the progress of education in some of the sister provinces.

After quoting the above, I could easily demonstrate the falsity and even the absurdity of the accusations heaped upon Catholic schools, both with regard to their teaching of secular branches and to their social, religious and moral influence. But no, I must remember what I promised to prove, and not allow myself to be carried away into side issues. My contention is that the non-Catholic public schools under the old regime were really Protestant schools. There is no doubt that the Catholic section of the Board of Education faithfully discharged the duty imposed upon them, that of establishing and controlling their schools, according to Catholic views. It is equally certain that the Protestant section of the same board were also faithful to their trust. They established and controlled their schools, according to Protestant views. Here is what their superintendent, J. B. Somerset, wrote, on page 27 of his report, already mentioned:

> The development of the moral nature is a primary requisite in any system of education. The board, recognizing this principle, has provided for the most careful inquiry into the character of its teachers, and for such

systematic religious instruction in its schools as may be given with the object of teaching the principles of Christian truth contained in the Bible, and accepted by all Protestant denominations.

I need not say that, in so writing, Mr. Somerset acted in the name and behalf of the Protestant section of the Board of Education; his official report, very elaborate and cleverly written, provoked no contradiction in parliament, nor in the press, nor anywhere else to my knowledge. The same report, pages 27 and 28, recites the regulations of the Protestant section of the board, regarding religious teaching, as adopted on the 2nd December, 1885, which were in force when Mr. Somerset wrote his report and continued to be so after:

"Every school established and in operation, under the authority of the Protestant section of the board of education for Manitoba, shall be opened and closed daily with prayers," consisting of "one or more of the forms of prayer printed on the cover of the authorized school registers, . . . always including the Lord's prayer, repeated together by teacher and pupils."

"The Bible shall be used as a text book in the Protestant schools of Manitoba."

"The scripture lesson in each school shall follow the opening prayer, and shall occupy not more than fifteen minutes daily."

"The pupils of each school, from standard three upward, shall be taught to repeat from memory the ten commandments and the apostles' creed, and one-half hour weekly may be devoted to this exercise and such other instruction in manners and morals as may be practicable."

In spite of all the proofs heretofore enumerated, some people contend that the Protestant schools were not sectarian. Surely they were not in the estimation of those who, very improperly, use the word sectarian teaching as meaning the teaching of Roman Catholic doctrine; but it is unquestionably certain that those schools were sectarian in the estimation of those who attach to the words the literal signification, or, if you like it better, I will say those schools were merely and simply Protestant schools. Protestant in fact, as well as in name; Protestant by those who controlled and directed them, as their section of the board, their superintendent, their inspectors, etc., etc. Those schools were Protestant in the selection of the books used by the teachers, pupils both in schools and libraries. They were Protestant by their religious exercises and their "systematic religious instruction . . . . accepted by all Protestant denominations." Those schools were Protestant by those who supported them, Protestants alone being called upon for that object; they were also Protestant for those who attended them, as Protestant children alone had the right.

It is so much the more astonishing to deny to those schools the true character which distinguished them, that at the time they claimed to be Protestant openly, sincerely, without hesitation as without intention to ensnare the good faith of anyone; those institutions were Protestant public schools as well as the others were Catholic public schools, both showing their true colors in accordance with the distinction foreseen and expressed in the constitution of Canada and in the constitution of Manitoba, and as fully provided by all the school laws of Manitoba under the old regime.

II. THE NEW REGIME.

Having proved that, before the 1st May, 1890, there were Protestant public schools in Manitoba, I shall proceed to demonstrate that the school system, now in vogue, is nothing but their continuation even when the law designates them under the title of public schools. My proof will cover the following subjects :

The administration and control of public schools ; the nomination of their inspectors, professors and staff; the choice of their books ; the determination and practice of their religious exercises ; the children who attend them ; the ratepayers who support them; the sympathies they elicit.

Administration and control—The Act 55 Vic., chap. 37, intituled : "An Act Respecting the Department of Education," reads as follows in its 18th clause :

From and after the first day of May, A.D. 1890, the Board of Education and the superintendents of education appointed under chapter 4 of 44 Victoria and amendments, shall cease to hold office, and within three days after said first day of May, said boards and superintendents shall deliver over to the provincial secretary all records, books, papers, documents and property of every kind, belonging to said boards.

The provisions of this law were carried into effect and without compensation, inasmuch as the Catholic section of the Board is concerned ; *all the Catholics having anything to do in the general management of schools were dismissed and no one was appointed or could accept an appointment under the new law.* It was not so with the Protestant section and its staff. Several of the members of the Protestant section were called to the new organization ; the inspectors had the same privileges.

Clause 1 of the said Act says :

There shall be a department of education, which shall consist of the executive council or a committee thereof, appointed by the lieutenant-governor in council.

Immediately before the passing of this Act the executive council had acted in such a way that no sincere Catholic could join or remain with them. The members of this executive council were, therefore, all Protestants ; the honorable the Attorney-General had caused his own appointment as superintendent of the Protestant school section of the Board of Education ; he continued the functions of that office as member and legal advisor of the Department of Education. His honorable colleagues, all eligible to the position of members of the

Protestant section under the old regime, became ex-officio members of the new school administration. Clause IV. of the same act says :

There shall be a board as hereinafter provided to be known as the advisory board,

and clause 5 says :

Said board shall consist of seven members.

The disposition of the law is such that it is morally impossible for Catholics to become members of this new organization ; the seven members will be and are Protestant as well as the five members of the executive council. Therefore, twelve Protestants continue the work of the twelve Protestants who formed the Protestant section of the board of education under the old regime. His Lordship, the Bishop of Rupert's Land, chairman of the old Protestant section of the board of education, is chairman of the new advisory board ; the Rev. Dr. G. Bryce, member of the old board, is also member of the new board ; all the clerks are not only Protestant, but some are the same as under the old law.

The Inspectors — All the Catholic inspectorships were abolished, but the Protestant inspectorships were preserved. Three old incumbents were maintained in charge, and the two others were replaced by Protestants. While dismissing all the Catholic inspectors a new inspectorship was created for the Mennonites, and one of their denomination was brought from the United States to fill the situation. The numerous functions of the new comer would seem strange under the new law, if that law was not in reality a continuation of the old system as far, at least, as Protestants are concerned.

Preparation of Teachers—Each section of the old board of education had its normal schools ; those for the Catholics were abolished, while the Protestant normal schools were quietly continued, and the principal of the Normal Protestant School of Winnipeg was maintained. I pray my readers to observe that I say nothing against the character or the qualification of any of those above mentioned ; but I say this : His Lordship the Bishop of Rupert's Land continues to be the head of the Anglican church in the province ; the Rev. Dr. G. Bryce is always the Rev. Dr. G. Bryce ; the other members of the school administration are as much Protestant to-day as they were previous to the 1st May, 1890. I am glad to believe it, all are honest and sincere ; therefore, it seems evident to me that they cannot have accepted the management, the control or the action they exercise in the schools attended by all the Protestant children of the province without being determined to protect the religious convictions of those children, in conformity with the desires of their parents. How is it possible for them to direct, to protect, to teach, to form the teachers and the pupils of the schools without a certain tendency to bias in conformity with their own personal convictions?

Is it possible for any one to be Protestant in every respect, everywhere, and always, except in the school, of which the same person has the control and direction, with the power of interpreting and executing the law? To illustrate the difficulty, let us suppose that the actual school laws should remain what they are to-day, but that a complete change is made of the persons who apply and interpret them; let us suppose that all the members of the government are Roman Catholics; that all the members of the advisory board and the staff of the Department of Education are also Roman Catholics; that all the inspectors, principals and teachers of the Normal schools will be also Roman Catholics; what would Protestants believe of the religious teaching in the schools of Manitoba? What would the "Equal Righters" think, say or write? Pardon my sincerity, I am also an equal righter, and I say that when all those connected with the schools are Protestant, it is but natural that such schools should be Protestant.

The Choice of Books.—No one can deny that the books used in the schools have a great influence on the teaching. As it has been shown, under the old regime, one of the duties of the Protestant section of the Board of Education was

To select all the books, maps and globes to be used in the schools under its control.

Under the new regime here is what is read in clause 14:

Said advisory board shall have the power to examine and authorize text books and books of reference for the use of pupils and school libraries.

Evidently the advisory board is in this the continuation of the Protestant section of the old board. Surely there is no temerity in adding that the school books used by the pupils and professors, and also the reading books placed in the libraries, will be at least in a great proportion Protestant, and very often absolutely hostile to Catholic ideas.

The most superficial examination of all that is said and written everywhere suffices to demonstrate the injustice there would be in placing Catholic children in the obligation of using books chosen only by Protestants.

Religious Exercises.—One of the numerous reasons proving that the schools, now called public, are but the continuation of the Protestant school of the old regime, is the fact that the exercises and religious and moral teachings are identically the same.

The prayers adopted and the passages selected in the Scriptures, by the Advisory Board, are nothing but what had been adopted and selected by the Protestant section of the Board of Education. The prayers and readings from the Bible are not the only religious exercises in use in the public schools; there is, under the title of "morals," a whole mine, which the professor can explore, in order to induce, in the minds of his pupils, the religious convictions he has himself, as it was formerly done in the schools called Protestant schools. As a proof of what I affirm, I offer to the examination of serious-minded people the resemblance—nay, the similitude—existing between the rules prescribed in the old Protestant schools and those prescribed by the Advisory Board in the schools now called public:

Programme of studies for the Protestant public schools of Manitoba, revised May, 1889.	Programme of studies for the public schools of Manitoba, adopted Sept. 1st, 1891, and readopted Sept. 1st, 1892.
Morals—(a) Duties to self. (b) Duties to others. (c) Duties to State. (d) Duties to animals. To establish the habit of right doing, instruction in moral principles must be accompanied by training in moral practices. The teacher's influence and example. Current incidents, stories, *memory gems*, sentiments in the school lessons. Examination of motives that prompt to action, didactic talks, learning the Ten Commandments, etc., are means to be employed.	Morals—(a) Duties to self. (b) Duties to others. (c) Duties to State. (d) Duties to animals. To establish the habit of right doing, instruction in moral principles must be accompanied by training in moral practices. The teacher's influence and example. Current incidents, stories, memory gems, sentiments in the school lessons. Examination of motives that prompt to action, didactic talks, teaching the Ten Commandments, etc., are means to be employed.

A great effort of imagination is not necessary to discover, in the above lines, a complete assortment of religious arms, offensive and defensive, put at the disposition of those whose mission it is to teach to children—those children so accessible to the most various impressions, and more apt than is generally believed to seize the thought of the professor and be guided by the influences to which they are submitted. As a rule, pupils think in the same way as their teacher.

There is still less doubt on the certainty of this result when a professor is guided by the preceding programme. What cannot be said by a talented and zealous professor, charged with the teaching of the Ten Commandments, having to help him, his influence and example, the recalling of current incidents; in narrating to his scholars stories, memory gems; in insisting on the sentiments in the school lessons and the examination of motives that prompt to action; in making didactic talks and adding to all that an etc. (*et cetera*) as large, if it pleases him, as his own religious ideas !

All these means put in the hands of an intelligent and clever person suffice, under the new regime, as well as under the old, "for the introduction in the school of a systematic religious instruction contained in the Bible and accepted by all Protestant denominations." The regulations used in public schools singularly modify the text of the Act that says : "The public schools shall be completely nonsectarian." These last words would not have been accepted as a criterion of truth by the noble lords of the Judicial Committee of the Privy Council, had their lordships known what happens here.

School Population.—There were in Manitoba, and that by law, some schools which could in conscience be frequented by Catholic children The new law wishes this no more, but continues in favor of Protestant children the schools they formerly had. Official documents show the unjust distinction introduced by the practice and application of the new law.

Under the old regime, Protestant schools were not for Catholic children, who had no right to them, and, as the schools of the new regime are but the continuation of the formerly Protestant schools, one must not be too much astonished to see that Catholic children are counted no more under the new organization than they were formerly. One may perhaps be surprised at the fact that schools boasting of being national, keep no account of the children of a notable part of the nation. What I say here would probably not be believed if I could not prove it by an official document whose authenticity cannot be denied. This document is entitled, "Report of the Department of Education, Manitoba, for the year 1891," addressed to the Lieutenant-Governor and signed by the Honorable Daniel McLean, member of the Government, and charged by the latter with the direction of the Department of Education.

The following table, taken from page 2 of the report, expresses in figures the systematic exclusion of which Catholic children are the victims under the new law.

	SCHOOL POPULATION.		*My Remarks on the adjoining statement.*
Year.	School Population.	Total Number of Pupils Registered.	
1871		817	These figures show but the Protestant children, and are taken from the reports of the superintendents of Protestant schools under the old regime.
1881	7,000	4,919	
1882	9,641	6,972	
1883	12,346	10,831	
1884	14,129	11,708	No account is taken and no mention made of Catholic children whose enumeration may be found in the official reports of the superintendents of Catholic schools under the old regime.
1885	15,850	13,074	
1886	16,834	15,926	
1887	17,600	16,910	
1888	18,850	18,000	
1889	21,471	18,358	
1890	25,077	23,256	
1891	28,678	23,871	

If the department had had in view to prove that the schools under its direction were but the continuation of the former Protestant schools, it could not have employed a stronger argument than the one contained in the figures of the preceding table. Formerly all the schools were public, the Catholic as well as the Protestant, and *vice versa*. The census taken under oath by each of the two sections were documents equally official, and are kept on record in the offices of the Government. How is it that the administration of the public schools of the day, which are also qualified as national, can leave out the whole Catholic school population and merely mention the Protestant children, and that when the statistics are gathered from 1871, when Catholic children were the most numerous? Why two weights and two measures? why should a part be counted for nothing and the other part taken as the whole?

Ratepayers.—Previous to 1890, the non-Catholic public schools of Manitoba were Protestant, in name as well as in fact: to-day the same schools have kept their character, but have lost their name; true, it is a loss, but the loss is compensated in a large measure. In all places where there was a Catholic district covering the same ground as a Protestant one, it was decided by the law that all assets of the Catholic schools would become the property of the Protestant schools, which would then be called public schools, to be supported by the school assessments of Catholics as well as of Protestants. Let it be kept in view, the provision of the law was the same, even in a district where there might be but one school with only ten Protestant children, although in the same place there would be schools enough to accommodate several hundred of Catholic children. Yes, by the terms of this law, in such a case, the school trustees charged with these hundreds of children would disappear, to make room for trustees named by the parents of the ten Protestant children. The new laws, while permitting the Protestant schools to continue to develop and to prosper, are so prejudicial to Catholic schools that already many have been closed and others are on the point of meeting the same fate, while the rest are maintained, but with difficulty. I give Winnipeg as an illustration: The Catholics have in the city five educational establishments, frequented by over five hundred children. Under the old regime, the Catholics of Winnipeg had their own school trustees, as the Protestants had theirs; the limits of the two districts were not similar, nevertheless, the Attorney-General in 1890 decided that the Catholic school trustees would not be recognized any more. This decision entailed the confiscation of all appertaining to the Catholic school trustees in favor of the Protestant board. Fortunately, the Catholic establishments belonged to corporations that the school law could not reach and the Catholic children remained where they were. There was something reached by the decision of the then Attorney-General; it is the assessment levied on Catholics. For three years past the school taxes of the Catholics, instead of turning to their benefit, are applied to help the schools where Catholic children do not attend. The Catholic schools of Winnipeg, deprived of the assessments of their supporters, deprived also of their legitimate share of the public money, are left to the good-will of the parents, helped by the self-denial of the teachers.

I have witnessed the beginning and the growth of the city of Winnipeg; at all times I have admired the liberality of its inhabitants; it is perfectly well established that the people of Winnipeg give freely and generously. How is it that in the same city we find an unjust meanness such as the one perpetrated against the Catholic schools of the place? I know that several of the best citizens are ashamed, when thinking that money is taken even from the poorest Catholics to help in educating the children of Protestants, even of some of the richest. Unfortunately, this sentiment has not reached the main body of the citizens, and the meanness is still being enacted. Its injustice is so much the more manifest that the School Board has not sufficient accommodation, we are told, even for the Protestant children. What embarrassment it would be for that School Board if, at a fixed day, all the Catholic children of the city would go and ask for their place in the public schools, to the maintenance of which their parents are forced to contribute. The ignorance of the financial position made for the Catholic schools by the new law can alone account for the affirmation made by the noble lords of the judicial committee of the Privy Council. Their Lordships surely were not aware of the bitter sarcasm they used when they said, "In such a case the Roman Catholics were really placed in a better position than the Protestants."

The Friends of the Public Schools.—In 1890, the government first intended to completely secularize the primary instruction, but it met with such remonstrance that it modified its bill, merely abolishing the Catholic schools and securing that the Protestants would be left with such schools as they had themselves framed by the "introduction of systematic religious instruction accepted by all their denominations." The partizans of secularization are dissatisfied with the religious practices maintained in the schools; they would like to see the disappearances of prayers, of the reading of the Bible and the "means to be employed," according to the programme prescribed in the new as well as in the old schools. Complete secularization is not without supporters in different classes of citizens, but the Protestant clergy "en masse" look at it as the most dangerous thing after the Catholic teaching. The rev. gentlemen accept with enthusiasm the new laws because, while repudiating the Catholic doctrine, they do not admit of secularization and because they are in reality but the continuation of the Protestant schools, such as some of the clergy and laity of the different denominations have made them, through the Protestant section of the board of education.

It is very difficult to imagine what has been printed in the press and what has been said in different political and religious meetings to prove, sometimes indirectly, but always with evidence, that the school question of Manitoba is purely and simply a religious one. I will not make any quotations, it would take a large volume to reproduce what has been said cooly and in a becoming manner, but it would take many large volumes to contain the violent language, the accusations and insinuations of all sorts against that scarecrow, that people dressed and stuffed according to their ideas, and which through stupidity or malice they call the " Romish church."

In the midst of this coarse and absurd trash, had anyone, just and disinterested, the courage to raise his voice to appeal to common sense or to the most elementary sentiments of justice, what has not been said against such persons? They were so many Judases, traitors to the Protestant cause, sold to Rome, to the Archbishop, to the hierarchy, and other stupidities of the kind. I beg the reader's pardon for making even a passing allusion to all these painful occurrences. I do it merely to prepare for the following question: Why become so blindly sectarian in upholding a school system, if not because the system itself is sectarian? Why such appeals to fanaticism, made in season and out of season, everywhere and on every opportunity, if not because the schools spoken of are in reality what the people pretend they are not, Protestant schools: but enough on that humiliating aspect of the question. I will now prove that the public schools of Manitoba have secured the official approbation and the support of the religious denominations, which had most contributed to mould the Protestant schools under the old regime.

The Presbyterians assembled in synod in Winnipeg, the 22nd of November, 1892. The question of public schools was again discussed at great length; the Rev. Dr. Robertson moved a series of politico-religious resolutions, which he supported by a speech of the same character; contending among other similar reasons:

That a system of separate schools (read Catholic schools) could tend to fortify a sentiment of annexation.

The Rev. Peter Wright:

Had very much pleasure in seconding and in cordially and gladly supporting the resolutions; the latter did not at all contemplate doing away with any of the existing religious exercises. If they did he would not second them. . . Engage only Christian men and women. While there were exceptions, there was no class of people for whom he had a higher respect than the school teachers; and a Sunday seldom passed that he did not give thanks from his pulpit for the help rendered him in church work by Christian school teachers.

The Rev. Dr. Pringle:

Regards separate schools as a curse to any province or any town. He was glad we were not left to the alternative of separate or secular schools; if we were, he would go in with his might for secular schools.

The Rev. Principal King opposed the last four resolutions of Dr. Robertson saying :

It was a mistake to bring such questions before this church court to make their beloved synod the tool of some political party. He washed his hands clear of the whole thing.

The venerable doctor also said :

That he could not agree with the sentiment of one speaker, looking to the relegation of religion to the church and family alone.

He moved as an amendment to Dr. Robertson's resolutions that all the clauses be omitted except the first one which reads as follows:

That this synod, in accordance with the position taken at previous meetings of synod, in favor of national schools established in Manitoba in 1890, desires to express its continued anxiety for their complete establishment throughout the bounds of this synod.

The proposition was adopted.

The Rev. Principal King then moved another resolution, seconded by the Rev. P. Wright.

That the synod, in harmony with the decision of the general assembly of 1889, on the subject of religion and instruction in the public schools, would earnestly deprecate any change in the existing school law of the province of Manitoba, in the direction of the withdrawal or the abridgment of the right now enjoyed by the people. . . . He thinks that such abridgment would be both dishonoring to God and injurious to the interests of the state.

The resolution was adopted.

I confess that I understand nothing in ordinary, language if all these assertions of the Presbyterian synod do not mean : (1) That the Catholic schools must be by all means done away with ; (2) that secular schools must also be opposed ; (3) that one must use every effort to maintain the actual schools with the continuance of their religious exercises. In other words, and according to my proposition, the Presbyterian synod proved that the actual public schools, are and should not cease to be but the continuation of the Protestant schools of the old regime. Dr. King, himself, in 1892, affirmed his views as similar to those in the general assembly of 1889.

One member of the synod, the Rev. Dr. Bryce, fearing that somebody might think there was in the resolution of his confrere something in favor of secularizing the schools "which was not so . . . read from the Act all the clauses providing for religious exercises in the schools," and to "prove that the synod ought to firmly and decidedly take a stand." The reverend speaker exhibited to the assembly a precious gem of the first sectarian water. People would hardly believe it, but the assertion was made in full synod and nobody was reported as having objected.

I beg pardon from the noble lords of the judicial committee in daring to quote the words of a most zealous champion of public schools, who in the midst of the synod of his church thought proper to say (The Winnipeg *Daily Tribune*, Nov. 23, 1892.):

> The action of the Presbyterian body as representing the strongest religious denomination in the North-west in declaring for national schools on two previous occasions, which declaration was sent to the Privy Council, had an important effect upon the decision which was given.

Were this affirmation made so solemnly, true, the judicial annals of Great Britain would have to record that the highest tribunal of the empire, under the pressure of the declarations of Presbyterian synods of Winnipeg, had given a decision contrary to the sacred interests of education among the Catholics of this province.

An Anglican synod met on the 11th January, 1893, in Winnipeg, under the presidency of His Lordship the Bishop of Rupert's Land. The meeting numbered more than one hundred and twenty members, comprising the chief of the clergy and laity of the church of England. The Right Rev. president delivered his charge; most of it being on the religious teaching in the primary schools. His Lordship expressed arguments and motives which are found in all Catholic treatises on the subject and substantiated by statistics. Here are quotations from the charge :

> The known exclusion of religious teaching makes religion itself felt as something extra and superfluous. . . . Pure secular education has been accompanied by the deterioration of tone and character in the young. . . . the efforts to supply religious education independently of the school failed. . . Religious instruction will be given systematically by few parents, not at all where most needed.

Speaking of "What would happen in England if the present assistance to separate schools were to cease," His Lordship described at the same time what would happen in Manitoba and says :

> Many schools would be closed, many others would give but inferior education, still enough will be carried on; that a government system of secular instruction might call itself national, but would be so in name not in reality.

I have already stated that the Metropolitan of Rupert's Land, after having been for nineteen years the president of the Protestant section of the board of education, is since president of the advisory board for the public schools. He is consequently perfectly aware of the value of the religious exercises, prescribed by each of these two boards and here is the enumeration and appreciation made by His Lordship.

> There is a short prayer concluding with the Lord's Prayer. There is a reading of a passage of the Bible. In the teaching of morals, there are the ten commandments. Now, these are not small things in themselves, but they are doubly important, because they carry with them for the teachers, a degree of liberty.

Yes, the bishop knows the value of what has been chosen and

prescribed, under his presidency, for teaching the children of his church, as well as other Protestant children, and he adds:

The teachers who ignore these exercises can hardly be realizing their position as Christian men.

After so speaking the president of the Anglican synod gave the following advice:

I think the synod would do well to pass a resolution, expressing the hope that there would be no interference with the present religious exercises in public schools.

The charge of the Metropolitan met with full approval and the committee appointed to report on it, presented the following:

(2) Resolved, that while this synod would gladly see a larger measure of religious teaching in our schools than at present prevails, it trusts that every effort will be made, both by the educational authorities and by the Christian public generally, to render existing regulations on the subject as widely operative and efficient as possible.

(3) This synod stands pledged to resist to the utmost any attempt to secularize our public schools.

The Rev. Canon O'Meara in proposing the adoption of the clauses of the report concerning religious education, reminded the synod that it is owing to the stand taken in 1890,

by the Bishop and the Rev. Dr. King of the Presbyterian church that the intention to fasten upon the country an utterly godless system was changed.

The Rev. T. H. Walton seconded the motion.

He argued that in the interests of children, the state, and the church, education should not be made purely secular.

After that the Metropolitan acknowledged that:

When the parish schools were given up there seemed to be no doubt that there would be a certain amount of religious instruction in the (public) schools.

It is evident that the Anglican Synod (1) repudiates the purely secular schools as dangerous to all; (2) that on the contrary it recognizes the absolute necessity of religious instruction in public schools; (3) that it affirms that the Anglicans in giving up their parochial schools, had no doubt that the public schools would continue to give religious instruction; (4) that the synod recognizes that in fact the public schools have religious exercises,

that are not small things in themselves, but that are doubly important, because they carry with them for the teacher a degree of liberty in his teaching.

(5) that the synod pledges itself to resist to the utmost any measure tending to diminish the religious instruction actually given in public schools. To all that, Mr. Mulock, a member of the synod, adds:

That as soon as the Protestant bodies agreed upon what they wanted, the government was willing to take action.

CONCLUSION.

As a conclusion of all I have stated, I cannot help being convinced that the actual public schools of Manitoba are nothing else but the continuation of the Protestant public schools, formerly established by law in the province and in force since the 3rd May, 1871, until the 1st May 1890. The two systems are the same, as far as Protestants are concerned, but the result of the introduction of the new system has been detrimental to Catholics. The old regime had consideration for all religious beliefs and placed the citizens on the same equal footing with regard to their religious convictions; the new regime on the contrary, while hiding under false names, pretends to offer the same advantages to all, but creates an essential distinction. Some may conscientiously accept, and in fact do accept, what the law gives, while others cannot conscientiously avail themselves of the same, and suffer by the practical conclusion to which they are condemned.

An effort is made to conceal such a painful distinction. The equality of rights is proclaimed, and we are told:

"It is not the law that is in fault. It is owing to religious convictions, which everybody must respect, and to the teaching of their church that the Roman Catholics find themselves unable to partake of the advantages which the law offers to all alike."

What a queer reasoning, laws favorable to Catholics were repealed, others were enacted contrary to their religious convictions—such religious convictions "which everybody must respect"; and it is said: It is not the law that is in fault, but it is the Catholic religion! Just as if it were said: It is not the fault of the Roman empire, if Christians were put to death under Nero and his successors, that was "owing to the religious convictions of those Christians and to the teaching of their church," which forbade to the faithful certain practices of the law declared equally advantageous to all alike.

The results secured by the two school systems of Manitoba are very different. The old regime has not failed to develop a remarkable advancement in the interest of education; a progress seldom achieved, if ever, in a new country and, in a way, precious to all, as related by Mr. J. B. Somerset, when he says:

"There has been an almost entire absence of the friction and disagreement that have marked the progress of education in some of the sister provinces."

Can anyone say the same with regard to the new system? Alas, no! It materially retards instruction, at least amongst Catholics. On the other hand, how painful it is to witness every day the friction, the disagreements, the injurious proceedings, the disunion and the uneasiness which prevail in the province since three years. The law was to unite, and it divides; it was to assimilate, and it enlarges the distinction.

The Catholics have undoubtedly to suffer, but that does not close their eyes to advantages offered by their native or adopted land. We may suffer, but we cannot be traitors. Why add to the difficulty of supporting our schools as under the new law, the unjust reproach of failing in our obligations to country and allegiance. Such grave accusations have been uttered against us and the reader will permit me to repudiate them before closing my remarks and to tell to those unacquainted with my position, what my faith requires from me, both in religious and in civil order. I am a Christian, as such I raise my aspirations far above the world. While looking towards Heaven my faith is increased in the Holy Church of my Saviour, as the way which leads to it. I give my allegiance to that Holy Church, listening to her teaching by which I am directed to love the Lord my God with my whole heart, and my neighbor as myself. Her sacred teaching tells me to do good to them that hate me or wish me evil, and as I would that men should do to me, do I also to them in like manner. I am a Catholic.

My allegiance to my church in the spiritual order is also my guide in the accomplishment of my civil or political duties. The sun of Canada has smiled upon my cradle, I hope it will also shine over my grave. For six generations, my ancestors were born on the banks of the St. Lawrence. Canada is my country. I never had and never will have another home. Manitoba and the Northwest have had my life, my labors and my affections for nearly half a century, they will have them until my last day. I am a Canadian.

I was born and I have lived in British possessions; my allegiance is, therefore, to the Crown of England; my conscience and my heart repudiate anything that should be contrary to my obligations as a British subject. I feel happy to live under the protection of the glorious banner of the British empire. Can I be a traitor to my allegiance because I desire that the soft breeze of liberty should wave the noble standard towards my co-religionists, as well as towards my other countrymen, in order that everyone may enjoy the protection and impartiality to which all are entitled in return for their allegiance?

†Alex., Arch. of St. Boniface, O.M.I.

CHAPTER III.

ADDRESS

Delivered by the Bishop of Rupert's Land before the Anglican Synod, December, 1889.

I have thought it might be well to publish in a separate form the remarks I made to the Synod on the subject of primary education. In addressing the Synod I did not think it desirable to discuss the probable change in the method of administration. I confined myself to the question of religious teaching. But identified as I have been from the beginning with the past administration of our provincial system of education, I do not think that it will be out of place for me to make some remarks on this subject in this publication. I believe that the Board of Education has been in the execution of its trust a faithful servant of the State, and impartial in its administration. It is my opinion, too, that the State has been exceptionally well served by the successive superintendents of education, and I think it is a subject of regret that the Province has lost the experience and administrative ability of the late superintendent.

There is grave objection to the Department of Education being treated like an ordinary department of the Government. Usually there is a Minister who decides everything in his department, and an assistant, with perhaps half the salary, who acts as Deputy Minister. But in this department the real administrator should be, if possible, a scholar of fair if not high university attainments, well acquainted with educational questions and methods. And as his value will be largely increased by experience and knowledge of the country gained by years of office, he should be a permanent official. Now, it is impossible to secure and retain a valuable man of such attainments without a liberal salary. To expect always these qualifications, even to a very moderate degree, in the statesman receiving for political reasons the Ministry of Education, is out of the question. And it would scarcely be right to make such a man the mere clerk of the politician for the time in office. Besides, it will be difficult for the Minister in this country to be credited with the absolute determination of all the questions rising out of school matters without giving suspicion of political partiality and embittering those whose wishes he disregards. On the other hand, I readily admit that it would be an advantage that the Government should have a closer connection with the Board of Education than it has had in the past. The expenditure of the grant for education as proposed by the board is now voted by the Governor-in-Council, and it seems right that the Government should thus be responsible for the expenditure. But the Board of Education feels that it is by its special information a more competent authority. Thus, there is apt to be friction, if the Governor in Council thinks proper to reject any of the estimates or proposals of the board. This would be avoided if, as I have suggested in the address to the Synod, one of the Ministers occupied the position of chairman of the Board of Education.

Criticisms that have been made on the addresses of Dr. King and myself, suggest one or two remarks. I have seen it represented that we would prefer the present system of separate schools to any merely secular system. And I do not hesitate to say that I would; but at the same time I think this an unfair way of putting the matter. There is much in the present system that is objectionable that could be removed. Under proper restrictions I see a measure of justice and no injustice in separate schools, and I do not think that it will be easy to do away with them. However the Roman Catholic authorities may approve of the subjects of religious teaching that Protestants would agree upon, they will accept no teachers but their own. The great majority of Roman Catholic children will, therefore, be sent to their own private schools, however inferior, rather than to State schools not under Roman Catholic instructors, whether there be religious teaching in them or not. If there is no religious teaching there will be but the stronger expression of dislike. The day will come when one, if not both political parties, will discover that it is undesirable for the State to have this inferior secular instruction, and unjust to the Roman Catholic section of the community, that while getting no State aid for its private schools it should have to contribute to the support of the state schools. And the separate schools will reappear—possibly in an objectionable form. If Protestants allow the threatened secularization of the the public schools, they may expect to see in a few years these two classes of state schools —Roman Catholic and secular. Will that be satisfactory?

It is sometimes said that the religious teaching at present in the Protestant schools does not amount to much. It is still far from sufficient, but there has been a gradual improvement. The Protestant Board of Education has, however, never been chosen to represent the opinions of the churches. I have been all along aware that several of the members did not share my views—at one time certainly I would have been in a small minority. But I have always regarded an attitude unfriendly to religious teaching in the schools for our children, as so unnatural for religious men, that I have hoped for the gradual overcoming of the prejudices so that a more satisfactory system might be introduced. As long as the school law placed no obstacle in the way of the adoption of a fuller system of religious instruction I felt able to work on the Board, and look forward to this. I am, indeed, perfectly satisfied with the religious subjects now prescribed for the Protestant section. I wish for nothing more—only

I desire them not only read or learned by heart but taught. And till this is the case, I must consider the religious teaching of our schools insufficient.

THE EXTRACT FROM ADDRESS TO THE SYNOD.

But higher education is not everything, and to-day there are circumstances that oblige me to refer to primary education. Though we have not now any primary schools, it is not because, in view of the church such schools are of small importance. The day was when we had a church primary school, wherever we had a clergyman. That was our position when this province was transferred to Canada, and it seems probable that the Dominion intended to recognize such efforts in the past, and to protect the school interests that then existed. But our church saw such advantages in a national system of schools, and such reason to have confidence in the administration of it, that it went heartily into it, trusting that the schools would be worthy of a Christian people and give an education in which the first, namely the religious, interests of the children would not be lost sight of. And I may say that the only reason which has led me for so many years to give up time that I could ill spare, to be a member of the Board of Education, has been the hope that by conciliatory action I might help in securing a measure of religious instruction reasonably satisfactory at once to ourselves and the other religious bodies.

The Roman Catholic Church alone continued to have separate schools. I may be mistaken, but I am of opinion that this privilege has been so worked as to give it an undue denominational advantage. I mean that in being enabled to supply the primary education of its members, it has been helped to give cheaply a higher education, that has drawn to it Protestant children, more particularly girls. If separate schools are aided by the state, I think the state should have the same securities for a sound secular education as in its other schools. Although there are separate schools in England there is only one council of education; there are common qualifications for all teachers; there is one system of inspection and one body of inspectors—there is one course of education. Further, in England separate schools only receive the share of the government grant. They get nothing from rates. This part of their support has to be supplied by voluntary contributions. If this provision be not adopted here, at any rate it should be seen that there is no opening for such an abuse as I have suggested. However desirable one system of national education may be, I think that the system of separate schools, as it exists in England, assures to the state the education it should require, and is at the same time eminently just, and one that should be open to any religious body.

The notice given to the Protestant superintendent of education has prepared us for some modification of the method of administration.

But on this I do not care, as bishop, to address you. I would simply say that I consider that the best way for the administration of our schools would be to adopt the English plan. In that case one of the ministers would occupy the position, which I have had the honour to fill for so many years and preside over the board of education. He could thus represent and carry out the policy of the government without any great call on his time, while a permanent official, a competent scholar, well acquainted with education questions and methods, as deputy minister or superintendent of education, could be the real administrator, and a small board of independent gentlemen, conversant with education, could still be responsible for the decisions come to.

But a more serious question is that of the education to be given in our common schools. It is certainly most desirable that the people of this country should be thoroughly amalgamated. I, therefore, greatly prefer that the young people of our communion should be educated with the other young people, with whom they will afterwards work. But we must ask what is the education to be given? Is it to be an education, that will keep out of view those Divine sanctions, which are the real foundation of morality, an education that is to take no notice of that to which we owe our modern civilization, and from which we receive the hope of our life—our Christian faith. I believe that such an education will in the end be a poor one both for the individual and the nation. The Bible reiterates, "The fear of the Lord is the beginning of knowledge," and again, "The fear of the Lord is the beginning of wisdom." The noble question that opens the Westminster Shorter Catechism—one of the standards of the Presbyterian churches, is "What is the chief end of man?" And the answer is "To glorify God and to enjoy Him for ever." It seems a miserable education for the future of the man that could ignore the very end of his being. Education should be a training for the future help and guidance of the man in all his interests. In the present day it is too much the notion that education is the filling of the mind with information on all possible subjects that may come in usefully, and every science and branch of knowledge puts in its claim, but after all the true education is not so much a laying in of facts as the training of the mind for its future exercise, and can that be called a wise and true training that loses sight of the most important principles for the guidance of the man? Those who most value education, who most recognize and appreciate its tremendous power, cannot but be constrained by their sense of the danger of any defect in this. I would call attention to an important passage in the report of the late Royal Commission on Primary Education appointed in England in 1866. This Commission contained leading men of all the chief religious bodies, and included prominent advocates of secular schools. But though they differed on many questions, and especially on the wisest way of imparting religious knowledge, they agreed in one most remarkable conclusion:—"That whilst we desire to secure for the children in the public elementary schools the best and most thorough instruction in secular subjects, suitable to their years, and in harmony with the requirements of their future life, we are also unanimously of opinion that their religious and moral training is a matter of still higher importance alike to the children, the parents and the nation." If this be admitted, the first practical question seems to be, how can this religious and moral training be best secured in the interest of the nation? And the conclusion of the minority, who favoured more or less a secular system, seems strange—that the State is bound to promote the best secular knowledge, but that it is no concern of the state to see after the other—no concern to see after that which is admitted by them to be of the first importance for children, parents, and the nation.

Various classes of objections have been raised to religious worship and teaching in primary schools, but only one seems to me a serious one, and that is that it is not feasible on account of our divided Christianity. Other objections seem to me without force in view of the greatness of the desired end. Those alleging want of reality and the encouragement of hypocrisy would, I fear, equally apply to family worship and divine service. Those pointing to a lessening of the regard for the Bible are mainly imaginary. I attended a school where there was daily Bible instruction; I also attended a Sunday school, and I am perfectly unconscious of any difference with regard to the Bible in the two cases, of any lessening of reverence or regard for the Bible from there being lessons from it in daily school, on the part of myself or any one having those lessons. Objections setting forth want of qualification on the part of the teachers simply point to another remedy, where this is felt to be the case. I have full confidence in the body of teachers in this province; and we may expect still greater reason for confidence when the country passes out of its pioneer stage. The minority of the English commission admit as regards England "it is with exceptional pleasure that we recall the deep impression which has been made upon us by the high moral quality of most of the teachers whom we have examined." It will be the fault of the country if this is not the testimony that we have a right to expect. I am sure that ordinarily we should all be only too glad of the help of the present teachers in our Sunday schools. As the eminent Principal of Queen's University, Dr. Grant, lately said: "If the teacher is an unworthy man and wishes to insinuate evil teaching, he can do so in connection with any subject. In that case he is not fit to be a teacher at all. This may be safely left in the hands of the trustees of each district." For myself, I heartily agree with the majority of the Royal Commissioners, "that it is of the highest importance that the teachers who are charged with the moral training of the scholars should continue to take part in the religious instruction, and that any separation of the teacher from the religious teaching of the school would be injurious to the moral and secular training of the scholars." There is still another class of objections to religious teaching in schools, on account of its insufficiency and neglect of what is considered the proper aim of religious teaching. Now, as far as results are concerned, I am afraid the same objection might be raised to the Sunday school instruction, which those objectors would depend on. There may, indeed, be the best religious teaching applied most tenderly to the heart and conscience, and yet there may be no loving response from the heart of the child to God. "Thy face, God, will I seek." But while we look to God's grace for the changing of the heart and drawing it to love and serve God, still we find that the Spirit of God deals with us as reasonable beings, and a provision of knowledge of the things of God is a divine preparation for the soil receiving the good seed. The Eunuch of Ethiopia was prepared for the message of Philip by an acquaintance with the prophecies of Isaiah. "How shall they believe in Him, of whom they have not heard?" The makers of this class of objections think little of any religious instruction which is not an application of certain special portions of God's truth to the heart. In that I differ from them. I think there is great value in the acquisition of the information given us in the Bible, and in the inculcation of morality from its divine source. So far I would agree with these objectors that it is not desirable that religious teaching according to their view should be a subject of daily practice. That I would leave largely to the Sunday school, though the judicious and faithful teacher will make use of proper opportunity. I am quite conscious that, as there may always be too much of the best, so there may be too much of religious teaching. The time given to it should be carefully limited and the subjects should be largely historical.

But even those who favor secular schools feel the necessity of some moral training. The minority of the Royal Commissioners give a long list of moral duties that they would enforce on the children. Most of the English school boards have regular religious instruction, but the Birmingham board is an exception. It has replaced the Word of God by "outlines" of lessons on honesty, truthfulness, obedience to parents, and some forty moral duties. Let us see the working of such a system, where it is in full force as in the Australian colony of Victoria. An inspector, we are told, when examining the children in a primary school asked the question "Why should we obey our parents?" The child referred to the divine sanction of the 5th commandment. The inspector replied—that he could not give any marks—the answer should have been, "because they feed, clothe, and educate me." Thus you see in this system obedience to parents is simply a moral duty as taught by the natural conscience—what is the real worth of this? When Bishop Horden began to teach the Indians of Rupert's House, he gave them a lesson on the 5th commandment. He had four men of the tribe placed before him. He asked the first who killed his father, the second who killed his mother and so on. Each answered 'I did,' and we are told, the confession excited no feeling in the crowded building. It had been the way of the tribe. When old people became a burden to the wandering family, they were told they had lived long enough and were put out of the way. We, indeed, beloved brethren, strike at the whole edifice of our morality, when we remove this foundation—"Thus saith the Lord." How often in the history of the world has this sentence of Holy Scripture been realized: "Professing themselves to be wise, they became fools." The conclusion of the majority of the Royal Commissioners seems unanswerable: "That the only safe foundation, on which to construct a theory of morals, or to secure high moral conduct, is the religion, which our Lord Jesus Christ has taught the world. That as we look to the Bible for instruction concerning morals and take its words for the declaration of what is morality, so we look to the same inspired source for the sanctions by which men may be led to practise what is there taught, and for instruction concerning the helps by which they may be enabled to do what they have learned to be right." It is very pleasant to find the Bishop of London, of the Church of England, Cardinal Manning and the Duke of Norfolk, of the Church of Rome, Dr. Rigg, an eminent Methodist minister, and other leading clergymen and laymen of the various religious bodies uniting in this important statement.

Now, how is adequate religious instruction to be given, if not in the primary schools? The answer is, in the home and in Sunday schools. I think we may soon satisfy ourselves that the home instruction would be very limited. As the Bishop of Rochester once said: "There are three things requisite for adequate instruction in religious as in other knowledge—leisure, capacity, and inclination." In how many a home would one or more of these necessary conditions be wanting? Alas! In these busy days in how few homes would they be combined? The instruction in Sunday schools is of course of great value, but that value is immeasurably increased where there is careful instruction in the day school. But at best it would be very partial in its extent and often, as we have reason to regret, not very efficient. As regards England, the commissioners report "that the evidence does not warrant the conclusion that religious and moral training can be amply provided otherwise than through the medium of elementary schools. That in the case of a considerable number of children, if they do not receive religious instruction and training from the teachers in the public elementary schools, they will receive none, and that this would be a matter of gravest concern to the state."

It is true that in this country the full effect of a secular system of education will not be immediately felt. We have a fine body of settlers. There probably is no town in which the people attend church better than in Winnipeg. I presume that in our present towns most of the children attend Sunday school, and though in the country districts they can only to a limited extent do this owing to the distance of children from Sunday Schools, yet the feeling would be in favor of attendance. But this country will not always be in this happy condition. We must look forward to larger populations and careless classes, as seen not only in the old countries of Europe, but in the United States. And then the result will be deplorable. We see in France secular education in its full development. "Not only is no word of religion taught, but the very name of God is in strictness forbidden to be uttered." Is it strange that unbelievers themselves almost tremble for the future of that country. The master of one of the schools in Paris, himself a professed materialist, when questioned, said that he believed that in ten years few of the boys in his school would even know the name of Christ otherwise than as a matter of history, and that he himself even viewed with apprehension the consequence of such a change, for although a materialist, he felt by no means certain that materialism would be capable of supplying the wants of a nation.

But it may be thought that there is no danger in a British colony of going on to this extreme. It is, dear brethren, only the legitimate end of the secular system.

I have already referred to the colony of Victoria. The school system there is not yet absolutely 'Godless,' as in France. It has yet only reached the stage of being 'Christless,' but it is stated that it has been seriously proposed to make the thin Theism still left in the text books still thinner by "omitting any statements that might be offensive to our Chinese fellow-citizens." But though the name of God is not yet forbidden, how Christ, our Saviour, seems to be dishonored. One of the text-books in English contains Longfellow's little ballad "The Wreck of the Hesperus." But it is given in a mutilated form. The touching stanza of the child in its distress has been cut out:

> "Then the maiden clasped her hands
> And prayed that saved she might be,
> And she thought of Christ, who stilled the
> Wave on the Lake of Galilee."

It is said by an Australian contributor to the *London Spectator* that all similar references to Christ and Christianity have been removed, and that Messrs. Nelson & Sons, the publishers, have had to publish special editions of their school series for this colony, and fully purged of all taint of Christian fact and sentiment. Thus the blessed name, which is above every name, is practically treated as an improper passage in a heathen Latin writer. Surely a Christian may well say that an enemy hath done this. It was not by such

hearted Christianity that our religion spread in its first days and our
fathers got the faith. In face of such a fact we may well ask, are we,
the Christians of to-day, at all awake to the preciousness of what has
been committed to us? Do we understand the vast responsibility that
rests upon us? What a condemnation the possibility of such results
is of our divided Christianity! How it calls on us to enter our inner
chamber and pray the last prayer of our Lord with His disciples
before His death " that they all may be one, that they also may be
one in us, that the world may believe that Thou has sent Me." And
how strange it is, even from a literary point of view, that in a day
when information of all kinds is crowded in on the pupils, it should
be thought proper to withhold the information which is absolutely
necessary for the intelligent reading of all our literature! Fancy a
reader of Milton ignorant of the facts of the Bible!

I have left myself little space to speak of that which is the really
formidable objection, that it is not feasible with our divided Christianity to formulate a scheme of religious teaching which will be acceptable to all religious bodies. With regard to this I simply say that
I think there should be no difficulty in drawing up a scheme, giving a
very considerable—to my mind a very adequate—amount of religious
teaching, which should not be inconsistent with the teaching of any
of the chief bodies. In the first place, I give my entire adhesion to
the following resolution, which I understood was passed unanimously
at the last general assembly of the Presbyterian Church of Canada:
" The general assembly still adheres firmly to the belief that the Bible
should be made in the public schools the object of regular systematic
instruction, and rejoices to believe that a rule to this effect, combined
with a conscience clause, giving full relief to every objector, and with
a clause empowering trustees to dispense with such instruction when
they consider it expedient, would be most acceptable to the different
branches of the Christian church." I think it perfectly possible to
agree on an adequate selection of lessons that might be taken either
from the authorized English version, the Douay version, or a
French version, as trustees of any school might prefer. In the
second place, I approve of a second resolution of the Assembly : " The
General Assembly acknowledges receipt of a communication from the
Anglican Synod of the Diocese of Toronto on the subject of religious
instruction in the public schools of Ontario, and expresses its
sympathy with the object therein contemplated." The communication referred to suggested the preparation by representatives of the
several religious bodies of a " Short Compendium of the Chief Truths
of Christian Faith and Practice." This I should like to see. I
think the compendium better be confined to the Apostles' Creed, the
Lord's Prayer and the Ten Commandments—which are the common
heritage of all Christendom. Such a manual would probably by no
means contain all even in these that everyone could wish said, but it

could contain the chief truths of our faith and yet have nothing objectionable. Further teaching could be given in Sunday Schools or when young people are prepared for Confirmation or the Lord's Supper.

The General Assembly appointed a committee, which among other duties, had to take steps to secure the co-operation of other branches of the Christian Church. I should be very glad if we were to intimate to their authorities here our desire to co-operate. Dear brethren in the Lord, we are a Christian people, and should be very jealous of our faith. This is the Divine assurance: "Them that honor Me, I will honor."

There can be nothing unreasonable in this that we should require in the education of our young people that which we regard as of primary importance for their future. There may be Jews and other unbelievers in Christ wishing to send their children to the public schools—there should be a stringent clause protecting their children from the religious instruction and guaranteeing that they suffer in no way from this.

The Roman Catholic Church might give its sympathy and aid in all that I propose, but we cannot look for this. In that case I simply say that I should infinitely prefer that the Roman Catholic Church should continue to have separate schools under satisfactory conditions for the State, to our schools being without religious instruction.

I have taken up a longer time than I like in speaking on this important subject. I hold no extreme views on this question. On the contrary, I am very conscious in addressing you that there are not many likely to fill my position, who may be expected to take a broader and more generous view of secular education or be more averse to giving to children unsuitable and excessive dogmatic teaching. And, therefore, some weight may be given to my words when I say that the establishment of a system of secular instruction means, I doubt not, a ceaseless agitation. At the present moment the members of the Church of England in England are paying yearly three millions of dollars (£600,000) in voluntary subscriptions to support 11,890 separate schools for 2,606,880 children in schools built by voluntary subscriptions, to the amount of seventy millions of dollars (£14,000,000). The members of our church here may not have much of this spirit at present, or, if they have, may not be able to show it, but the day may be expected to come when they will. Having spoken already at such length, I cannot touch on other matters to-day. I desire, then, simply to commend our deliberations to the guidance of God's Holy Spirit, that our Church may be an instrument for promoting the glory of God and the salvation of men.

CHAPTER IV.

Extracts on Primary Education from the Address of the
BISHOP OF RUPERT'S LAND
To the Synod of the Diocese, January, 1893.

In addressing the synod I abstained from remarks on primary education, as the courts had before them the question whether the provincial school act was constitutional or not. Even now only the grave consequences to be apprehended force me to take up the subject. For the question enters somewhat into that political strife for which it is well for the Church, if possible, to keep away, and there is evidently much difficulty in the existing circumstances of the province in securing what the friends of religious education would wish.

There are some who speak of religious education as something that is outside the province of the state. I feel a difficulty in understanding such a position in the case of anyone who realizes its importance either for the individual or for the state. For as regards the state and civil government, belief in a personal God behind the moral law is surely the strongest, and in fact the only, satisfactory support for it, and experience shows that this belief is the most influential motive for inducing obedience even to the laws of the state. The state, therefore, for its own advantage should seek that its children should have a religious education. For a Christian state to set itself against this seems a dishonoring of God and disastrous to its best interests. But in enforcing the necessity of religious education there must be no depreciation or disparaging of the best secular education. No one can desire to return to a state of things common enough not long ago, when there was little instruction of any kind even of a religious character. This is practically the case among those Roman Catholics whose ignorant condition and large proportion of criminals are sometimes thrown against the friends of religious education. Still a thorough teaching of the Bible with wholesome home discipline will, with very poor secular instruction, train up a thoughtful, intelligent, honest, and capable people. This was the case in Scotland in days of the old parish schools. In England until recent years there was no state provision for education, and in general there was no proper instruction for the common people —in country parishes often only a dame's school conducted by a respectable elderly woman who could do little but read. One thing is clear. A good secular education is a necessity of our age. The question is what is its probable effect if unaccompanied by religious instruction. For education is not simply the imparting of useful knowledge, though as much of this as is consistent with the real training of the mind is well, but education is above all the inculcating of sound principles of life, and the strengthening of the mental powers and conceptions. Tennyson well said in his "In Memoriam."

> "Who loves not knowledge? Who shall rail
>   Against her beauty? May she mix
> With men and prosper? Let her work prevail!
>
> But. . . . Let her know her place!
>   She is the second, not the first.
>
> A higher hand must make her mild,
>   If all be not in vain, and guide
>
> Her footsteps, moving side by side
>   With wisdom, like the younger child:
>
> For she is earthly of the mind,
>   But wisdom, heavenly of the soul."

As the Archbishop of Canterbury said in his opening address at the Folkstone congress:

It is on character infinitely more than on material knowledge, that all which is vital to the power and estate of England turns. It is truth which has made her free.

He quoted the following passage of William Law:

The youths that attended upon Socrates, Plato and Epictetus were thus educated. Their every day lessons and instructions were . . . upon the immortality of the soul, its relation to God, the beauty of virtue and its agreeableness to the divine nature, upon the dignity of reason, the necessity of temperance, fortitude and generosity, and the shame and folly of indulging our passions. Now, as Christianity has, as it were, new created the moral and religious world, and set everything, that is reasonable, wise, holy and desirable in its true point of light—one might naturally suppose that every Christian country abounded with schools for the forming, training and practising youths in such an outward course of life as the highest precepts, the strictest rules and the sublimest doctrines of Christianity require. This lofty ideal may be unattainable, but it is hard to imagine that any religious person can do other than aim at a measure of it and regret that any difficulty should be in the way of religious instruction. But the differences in belief certainly create a very real difficulty. The question is whether the loss from the absence of religious teaching is not so grave that every effort must be made in the interest alike of the child and the state to overcome the difficulty as far as possible. This is simply all that time will allow me to consider with you to-day.

There has been now considerable opportunity for forming a judgment on the probable effects of pure secular education. Such an education has existed in France for over ten years, and in the Australian colony of Victoria for twenty years. So perfect is the educational system in this colony that only one out of two hundred of school age was absent from school. Very full evidence has been collected of the effects, more or less traceable to this instruction. I cannot, in my limited time, lay it but very partially before the Synod; but, with the consent of the Synod, I shall, at my own expense, place some valuable papers and speeches on the subject in the appendix of the Synod report. At present I wish to point out certain inferences that may clearly be made out from these papers.

1. Pure secular education leads to a growing want of appreciation of the importance of religion—and so to an indifference, if not hostility to religion. The known exclusion of religious teaching makes religion itself be felt as something extra and superfluous, with which the children should not be troubled, and which is of secondary importance. This has a most deadening effect on the religious feelings of the young, and thus, as has been said, silence on religious topics during the school hours proves to be a measure of positive hostility to faith.

This is found to be the case under the most favorable circumstances, when the parents are church-going and there is still in the community a degree of religious earnestness. Thus in Wales, where the people are professedly religious, but in which most of the board schools, especially numerous there, have established pure secular education, we are told that, while the young weaver or tinplater used to go to Church, Chapel, and Sunday School almost without exception, now they loaf about the country lanes on Sundays in dozens.

It need not, then, be wondered at, that where the tone of the community, as in France, is largely antagonistic to religion, the supposed neutrality of secular education develops into a vehicle for infidelity and atheism. Many Frenchmen affirm that religious neutrality has proved unattainable. They say it is impossible.

2. Pure secular education leads to a growing unfamiliarity with Holy Scripture.

"The fact has to be faced," reports Mr. Russell, a teacher of long experience, and now inspector of schools in Victoria, "that a very large percentage of our state school pupils are growing into adult life with little or no knowledge of the Bible."

And this unfamiliarity is not at all confined to those who do not attend Sunday Schools. An English clergyman thus writes of the Sunday Schools he visited in Victoria and New Zealand:

"I noticed the ignorance of the Bible, which extends to familiar Scriptural biographies. While in respect of intelligence and general knowledge the children were quite up to the level of children of the same age and class educated in the best elementary schools in England, they fell considerably below them in religious knowledge."

Archdeacon Stretch, of Melbourne, says that once there was not this deficiency. He remembered when the elder classes could pass a highly creditable examination in both Testaments; but now a child is rarely found who knows anything of the old Testament, and as for the knowledge of the new, it is for the most part of the very thinnest description. It seems, then, that the efficiency of the Sunday School depends on the possession of an amount of religious knowledge not there acquired.

3. Pure secular education has been accompanied by a deterioration of tone and character in the young, as marked by want of respect for parents, elders, masters and superiors, by a neglect of the Sabbath, by a lawless and insubordinate carriage, and the grievous fact of rather an increase of crime than that decrease, which should follow the very improved secular instruction, if it was healthy. The Victorian Year Book states that 12,169 male criminals were convicted in 1880, and 20,189 in 1890—that 31 were convicted of murder or manslaughter in 1880, and 56 in 1890—that 245 were convicted of crimes of robbery with violence in 1880, and 465 in 1890, while the proportion of educated criminals in 1889 was 74 per cent., and in 1890, 89 per cent. We read that in France the houses of correction are gorged with boys and girls. Juvenile crime is increasing at a truly frightful rate. In 1886 there were 5,606 prisoners under 16; in 1888 there were 7,351; yet in France the number of children of school age is actually decreasing. The late chief of police in Paris, after stating that the young criminals sprang up like weeds between the cracks of the pavement, said it was the natural fruit of the "secularization law." One of the French judges has called public attention to the fact that the increase of juvenile crime was beyond doubt coincident with the changes introduced into public instruction. The official report to the Prefect of the Seine, by the inspectors of workshops and factories in Paris, states :

> We have noticed with pain the lack of moral instruction in those children (the juvenile employees), although they have attended the courses of morals in the schools they show little trace of it. It is an unpleasant duty to report, Mr. Prefect, that for want of moral education the children are losing all notions of respect and duty, and are becoming addicted to bad language. Their conduct in the public street is often scandalous, and many employers will no longer engage apprentices, on account of the troubles they cause. It is high time to put an end to these moral disasters.

In Wales there is a general complaint with respect to the young of waywardness of conduct, bad language, disobedience to parents, intolerance of reproof.

4. The attempt to teach morals apart from the Divine sanction of the Bible utterly fails.

In France, while all religious instruction is forbidden, provision is made for instruction in moral and civil duties. The minister of public works instituted an inquiry and appointed a commission to conduct it. Reports were made by the inspectors of schools. The conclusion of the commissioner was:

> The religious sentiment is inseparable from morality. Moral teaching cannot be effectively given without its aid.

We have exactly the same report from Victoria. The reports of the inspectors of schools, all laymen, tell one story. Extracts will be given from a number of them in the appendix. Time will only allow me to say that the purport of their reports is that there is now little moral teaching in the Victoria schools, that that little is felt to be perfectly ineffective, and that the want of a standard of appeal, such as the Scriptures, is a fatal objection to the expedient of using a text book in morals instead of teaching religion.

5. The efforts to supply religious education independently of the schools fail.

Three ways suggest themselves: By family instruction, by week day instruction out of school hours, by Sunday school.

As to the first, religious education will be given systematically by few parents, not at all where most needed. The Bishop of Manchester, formerly Bishop of Melbourne, thus explains what happened with the other methods in Victoria:

> The ministers of the different bodies met the children on the week days. Lessons were tried before the schools began, after they finished, and on the Saturday holiday, but they universally and signally failed. But you may say surely the churches did something on the Sunday, if they could not on the week day. I was told, "Oh, yes, the Sunday schools will make up for all the defects of the secular system." But these are the facts. In 1883 there were 71½ per cent. of the children of school age attending Sunday schools. Seven years later, in 1890, there were only 39 per cent. No wonder! If parents and children alike believe that religious instruction may be neglected, how can you expect them voluntarily to attend a Sunday school?

In France the experience has been the same. The schools were closed on one day in the week besides Sunday, " that parents, if they so desired, might have the opportunity of getting their children instructed in religion outside of the school buildings." And the Protestants, overjoyed at the abatement of the priest's influence, and relying on the potency of their Sunday and Thursday classes, welcomed in fact the new law without reserve. But they have been undeceived. They now agree in declaring its results deplorable. The Thursday classes have failed them. The religious instruction on one day is found insufficient, and even the attendance on Sunday schools has fallen off.

Lastly, a system of pure secular instruction fails to be a national system with any truth. Denominational schools gradually rise up, and are maintained at great cost. Notwithstanding the excellent secular instruction in the French schools, out of the whole five and-a-half millions of primary scholars in 1890, more than one-fifth (in Paris two-fifths), were in private and denominational schools, and yearly the difference lessens. In 1890 the whole number of scholars in primary schools fell off by nearly 22,000, owing to the decrease in children of school age, but while the public schools lost over 40,000, the other schools gained nearly 20,000. I have hitherto avoided referring to the United States, as, though the evils of which I have spoken are lamentably apparent there, it is difficult to separate the causes on account of the enormous immigration and its mixed composition. But on this head the statistics speak plainly. The Federal Commissioner, whose duty it is to collect, at the central bureau in Washington, educational statistics from the several states, reports that there is continually going on a transfer of pupils from the state schools to private and denominational ones. In 1888 the enrolment of scholars in these voluntary schools exceeded a million, and the numbers on their books increase from year to year much more rapidly than those in the state schools. Mr. Fitch, one of Her Majesty's chief inspectors of schools, was commissioned by the British Government to report on the school systems of America and France. This is how he explains this constant outflow from the state schools:

"By far the most potent of all the influences that are thus detaching so many scholars from the common schools are to be found in the religious objections to the school system."

He adds:

"At great personal sacrifice many of the congregations keep up elementary schools at their own cost, in order that they may impart in them the religious instruction to which the several religious bodies attach most importance."

The conclusion of Mr. Fitch is:

"Where the state system absolutely excludes religious instruction from its purview, there grows up side by side with it a rival system outside of the national school organization, and in part hostile to it, administered by religious bodies, maintained at their own cost and that of the parents, receiving neither aid nor supervision from public authorities. Experience seems to prove that in such circumstances the number of voluntary and denominational schools tends to increase, and the separation in feeling and interests between such schools and the common schools more marked, while the area of the state's influence over public education becomes *pro tanto* restricted."

This is his inference from his observation:

"A secular system, pure and simple, it would appear, is incapable of becoming a truly national system."

There can be no doubt what would happen in England if the present assistance to separate denominational schools were to cease. Since 1870 the Church of England has raised for its parish schools ninety millions of dollars. It is providing for the education of two and a-half millions of children. The church that has made such sacrifices to secure a full religious education for its children would not be found wanting. Many schools would be closed, many others would have inferior instruction, but so many schools would still be carried on that a government system of secular education in England, that some strive after, might call itself national, but it would be so in name, not in reality.

Now, what is the position of primary education with ourselves? There is no religious instruction, and yet we should be thankful that we are much farther yet from the position of France and Victoria than many perhaps think. There is a short prayer, concluding with the Lord's prayer, acknowledging the need of divine guidance and blessing, and asking God for these gifts. "The fear of the Lord is the beginning of knowledge." There is the reading of a passage of the Bible thereby confessing the unique and supreme position of the word of God. "Wherewithal shall a young man cleanse his way, even by taking heed thereto, according to Thy word." Then in the teaching of morals there are the Ten Commandments, thereby recognizing the Divine sanction for the moral law. Now, these are not small things in themselves, but they are doubly important, because they carry with them for the teacher a degree of liberty in his teaching of what may come before the classes in their literature or otherwise. God is not excluded as in France, nor the name of our Lord Jesus Christ, that blessed name that is above every name, suppressed as in Victoria. But what would be the position if prayer were forbidden—if the Bible were made a sealed book—if the Ten Commandments were excluded? It is very clear that if the Legislature were to make these changes, then our teachers would be in the painful position of those in Victoria. Mr. Rennick, inspector of the schools in that colony, reports:

"The teachers feel in giving these lessons (on morals) they are treading on debatable ground, while the sanctions of Scripture are expressly forbidden by the department."

The teachers who ignore these exercises can hardly be realizing their position as Christian men, if as a result of the indifferentism of themselves, of many school trustees and others, the Legislature should forbid all religious exercises. Surely the principle at the root of such a prohibition must be carried out far beyond the mere exercises. Words and ideas would be daily meeting them in history and literature that would have to be passed over in silence, unless the example of Victoria was also followed in expurgating the text book. As to the charge that these religious exercises make the schools Protestant, I think it sufficient to say that in the English school boards the members of the Church of England mainly rely on the help of the Roman Catholic members to secure in the board schools a measure of religious instruction, and, therefore, I think I am warranted in saying that such an objection here, whether made by themselves or by others for them, is rather with the ulterior object of making the present schools more obnoxious to many than they even now are. But regretable as the removal of these exercises would be, they are only palliative. Potent forces are, I believe, for the time in action within our small community stimulating church attendance and church interest, but by and by, we shall have a larger population and then the evils that show themselves elsewhere from the want of religious instruction, will, I have no doubt, present themselves here. But however dissatisfied we may be with the position of religious instruction, for the present we are helpless. If we attempt anywhere a separate school there must be no deficiency in the secular instruction. Even our best town parishes are not in a financial position yet to do this, and discharge the pressing duties for the Church upon them. But if things remain as they are, and still more if they get worse, our clergy must be very different from the 20,000 clergy of the mother land, if after some years when it becomes practicable, they do not encourage schools of our own.

Into the wide and difficult question of securing more satisfactory arrangements with the state I cannot now enter. But I think the Synod might do well to pass a resolution expressing the hope that there will be no interference with the present religious exercises and authorizing the appointment of a committee to deal with any opportunity that may present itself in conference with other bodies or otherwise, for securing a measure of religious instruction. In the meantime we should do all we can. The clergy should exert themselves to establish Sunday schools. Care must be taken that they do not occupy the time merely in interesting the children with stories or in giving addresses with good advice, but that they instruct their classes in the fulness of the Christian faith. That is often a different thing. In the Catechism with its teaching on the Commandments, Lord's Prayer, Creed, and Sacraments, and in the collects, epistles, and gospels bringing before the children during the year a very full view of the counsel of God, we have an admirable course of instruction. With this there should be combined Scriptural lessons partly historical and partly exhibiting the teaching of the day or season. A union school can never adequately take the place of a Church school. It may be very useful where a Church school cannot be maintained as long as it is not made subservient to the interests of some special denomination, but the usual instruction of a union school, however useful in its place, can only supply the scriptural foundation for the full systematic instruction in the faith, which the children of the Church should have.

Secondly, the clergy should impress on their people the duty of bringing their children and young people to Church, and of having them sit beside them. The Sunday School is invaluable, but it must not take the place of the Church of God.

After the formal opening of the afternoon sitting Archdeacon Fortin presented the report of the committee appointed to consider his Lordship's address. The report was as follows, so far as relates to education :—

Your committee, in common with the whole synod, have heard with profoundest interest the weighty and supremely important deliverance of his lordship as to the disastrous effects of a purely secular system of primary education. In view of the facts cited and the considerations urged by his lordship, this committee would propose the following motions for the adoption of the synod :

1. Resolved, that this synod cordially thanks his lordship, the metropolitan, for the words which he has addressed to it on the subject of primary education; and would respectfully request him to allow of the combination into one pamphlet of that part of his charge, along with those other papers on the same subject to which he referred, so that such a pamphlet may be very widely circulated through the whole province, with a view to informing and moulding public opinion on this subject.

2. Resolved, that, while this synod would gladly see a larger measure of religious teaching in our schools than at present prevails, it trusts that every effort will be made, both by the educational authorities and by the Christian public generally, to render existing regulations on the subject as widely operative and efficient as possible.

3. Resolved, that whatever changes in the school policy of this province may in the future be required for the satisfactory solution of the educational problems with which, as a province, we have to deal, this synod stands pledged to resist to the utmost any attempt to secularize our public schools.

4. Resolved, that his lordship the metropolitan be requested to name a committee of this synod whose duty it shall be to give special and continuous attention to the subject of religious education both in its general bearings and in its special relations to the educational policy of this synod, with power to take such action as may seem to them from time to time to be desirable.

CHAPTER V.

EDUCATION : NOT SECULAR NOR SECTARIAN, BUT RELIGIOUS.

—BY THE—

REV. J. M. KING, D.D.

A Lecture Delivered at the Opening of the Theological Department of Manitoba College, Winnipeg, October, 29th, 1889.

The subject of common school education is one which is likely to engage in the near future the public mind in this province to an extent which it has not hitherto done. Important changes are foreshadowed as in contemplation. An attempt is to be made, it appears, to terminate a system which, however accordant with the views of a section of the inhabitants, can never, and especially as it has been wrought, be other than unacceptable to the great majority. The best thanks of the country are due, one need not hesitate to say, to any government which makes an honest endeavour to remedy the existing evils and place the matter of public school education on a more satisfactory basis.

The subject is confessedly one of more than ordinary difficulty, even as it is one of the very last importance. It has not, indeed, any very close or obvious connection with the work with which, whether as arts or theological students, we are to be engaged. It is neither a question of philosophy nor of theology, strictly speaking; yet it has claims upon our attention at this moment as one of the colleges of the province, which only a few questions, whether of philosophy or theology, possess. It is at least a live question and may soon become a burning one. The present lecture is given, not as an adequate or exhaustive discussion of the subject, but as a humble aid to its better understanding by the people of this province, with whom, it is to be hoped, its ultimate settlement within the limits of Manitoba will be found to rest.

Numerous questions are raised when we direct our minds to the consideration of this subject. What form should public school education assume; education, that is, the details of which are determined and its cost met in part at least by the state? Should it be restricted to the elementary branches, or should it embrace the higher branches also? Should it be entirely free or only partially so? In particular, should it be purely secular? or should it be at the same time religious, and if religious, in what

[179]

form is the religious element to find place? What I have to say this evening will have reference to the last only of these questions, which, however, is also by far the most important.

A purely secular system of education: one, that is, in which there should be no attempt to combine religious instruction or religious influence with the teaching of reading, grammar and other such branches, has some strong and obvious recommendations, especially in the present divided state of religious opinion. First, it is in strict accord with what appears to be the modern view of the function of the State. According to this view, it is no part of this function to teach religious truth. That lies wholly within the domain of conscience, a domain which a power wielding the sword may not enter. Civil government, it is claimed, has been instituted for quite other purposes than that of propagating religious opinions, however true and however important. To use its resources for this end is to misuse them, and in doing so even to render a doubtful service to the truth which it has espoused. Again the purely secular system of education escapes numberless difficulties which are apt to arise when religious teaching is made to form an integral part of the system. There is no longer any question of what kind and amount of Christian instruction should be imparted. There is no more any room for the jealousies of rival denominations, so far as the school system is concerned. No branch of the Church, Protestant or Catholic, can feel that another is getting the advantage of it, when all are treated alike, the religious opinions of all being equally ignored. Within one domain, at least, there is absolute freedom from ecclesiastical quarrels, the bitterest of all quarrels as our legislators are accustomed to say, with that happy blindness to the character of their own contentions which is so common. Now, even admitting that the statement proceeds on a somewhat exaggerated estimate of the danger to peace and good feeling arising from religious instruction finding a place in the public school, it is an obvious gain to have in its exclusion the door shut against one element of jealousy and discord. It may be added as another advantage, that with religious teaching relegated to the home and to the church, so much more time is left for those secular branches which all admit ought to form the staple of public school instruction, and which in our day have become numerous enough to tax the brain and the time both of teachers and pupils. In the light of such considerations as these, it is not, perhaps, astonishing that a purely secular system of public school instruction should present itself to many persons as the best, or if not the absolutely best, yet the best practicable in a community where such diversities of religious opinion exist as exists among ourselves. Is it the best, then, or even the best practicable? Is it good at all? I do not think so, and it will be my aim in the first part of this lecture to support this opinion in the calmest and most dispassionate manner in my power. First, then, I ask you to notice, that when the purely secular system of education is supported on the plea that it is no part of the function of the State to teach religious truth, consistency demands the exclusion of all religious ideas from the authorized text books, even to that of the Divine existence, which is not only a religious truth, but the fundamental truth of religion. If there must not be religious instruction in the public school, if the reading of the Bible even must form no part of the exercises, because the State, which sustains the school, transcends its legitimate and proper sphere, when it undertakes to teach religious truth, then, on the same ground, any literature which expresses religious opinions or appeals to religious sentiments or enforces religious obligations, must be excluded from the books used in the class-room, or these must be purged of the obtrusive if not obnoxious element, prior to their admission. The principles of morality, if enforced at all by the teacher, must be enforced by considerations altogether distinct from the authority, the character or the will of the Creator. The Ten Commandments, giving the summary of the Divine will in relation to man and the basis for over three thousand years of human morals, cannot be taught. Such are the conclusions which we are compelled by a resistless logic to accept, if we adopt the fundamental principle of secularism, viz., that the state oversteps its proper sphere when it undertakes to teach religious truth, and on that principle argue for the exclusion of the reading of the Bible or any definite religious instruction from the exercises of the public school. And some have not hesitated to accept them in their entirety. France, logical, if anything, has done so. It has not, indeed, adopted the blasphemous atheistic catechisms which have been long current among a certain class of the population, but it has, if I am rightly informed, with an unhappy consistency, entirely removed the name of God and the whole group of ideas connected therewith from the text-books which it puts into the hands of its youth. An Australian colony, too, has not hesitated, in conformity with the secularistic principle, which it has adopted, to excise from a passage of Longfellow the lines expressive of religious sentiment, before giving it a place in the book of lessons. The people of Manitoba, I feel sure, are not prepared for any such course in the matter of public school education. And in rejecting it—in regarding it with instinctive revulsion—they must be viewed as at the same time repudiating the purely secular view of the state and its functions on which it is based and of which it is the logical outcome.

So far, however, the conclusion is a purely negative one. Religious instruction in the public schools is not ruled out by the character of the state as a civil institution. But even if admissible, is it expedient? Is it requisite? The answer to this question, which is one of the very highest importance, can only come from a consideration of the end contemplated in public school education. What, then, is the aim of the state in instituting and maintaining public schools? There will probably be very general accord on this point. The aim surely is, or at at least ought to be to make good citizens, as far as education can be supposed to make such; citizens who, by their intelligence, their industry, their self control, their respect for law, will tend to build up a stong and prosperous state; citizens whose instructed minds, whose trained powers, whose steadfast principles will serve to promote the public welfare. This, and neither more nor less, must be the aim of the public schools in the view of the state, and as far as supported by it; not more,—it overshoots the mark when it seeks to develop the purely spiritual qualities, the graces of a religious life, except as these are subservient to the origination and growth of civic virtues; and not less, it falls as far short of the mark when it is viewed as designed simply to give instruction in reading, arithmetic and other such branches, and thereby to promote intelligence and to train intellect. The idea of the institution is most defective, so defective as to be virtually misleading, which makes the school simply a place for imparting knowledge, or in addition, an intellectual gymnasium. It should be beyond question, that the state, in undertaking the work of education, can only find an aim at once adequate and consistent in the preparation of the youth, so far as public education can prepare them, for the parts they have to play in civil life. In a single word, the aim of the public school is to make good citizens, or to train the youth of the state, that they shall become good citizens. But to make good citizens, the school must make good men. Character is at least as requisite as intelligence, virtuous habits as trained intellect, to the proper equipment for life. The prosperity, whether of the individual or of the State, rests on a treacherous basis, which does not rest on integrity and self control. It is often the precursor of ruin. Against that ruin, learning whether of the school or of the college, is but a feeble barrier. Nay, learning divorced from morals, disciplined intellect disengaged from the control of virtuous principle may only make that ruin more speedy and more complete, may have no other result than to give us more skilful swindlers, or more expert thieves. In this way, the school instructing the mind and cultivating the intellectual facilities while disregarding the moral nature, constitutes a real danger and may become a positive injury both to the individual and to society. In any case it must be obvious that the good man is necessary to constitute the good citizen, and the education therefore, which is to promote the society and welfare of the state must be capable of forming good men—it must at least aim at doing so.

But to make good men there must be moral teaching and moral training; that is, there must be both instruction in the principles of morality and the effort to see that these principles are acted out by those in attendance on the school. The virtues of truthfulness, purity, gentleness, self-control—the virtues which go to make good men if in any sense native to the soil of our fallen nature, find much in it to retard their growth. They need to be cultivated. The opposite vices, falsehood, selfishness, angry passion, will show themselves more or less in every school room, and every play ground. They will need to be wisely but firmly repressed. The school, if its aim be to make not simply expert arithmeticians, correct grammarians, but truthful and upright men, pure minded and gentle women, cannot disregard the workings of the moral nature, as these come out from day to day within it, now on their better side, now on their worse. The better must be fostered and encouraged, the worse checked and in some cases punished. The conscience must be appealed to. The sense of duty must be cultivated. The habit of obedience must be taught. It is true that the public school is not primarily a school of morality any more than it is primarily a school of religion, but a teacher charged with the oversight of children for five or six hours a day during the most formative period of life, may not ignore the moral nature, as it reveals itself every hour in his presence. He must rebuke or punish indolence, falsehood, rudeness, malice, even as he must encourage diligence, truthfulness, purity and gentleness. For him to be indifferent or neutral in the conflict between good and evil, which goes on in the school-room and the play-ground, as really as in the business mart or the legislative hall, of which the heart of the youngest child is the seat, as undeniably as that of the busiest adult, is virtually to betray the cause of right; and in mercy at once to the child and to society, he must make his sympathy with goodness, with right character and right conduct, clearly and decisively felt. At any rate, if the public school is to be the seed-plot of noble character, of generous virtues, and not simply of scholastic attainments, if it is to furnish society with good citizens, and not simply with smart arithmeticians or possibly with apt criminals, there must be found in it, not only methodical instruction and careful intellectual drill, but amid all else, as the occasion offers or requires, moral teaching and moral influence. The presiding genius in every school, a genius which may be often silent but which should never sleep, ought to be a lofty and generous morality.

But (and this forms the last link in the argument against a purely secular system of education) moral teaching, to be effective in the highest degree, or in any degree near to the highest, must lean on religion and be enforced by its considerations. It is this position especially that the apologist for a purely secular system refuses to accept. It is claimed that it is possible to teach morality, and morality of a high kind, without introducing the religious element in any form. Everything turns here on what is meant by the teaching of morality. If by this is meant simply pointing out in words what is proper and dutiful in human conduct, defining the duties which men owe to each other, then it is possible. The summaries of morals which are found in the agnostic literature of the period, not the less excellent that they are, in good part, borrowed without acknowledgment from the Bible, demonstrate its possibility. But to how little purpose are duties pointed out in the school-room, or anywhere else, if there are no considerations presented enforcing their performance, no sanctions of a high and sacred kind to secure them against neglect or violation. The whole end contemplated in the teaching of morality, is to bring the teaching into practice, to have the precept translated into action. And the main difficulty in the attainment of this end, as everyone knows, has always been in connection, not with the rule, but with the motive; it has always been, not to point out the direction in which the life should move, but to cause it to take this direction, in spite of the deflecting force at work. The failure of Pagan systems of morality was far more due to defective sanctions, than to wrong rules of conduct; and the vice and crime which are found in every Christian country to-day are in only a small degree the result of ignorance of what is right. They are mainly due to sinful dispositions, some of them inherited, to unbridled appetites, and to the force of bad example. Now the problem is, to find and to bring into play a motive or a cluster of motives powerful enough to overcome these forces of evil, and to carry the life in spite of them towards what is good. In the absence of religion, with that sphere closed, where is the public school to find such a motive? Denied access to those which religion supplies, by what considerations is it to enforce obedience to the moral rules which it lays down? There are, of course, considerations of expediency, of self-respect, of the authority of the teacher, and the fear in extreme cases of the rod which he wields, to which appeal can be made, but who would expect noble and generous character or action as the result? It is undeniable that the highest and most powerful motives of right conduct lie within the religious sphere. Even if it does not require the idea of God to render the conception of duty intelligible—to ground it—as many think it does, it is certain that the being and character and moral government of God give to the word duty a new force, and invest the whole details of duty with a new sacredness, presenting them as the embodiment of the Creator's will. It is not less certain, that added hatefulness and terror gather round falsehood, selfishness, injustice, all that is undutiful and wrong, when it is viewed as the object of His displeasure "in Whom we live and move and have our being;" while a whole circle of moral excellencies, patience, meekness, gentleness, considerate regard for others, self-denial, do not so much gain added charms, as they almost come first into distinct sight, when they are enjoined in the words and displayed in the life of the Saviour of mankind. There may be a select few—persons of philosophical thought, who can dispense with these sanctions of morality or who think they can; whose observance of duty rests on some other grounds, but to the great bulk of mankind, and very specially to children, they furnish the strongest and most appreciable motives to virtuous action—they are the indispensable supports of right conduct. To me, therefore, it is as certain as any moral truth can be that to shut out religion from the public school, and thus to refuse to the teacher the employment of these sanctions, is to render the moral teaching weak and ineffective and therefore to defeat the very end which alone justifies the state in maintaining the school, the training of good citizens, or at the very least, to make the attainment of that end far less complete than it might be. Even Huxley says: "My belief is that no human being, and that no society composed of human beings, ever did, or ever will, come to much unless their conduct was governed and guided by the love of an ethical idea, viz., religion. Undoubtedly your gutter child may be converted by mere intellectual drill into the 'subtlest of all the beasts of the field,' but we know what has become of the original of that description and there is no need to increase the number."

The necessity of religious truth to effective moral teaching would be admitted by some, not by all, of the advocates of a purely secular system of public education. It would be more or less fully admitted by most of them who are professedly Christian men. But the ground is taken, that while the knowledge of religious truth is desirable, even indispensable, it is best, especially in the divided state of opinion on religious questions, that religious instruction should be communicated by the parent and by the Church, and that the school should confine itself to instruction in the secular branches. This is plausible; it is no more. I believe the position to be essentially unsound. For, first, if moral teaching, enforced by religious considerations, is requisite in order to make good, law-abiding citizens, that is, in order to promote the security and the well-being of society, the state ought to be able itself to furnish it, and ought to furnish it in the schools which it maintains. It is not denied for a moment, that there is a kind and amount of religious instruction which is more competent to the parent and to the Church, that there are aspects of religious truth, as for example, the nature and the necessity of regeneration, the work of the Holy Spirit, with which perhaps these alone should be expected to deal, but the more general truths of religion, as the existence, the character and the moral government of God—such truths as, we have seen, add to the sanctions of virtue and strengthen the sense of duty —these it must be competent for the state to teach, otherwise it does not possess the means for its own preservation and for the protection of its own well-being. Second, the restriction of the school to purely secular instruction, with the relegation of religious instruction and even moral on its religious side, to the home and the Church, gives no security that the latter will be supplied at all in many cases. There are not a few parents, even in our favored land, who are too indifferent to impart moral and religious teaching to their cihldren, not a few whose own character and habits render them quite incapable of effectively doing so. And while the churches, Protestant and Catholic, are active, there are no doubt many children and young persons not found in attendance on the Sabbath schools with which they have dotted the surface of our vast country. The scattered nature of the settlements renders attendance in these more difficult, and, in any case, the churches have no authority to enforce it, if the youth are indifferent or indisposed. Make public education strictly secular, and it can scarcely fail to happen, that in cases not a few the youth of the province will get their arithmetic and grammar from the school, their morals from the street corner or the saloon. This is not a result which any thoughtful and patriotic citizen can contemplate with satisfaction. And lastly on this point, the division of instruction into secular and sacred, with the relegation of the one to the public school and of the other to the home and the Church, which is the ideal of some who should know better, proceeds upon a radical misapprehension of the constitution of man's being, in which the intellectual and moral nature are inseparably intertwined, and in which both parts are constantly operative. It ignores the fact that man is a single and indivisible entity. It is possible to divide the branches of knowledge, but it is not possible to divide the child to whom they are to be taught. Above all, it is not possible to keep the moral nature in suspense or inaction, while the intellectual is being dealt with. This is the point on which the whole question before us turns. The opinion of one who has not taken it into account is very little. The child can pass from one branch of secular instruction to another. He can be taught arithmetic this hour, grammar that, and in learning the second he ceases to have anything to do with the first, but in learning the one and the other he continues to be moral; he cannot cease to be this any more than he can cease to breathe and yet live. During the whole six or seven hours daily that he is withdrawn from under the eye of the parents, who are supposed to be primarily if not exclusively responsible for his moral and religious training (for the two in any effective sense must go together), amid lessons and amid play his moral nature is operative, sometimes very actively operative, the principle and habits of a life time are being formed under the teacher's eye. Has the teacher any responsibility in the premises: Must he not hear the profane word in the playground? Must he not observe the falsehood that is spoken in the class-room? Must he look with indifference on the display of selfish feeling as he might look upon a wart on a pupil's hand? Who will say so? The very idea is abhorrent to every right mind. But if he has responsibility for the moral development of his pupil, then there must not be denied to him the most effective instrument, if not for correcting improprieties of conduct, yet for evoking noble and virtuous action, religious truth, the truths of our common Christianity—in other words, the education must not be absolutely secular. The welfare of the child and the welfare of the state alike forbid it.

The consideration that recommends a purely secular system of education to many, notwithstanding its obvious drawbacks, is, if I mistake not, the belief that only through its adoption can the separate schools of the Roman Catholic church be abolished without even the shew of injustice to their supporters. The belief is, in my humble opinion, a mistaken one—but even if it were not a mistaken one—even if it were a fact that separate schools could only be equitably got rid of through the entire secularization of our public school system, much as this end is to be desired, I could not consent to purchase it at such a cost. If the thing is wrong in principle, and likely to be pernicious in operation, is it necessary to say that a right-minded man will feel that he has no liberty to employ it to accomplish any end, however desirable? Truth and right disdain the aid of such weapons. The Roman Catholic church errs, indeed, as most Protestants think, in claiming the absolute right to regulate and control the education of its youth. It is a claim which the state, if it would preserve its independence, cannot afford to concede—cannot allow to be put in operation in schools supported by public funds. But that church has hold of a great truth when it asserts, everywhere and always, that education should be religious, that instruction in the fundamental principles of morality should go hand in hand with instruction in reading and arithmetic. As a Protestant, I am unwilling that it should be left to it to be the only witness for this important truth—important alike to the State and to the Church, and that the Protestant churches, through their abandonment of it, should be to that extent placed at a disadvantage in the conflict, whether with sceptical thought or with depraved conduct. In the interests of Protestantism, therefore, as well as of the public well-being, I would venture to ask those whom my words can reach, or my opinions can influence, to think twice before they give their consent to the banishment of the Bible and religious exercises, and the fundamental truths of the Christian religion from the schools in which the youth of this province are to be taught. If Rome desires to see Protestantism weakened, as we may presume it does, it could wish nothing better than to see it take the twin systems of agnosticism and secularism for its ally in the matter of public school education. A purely secular system of education being open to these grave objections, it is only what we might expect, to find it condemned more or less strongly by the various Christian bodies. Our own church has testified during recent years with increasing unanimity and force, to the importance of the religious element in the instruction given in the public school, and to the desirability of its being enlarged rather than reduced and far less eliminated. And in this respect it has only reflected the trend of opinion among thoughtful Christian people in general. Accordingly corresponding action has been taken by the courts of the other churches. A voice may have been raised here and there in favor of a purely secular system, under the idea that it is demanded by the principle of the separation of Church and State, but the prevailing opinion has been and is unmistakably against it or any approach to it. The truth is, it is not difficult to observe the existence throughout the country of a deepening conviction of the danger to the state and to public morals, without which the state can have no stability, of a system of education in which religion has no place. As it is in our country, so is it elsewhere. In some of the Australian colonies, where the system has been for some time established, it encounters only a fiercer opposition from the Christian bodies as its results became more apparent.

It is not easy to state with exactness what the results have been of the purely secular system of education, where it has been introduced, how far it is responsible for the greater prevalence of certain forms of crime in our day. It is easy to state what, reasoning from general principles, we would expect the results to be; but it takes time, not one year but many to develop fully the consequences of of such an experiment. I could not help, however, being struck with a paragraph in the *Edinburgh Scotsman* for September 21st. In Scotland, if I mistake not, the question of religious instruction is left with the school board of each locality. At the time when the system was introduced great opposition was offered in a certain stirring and somewhat radical border-town of Scotland, to any form of religious instruction in the public school. Now, in the paragraph referred to, the provost of that town is reported as saying, " Matters were getting so bad that he thought the magistrates would have to meet and appoint a public whipper. They were reluctant to send boys of such tender years either to prison or the reformatory, and he thought the appointment of a public whipper was the only way of successfully coping with such misconduct. Not only parents, but teachers were greatly to blame for the reprehensible conduct of the youth of the town who did not seem to be getting the right kind of tuition at school." Is the alternative, then, the Bible in the school, or the whipping post at the police court? And, if so, who would hesitate which to choose?

With these words I pass from the consideration of the purely secular system of public education. I do not know for certain that it is the intention of the government, or of any member of it, to propose its introduction into Manitoba. Hints, indeed something like assurance to this effect, have found their way into the public press. Should this prove well-founded, and the attempt be made to institute a system of public school instruction, in which religion shall be recognized only by its exclusion, I find it difficult to believe that the present House, numbering many thoughtful, Christian men, when it is fully seized of the question, will give to such a measure its sanction. In resisting the attempt, if it is made, members may count on the hearty approval and support of many whose voices are seldom heard, perhaps too seldom, on public questions. The hope may be entertained that a bill seating secularism pure and naked in the public schools will not be suffered to obtain a place on the statute book of this fair province. If the considerations adduced in this lecture have any force, it should encounter the opposition, not only of Christian men, but of thoughtful and patriotic citizens. In my humble opinion, and I trust it is the opinion also of many whom I address, a system of public school instruction, which makes no provision for the recognition of God, which does not even allow such recognition, in which the Bible shall be a sealed book and the name of the Saviour of mankind may not be spoken, and in which the highest sanctions of morality and the most powerful persuasions to right conduct,—those, I mean, which religion and religion alone supplies—are not allowed to be employed—such a system could scarcely fail to be prejudicial to the state, as it ought to be intolerable to the conscience of a Christian people.

At the opposite extreme there is the system of separate or denominational schools, such as to some extent now obtains in this province, a system under which not only is religious instruction given, but the distinctive doctrines and practices of individual churches are taught. Does the continuance and extension of this system promise a solution of the educational difficulty? By no means. Less injurious probably in its operation, it is even more indefensible in principle than the one which has been so freely criticised.

First, it is in direct violation of the principle of the separation of Church and State. It is unnecessary, indeed it would be quite irrelevant, to argue this principle here. It is that on which, rightly or wrongly, the state with us is constituted. I do not understand it to mean that the state may not have regard to religious considerations, such as it shows, when it enforces the observance of the Sabbath rest, or, that it may not employ religious sanctions, as it does when in its courts of law it administers an oath in the name of God; but I do understand it to mean that the state is neither to give material aid to the operations of the Church in any of its branches, nor to interfere with its liberties. Each, while necessarily influencing the other, has its own distinct sphere, and must bear all the responsibilities of action within that sphere. Now, when the right of taxation, and in addition grants of money are given by the state to schools, in which distinctive doctrines and rites of any church, whether Protestant or Catholic, are taught, schools which, while giving instruction in secular branches, are used at the same time to extend the influence, if not to increase the membership of that church, then the principle of the separation of church and state is violated almost as much as if the officiating minister or priest were taken into the pay of the state, and the violation (I say it with all frankness, but without any feeling of hostility to any class), is not more easily borne, that it is mainly in the interest of a single section of the church. The public school is surely meant to be the school of the state by which it is supported. It does not exist to initiate the youth of the province into the details of Christian doctrine, or to prepare them for communion. Its main, if not indeed its sole aim, is to make good citizens; intelligent, capable, law-abiding citizens. But under our present system, schools exist and are maintained by the state which are church schools in everything but in name, which are in fact proselytising agencies. Their establishment in the early history of the province is an inconsistency which is not, perhaps, difficult to explain, but their perpetuation can scarcely fail to be felt by the majority of the inhabitants as a misappropriation of public funds and an injustice to a large section of the community.

Second, the system of separate, or sectarian schools operates injuriously on the well-being of the state. However useful it may be to the church or churches adopting it, enabling them to keep their youth well in hand and to preserve them from any danger to faith or morals which might result from daily contact with those of a different creed, it is in that measure hurtful to the unity, and therefore to the strength of the state. It occasions a line of cleavage in society, the highest interests of which demand that it should, as far as possible be one. It perpetuates distinctions and almost necessarily gives rise to sentiments which are at once a reproach and a peril. I do not think the religious differences between the Roman Catholic and the Protestant churches, small or unimportant. As a Protestant, sincerely and firmly believing our faith to be more scriptural, I could not wish these differences to be thought of little account, but surely it is possible for the one party and the other to maintain steadfastly their respective beliefs without cherishing sentiments of distrust and hostility to the manifest injury of the public weal. And yet they are the almost necessary result of a sectarian system of education. The youth of the country, its future citizens, are separated in the school and in the playground. Separation results in mutual ignorance, and ignorance begets indifference, misconception, sometimes even contempt. This is no fancy picture. One has only to listen to the language and mark the countenance of the children of Winnipeg to-day, when reference is made to those of the other faith, in order to see how much ignorant scorn exists, which could not exist did children of all faiths meet in the same school and associate in the same playground. Surely the state should not, unless compelled to do so, lend the authority of law, and the support of public moneys, to a system of education which so injuriously affects its unity and therefore its stability and well-being.

I do not know whether the province has the power to change the existing system. That is a question of law with which I feel myself incompetent to deal, and which in any case could not be suitably discussed on an occasion like this. One may certainly wish that it may be found to possess the power, or if not, that it may receive it. The system itself of separate or sectarian schools appears to be incapable of justification on any ground of right principle or even of wise expediency. I do not expect to see any permanent contentment in relation to the question while the system is maintained. The conviction will continue to be deeply and generally cherished, that the equities of the situation have been disregarded and that the interests of the state have been sacrificed to meet the requirements of the Church of Rome.

But if a purely secular system of education is deemed in the highest degree objectionable, and a denominational or sectarian system only less objectionable, what is it proposed to establish in their place? I answer, a system of public, unsectarian, but not non-religious schools. It is admitted on all hands that the main work of the school ought to be instruction in the various secular branches. Its primary aim is to fit those in attendance for the active duties of life. But as not inconsistent with this aim, rather as in a high degree subservient to its attainment, it is desired that the religious element should have a definite place assigned to it in the life of the school; that it should be recognized to this extent at least, that the school should be opened and closed with prayer, that the Bible, or selections from it, should be read daily, either in the common, or in the Douay version, as the trustees may direct, that the morality inculcated should be Christian morality and that the teacher should be at liberty to enforce it, and should be encouraged to enforce it, by those considerations at once solemn and tender, which are embraced in the common belief of Christendom. A system of public education of this kind, in which religion has a definite but at the same time strictly guarded place assigned to it, ought to be acceptable to the great majority of the people of this province. It has certainly much to recommend it. It has no sectarian features and yet it is not godless. Religion is recognized in it in such form and degree as to make it possible to give a high tone to the life of the school, as to secure more or less familiarity with the contents of Scripture on the part of every child, and as to make available for the teacher those lofty and sacred sanctions which have in all ages been found the most effective instruments in the enforcement of morality.

I can understand it to be objectionable to agnostics and Jews, possibly also, though one would desire not, to the Roman Catholic church. But with a conscience clause, such as would be properly included, excusing attendance on the religious exercises, where so desired by the parents, there would be no just complaint in the case of the former. The number of people in the province who do not accept the New Testament, even with the addition of those who accept neither the Old nor the New, who do not believe in God, is not large, it may be hoped, will never be large; it cannot be reasonably claimed that the Bible should on their account be excluded from the public school. It would be a travesty alike of justice and of popular government that a mere fraction of the community should virtually dictate the form which public education is to assume contrary to the wishes of the great majority. The people of the province as a whole abide by the Christian faith. The statistics of the several Christian bodies, the amount of money contributed within the province for religious purposes, show the keen and general interest which the inhabitants take in the matter. Well, the schools are theirs, are sustained by their money. Surely they have the uncontestable right to give a place in them to their common Christian beliefs, especially where these are seen to be in a high degree helpful, if not indeed indispensable, to the ends for which the schools exist.

The system, while so far meeting the views of Roman Catholics, as it is distinctly religious, will possibly be objectionable to them as a body, though certainly not to all, as not going far enough. They would desire that the public schools should be free to teach, not only the great common beliefs of Christendom, though these surely embrace, if not all that is most vital, yet enough to enforce the highest morality, but also the distinctive doctrines and rites of the Roman Catholic Church. The teacher, while sustained by public funds, must be free not only to read the Holy Scriptures in the version most approved by the parents, but to read out of them, or to read into them, the worship of the Virgin Mary, the invocation of saints and whatever is held by the Church of Rome. Now I would not willingly be a party to inflicting injustice in any section of the community, and there are special reasons why the claims of our French-speaking Roman Catholic brethren should be fairly and, if possible, even generously considered. They were early in this western land. They have done much, and at great cost—cost not of money only, but of toil and suffering from the native races. But this claim —the claim to teach the distinctive doctrines and rites of their Church in schools sustained by public moneys — is one I have no hesitation in saying, and as entertaining much regard for some among us by whom it is made. I say it with regret which the state ought not to concede, should not feel itself at liberty to concede. It is a privilege, which under the system proposed, is not granted to any other church. No other desires to have the opportunity to teach the distinctive doctrines of Presbyterianism, or Methodism, or even of Protestantism, in the public school, or if any cherish such a wish it would be very properly denied them. There is no room, therefore, to speak of injustice to a class who happen to be in the minority, when exactly the same privileges are granted to them which are granted to other classes of the community. If it is a matter of conscience with the Roman Catholic church (it is obviously not with all its members) that the whole body of the faith, as held by it, should be taught even to the youth in attendance on school and in the day school. I see nothing else for it than that they should establish and support from voluntary contributions the schools in which such teaching is to be given. But it were surely far better that our Roman Catholic fellow-citizens should unite with us in securing a distinct recognition of our common Christianity within the public school, leaving what is distinctive, and what many on the one side and on the other feel to be very important to be taught to the children in the Sabbath school, or in the church, or, better still, in the home.

The statement is sometimes made—it has been made more than once of late in our city—that the ground now taken implies a denial of right to the Roman Catholic minority in the province, one as real as if the privilege of separate schools were withdrawn from the Protestant minority in Quebec. But the schools of the majority in Quebec are, as we might expect—distinctively Roman Catholic. The catechisms and formularies of the Church of Rome are taught in them. It is surely to presume on our ignorance to institute in these circumstances a comparison between the position of the minority in our own province and that of the minority in the province of Quebec. It is to trifle with our intelligence to affirm that the denial of separate schools in the one case would be on a par with its denial in the other. The two cases are really essentially different. No well instructed and impartial mind can put them on a level.

The attempt will no doubt be made to belittle in various ways the importance of such recognition of religion in our public schools as has been advocated.

It will be said, as it has been recently said by a journal published in another province, but with special reference to the situation in this one, that little importance is to be attached to religious teaching of a general character, teaching, that is, from which the distinctive doctrines of the several Christian bodies have been eliminated. For such an assertion there is no good ground whatever. The reverse of it would be nearer the truth. All the most powerful motives to good conduct, all the most effective supports of morality, are found within the common creed of Christendom. They are not the exclusive property of any of the churches. If the unsectarian teaching, therefore, of the public school would not be influential and influential for good, it would be due rather to the lack of skill or of earnestness on the teacher's part, than to the poverty of the resources from which he was privileged to draw.

It is also said that the opening and closing of the school with prayer and reading of the Bible is too small a matter altogether to have much importance attached to it, one way or another. It certainly does not bulk largely in the general exercises. But that settles nothing as to its importance or non-importance. Our national flag is a small thing—a piece of bunting which can be bought for a dime or two. Nevertheless, as it floats over our homes, it represents the power of England. And even so, the divine name invoked in the opening exercises, the open Bible on the desk, holds up to teacher and scholar alike, the presence and the majesty of God. It is true, the exercise may be in some cases little more than a seemly form, just as the exercise of private or domestic worship may be only a form, under cover of which the worshipper dismisses himself only the more securely to a day of unrelieved worldliness. But this possibility is not supposed to constitute a valid reason for discontinuing the exercise in the latter case; nor should it be in the former. It is a reason why school trustees should have more regard to Christian character than they often have, in the choice of persons to be the moral as well as intellectual guides of our youth.

This suggests another objection which is sometimes raised. How few public school teachers, it is said, are really fit persons to conduct the religious exercises referred to? My acquaintance with the teachers of the province is not sufficiently large to enable me to answer this question. Some of them, I know, are among the best, the most consistent and earnest members of the several churches, and if others are of a different character—if the religious principles or the habits of any of them are of such a kind as to make the conduct of public prayer by them, or even the public reading of the Bible, an incongruity, something like a farce, then in any case, whether there are religious exercises or not, they are obviously not fit persons to superintend the intellectual and moral training of the youth of this or of any other province.

It is not the least important consideration connected with this question, though it is often one lost sight of, that the mode of its settlement must have a very marked influence on the character of the public school teachers as a class. Eliminate the religious element entirely, make the relation of the teacher to his pupil, just such as that of the tradesman to his apprentice, only that the one teaches reading, writing and arithmetic, the other a trade or handicraft and the general character of those in the profession will be lowered. There will still be those engaged in it of high moral and religious principle, but the prospect of exercising the profession, and the actual exercise of it, will no longer furnish the same incentive to the cultivation of such principle. Almost the reverse. Religion will be a sort of disqualification, or at least inconvenience, inasmuch as the teacher's mouth must be shut within the school, not only on all which he holds most sacred, but on all which he has found most helpful to his own goodness. Now the real attainment may fall below the standard, will often fall below it in this imperfect world. It will seldom rise above it. With the standard changed, with the position of the teacher lowered by the elimination of the religious element from his sphere, the character of the profession as a whole will be in time lowered also to the invariable injury of the youth and, therefore, of the country.

The final settlement of the question, which is now agitating the community, may be remote. It is possible it may be the work of years. Let us cherish the hope, that, when it is reached, it may be one which will not signalize the triumph of any political or ecclesiastical party, but one in which good men of all parties can take pride, and as the result of which the care and training of our youth shall become an object of greater solicitude to the people of the province, and the profession of the teacher, accordingly rise in general estimation. Gentlemen of the college—whether in the theological or in the arts course, be prepared to contribute your part in accomplishing such a settlement. Your experience in this institution may perhaps throw valuable light on the question to you, as it has helped, if not to shape yet to strengthen, my convictions on the subject. On the benches of this college there have sat during the six years of my connection with it, and there sit to-day representatives of almost all the religious denominations in the province, Episcopalian, Methodist, Baptist, Roman Catholic, and, of course, Presbyterian. The Bible has been read every morning and its teachings have been enforced, as occasion offered or seemed to require. In addition you have been led in prayer by the members of the staff in turn. No one, so far as I know, has taken offence. No one has asked to be excused attendance at the religious exercises on conscientious grounds. We have all, I am sure, been helped by these exercises. The tone of the college life has been assuredly raised thereby. Why take away then altogether from the public school that which we have found at once so inoffensive and so useful? Let the politician give us some better answer than this, that the Roman Catholic Church, her priests at least, demand that we shall either tolerate her sectarian schools or expel the Bible—their Bible as well as ours, from the public schools, and expel it from the public schools with what result? To make it possible for them to recommend or even sanction the support of these schools by their peoples? Not at all; their avowed principles would forbid it; but to give them obviously and undeniably the godless character which will go far to justify their condemnation and rejection of them.

CHAPTER VI.

THE REV. PRINCIPAL GRANT.

(Letter to The Sun—November 16th, 1889.)

I accept your invitation to address a Manitoba audience on the subject of Religion in the Schools, and will endeavor to be brief.

Public schools are a necessity in a free state. Freedom cannot exist where the people generally are uneducated. For freedom is not the mere power of choice, or the right to choose good or evil. No one has a right to do wrong. Freedom means insight of what is good, and the power to do the good, against all forces of prejudice or passion. Educate the people, therefore; that is, make them intelligent and moral if you wish them to remain free.

The state is bound in self-defence to see to it that a public school is maintained in every district. The matter cannot be left in the hands of parents, for many of them are either careless or blindly selfish.

The best school is the family. That, then, is the best public school which is most like the family. The teacher is in the place of the parent for the time being, and what would be thought if the state said to the parent: 'You must not refer to religion when speaking to your children!' Schools will be good only if you succeed in getting good teachers, and you will not get good teachers if you deny them reasonable liberty in their work, that is, liberties within the boundaries of regulations laid down by the government as expressing the reason and conscience of the community.

As a rule, there can be only one school in each district. That is the case in every one of our provinces. It is especially so in Manitoba, where for various reasons population is more sparse than in the older provinces. A system that is dual from top to bottom is, therefore, a great political blunder..

What should be the character of the religious exercises or instruction in the school? This is the question that divides men most, and yet I have always found the difficulty to be theoretical rather than practical. Now, in political arrangements there can be no greater mistake than blindly following a theory, without regard to facts. It is asserted vehemently that the school must be wholly secular in character, because there are differences of religious opinion in the district. But there are far wider and more numerous differences in the country than in any one school district, and yet that does not hinder the Senate from having a chaplain, and the House of Commons from being opened with prayer. No one objects to the appointment of publicly paid chaplains to our penitentiaries and asylums, or to our army and navy; or, where the ship is small, to a regulation that the captain or doctor shall read prayers. A day of thanksgiving to God is annually ordered. One day in seven is rigidly protected by law, and ordinary labor is forbidden thereon. All these things may seem unjust and even oppressive to some individuals, but the state is not likely to forego common rights on their account. We are a Christian people, and the only universally recognized text-book of religion and morality is the Bible. Let the public school then be opened with prayer, and let instruction be given in the Bible or in selections approved by the different churches, or according to a scheme of readings drawn up by a proper committee. There is no practical difficulty in this being done. Let prayers and Bible-instruction be given in the first half-hour of the school-time, so that a strict conscience clause declaring that no child need be present that half-hour whose parents objected shall be workable. How many parents will object? Perhaps one in a thousand, and that one is protected. He gets fuller protection than the man who wishes to work on Sunday, or who objects to paying taxes for chaplains for rascals. I may add here that I do not mean "Reading the Bible without note or comment." Bible-reading is not a fetish. If I could not trust the teacher of my boys to explain the meaning of a Bible-lesson, or allow them to ask questions on it, I would not trust him to teach history or to ask them to sing "God Save the Queen."

But, it may be asked, what would you do in the case of a possibly compact dissentient minority, like Protestants in Quebec or Roman Catholics in Ontario and Manitoba? It seems to me that the Ontario Separate School Law, in its original form might be taken as the basis of a compromise in such cases. It enacts that those who desire to establish separate schools may do so, where they are strong enough to support them. The trustee elections for such, must be the same as for public schools, the teachers must be duly certified, the regular text books on ordinary subjects must be used, and there must be public inspection, and a conscience clause. Each teacher now teaches only from ten to fifty scholars. If there are enough scholars for two schools in one district, the one might be public and the other separate, possibly with good results to both. This matter of separate schools I would leave absolutely to each province. The provision in the Confederation Act, that if separate schools should exist or be established by a province, that province shall not be allowed to abolish them if the more matured intelligence of the people so deserves, is most unwise. People do not care to put even a silk collar around their necks if they are told that they can never take it off.

GEORGE MONRO GRANT.

CHAPTER VII.

SERMON BY REV. DR. DUVAL.

(Preached 25th November, 1889.)

Isa., 54:13—" And all thy children shall be taught of the Lord ; and great shall be the peace of thy children."

I had intended to speak to you upon the public school question some weeks past, but, understanding that the honored principal of Manitoba college intended to make it the subject of his lecture at the opening of the theological department of the college, I felt it most courteous that the field, so far as Knox church pulpit was concerned, should be left untrammeled. And no matter what may be the various shades of opinion upon the subject I am sure we shall all feel deeply grateful to Dr. King for his very able introduction to, and discussion of, the question which, more than any other, is now engaging the public mind.

In the briefer space allotted to me I shall not be able to deal with the question in full, but can discharge at least my sense of duty to the formation of public opinion upon the subject. The matter is one that deals with the highest moral well being of individuals and society—this is its apology for a place in the pulpit. It is your concern and mine to see that our children shall be taught of the Lord, that great may be the peace of our children. And I wish to say at the beginning, the very dignity and sacred concern of the subject should keep all who speak upon it, in the attitude of striving for truth more than victory, and clothe them with a charitable spirit, that the spirit of Him whose essence is love, may guide us to a wise and beneficial issue.

In the *School Times* for November, an editorial, upon the desired change of the University from a mere examining body to a teaching body, speaks of the ministers of the council in this disrespectful language: "The clergy, as a matter of course, are opposed to the change."—which was not true—"but," it goes on to say, "the clerical mind is a mystery anyway, and we would not be much surprised at them opposing anything." Is that a proper way for an organ devoted to education to put before the mind, that is being educated, the whole body of men whose end in life is to teach religion and morals? Comment is unnecessary. I do not know the writer of that editorial, but it savors more of the petulancy of immaturity than the wisdom of experience—the unguarded expression of one who has felt little of the weight of the moral responsibility which attends the formation of minds that are to form society and shape the destiny of the state, and which, in those of experience, has begotten at least the grace of prudence.

Reformers are engaged in work too vital to be carried away with uncalculating enthusiasm.

And the reform we have now before us is a matter of such gravity that we should deal with it kindly, patiently, prayerfully—suffering no sentiment tinctured with prejudice, petulance or political policy to militate against the highest well-being of the people considered as a whole—for the end of the state is the good of the people. Now it is a well digested judgment that the perpetuity of a free state demands the general education of its people.

The state must therefore inquire what is the best mode of securing education, both to maintain itself, and to secure the end for which it exists, namely, the highest well-being of the people—Can it be left to private enterprise?

Centuries of failure have proved this impossible. Can we accept the Roman Catholic idea that the church is the only authorized teacher? Without halting to controvert that dogma upon theological grounds we find (1) That it would be such bad economy as to defeat it. Each denomination cannot sustain schools. And when you make the unjustifiable division into Protestant and Roman Catholic, it is still a serious violation of economy. And if the state should give up the whole matter of education to the churches, permitting the Catholic to make his collection for his schools, and all the rest in a general way unite to make collections for their schools, you would find (2) gross inefficiency. There would remain a vast residuum who from reasons of indifference or poverty, failing to unite, would be left in ignorance; the state would suffer. The only way that the Roman idea could be carried out would be to make the whole state Roman Catholic; that is the old mediaeval notion, and since that church is *semper eadem*, it is not yet out of it. But the world is out of it, and it does not seem possible ever to get it back into it again. It seems necessary, therefore, in order to efficiency and economy, that the state government should take control of what we call public education. (1) The state can tax for its support and gain the greatest results for the least expense. (2) A system of state education creates national sentiment which is much needed. (3) It would insure a coherence of the elements, which by separate schools is sure to nurture hostility. We have no question of the fundamental right of the state to do away with separate schools. If, by the constitution, one class has been specially enfranchised—that I shall leave to constitutional lawyers to decide; but even if it be so, it involves an inequity which, though for peace's sake it has been compromised with, can never stand in the development of constitutional principles which will trend gradually, but certainly, toward equality of rights.

The plain ground taken in the United States is that the government has no power to specialize any denomination or class to a right not enjoyed by all others. And Roman Catholics ought not to claim it for themselves. And the more so because in their schools the education is not simply to make good citizens, but Roman Catholics. On the contrary you could not tell in one of the so-called Protestant schools to what denomination teacher or pupils belonged, except upon special enquiry. Teachers there are simply seeking to bring up the children to Christian morality, leaving all peculiar tenets to the respective churches and families whence they come.

It is an error, therefore, for any one to think that the Province of Manitoba is seeking to do with a Catholic minority what it would not like Quebec to do with a Protestant minority. Manitoba proposes to do away with even the name Protestant schools, much less Protestant influence. She proposes state schools in which you could not distinguish the denominational bias of any teacher. If Quebec will do this, we will all be satisfied—and this can be done. In the State of Ohio I have had a sweet spirited Roman Catholic lady teaching my children in one of the classes of the public schools, and she never obtruded any peculiarity of her church upon them.

But while it is unwarrantable for the respective sects to set up separate schools, upon public funds, to propagate their peculiar tenets, and while I believe the government should inaugurate one system of schools for general public education, I believe it necessary that these schools should have some religious influence exercised over them—it might be as simple as the solemn reading of God's word and prayer.

This is not inconsistent with the separation of Church and State. The prophet can ever exhort the king while he does not rule him. Religious influence is not ecclesiastical influence. The church does not monopolize prayer--prayer is native to the soul. Tacitus, the heathen, speaks with surprise of a tribe of Fins so degraded as not to pray. It was Franklin, not a confessed Christian, the philosopher friend (not in every sense) of Voltaire, who with tremulous solicitude for unity of spirit in the founders of the great American republic, pleaded in terms akin to inspiration, notwithstanding the principle of separation of church and state, for prayer to the source of all Grace for guidance in the national councils. If, then, the people desire prayer at the beginning of their children's studies for grace to mould the mind and purify the heart, it is their natural right to have it. No minority, be it agnostic, infidel, Jew or Roman Catholic, has the right to deny to the majority this natural right; while, on the contrary, the majority has no right to compel the minority to conform in any attitude of mind or heart contrary to its conscience; nor does the majority wish them to conform. Members of Congress have the right to stay away from prayer; so in our schools those who wish can be excused. And that is all the right that the minority has in such a case. Suppose an infidel should go to Congress and say, "I am elected to Congress, but so long as your great majority have prayer I will not come in." What would the majesty of sixty millions of people reply? Would it say, "Well, we will just put it all away to satisfy you?" No; but they would say: "We do not interfere with your conscience, you can come in or go home, just as you please. You can attend prayer or come after it. The Sovereign Law is the state's collected will, which sits empress crowning good and repressing ill."

(2) And what is said of prayer applies to the reading of the Bible; the church does not monopolize the Bible. It is the good book from which churches draw their instruction and strength. But it is also the source of intellectual and moral strength to countless souls that are not allied to any church. Christ is the Light of the World. The Christian principles which that book contains, have for ages been a part of the common law of European civilization, and especially of the people of the British Isles and their colonies. When our fathers came to this continent they came in a general sense as a Christian and Bible-loving people. They read it before starting on their dangerous voyage, and prayed to the common Lord, of whom it speaks, for protection by the way. By its instruction and in its Spirit they gave thanks upon their arrival. They set up homes in its faith; their hearthstones were blessed by its presence; their marriages and baptisms were solemnized under the sanctions of its truth; their funerals were conducted with the sympathy of its grace. It has been with us the symbol of the presence of God guarding the sanctity of the oaths of testators and witnesses in courts of law. Our liberties were born out of it and are sustained by its spirit. Our literature is filled with it. It is the warp and woof of our whole social character and there are few, indeed, to dispute that it is the secret of the virtue and greatness of the peoples whose lives it controls. This being so, call it what you will, "Word of God" by the Christian; "Great Work in Moral Science" by the Agnostic—the people have in it a great heritage, and the majority of the people have *a prescriptive right* to continue its influence in some way as a factor in public education, especially when they impose on no one's conscience—religious or non-religious scruples—excusing all who desire to be excused, from any participation in its instruction. Our Jewish fellow-citizens, Agnostics or Roman Catholics, could not ask more if they have any regard for the rights of the majority, the integrity of the country, and the conscientious duty of that majority to regulate the country and guide it toward what they deem its highest well-being. And

especially do I not see why our Roman Catholic fellow-citizens should object to such an adjustment, seeing that they can hold their own Bibles in their hands, or, if in the majority, choose the Douay version to be read, or be excused from all, as they may elect. The province does not wish to do them injustice. To leave the Bible out of the schools would seem to make those schools more objectionable to them, upon the plea of Godlessness. And as Dr. Duryea well points out, it is not a matter of "the faith" in the Catholic Church that the Scripture shall not be read, but it has been the policy of the leaders of that church, for what seemed to them good and sufficient reasons, to discourage its reading among the common people, and "a matter of policy," he well says, "cannot bind the conscience." And Roman Catholic authorities are not agreed in objection to the reading of the Bible in public schools. Cardinal Manning has published his views to the world by saying "I am glad that the Bible is read in the public schools of England."

The Catholic and Protestant Christians have many fundamental principles in harmony; enough, indeed, to unite in a system of national schools under Christian influence, but not under ecclesiastical control. And a refusal to join in some plan, equitable to all, that will make the province homogeneous, progrsssive and safe, cannot fail to impress the public mind with the belief that our Roman Catholic citizens continue the mediaeval pretensions to the right of absolute control; and, in the absence of that, the policy of the non-affiliation and disposition to draw from the country the strength to ultimately control it. I hope we may not have reason even to suspect it.

And now with regard to those of non-Christian sentiments, I appeal to them to think seriously before they oppose Christian influence in the public schools. And to those younger men who with generous impulses are ready to do what seems broad and generous; I appeal to them to think carefully. The idea of a system of schools without any religious influence, where the Jew and Christian, agnostic and infidel, can all be on the same footing, seems indeed broad and generous. But it is as specious as broad, as dangerous as generous. You are to ask on whose footing you are putting all. Is it not bringing all down to the footing of the agnostic? Is it not asking, perhaps, ninety per cent. of the people whose souls have grown to the idea that in all their ways they should acknowledge God, that He might direct their paths, to say in this most important way, "We will not acknowledge Him, and don't care whether He directs our path or not?" And you ask men of position, faith and Godly principle, to do this for the sake of a small minority who are at best negative on the subject. And you do it heedlessly. You do it while this great majority is willing to excuse this minority from any participation in the feature to which they object. (2) You do it to try a dangerous experiment. *Daniel Webster*, in a masterly discourse upon this subject, puts the question: "In what age, by what sect, where, when, by whom, has religious truth been excluded from the education of youth? Nowhere! Never! Everywhere and at all times it has been regarded as essential." Are we ready to venture the moral well-being of this province upon a nostrum that has had no historic warrant from the various schools of reputable psychic physicians? The experiment has proved a failure in higher education and how much more might we expect it to fail among those less able to appreciate the motives furnished by philosophy.

I have in a letter from Dr. Duryea the case of Cornell University. It was "founded as a secular school and all religious teaching was to be omitted, if not prohibited. The object was to prevent religious bias in the pursuit of intellectual work and scientific investigation."

After the experiment had been fairly tried, and while President White was absent on his foreign mission for the government, the vice-president, himself an avowed agnostic, entered the parlor of the Congressional pastor, the Rev. Mr Tyler, one Saturday night, and abruptly said: "Mr. Tyler, we must have preaching at the University." The pastor with surprise, replied, "What? Do you say that? And pray why?" "Because we cannot do our work without it." "Why not?" "Because we cannot get scholarship." "How is that?" "We have not the motives by which we can get the right spirit and the needful application on the part of the students; they must be moved. And as matters are, they can be moved by moral considerations and religious sentiments." The result was the building of Sage Chapel and the endowment of its pulpit by Mr. Sage's son. And since this, Mr. Sage has endowed a chair of ethics from which principles are set forth in sympathy with the teaching of Christ.

I am lately also informed of another college in the west founded on agnostic principles, but which had to be surrendered to a Christian control for motive power to run it. It is now a Presbyterian Synodical college. This is simple verification of the truth declared by that great German Luthardt, "Religion is, as it were, life's forcing power (Triebkraft), and "it is an actual historical fact that human life owes to religion its best and fullest development." The trouble with all these "no religion" schemes is, they mistake the end of education. When a student in Princeton I learned from Dr. Arnold Guyot, as from no other man, that the end of education was moral well-being. He was not a member of that clerical class who unjustly get the credit from some supposed wise men of having no thought untinctured with religious prejudice — a judgment itself born of narrowness and inexperience. It was Dr. Guyot, the classmate and compeer of Agassiz who, as professor of geology and physical geography, revolutionized America in the study of geography, who delivered five hundred lectures on the moral development of the world; who in his own study said to me: "It makes no difference whether a man is Atheist or Theist, Pagan or Christian, he can never be in harmony with the universe until he accepts and walks by this law that the dirt is to serve the vegetable, the vegetable the animal, the animal the intellectual, the intellectual the moral, whose soul or animating substance is the spirit of God." Such thought from a scientist leads us not only to the truth that the moral is the true end of education, but that its perfection is gained through religious unity with the spirit of God; and this truth is being more and more felt by deep thinkers. If, then, education is to be looked upon, not as a lop-sided, but full development of the whole man in the harmony of all his parts, we must not neglect to daily weave, in the textures of our children's character, the sentiments of reverence and love, trust and gratitude toward God; for if these be lacking, the texture will be coarse, the character incomplete and mean, and the coming generations will fail to manifest those sentiments toward their fellow-men in the degree that they are due. You get no power to make your grateful flowers grow that is not from the sun in the heavens.

If there are men who will not listen to a preacher of the gospel on the subject, let them listen to men of science and philosophy. And to those who think intellectual culture will accomplish everything let them know that the ante-Christian civilizations had their highest intellectual culture synchronous with their most beastial depravity. While philosophy controls in a good degree a few deep thinkers, it has never held back the mass of society from corruption. Not only is intellectual culture unable to give moral security—it often destroys it. Victor Cousin, the profoundest of the French philosophers, in an address before the Chamber of Peers, declared that "any system of school training which sharpens and strengthens the intellectual powers without supplying moral culture and religious principle, is a curse rather than a blessing." Gentlemen, this is worthy of your thought. Mr. Herbert Spencer, after profound research in human culture, says: "The belief in the moralizing effects of intellectual culture is absurd." Dr. Thomas Arnold, the eminent educator, of whom it was said, "If elected to Rugby, he would change the face of education all through the public schools of England," has said, " If, having learned all that they (scientific and literary institutions) can teach us, the knowledge so gained shall hide from us our moral ignorance and make us look on ourselves as educated men, then they will be more than inefficient or incomplete—they will have been to us positively mischievous." Professor Townsend quotes as indisputable the aphorism that "mere intellectual training does not inspire patriotism or reduce crime," and before we make haste to set aside that great book from a controlling influence in public education, let us hear the words even of Professor Huxley: "I have always been strongly in favor of secular education, in the sense of education without theology; but I must confess I have been no less seriously perplexed to know by what practical measures the religious feeling, which is the essential basis of conduct, was to be kept up in the utterly chaotic state of opinions on these matters, without the use of the Bible. By the study of what other book could children be so humanized?" The idea of the respective churches and families being sufficient to offset the moral defect in every-day public education, has its fallacy in a misconception of the nature of the soul, which is a unit. You cannot say to Professor B.: "Take my boy and educate his intellect, and then I will send him to Dr. C. to train his spiritual nature." You might as well say to A., who has been eating immoderately, "Go now and pray the pain away." Religion is to condition the whole life of a man, to bring his every thought, feeling, and action into harmony with virtue. This position I took in a lecture before the Educational Association of the State of Delaware in 1882, and, so far, have seen no reason to change it. Prussia says: "Whatever you would have appear in a nation's life you must put in the public schools." I have no alternative to mention; I believe the province should have one system of public schools; that they should be under Christian influence, and that, with the proper concessions to the consciences of individuals, there will be no injustice to any man. And I am willing to trust the people of Manitoba, under the guidance of God, to keep with integrity that heart which has hitherto thrown, through all their social body, the pure red blood of their better life.

CHAPTER VIII.

EXTRACT FROM A

SPEECH OF MR. JAMES FISHER, M.P.P.

(Delivered in the Manitoba Legislative Assembly, 2nd March, 1892.)

I now turn to another, and a different phase of the question. I suppose it will not be denied that there is a general opinion among the Protestant majority in this province that the educational clauses in the Confederation Act, protecting or purporting to protect the Catholic minority, were incorporated in the constitution at the instance of Roman Catholics. I think I am safe in saying that it is the universal impression in Protestant circles that the Roman hierarchy, or Sir George Cartier, managed shrewdly to protect Catholic interests by the insertion of those clauses. And how often have we heard it remarked that if the public men of the Protestant faith had not failed in their duty, through pandering to the Catholic vote, these clauses would never have appeared in the constitution. Just to give you an idea that I am speaking correctly as to what the general impression is, I will quote from Mr. Dalton McCarthy. Addressing a great Protestant meeting in Ottawa in December of 1889, he said ;—

What have we to boast of as the outcome of the Act of Union? A separate school system imposed on the people of free Ontario by their own votes? No. Search the records and you will find that the Act for the settlement of the separate school question was imposed on the people of the Upper Province by the vote of the people of the Lower Province, and against the will of the people of the Upper Province.

It is entirely correct to say that it was by the votes of the French representatives of Lower Canada, and against the votes of the representatives of Upper Canada, that the separate school system was finally settled in Upper Canada in 1863, and so far I quite agree with the speaker. Mr. McCarthy then takes up the education clauses in the B. N. A. Act, and continues :—

Search the B. N. A. Act and you will see that it was attempted to be fastened on you for all time by this organic law, the B. N. A. Act, as a part of the bargain made at the time of Confederation. That and similar enactments have we to thank for the present state of affairs ; that is the result of Lord Durham's well meant labours. He brought us together, thinking that the English majority would ultimately govern ; he brought us together with the belief that he was doing the greatest possible benefit to us and to them. We came together ; we assembled in a common parliament, but by the skilful direction of the French Canadian vote, and the desire for power among the English and consequent division among them, the French Canadians were ultimately able to place their feet on our necks and impose laws on us contrary to our will, and we came out of partnership taking the smaller share of the assets.

Possibly this language may be open to two meanings, but I understand the statement that the separate school system was "attempted to be fastened on us" by the B. N. A. Act, to mean that it was something sought to be fastened on Protestants by Catholics.

That may be Mr. Dalton McCarthy's opinion, but I want to say if that be his meaning that there is not a word of truth in it; and to prove that I am right let me give you in a few words the situation of the Protestant minority of Quebec before the Union. Quebec, of course, as you all know, is filled chiefly by a French Canadian population. The immense majority are French Roman Catholics. They had in the province two systems of schools as they had in this province before 1890. In Ontario the Catholics had their separate schools; in Quebec the Protestant minority had their dissentient schools. When the proposition for Confederation came up the Protestant minority in Quebec were exceedingly afraid that they would be put under the control of the Catholic majority of that province in respect to education. They made two demands as a condition of union, first, that there would be a provision in the constitution whereby any rights that they had at the Union in respect to their schools should never be taken away from them, so that the legislature of Quebec should have no power to interfere with these rights, and second, that before they entered the Union the school law should be amended so as to remove certain objections then made to it by the Protestant minority. They demanded that the school law should be improved so as to satisfy them, as a minority before the Union, in order that in the future they would have the law as amended guaranteed to them. One of the changes they demanded, as I recollect the history of it, was that they should have a separate board of education. Now it is fair to state that the position of the Protestant minority in Quebec was in my opinion different altogether from that of the Catholic minority in Ontario. In the latter the system of the majority was non-sectarian, in Quebec it was a Catholic system. It was natural therefore that the Protestant minority in Quebec should be anxious about their position in the Union. I now propose to show the demand made by that minority for protection against the provincial legislature.

Mr. L. H. Holton was then, as you will remember, one of the leading Protestants representing Lower Canada. Speaking in the Confederation debate on behalf of that minority at an early period in the debate, he said:

> Another question which he had proposed to put had reference to the educational system of Lower Canada. The honorable gentleman (Sir John Macdonald) must be aware that this was a question on which there was a great deal of feeling in this section of the province amongst the English-speaking or the Protestant class of the population. Among that class there was no phase or feature of those threatened changes which excited so much alarm as this very question of education. Well, the Minister of Finance had said that the

Government would bring down amendments to the school laws of Lower Canada, which they proposed enacting into law before a change of Government should take place, and which would become a permanent settlement of that question. The question he desired to put was whether they intended to submit these amendments before they asked the House to pass finally upon the scheme of Confederation, as it would undoubtedly exercise very considerable influence upon the discussion of the Confederation scheme, and probably in the last resort from several members from Lower Canada.

On a subsequent date Mr. Holton said:

The English Protestants of Lower Canada desire to know what is to be done in the matter of education before the final voice of the people of this country is pronounced on the question of Confederation. To this statement Sir John Macdonald replied : "There was a good deal of apprehension in Lower Canada, on the part of the minority there, as to the possible effect of Confederation on their rights on the subject of education, and it was the intention of the Government, if Parliament approved the scheme of Confederation, to lay before the House this session certain amendments to the school law to operate as a sort of guarantee against any infringement by the majority of the rights of the minority in this matter. . . . Before Confederation is adopted the Government would bring down a measure to amend the school law of Lower Canada protecting the rights of the minority."

Mr. Holton was not satisfied with that, for a few days afterwards he returned to it again and said :

I would like to ask the Hon. Minister of Finance as to the course to be pursued in reference to the Lower Canada school law, which was promised to be introduced this session.

To this the like reply was made as before, but still Mr. Holton was not satisfied, and repeatedly thereafter he brought up the question again, indicating the intense interest felt in the situation by the Protestants of Lower Canada.

Hon. Mr. Sanborn, another Protestant representative from Lower Canada, gave expression to the same feeling as follows :

The English, who were a fourth of the population, and who, by habit and tradition, had their own views of public policy, were left entirely without guarantee other than the good feelings and tolerant spirit of the French. Was this safe ?

In the hope of disquieting these fears of the Protestant minority from his province, Mr. D'Arcy McGee, an Irish Catholic from Lower Canada, said :

I have no doubt whatever, with a good deal of moderation and a proper degree of firmness, all that the Protestant minority in Lower Canada can require by way of security to their educational system will be cheerfully granted to them by this House.

The Hon. George Brown, the noted champion of national schools in Upper Canada, had given special attention to the education clauses, and he recognized fully the deep anxiety felt in Lower Canada on the question. Referring to the satisfaction that existed in Upper Canada with the existing arrangements as to education, he declared that :

> It was not so as regards Lower Canada, for there were matters of which the British population have long complained, and some amendments to the existing school Act were required to secure them equal justice. Well, when this point was raised, gentlemen of all parties in Lower Canada at once expressed themselves prepared to treat it in a frank and conciliatory manner with a view to removing any injustice that might be shown to exist ; and on this understanding the educational clause was adopted by the Confederation.

Sir E. P. Taché, then Prime Minister, in further reply to the fears expressed by Mr. Sanborn, said :

> Mr. Sanborn gave expression to the fear that the Protestant English element of Lower Canada would be in danger if this measure should pass. He said as much as this, that in the Legislature of Lower Canada Acts might be passed which would deprive educational institutions there of their rights, and even of their property. But if the lower branch of the Legislature (that is, the provincial one) were insensate enough and wicked enough to commit some flagrant act of injustice against the English Protestant portion of the community, they would be checked by the general (that is, the Federal) government.

Hon. Mr. Dorion, the chief of the Rouge party of Quebec, referred to the demand made by the Protestants of Lower Canada for protection, and expressed his sympathy with them in these terms :

> There is at this moment a movement on the part of the British Protestants in Lower Canada to have some protection and guarantee for their educational establishments in this province put into the scheme of Confederation, should it be adopted ; and far from finding fault with them, I respect them more for their energy in seeking protection for their separate interests. I think it but just that the Protestant minority should be protected in its rights in everything that was dear to it as a distinct nationality, and should not lie at the discretion of the majority in this respect, and for this reason I am ready to extend to my Protestant fellow-citizens in Lower Canada, of British origin, the fullest justice in all things, and I wish to see their interests as a minority guaranteed and protected in every scheme which may be adopted.

Hon. Mr. Laframboise, a French Catholic from Lower Canada, expressed himself in this candid way :

> There is one certain fact, and that is that the Protestants of Lower Canada have said to the Government, "Pass a measure which shall guarantee to us the stability and protection of our educational system and of our religious institutions, and we will support your scheme of Confederation ; unless you do so we will never support you, because we do not wish to place ourselves at the mercy of a local legislature, three-fourths of the members of which will be Catholics." I admit that in doing this they have only done their duty ; for who can say, after all, what ten years may bring forth.

Sir John Rose, one of the most prominent representatives of the Lower Canadian minority, expressed his sense of the keen feeling that prevailed among his people in these terms :

> It is a very grave and anxious question for us to consider, especially the minority in Lower Canada, how far our mutual rights and interests are respected and guarded.

Again Sir John Rose returns to the subject in these words, referring to the Protestant minority :

> I know you must satisfy them that their interests for all time to come are safe; that the interests of the minority are hedged round with such safeguards that those who come after us will feel that they are protected in all they hold dear.

And again he says :

> Looking at the scheme, then, from the standpoint of an English Protestant in Lower Canada, let me see whether the interests of those of my own race and religion in that section are safely and properly guarded. There are certain points upon which they feel the greatest interest, and with regard to which it is but proper that they should be assured that there are sufficient safeguards provided for their preservation.

And once more Sir John Rose declares :

> I believe this is the first time almost in the history of Lower Canada that there has been any excitement or movement or agitation on the part of the English Protestant population of Lower Canada in reference to the common school question. (Hear, hear.) It is the first time in the history of the country that there has been any serious apprehension aroused amongst them regarding the elementary education of their children. . . . I would ask my honorable friend, the Attorney-General East, whether the system of education which is in force in Lower Canada at the time of the proclamation is to remain and be the system of education for all time to come ; and that whatever rights are given to either of the religious sections shall continue to be guaranteed to them.

To this last question of Sir John Rose, Sir George Cartier answered :

> It is the intention of the Government that in that law there will be a provision that will secure the Protestant minority in Lower Canada such management and control over their schools as will satisfy them.

Col. Haultain, a militant Protestant from Upper Canada, said :

> An opposition to this scheme has been very decidedly expressed by a certain section of the Protestant minority in Lower Canada. I am aware from personal intercourse with many gentlemen belonging to that section of the community that they do feel a very strong aversion to this scheme because, as they say, it will place them at the mercy of the French-Canadians. . . . And I must say, for my own part, that I do think the Protestant minority have some grounds for this fear. . . . I speak what I know when I say there is a feeling of distrust on the part of a great many of the Protestants of Lower Canada.

I have troubled honorable members, Mr. Speaker, with somewhat long extracts from the Confederation debate. I wished to impress on the House that throughout that discussion, from the beginning to the end of it, there was hardly a question raised about the rights that were to be protected by these educational clauses, except for the Protestants of Lower Canada. Hardly one word. The only suggestion that was made on behalf of Roman Catholics was, that if, in answer to the demands of the Protestants of Lower Canada these safeguards were given, it would be only fair that the Catholics of

Upper Canada should have the same protection accorded them. And the broad and fair and tolerant spirit of Protestants like George Brown and Galt, Mackenzie, Macdougall and others prompted them to provide as a matter of course that the same rights which were conceded by Catholics to the Protestant minority, at the urgent demand of the latter, should be conceded to Roman Catholics in the provinces where they were in the minority. Thus it was that the settlement was aimed at in a manner satisfactory to all classes. The House will now see how utterly far from the truth is the oft-repeated and generally accepted statement that the educational clauses of the Confederation Act, protecting the rights of the minority in respect to education, was a concession to Roman Catholic demands.

I now desire to refer to another circumstance connected with this same matter—a circumstance even more striking than that I have referred to—and I dare say some of my honorable friends on the Government benches have not heard of it.

The debate I have quoted from took place in the old Parliament of Canada in 1865, some time before the Confederation Act was adopted. That Parliament was then discussing the Confederation resolutions that had been agreed on between the two Canadian provinces and the Maritime provinces The provision with respect to education, embodied in these resolutions, protected only those rights of the minority which existed at the time of the union, but there was not one word in them indicative of an intention to preserve under Confederation any rights that they might acquire afterwards, although such a provision was afterwards put in the Act. How did the change come to be made? Here's an interesting bit of history that I want to tell you, and you have only to study the debates on the question to find out the truth of it. I read you the promise made by the Government in 1865, that before that session was over they would amend the legislation so as to satisfy the Protestant minority. There was a calamity befell the Government, however, that prevented this being done. There was a defeat of the union scheme in New Brunswick, and the Legislature had suddenly to prorogue without passing the amended law. The Protestant members from Lower Canada protested, but Sir George Cartier, Sir A. T. Galt and the rest of the leaders said, "We promise you we will pass the law next session," and they had in fact another session before the Confederation Act was passed. Well, the Parliament met in 1866, and a bill was introduced to amend the law as desired by the Protestant minority. What became of it? Somebody in the House got up and moved that if that privilege be given to the Lower Canadian Protestants a like privilege ought to be granted to the Catholics in Upper Canada. The Protestant majority of Upper Canada kicked against this, and the Government, seeing that they would be defeated on it, either withdrew the bill or it was defeated.

on coming to a vote. They failed, at all events, to carry out the promise given the Protestants in Lower Canada. What was done about it? It is worth while to recall those interesting events in connection with our position to-day. The Government were thus placed in a most awkward position. The Protestant minority of Quebec had positively refused to come into Confederation if they could not get their law amended, and they had been told that they would never be asked to come in until they got it, and unless it was guaranteed to them for all time to come. The difficulty thus threatening the Union was solved by Sir George Cartier, the great chief of the Catholic Frenchmen representing Lower Canada. He said to the Protestant minority of his province, in effect: " I ask you Protestant gentlemen of Lower Canada to take my word for it, and I now give you my pledge, that when Confederation is formed, and when Quebec has a parliament of its own, one of its first Acts will be to put upon its statute book the law that we could not get on our statute book here to-day." That, I say, was the promise given by that French Catholic chief, and the Protestants of Lower Canada took his word for it. They believed that the promise of a public man, solemnly given on a solemn occasion and respecting a solemn claim of a section of the people, would be solemnly respected, and it was respected. I don't know whether it was in the first or the second session of the Quebec Legislature that it was done, but that promise was carried out in good faith. Sir George Cartier was himself elected to that Legislature, and I believe he sought election with the one purpose of being in a position to carry out his solemn pledge, and so he got the promised law passed The educational clauses adopted in 1865 provided, as I have said, only for the safeguarding of rights the minority had at the time of the union. Sir George Cartier therefore found himself in this position. He could not, before the establishment of the union, give the Protestants of Quebec what he had promised to give them; he had to go and get the Legislature of Quebec to give it. But the Confederation scheme, as then settled, did not provide for protecting or safeguarding rights that might be created by the Legislature of Quebec after the union. To effect this purpose it was necessary to modify, or rather to widen, the educational clauses. When, therefore, the Government completed their draft Confederation Act they inserted in it this further provision, that not only should the rights of the minority at the time of the union with respect to schools be perpetuated and never taken away from them, but that if any legislation was passed with regard to them after the union, by any provincial legislature, the rights created thereunder could never be taken away from them.

I have attempted to show you, Mr. Speaker, and I trust I have offered sufficient evidence to satisfy the House that there has been a misapprehension, to say the least, as to the cause of these clauses appearing in the Confederation Act for the protection of the minority as to education. I hope I impress some of the hon. gentlemen present, at least, that these provisions were not, as some have thought, the work of either pope or archbishop, but that they were placed in the statute with a view chiefly to protecting the Protestant minority in the maintenance of what they thought their legal and just rights. I want to know if it will ever be charged again, in Manitoba at least, that this was a scheme of the Roman Catholics. And yet I read a few minutes ago from a speech of Dalton McCarthy's, delivered in 1889, in which he said it was. I have another speech of his here, delivered in February, 1890, in which he uses the following language to the same effect :

> I do hope that before long the delegation from the Province of Ontario will call on this House for its aid to blot out the separate school clause from the British North America Act, which limits and fetters the people of that province. That clause was carried by a majority of French-Canadians, and was imposed upon the people of Ontario against their will. . . . and I am sorry to differ from my hon. leader on that question. He tells us—and I never feel more humiliated than when I hear him speak on that subject—that he participated in imposing that separate school system upon us.

If Mr. McCarthy was speaking of the imposition of the school system on Upper Canada in the first place, he was speaking the truth, but if he applied it to the B. N. A. Act his statement was utterly without foundation.

As a matter of fact, Lower Canadians were more strongly decided —I mean their leading men were—against Confederation than Upper Canadians were. It was the Upper Canadian members, indeed, that carried Confederation, and many of the leading Frenchmen of Quebec were against it, so that it could not be true, as suggested by Mr. Dalton McCarthy, that these limitations in the B. N. A. Act were imposed upon us at the dictation of Lower Canada.

CHAPTER IX.

THE REV. DR. LAING'S LETTER TO MR. EWART.

THE MANSE, DUNDAS, ONT.,
JOHN S. EWART, ESQ. *March 22nd, 1892.*

Dear Sir,—Your two open letters on the Manitoba School Question* have been put in my hands by a friend. I have read them with interest. In their main positions I fully agree. The question as we see to-day in the Prussian agitation, and the proposed 16th Amendment to the Constitution of the United States, is world-wide, and will not be settled as long as a Rome claims (1) to be THE Church; (2) as such to have dominion over kings and legislatures, and to absolve from obedience by the faithful to all laws declared by Rome to be wrong; (3) to have the right to interfere in civil affairs, and be recognized as possessing *civil* rights *as a church* in every nation. The conflict between this Absolutism and Liberty will never cease until the latter has won the day. All this I acknowledge and, therefore, to use Hon. A. Mackenzie's phrase, as a "political exigency," owing to shameful party feeling among non-Roman Catholics, the education of the young must be conducted in view of the *fact* that the Roman Hierarchy claims the *jus Divinum* to compel the people which it dominates to submit their judgment and will to its dictations and control.

Seeing this, I presume in Manitoba, as in Quebec, we shall have separate state-supported schools for Roman Catholics.

I am far from thinking that the public school system of Ontario, or of 1890 in Manitoba, is ideally or theoretically the right one, viz., "Secular education with a vestige." I am strongly in favor of use by the State of the Bible as the text book in morals which is preferable to any other. In this I am glad to have the support of Prof. Huxley. What I complain of is, that while in Quebec the Protestant schools can and do teach religion as they deem best, the liberty to do this is taken from us in Ontario and Manitoba, and devotional exercises are put in place of religious or rather Biblical moral instruction. And why is this done? (1) We are told because Protestants cannot agree among themselves. This I believe to be untrue; we can, if we get the chance. (2 Because it would be unfair to Jews and Agnostics to put in the Christian Bible. Not to dwell on the conscience clause, this is also a false reason. If the

---

*See pages 219 and 231.

Bible is the best moral guide, *confessedly* it should not be rejected because there are in it certain statements to which Jews object; or because Agnostics say that there may be no God and the Book is not inspired. You will say intolerance may be negative as well as positive, and it is intolerant to say; Christian people may not get the best book because others think it is not what Christians affirm it is, viz., the Word of God. (3) Because in Ontario we have found, as claimed by the late Archbishop Lynch and Father Stafford, that the Roman Catholics not only have the *exclusive* right to have their schools controlled by the hierarchy, but that the hierarchy, *as representing* the Roman Catholic taxpayers, who may be public school supporters, have the RIGHT to object to any book that is opposed to the Roman Catholic doctrine or Church interests. It is the Roman Catholic *priesthood* in Ontario, not the people, who prevent our Protestant youth being instructed in the Bible. They do not wish the Bible to be in schools which the Roman Catholic youth may attend, to the number of 30,000.

On page 4 of your first letter you say "all Protestant denominations have had the right (in Ontario) to establish Separate schools for themselves should they desire to do so. But with trifling exceptions there has not been a symptom of an effort on the part of Protestants to avail themselves of the privilege." Now you will pardon me when I say that statement is far, far from fair or according to law or fact.

(1) No *denomination* can have a school as such. A Separate school cannot be known as Episcopalian, Methodist or Presbyterian; in law it is only *Protestant*, *i.e.*, non-Catholic.

(2) A Separate Protestant school can only be established when a Roman Catholic teacher is employed in the public school of that section. In many places a Roman Catholic teacher is employed in the public school: the law allows this; but unless there is priestly interference or Roman Catholic text-books are illegally used, or altars put up and Roman Catholic worship practised in the schoolhouses no objection is made. In some places the priest, who by law cannot be a trustee, nevertheless through Roman Catholic trustees gets the control of the school.

(3) As a matter of fact, efforts to have Separate schools have been successfully opposed, and in one instance valuable school property was sold for $5 to the Roman Catholic Separate School Board.

(4) If a Protestant Separate school is established, it cannot exercise the privileges conferred by law on the Roman Catholic Separate school. A study of the Ontario Act will prove this exclusively. If Protestants had like privileges our Public School system would not exist for a year. Hence everything has been done to make Protestant Separate schools die out, while Roman Catholic schools have been sedulously cherished.

(5) If the Church of England people could establish a church school, have all their taxes diverted within a radius of three miles to the Church of England Separate school it would be done in many cases, and the public school would be hopelessly crippled, but the law will not allow this. The same might be done by Presbyterians and Methodists; but the law forbids these to do what the Roman Catholics claims as a RIGHT. See preamble of School Act, 1863.

You will see, therefore, the injustice of the Ontario law : (1) It gives the Roman Catholic denomination RIGHTS denied to all others. (2) It allows their priesthood, who are not ratepayers, to control the Separate schools, while Protestant clergy have no power, except as ratepayers and visitors in the Public schools, which latter privilege belongs to the priest also. (3) It allows Roman Catholics in a district, through their priests, to manage the public schools ; and practically the right has been acknowledged by Hon. A. Crooks, G. W. Ross, and O. Mowat, if the Roman Catholic clergy *as such* do object, to revise and interfere with the books used in our high and public schools.

If the Quebec system were in operation here it would be at least fair. (1) All schools be either Roman Catholic or Protestant. (2) All schools be managed by Roman Catholics or Protestants without the interference of the other. (3) All property of each be taxed for their own schools and not for the support of the other. (4) Religious instruction be given in each as the parents desire. This would be fair.

Now, sir, when I took this in hand I did not mean to write at such length. I take the liberty of sending you what I have published on the question, I look with anxious concern on the important issue of this school question, not only in Manitoba and Canada, but in Germany and the United States. There can be but one final issue, liberty to parents to educate their children, but before that is reached there may be much trouble.

Asking your kind forbearance, I am, yours truly,

JOHN LAING.

N.B.—Dr. Laing desires that it should be understood "that the above letter was not written for publication, but *currente calamo* in answer to a private note. It is not, therefore, to be regarded as a full statement of Dr. Laing's position—that he has carefully stated in two pamphlets published in 1884 and 1887. His chief desire is to have religious instruction given in the public schools ; and he contends against the wrong done to other churches by allowing state education to be controlled by the Roman Catholic clergy, while Protestants cannot be allowed the use of the Bible even in giving religious instruction to their children, because, forsooth, 30,000 Roman Catholic children in Ontario attend the public schools."

CHAPTER X.

MR. EWART'S REPLY TO THE REV. DR. LAING.

WINNIPEG, *29th March, 1892.*

DEAR SIR,—I have read with much interest and gratification the letter and pamphlets which you were kind enough to send me. I am glad to have you say that the Quebec system is a fair one. It was that system which was in force in Manitoba from its establishment as a province until the Act of 1890. It is for the restoration of that system that Roman Catholics in this province are fighting.

You make a strong case for its introduction into Ontario when you argue that as Roman Catholics have their schools to themselves Protestants should be accorded similar privileges. You do not ask, as I understand you, that each Protestant denomination should be allowed to separate itself, but that all Protestants together should constitute a class (p. 11 of your "Letters"), and be permitted to model their schools to suit themselves. That right the Protestants had in Manitoba until the Act of 1890 took it away and placed all schools under statutory management.*

We are therefore agreed upon the fundamental parts of the case. But I would like to add a few words for your consideration upon two points suggested by your Letters and Pamphlets.

1. You think that the controversy will never be closed "as long as Rome claims," etc. To my mind these "claims," as such, have no bearing upon the question. The *claim* "to absolve from obedience by the faithful to all laws, etc.," does not in any way affect our legislation or the enforcement of our laws. In Quebec the question of education is well settled, but the pretensions of the church are as vigorously asserted* there as any elsewhere in the world. In Manitoba there was the same settlement, and it was not the *claims* of the Roman Catholics, but the intolerance of the Protestant majority, which disturbed it.

The church *claims* to control legislation in Canada as to education you say. Well, many a man asserts unfounded claims to his neighbor's property. It is not a wrongful claim which hurts; it is the power to enforce it that is injurious. Catholics have no power to accomplish anything in Canada other than through lawful and

---

* And Manitoba Protestants approved of the deprivation. —(ED.)

constitutional means, equally open to all. That they claim to have authority is unimportant. They must play the game with the same counters as other people. The Legislature does not grant privileges to Roman Catholics, and withold them from Protestants, because of any "claim," but for other reasons.

And this brings me to the second point, which is that Roman Catholics play more skilfully and earnestly than Protestants; and hence alone (as I see it) the denunciation of them. What do we charge against them? That they are better disciplined, act better together, are more homogeneous, and, taking their creed by authority from their church, instead of by authority from the Bible, they naturally subordinate their views to those of their Bishops. As fittingly might well-justified rebels complain of the discipline of the regular army. It hurts them, it easily overthrows them, but what is the remedy? Clearly not assertion that discipline is unfair, but counter discipline. You cannot properly object to the Bishops and Priests acting as officers. Your clergymen are the opposing officers, and once a year you hold a council of war—but your army will not fight.

You say that Protestants want religious education in the schools. I think it is the Ministers, and not the people who so advocate; just as you think it is the priests, and not the Catholic people, that want their religion taught in the schools. And I put this to you: The Protestants can obtain in Ontario anything they really desire in reference to the schools. Why do they not take what they want? You answer me, Politics. But I reply, Politicians play to the majorities *when they are in earnest.* Do you not sometimes feel oppressed with the indifference, the dead inertia, of Protestants, not only with reference to this subject, but to others which to you seem far more important? Believe me, Sir, if Protestants for six months set their hearts upon Protestant religion in the schools, the politicians would tumble over one another, that they might be the first to give it. Test Catholic sincerity in the same way. Here in Manitoba where there is no pretence, or little, of the people being priest-ridden, the politicians know perfectly well that Catholics vote, almost to a man, for religion in the schools. The liberal candidates in the last Dominion election know it to their cost.

Perhaps you may have noticed in the *Week* a criticism of my pamphlets. I have sent a reply, of which I send you a copy. It bears upon the second point to which I have alluded.

With kind regards, I am, yours sincerely,

JOHN S. EWART.

CHAPTER XI.

OPEN LETTER FROM MR. EWART TO THE HON. MR. GREENWAY.

2nd January, 1892.

To The Honorable Thomas Greenway:

SIR,—Believe me it is only after much hesitation that I have determined to write a word of criticism upon the policy of your Government. Nearly four years ago I welcomed your accession to power as the introduction of a new and brighter era of Government in Manitoba. Mr. Norquay's Government, I had believed, was not only incapable and subservient, but extravagant and corrupt. I hailed the advent of a Liberal administration, as promising relief from Ottawa domination, and from usless and knavish dissipation of our income.

I must needs, therefore, have some more than ordinarily good reasons for publishing any adverse criticism of your conduct of affairs, immediately, or shortly, before your appeal to the constituencies. Not that I boast myself much of a factor in elections, for which, indeed, I have long since been convinced I am singularly ill adapted. But I do think that you should either have the benefit of my vote, and any influence I may possess, or that I should be able to offer to myself, and others, satisfactory reasons for witholding them.

Judging from recent public utterances you appear to have determined to appeal for support, not upon the general character of your Government, but upon the very worst feature which has distinguished your tenure of office. You thus challenge an expression of opinion upon one question; and if you are successful you will properly claim that your views have received public endorsation. You do not ask us to vote confidence in your Government, but to give you a mandate and justification for a continuation of your efforts to abolish all distinction between Protestant and Catholic in reference to education, even to the amendment of our constitutional Act should its provisions be found to stand in your way.

We are, therefore, not asked to vote for, or against, a Liberal Government, or a good Government, but for, or against, the indefinite continuation of the present deplorable ferment and turbulence anent the school question. Upon that question my mind is made up. I have recently had occasion to make as thorough a study of it as my ability permits. It is one requiring study and dispassionate consideration. It is a many sided question, but yet one upon which people are liable without reflection to jump to unwarranted conclusions. May I ask a patient ear, and a tolerant mood, while I shortly review the subject.

I base my complaint against your Government upon two grounds: (1) Upon the ground that your legislation and policy are in direct violation of election pledges, and (2) upon the ground of their inherent badness.

The St. Francois Xavier election was held on the 12th January, 1888. Every one knew knew that the life of the Harrison administration depended upon the success, in that contest, of the Hon. Mr. Burke; while his defeat would mean your accession to office. The constituency was largely French and Roman Catholic. Mr. Burke was of that nationality and denomination. His opponent was an English Protestant. Politically, the majority had hitherto been favorable to the Conservative Government. You undertook the difficult, and seemingly hopeless, task of turning the Conservative majority into a Liberal one; of prevailing on the French Catholic Conservatives to support the English Protestant Liberal. You appealed to the electors for government condemnation upon the ground of extravagance, wastefulness and general mismanagement. In this appeal you were meeting wtih unexpected success. To offset your arguments strong efforts were made by the Government to induce the electors to believe that the Liberals were the natural enemies of the French and the Catholics. Mr. Joseph Martin and other Liberals, with great earnestness, repelled the charge, asserted that they were entirely in sympathy with the French Catholics, and distinctly promised that their language and institutions should be conserved.

By means of such promises the Liberals carried the election, and four days afterwards you, sir, were sent for to form a new administration. To assist you in this work you personally called upon His Grace, the Archbishop of St. Boniface. You found him too ill to meet you. At his request you made your communication through Vicar-General Allard. You proceeded to assure the Archbishop that you were in entire sympathy with him upon the two questions of Catholic schools and French language; that it would be the policy of your Government to maintain them inviolate, and you requested that His Grace would name some one who would be acceptable to his people as a member of the Cabinet. The Vicar-General listened to your promises and request, and agreed to meet you in Winnipeg at nine o'clock the next morning. He did so meet you, and then told you that His Grace was extremely gratified with your protestations of good will; that he believed that Mr. Prendergast had the confidence of his people, and that inasmuch as politics, apart from defence of his flock, were outside his sphere, no opposition would be made to the Government as far as he was concerned. You gave the same assurance to the Liberal French members of the House; and you thus were enabled to meet the general elections with Mr. Prendergast as a colleague in your Cabinet, and several French Catholic candidates in your ranks. After the election you had as supporters five out of the six French members.

These pledges, sir, have all been broken; and power obtained with the assistance of Roman Catholics has been prostituted to their overthrow. This is my first argument against you.

What answer have you to make? It is not that there suddenly arose any public demand for the reversal of a system in which everyone had acquiesced for nineteen years. No, sir, the public mind was at rest upon that question. It was not, I am convinced, that your Cabinet had carefully considered the question, and had determined that there was something so essentially detrimental in the existing system that an instant end must be put to it.

Your action, therefore, has the appearance of mere wanton violation of pledges and excitement of religious animosities. From this charge, however, for my part I am glad to relieve you. The story, as I read it, runs thus: Mr. Joseph Martin, your capable but impetuous and head-strong Attorney-General, with that utter disregard of the feelings, interests or rights of others which did so much to mar the usefulness of his efforts, of his own mere motion, determined to abolish both the Protestant and Roman Catholic schools, and to set up in their stead a system of purely secular schools, without any vestige of religious instruction or religious exercises. No sooner thought than said; and, at Portage la Prairie, he announced that at the next session it should be done. You did not attempt, sir, to conceal that this announcement was made without your knowledge or approval. You made no secret of the fact that you entirely disapproved of it, but you were not strong enough to thwart Mr. Martin's purpose, and you allowed yourself (under threat of resignation, probably) to be driven into acceptance of his policy. But the public had to be reckoned with. Some Protestants insisted upon the retention of their schools (waiving the use of the denominational title, which was of no value), and, being strong in votes and influence, their insistence was rewarded with substantial success. The Catholics were weak, and their protests were unavailing. So came about the Act of 1890.

I blame, therefore, Mr. Martin principally in this matter, and you, sir, only in so far as you failed to precipitate a rupture in your Government, rather than adopt a policy of which you did not approve. I had, therefore, hoped that upon Mr. Martin's retirement from the Government (which was always imminent) the policy would have ceased to constitute a plank in your Government's platform. I had hoped that were the Catholics successful in the Privy Council the agitation would have ceased and quiet be again restored.

Could I still retain this hope I should now be silent. But recent events indicate too strongly that while the elections of 1888 were fought in alliance with the French Catholics, those now at hand are to be carried (if at all) by the cry of "Down with the Catholic schools."

I think it important, therefore, that this old question should be restated and discussed; and I have some hopes that a presentation of the considerations which finally triumphed in Ontario in 1863 (after many years of discussion) may not be without effect in Manitoba, no matter how feebly I may be able to state them.

You are aware, sir, that the general acceptance of the doctrine of the duty of the state with reference to education is of very recent date. You are also aware that notwithstanding the indifference of the state towards education, nations thrived and flourished and grew patriotic and vigorous. The "good old times," sir, were such without the help of the national schoolmaster.

In recent years the state has busied itself about the education of the people, and is already beginning to exhibit strong symptoms of the same fatal inclination for uniformity, dead-level, and drill-sergeants which too frequently enters into its conception of government. Up to date children have been educated as their parents desired. Now, having at last got into action, the state looks about for an ideal form of education, cannot agree about it, shakes up the ballot box over it, and having by "count of heads" settled the ideal, wants everybody to be educated in this particular way, and no other.

Pause for a moment, sir, and ask yourself: "Were I in the minority, how would this suit me?" What would Protestants in Quebec think of the doctrine? I may be told that the cases are different; that in Quebec the ideal would be a Roman Catholic education, whereas here it is secular, with the least possible recognition of religion. Yes, sir, the cases are different, but they are based upon the same principle, that the state has the right to determine the character of education—I mean whether it is to be secular or religious, and if the latter, of what order; and that principle is unquestionably wrong.

It is upon this point, the character of education, that Protestants and Catholics are fundamentally at variance; not whether children shall be educated (on that they are agreed), but what shall be the character of the education. The great majority of Protestants think that secular education during the week, with little more than the acknowledgment of the Deity twice a day is good enough for their children. A true Roman Catholic abhors this system and insists upon all education being permeated with religion. A Protestant is trained secularly, and religion is relegated to Sunday. A Roman Catholic is trained to be religious as well as intelligent during all days of the week. They cannot agree, and perhaps never will.

I do not stop to discuss which is the better system in theory or practice. It is sufficient for my purpose to point out the fundamental antagonism, and to protest against the adoption in Quebec, or Manitoba, of the principle that the state ought to control the character of education. In England it is not done (the denominational system, aided by the state, is there in full force); in Ontario it is not done. John Stuart Mill says:

> The spirit of improvement is not always a spirit of liberty, for it may aim at forcing improvements on an unwilling people; and the spirit of liberty, in so far as it resists such attempts, may ally itself locally and temporarily with the opponents of improvement; but the only unfailing and permanent source of improvement is liberty.

I concede that the state does well to insist upon the education of all children, and may fairly require of parents that their children shall attain to a certain standard of knowledge. But I contend that if parents of their own accord provide for such education, the state has no right to do more than see that the standard is reached. So, too, I argue that several heads of families may combine and form a school for the instruction of their young. And so also may a whole religious denomination. This last would amount to voluntary separate schools, and no one would, I think, suggest the violent suppression of such schools, even as no one would deny the right of the state to see that they were of standard efficiency. John Stuart Mill is arguing on the same line when he says:

> The objections which are urged with reason against state education, do not apply to the enforcement of education by the state, but to the state taking upon itself to direct that education, which is a totally different thing.

Dr. Duval was undoubtedly right* when he said that if:

> The people desire prayer at the beginning of their children's studies for grace to mould the mind and purify the heart, it is their natural right to have it.

And he would get the Catholics' hearty support of his remark :†

> The idea of a system of schools without any religious influence, where the Jew and Christian, agnostic and infidel, can all be on the same footing seems indeed broad and generous. But it is as specious as broad, and as dangerous as generous.

The natural right here conceded, is not to be limited to a commencing prayer, but extends to the whole day's studies. I think the worthy Doctor would agree to this.

You will observe, sir, that my present point is that while the state may properly interfere with the natural right of the parent, so far as to protect itself from ignorance and consequent vice, it ought not to meddle with the religious aspect of the question. To declare that, in Manitoba, education is to be entirely secular, or that, in Quebec, it is to be Roman Catholic, would alike be, in my view, so to meddle with this religious aspect, and would be alike vicious and unwarranted.

---

* See page 200.   † See page 202.

But you may tell me that the education afforded by the Catholic schools is not equal to that obtained in other schools. This is disputed, but my answer does not depend upon the settlement of the dispute. It is this, that the education is, at all events, sufficient to provide against absolute ignorance, and consequent vice, and, therefore, there is no such inefficiency as alone furnishes warrant for the interference of the state.

Now, sir, what do the Catholics ask? Merely this, that so long as they provide efficient education for themselves they should be permitted to do so at their own expense—that they should be taxed for their own schools, and that Protestants should be taxed for their schools. This must commend itself to every one as extremely reasonable and fair, and something which ought to be accorded, unless it can be shown to be detrimental to the Province in some degree more serious than would be the refusal, to a large body of the population, of so reasonable a request.

It is objected by many that if Catholics are allowed their schools, other denominations cannot be denied equal liberty, and so public schools become impossible. To this various replies may be made:

1st The objection assumes that everything ought to be made subservient to the absolute similarity of all schools. Such was the English idea until quite modern times. Queen Elizabeth, in an injunction set forth in the first year of her reign, ordained that:

> No man shall take upon him to teach, but such as shall be allowed by the ordinary and found meet, as well for learning and dexterity in teaching, as for sober and honest conversation, and also for right understanding of God's true religion.

And by Canon 77 of 1603 there was added that

> He first subscribe to the 39 articles of religion, and to the two first clauses of the second article concerning the Book of Common Prayer.

With what pity, if not contempt, do many Protestants now regard such regulations. And yet with what do they propose to replace them? They also demand a system of uniformity, but one the exact opposite of Queen Elizabeth's. The good Queen wanted everybody to be educated in the one religion, but now there is to be substituted an education in which there is no religion at all, or next to none. The new notion may indeed be better than that of Queen Bess. I do not stop to argue that. I merely plead for liberty. I point out that both systems suffer from the same vice of intolerance, and that each of them is an undue interference with the liberty of the subject, and the natural rights of parents. If I had my way I would require that every one should read Mill's essay on Liberty, especially the chapter on "Individuality as one of the elements of well-being," and the "Applications," before expressing himself upon the school question.

2nd. The objection applies to churches as well as to schools. If everyone is allowed to worship as he thinks proper, a national *church* becomes impossible. And yet, sir, what a splendid conception is that of a national church. What a blessing, particularly in Manitoba. Observe the useless, I had almost said senseless, waste of money, power, and energy, attendant upon the sectarian system. Every little hamlet with its three or four impecunious congregations striving, in ungracious rivalry, for the possession of the few villagers. Why should not the State compress all these denominations into one grand national church? Ought not the State to protect itself from vice? And is not an effective church the best antidote? Ah! sir, one would argue a long time before making a single convert to such a scheme. And why? Because experience has taught that people will not, and cannot, be made to agree on matters of religion, and that it is unjust to insist upon harmony in such matters. And yet, sir, you do not see that while subscribing to this principle, you are transgressing it, in providing for a non-religious education, without escape except upon penalties. Do not think that you can successfully distinguish between a State *selection* of religious education, and a State *suppression* of religious education, when discussing the right of the State to interfere with the natural rights of parents.

3rd. The objection assumes that if the Catholics are allowed their schools the other denominations will demand sectarian schools, and so public schools will become impossible. Nothing is further from the truth.

(a) Prior to 1870 the Episcopalians, Presbyterians and Catholics had schools in this territory. During the first session of the Legislative Assembly an act was passed which provided in a few pages for the establishment of Protestant schools and Catholic schools. There was to be an advisory board of fourteen, one half Protestant and the other half Catholics. The Protestants were given sole and complete control over their schools, with *carte blanche* to make them as they pleased. Now, sir, allow me to call your particular attention to the character of the schools set up by the Protestant section of the board, at which sat five clergymen and two laymen. These Protestants, sir, coming directly from their own sectarian schools, established schools which are almost the exact counterpart of the schools attempted by you under the Act of 1890. And not only so, but the Episcopalians willingly gave up to the State the schools and organization which they had established, entering heartily into the new arrangement. Allow me to quote from the report of the superintendent of Protestant schools (Rev. W. Cyprian Pinkham, now Bishop of Saskatchewan) for the year 1871 :

> Each parish school as it had existed previous to the passing of the School Act was practically taken on by the Government when it enacted, etc.
> Our section of the Board after most mature deliberation determined to exclude all distinctive religious teachings from its schools, but has enjoined the reading of the Holy Scripture, and the prayers as published in the by-laws and regulations, at the opening and closing of the school."

15

Now observe that by your Act of 1890 the Legislature showed that it too was "determined to exclude all distinctive religious teaching from its schools," but permitted religious exercises (*i.e.*, reading of the Holy Scriptures and the prayers as published by the Advisory Board) before the closing hour in the afternoon. Protestants can hardly find fault with so careful a copy of their own acts, or pretend that it does not suit them.

(*b*) From 1871 until the Act of 1890 the Protestant denominations showed no signs of unrest, or of a disposition to demand separate schools. On the contrary, when your Act was passed the Presbyterian Synod by resolution distinctly approved of it. His Lordship the Bishop of Rupert's Land does not like the new Act, which takes away the power of Protestants to mould their schools to their liking, and introduce more religion should they think proper to do so. But he was never dissatisfied with the Act of 1871. All his complaint was that he did not quite approve of the way in which Protestants used their power to do as they pleased. The Act was all right, but his views were those of the minority and did not prevail, and he did not insist upon them.

(*c*) The assumption may further be shewn to be erroneous by reference to the Province of Ontario. There the Catholics have for many years had their schools, and all Protestant denominations have had the right to establish separate schools for themselves should they desire to do so.* But with trifling exceptions there has not been a symptom of an effort on the part of Protestants to avail themselves of the privilege.

These considerations, sir, show conclusively that the assumption, that if the Catholics are allowed their schools, the other denominations will demand separate schools, and so national schools will become impossible, is without foundation.

Before leaving this point allow me to remind you that the separation of the Catholics does not affect materially even the economical management of other schools nearly as much as may be generally supposed. With the exception of the cities there are very few places in which the population is of a mixed character. In the districts in which the Catholics have schools there are very few, and sometimes no, Protestants. You will therefore see that the Catholics being in this way grouped, the Protestant schools are not affected by their existence to any appreciable extent.

Should the reasoning from principle, sir, which I have attempted, appear to you too abstract and inconclusive, allow me to put the matter before you in practical form, admitting, as I do, that abstract principles of government must oft-times be modified by circumstances.

The object of school legislation is the education of the people.

---

* This statement is not quite accurate (see the Rev. Dr. Laing's letter page 215), and the argument thereby loses much of its force. See, however, the reply to Dr. Laing page 217.—

This is to be attained by (1) setting up schools, and (2) getting children to attend them. Attendance may be secured (1) by coercion, or (2) by persuasion. Persuasion is preferable, and coercion only to be resorted to as an extreme measure. Thus far you agree with me. Let us apply our notions to Manitoba. There are here (for the purposes of my argument) two bodies of people. (1) The Protestants want their children to attend undenominational schools, with a vestige of religion in them. (2) The Roman Catholics make it a matter of conscience that their children shall attend Catholic schools—to them undenominational (that is irreligious schools) are wrong. Now, sir, having in mind that our practical object is to get the children to go to school, what are we to do? We can select one of four courses. (1) We can please one of the bodies, and set up undenominational schools (with a vestige); (2) we can please the other body, and have the system altogether denominational; (3) we can please neither of them by setting up purely secular schools; or (4) we can please both of them, by allowing all those who want undenominational schools (with a vstige) to have theirs that way, and those who want Catholic schools to have them also. You pay your money and you take your choice. Recalling, once more, that our object is to persuade people to send their children to the schools, which of the four systems would you select? Is it not clear that children will be sent to schools approved by the parents, and witheld from those to which they, rightly or wrongly, object? How then are you going to fill your schools? By having them approved by the whole public, or by a majority only? You see my point.

But you may reply, that if the Protestant denominations are willing to give up denominational schools for the sake of the advantages to be derived from common schools, the Catholics should also be willing to do so. If there is no use in repeating that Catholics cannot do so (which is a sufficient answer), let me point out that Protestants give up nothing. As between denominational and common schools, they *prefer* the latter. And none of them would argue that the example of the Catholics in refusing to agree with them would cause them to change their opinion. Catholics have separate schools in Ontorio, but that has never been given as a reason why Protestants should give up the undenominational schools they enjoy, and each sect set up for itself. As you see, sir, and know, the Protestants are satisfied with the non-sectarian schools—the vestige being still visible, and they will be satisfied with nothing else. It is useless, therefore, to assert that they give up something for uniformity's sake, and to argue that Catholics should be willing to follow their example. They give up nothing, but Catholics are asked to surrender what to them is sacred. It is neither fair, nor just, nor reasonable to expect them to do so.

But perhaps your desire is to bring the Catholics into line with

Protestants upon the question of education; to remove religious animosities by uniting the children in common schools? And do you seriously believe, sir, that the best means of ending intolerance is to commence the Governmental practice of it; that Catholics can be coerced into brotherly love; and that the first and last step towards the removal of antipathies, is to aggravate them? Should I desire your friendship, sir, do you think I should commence by giving you a slap in the face? You are not ignorant, sir, of history, nor are you unfamiliar with human nature. A moment's reflection would tell you that your present course is the very worst for your asserted purpose. All experience shows that people will not be driven into the acceptance of an opinion or course of action. But the spirit of intolerance and religious animosity burns still as fiercely as ever in many breasts, and once more it is thought that coercion must succeed in establishing the much sought for uniformity. It will fail, sir, as it always has failed when attacking religious opinions. Do you imagine that you can succeed where kings and czars and autocrats and parliaments and physical persecutions have failed? Do you not see that as coercion ceases, better acquaintance and natural kindness heal the breach and make for the desired harmony and unanimity? Believe me, sir, Protestants and Catholics are mutually intolerant because they are mutually misunderstood. Did you ever read Cardinal Newman? Let no Protestant pretend that he can argue the Catholic question, intolerantly asserting that they are stupidly wrong, until he has read their controversial writers.

Your plan was tried, sir, as you are aware in Upper Canada. You remember the bitterness of the struggle. For years Separate Schools, and Representation by Population, were the leading questions upon the platform and in the press. George Brown and Alexander Mackenzie fought fiercely against the re-establishment of separate schools. Orangemen and Catholics threshed away at the old, old questions, and left them where they found them. It was a fierce and savage fight—Protestant and Catholic once more proving how little education had done for either of them. It ended in 1863, as it only could end, by the full concession of the separate school principle. Mr. McKenzie's words, with reference to this memorable contest, spoken twelve years atterwards, ought to have weight with you, and with every one who seeks to form an opinion on the subject. He said:

> I believe in free schools, in the non-denominational system; and, if I could persuade my fellow countrymen in Ontario and Quebec, or any other province, to adopt that principle, it is the one I would give preference to above all others. For many years after I had a seat in the Parliament of Canada, I waged war against the principle of of separate schools. I hoped to be able, young and inexperienced as I then was, to establish a system to which all would yield their assent. Sir, it was found to be impracticable in operation, and impossible in political contingencies.

You will also remember the New Brunswick phase of the question. Litigation revealed the fact that in that Province the Catholics were completely at the mercy of the majority, and the majority appeared to be disposed to deal harshly with them. The matter was debated at length in the Dominion House of Commons in which you then had a seat. You listened, I have no doubt, to Mr. Mackenzie's speech in which he declared that the Upper Canada settlement of the question in 1863 was a fair and reasonable settlement and that he felt bound to give his sympathy to those in other Provinces who believed they were laboring under the same grievances that the Catholics in Ontario complained of for years."

You cannot have forgotten sir, that after listening to that speech you joined with the great majority of both sides of the House in passing a resolution which requested the Imperial Government to use its influence to the end that the Catholics might have their schools.

While quoting let me also cite the opinion of Principal Grant, who is not deficient in Presbyterian combativeness. In his opinion the concession made in Upper Canada to the Catholics was "a good practical compromise."

And now, sir, for what purpose would you re-open this question, surcharged as you know it to be with all bitterness and angry disputation? How amicably Protestant and Catholic, in Manitoba, have worked in matters relating to education has been a matter of thankful remark. You throw them into discord and enmity by arousing the long dormant sectarian antipathies. You may, sir, live to see them at peace again, each with schools after their own design, and perhaps you may learn to say with George Brown:

I point with glad thankfulness to the banishment of religious jealousy and discord that so long rent our country.

Yes, sir, you may live to be thankful, but it will be because of the early defeat of your present policy; and your thankfulness will be mixed with the bitter regret that it was your hand that fanned the flame, if it did not light the match. For what purpose, again I ask, do you pursue this course? You are aware, sir, that in doing so you are out of sympathy with the Liberal party, and that your policy is hurtful to that party, as antagonizing Catholics in all parts of the Dominion. It is not, then, for party purposes that you do it, and I have said that it is not of your own designing, and has not your approval.

For what purpose then? Am I driven to the conclusion that it is merely to sustain your own Government in power—for merely personal purposes? Are you willing to violate election pledges; to renounce political principle; to injure your own political party; to provoke ferment, unrest and confusion in so important a matter as education; to set divines at each others throats; to arouse all the passions and hatreds and contempts inseparable from religious controversies—to keep yourself in office?

It is announced, that should you be beaten in the Privy Council you intend to continue the agitation and seek an amendment of the constitution. You are perfectly aware that an amendment cannot be obtained; that both parties in the Dominion parliament would almost unanimously vote against it. You could not even pretend that Manitoba had a peculiar grievance, for she has the same control over education as Ontario and Quebec. Knowing then that an amendment cannot be obtained, why would you seek it? Why perpetuate and intensify the animosity and turmoil which you have aroused? Why continue to injure your political party, and violate your pledges and principles? Much as I regret it, sir, I can see no reason other than—to keep yourself in office.

I presume I need not ask you frankly to tell me whether you have not more or less contempt for people whose votes you can wheedle out of them in this way—who have passions, there, ready to take the place of their judgments, at the bidding of a politician at election times? Sir John A. Macdonald carried the last elections by appealing to passions. You, sir, may do the same. Or possibly you may find that you have not, with sufficient dexterity, stirred up, to proper intensity, religious animosity—that your jacks have not, for some reason, jumped at your pull of the string; in which case, sir, you will serve for a parable, and be likened "unto children sitting in the markets, and calling unto their fellows, and saying: We have piped unto you, and ye have not danced; we have mourned unto you, and ye have not lamented!"

One word more. I see that some would advocate that if Catholics are entitled to be separate in this matter of education they should be left to get along as best they can; that they should be left disorganized. Can religious antipathy suggest a more unreasonable proposal? It means this: That if the Catholics are by law entitled to have separate schools you would prefer seeing them weak, struggling and inefficient, rather than organized and capable—you would have Catholic children uneducated, rather than educated as Catholics! Such intolerance is not creditable to those who advocate the course, and is not indigenous to the western prairies, I think, or capable of transplantation there.

I would that I could see anything but an election cry in this agitation. I believe that our province is indebted to your Government for many things. But you have cast your pledges, your principles, your party and your record to the winds, and have adopted a cry which, while it may answer your expectations for a time will certainly recoil upon you ere long; and meanwhile will work incalculable and irremediable mischief.

I am sir, yours with much regret,

JOHN S. EWART.

CHAPTER XII.

MR. EWART'S REPLY TO CRITICISMS.

20th January, 1892.

To the Editor of the Free Press:

Sir,—My letter to the Hon. Mr. Greenway has evoked countervailing arguments of various kinds and qualities. I shall reply to one kind first—the kind which answers arguments by personal attack :

1. "You are a lawyer, and were paid to write the letter." True, I am a lawyer. Untrue, that I was, or am to be, paid or remunerated in any way by Catholics, *Free Press*, or other body, paper, or person, whomsoever. The letter was written without the knowledge or solicitation of anyone.

2. "You wrote another former letter, inconsistent with the present one, and the *Free Press* refused to publish it." The document referred to was an essay (not a letter), written, as are many such for my own delectation and self-improvement. It was not "inconsistent with the present one." It was not refused publication by the *Free Press*, or any other paper. It is in my house, and may be read by anyone who will honor me with a visit.

3. "You have deserted your party." Query: If Mr. Greenway abandons the Liberal party, must I do the same in order to—remain a member of it? If Mr. Greenway votes one way in 1875, and another way in 1890, must I change my vote in order to—vote the same way as before? If the Liberal party advocated separate schools for New Brunswick, where the law gave them none, am I a renegade if I advocate separate schools for Manitoba, where the law provides for them? I shall be content to be called a traitor when I act as such, but I reject the title when bestowed merely because I refuse to duplicate the vacillations of any particular fugleman.

Most of the other arguments (published, as well as privately communicated) may best be met, I think, by a re-statement of the case. But first let us see how far all (or nearly all) can go together.

1. The state may protect itself from ignorance and consequent vice, and for that purpose insist upon a measure of education.

2. It may do so by erecting schools ; and compelling, if need be,

[231]

children to attend them. It is much better to secure voluntary attendance. John Morley recently said (On Compromise, p. 102):

> Those who have thought most carefully and disinterestedly about the matter are agreed that in advanced societies the expedient course is that no portion of the community should insist on imposing its own will upon any other portion, except in matters which are vitally connected with the maintenance of the social union.

3. The state has nothing to do with religion. It has no opinion upon the question of Protestantism *v.* Catholicism, or both *versus* Agnosticism. In its view all classes are equally sensible and sincere. Mariolatry and Predestination are to it equally right and equally wrong—which is right cannot be known. In its opinion all are entitled to exactly the same rights and privileges. "Absolute liberty, just and true liberty, equal and impartial liberty, is the thing that we stand in need of," (Locke's Introduction to his Letters on Toleration). These are the principles frequently cited against me. I adopt them, and ask that my opponents will not refuse to pursue them to their logical conclusions. Let me hereafter speak of them as the third admission.

4. As a corollary: Legitimate ends of government (such as education), ought to be attained in such way as will least conflict with religious freedom.

5. Subject to the principle of state self-protection, parents have a right to mould the character of the education of their children as they please—that is to make it Episcopalian, Presbyterian, Catholic, secular or otherwise.

6. The great majority of Protestants believe in secular schools with religious exercises. (This is the meaning of the passage in my former letter, that Boreas misunderstood, and therefore condemned as bearing "absurdity and insincerity on its face.") The great majority of Catholics are opposed to such schools and desire denominational schools. For the purpose of the argument let it be assumed that the community is divided into these two classes.

For the sake of those who refuse adhesion to the third admission I beg to quote from John Locke's first letter on Toleration. (Letters, they were, more needed, perhaps, in 1689 than 1892; yet still much needed).

> But if one of these churches hath this power of treating the other ill, I ask which of them it is to whom the power belongs, and by what right? It will be answered undoubtedly, that it is the orthodox church which has the right of authority over the erroneous or heretical. This is, in great and specious words, to say just nothing at all. For every church is orthodox to itself; to others erroneous or heretical. Whatsoever any church believes, it believes to be true; and the contrary thereunto it pronounces to be error. So that the controversy between these two churches about the truth of their doctrines, and the purity of their worship, is on both sides equal; nor is there any judge, either at Constantinople, or elsewhere upon the earth, by whose sentence it can be determined. The decision of that question belongs only to the Supreme Judge of all men, to whom alone belongs the punishment of the erroneous.

And again (3rd Letter):

God never gave the magistrates authority to be judge of truth for another man.

Dr. Bryce wrote as follows (*Free Press*, 18th Dec, 1889):

Prelate and Presbyter, Canon and Salvation Army captain, Agnostic champion and Methodist exhorter, and their followers, should in the eye of the state all be equal.

Now, remembering this third admission, let me answer the objection most frequently urged. It is this: "The common schools are not Protestant. They are entirely unsectarian. There is no religion taught there, and therefore no reason why Catholics should not attend them." My Protestant friend, can you believe that it is precisely because "no religion is taught there" that Catholics disapprove the place? Catholics believe (as do also in a modified form His Lordship the Bishop of Rupert's Land, the Rev. Principal King, and a large number of Protestant divines) that teaching should accompany and permeate the secular lessons; that one ought not to be separated from the other; that history, philosophy and the rest should be taught with their religious aspects constantly in view; and that separation of teaching into secular and religious leads to infidelity and vice. I do not ask you to believe this, I do not myself believe it (using the word "religious" as they use it) I merely wish you to acknowledge that such is their belief, and so far as the state is concerned—which is right cannot be known. Perhaps I can help to make my point clearer by putting "the boot on the other leg." Suppose that the state were to set up music halls throughout the province and provide by local taxation for Sunday lectures of educational value garnished with classical music. The Protestant conscience would be outraged. Catholics would see nothing improper and might reply: "Why do you object? There is no religion there." "That is exactly the ground of my objection," would retort the Protestant. "You are unreasonable," might answer the Catholic; "surely if you go to church in the morning you can attend a lecture in the afternoon. Too much religion is unreasonable." My Protestant friend, you have no more right to judge how much religion Catholic children ought to have during the week, than have Catholics to prescribe your limit on Sunday. Which is right cannot be known.

Again, Catholics believe their maxim, "*Extra ecclesiam nulla salus*; or, as taught at St. Boniface "*Hors de l'Eglise, point du salut*—Outside the church no salvation." (Certain explanatory qualifications are unimportant here). If any Presbyterian should denounce this claim as so absurd and unreasonable as to fairly merit their disregard, I refer him to the Westminster Confession, chap. XXX, sec. 2, where he may read with elaborate notes to prove it:

To these officers (church officers) the keys of the kingdom of heaven are committed, by virtue whereof they have the power respectively to retain and remit sins, to shut the kingdom against the impenitent, both by words and censures; and to open it unto penitent sinners, by the ministry of the gospel, and by absolution from censures, as occasion shall require.

Once more, I do not ask you to believe all this, but it is necessary that you should admit that Catholics do most heartily believe it and that as between you and them the state insists—Which is right cannot be known.

If I have carried you this far, you will agree with me that it is the most sacred duty of Catholic parents so to shape the opening and maturing intelligence of their children that they shall be protected from a secular education (leading, as they believe it does, to infidelity and vice); and shall be subjected to such daily and hourly influences as will insure their cordial and unswerving adhesion to the Catholic church. You and I, my Protestant friend, think that such adhesion is unfortunate and fettering; and we would wish that Catholics were Protestants. But remember the third admission, and let the state reiterate—Which is right cannot be known.

We are now in a position to formulate a school law. We have before us the principles which must govern our draft, and we know the people for whom we have to legislate. Let us proceed :

1. Schools to which all children will go are ideally the best. Let us try then and devise a system acceptable to both classes in the community. We try and fail. Catholics will not go to schools after the Protestant notion, and *e converso*.

2. What are we to do now? Each party is equally sensible and sincere; each is entitled to exactly the same rights and privileges; which is right cannot be known. (Do not stumble at this now). What are we to do? Shall we give up our project because the ideal manner of attaining it is impracticable? Or shall we seek the practicable, remembering that the ideal is almost always unattainable? Let me quote Morley's book again (p. 122):

> It is the worst of political blunders to insist on carrying an ideal set of principles into execution where others have rights of dissent, and those others, persons whose assent is as indispensable to success as it is impossible to attain.

Burke is to the same effect :

> All government, indeed every human benefit and enjoyment, every virtue and every prudent act is founded on compromise and barter. We balance inconveniences; we give and take; we remit some rights that we may enjoy others. Man acts from motives relative to his interests; and not in metaphysical speculations. (Speech on Conciliation of America).

3. Let me recall what we want to do. It is to educate the people. One system of schools would be the best. That is impracticable, because the people will not amalgamate. We must adopt then one of the following courses: Establish (A) schools liked by neither party; or (B) schools favored by the majority; or (C) two sets of schools. Let us consider B and C, assuming that the contention

must be narrowed to these; and let us ask which conforms to our agreed principles taking these seriatim. (Please refer back, and save repetition of them).

1. Education of the majority of the children will be attained by B; but of all children by C. (Shall we score one for C.?)

2. Or, if all are educated by B., it will be by *compelling* Catholics to go to the schools, which is undesirable. (May we not now score for C.?)

3. B, although the choice of the majority, may be wrong. It would certainly be so either in Manitoba or Quebec. All are entitled to exactly the same rights and privileges. Catholics are as much entitled to have religious schools, as Protestants are to have secular (with a vestige). Which is right cannot be known. These principles condemn the establishment of B and necessitate the adoption of C. (Another goal for C, I think).

4 and 5. B is an undue interference with the right of parents to control the character of education. Were B necessary in order to secure education, then this interference might not be undue. Being not necessary it is unreasonable (C has 3 to 0).

Once more: Suppose the Catholic system to be injurious, then, as Morley tells us, " the only question that we need ask ourselves turns solely upon the possibility of breaking it up and dispersing it, by methods compatible with the doctrine of liberty " (84). In other words, people must sometimes be led and not driven. It is the disregard of this principle of political action that constitutes the stupidest and most disastrous feature in Mr. Greenway's policy. (According to my umpiring, C wins by 4, love.)

At this point I feel the impatience and intolerance of strength arising; the hot inclination of the majority to have its way, asserting itself as against cold reasoning. And I hasten to uphold our admissions with the remark that intolerance may be exhibited as well in a negative as in a positive command; as well in compelling abstinence, as in obliging performance; as well in the decree that *no man* shall ask a petition of any one but Darius, as in the requirement that *all men* shall "fall down and worship the golden image that Nebuchadnezzar the king hath set up"; as well in compelling children to be educated in no religion, as in any particular religion; as well in limiting the amount of religious instruction to be given to a child, as in prescribing that he is to have nothing else. Locke says (1st Letter):

> As the magistrate has no power to impose by his law the use of any rites and ceremonies in any church, so neither has he any power to *forbid* the use of such rights and ceremonies as already received, approved and practised by any church.

Catholics desire that all education should be of a religious character. Have you a right to say that he shall not have it so? Your only plea would be that so much religion is wholly unnecessary. And why should you, my homœopathic friend, be the one to measure out religious doses? Why not some one of allopathic generosity? Why not the Rev. Principal King, who would have "the being, the character and the moral government of God" taught in the schools, but not "the nature and the necessity of regeneration," or "the work of the Holy Spirit?" Why not the present government, with its belief in purely secular schools? Why not Thomas A. Kempis? You never read the celebrated "Imitation of Christ," my Protestant friend. You can get it in English for sixty cents, and it would not hurt you. Here are a few words:

Christ (loq.) let my words be thy *principal* study; for these awaken attention, enlighten the understanding, kindle a holy zeal, provoke true contrition and heal the wounds they would make with a spiritual labor of grace and solid comfort. Let not the growing wiser, and more learned, be the end thou proposest to thyself in reading; but read that thou mayest be qualified to practice, and let thy knowledge be seen by subduing thy vices and passions. (Cap. XLVIII.)

And again:

How shall we follow a pattern which we but little think of? The first step, therefore, toward thus copying after Him, is the employing our thoughts with great frequency and serious attention upon the perfection of this divine original. (Cap. I.)

Once more:

The great occasion of the fantastical opinions, and dangerous corruptions, with which the world is pestered is certainly this, that men propose no end to their studies but to be great, and to have other people think as highly of them as they do of themselves. (Cap. III.)

All fudge and poppy-cock, you say. But suppose that a section of the community desire to adopt this style of education, with firm belief in its efficacy, have you a right to prevent them, or even to make it difficult for them?

Could the state but know, for certain, exactly how much religious training is enough, a regulation might well be made upon the subject. But it does not know, my friend, nor, I think, do you. Can we not agree, then, that the extent to which a child is to be surrounded with religious influences is a matter for the parents and not for the state? Remember that while the state may insist upon education it ought to attain that end in such a way as will least conflict with religious freedom.

Let me now answer directly some objections. I am reminded that the same liberty claimed for Catholics must be accorded to Protestants. Certainly, I reply, and Protestants in Quebec, I assure you, appreciate to the full the value of the arguments in favor of liberty for the minority. Dr. Davidson, of Montreal, besought the Equal Rights Association to make no attack upon the doctrine of separate schools, for, said he, what shall we do without our nine hundred Protestant schools in Quebec?

"And if all the different sects demanded separate schools, education of the masses would be almost impossible." It would be much hampered, I reply; and if all Manitoba children were deaf or blind their education would, I believe, be extremely difficult. But they are not; and we need not speculate as to what we would do if they were. Happily for us, there are but two parties in Manitoba to be considered in dealing with the subject of education. And it is for idle men, merely, to cope with the imaginary difficulties of non-existing conditions.

Another objection may be put in this way: "The state is justified in setting up national schools. All idea of national schools is gone if any sect is left outside their operation. The subtraction would not qualify merely the nationality of the schools, but destroy it. There can be no national schools if the Catholics have separate schools. If we cannot have national schools, then let every denomination set up for itself." Let us not be fooled by phrases, or misled by the improper use of an adjective. "National highway" was applied to the C. P. R. wherewith to conjure votes, and so "national" applied to schools may help to cloud the issue. Schools in Manitoba are not, and by reason of the Canadian constitution never can be, properly called national. Let us assign them the most soaring adjective which we can truthfully apply, and dub them "provincial schools," and the strength derived from the misappropriation of the adjective is almost gone. It weakens, we see, in proportion as the ideas associated with provincialism are less stirring than those aroused by nationalism. The schools of 1890 are, as by statute they are called, not national schools, but "public schools."

If this answer be thought insufficient, take another. In England there is a national church, but yet there are many others. In Canada there may be a national highway, but it has not swallowed up all the others. There may be national schools, or that which you may choose to call such, and also separate schools, which may also, just as properly, be called national schools.

Yet another answer. You want one set of schools. If that be practically unattainable, what is your next choice—some system which approaches your ideal, or that which is furthest removed from it? Your system you argue the best for two reasons: (1) that it is the cheapest, and (2) that it tends to homogeneity and good-fellowship. Your ideal system being unattainable—the highest possible degree of economy and homogeneity being out of the question, do you argue in favor of the greatest extravagance and heterogeneity? One set of schools being impossible, do you then argue in favor of their indefinite multiplication? I think you will not. You will agree with me that if we cannot get along with one church, better have two than twenty ; and if not with one kind of school, your purposes of economy and good-fellowship will be best subserved by taking the lowest practicable number.

A criticism of the Brandon *Sun*, in a well written article, is as follows : " It is more singular that he should have deliberately closed his eyes to the main features of the issue. He knows that the demand for a national school system is, in part, to do away with class legislation, to obliterate all lines of demarcation in the state that distinguish classes and creeds, to establish uniformity, to promote harmony and good-fellowship, to be able to provide the necessary means to establish and maintain the most efficient constitutional system, to provide approved checks for the suppression of crime, and, in a word, to lay the foundations of a homogeneous nationality upon which, etc."

Queen Elizabeth's parliament over three hundred years ago passed an Act to establish uniformity It proposed to "obliterate all lines of demarcation in the state that distinguish creeds, to establish uniformity, to promote harmony and good-fellowship," by dint of statutory pressure. When the Emperor Ferdinand interceded on behalf of the Catholics he was told :

> The Queen declares that she cannot grant churches to those who disagree from her religion, being against the law of her parliament, and highly dangerous to the state of her kingdom, as it would sow various opinions in the nation to distract the minds of honest men, and would cherish parties and factions that might disturb the present tranquility of the commonwealth. (Hallam's Hist. of Eng., cap. III.)

The author adds :

> Yet enough had already occurred in France to lead observing men to suspect that severities and restrictions are by no means an infallible specific to prevent or subdue religious factions.

Of course, the statute failed in its object, as have always, and in every place, failed all similar ordinances. With such experience to aid our judgments, I would hardly have imagined that any one now living believed that such objects could be so accomplished, and would argue in all seriousness what Lowell wrote in satire :

> I du believe wutever trash
>   'll keep the people in blindness—
> Thet we the Mexicuns can thrash
>   Right inter brotherly kindness,
> Thet bombshells, grape, an powder 'n' ball
>   Air good-will's strongest magnets,
> That peace, to make it stick at all,
>   Must be druv in with bagnets.

If Mr. Greenway really is moved by kindly feeling towards the Catholics, and is legislating for their good, does he not, by confiscating all their school houses, furniture and apparatus, purchased with their own money, at least leave himself open to the question:

> Perhaps you did right to dissemble your love,
> But why did you kick us down stairs?

JOHN S. EWART

CHAPTER XIII.

ARTICLE IN "THE WEEK"

March 25th, 1892.

The introduction, in the Dominion Parliament, of Mr. McCarthy's Bill to repeal the dual language, and separate school, provisions of the North-West Act suggests the renewal of the struggle which is probably not far distant in respect to Manitoba. The principle involved is substantially the same in both sections. That principle is still being earnestly discussed in Manitoba. We have just been reading what is perhaps the latest important contribution to it, in the shape of two vigorous pamphlets by Mr. John S. Ewart, of Winnipeg. The first is "An Open Letter to the Hon. Thomas Greenway"; the second "A Reply to Criticisms," reprinted from the Manitoba *Free Press*. In these pamphlets we have the advantage of a forcible re-statement of the arguments in favour of the separate school system by a clever advocate who is at the same time a Liberal, and consequently on general principles a supporter of the party by whom the law abolishing that system has been put upon the statute book. Into the charges of bad faith which Mr. Ewart presses against Mr. Greenway and his Government we need not enter, as they do not affect the general argument. Mr. Ewart does not rest his case upon the constitutional question, hence we are free from the complication which is caused by that issue. His letters are a frank and able attempt to defend the discarded system on its merits, and as such are worthy of careful study by every one who wishes to reach a sound conclusion in regard to the right and wrong of a controversy which is likely, at no distant day, to stir the whole Dominion, and in the final settlement of which the future peace and progress of the great North-West provinces of Canada may in no small degree be involved. Within the limits which necessarily circumscribe our discussion of such a matter we can attempt nothing more than to point out what seem to us to be certain misconceptions, or invalid assumptions, upon which Mr. Ewart's arguments are based, and the removal of which would cause the whole structure to topple. The most fundamental of these misconceptions or assumptions is that contained in the following and similar passages :

> It is upon this point, the character of education, that Protestants and Catholics are fundamentally at variance ; not whether children shall be educated (on that they are agreed), but what shall be the character of the education. The great majority of Protestants think that secular education during the week,

with little more than the acknowledgment of the Deity twice a day, is good enough for their children. A true Roman Catholic abhors this system and insists upon all education being permeated with religion. A Protestant is trained secularly, and religion is relegated to Sunday. A Roman Catholic is trained to be religious as well as intelligent all days of the week.

Again :

As you see, sir, and know, the Protestants are satisfied with the non-sectarian schools—the vestige (of religion) being still visible, and they will be satisfied with nothing else. It is useless, therefore, to assert that they give up something for uniformity's sake, and to argue that Catholics should be willing to follow their example. They give up nothing, but Catholics are asked to surrender what to them is sacred.

We maintain that it is a misconception to regard the question as one between Catholics and Protestants. It is rather a question between Catholics (primarily the Catholic clergy) and all other classes of citizens. It is a misconception, not to use a stronger term, to say that Protestants (note the unfairness of making the comparsion between Protestants generally and *true* Roman Catholics) think that "secular education during the week etc.," is good enough for them, and that they surrender nothing. The *true* Protestant certainly attaches no less value to religion as an indispensable factor in all education, every day in the week than the most devout Roman Catholic. The difference is that he, as a citizen of the state, recognizes the rights of all other citizens and declines to force the teaching of his own religious views upon them or their children, and as both Christian and citizen he denies that it is within either the power or the duty of the state to provide for genuine religious teaching. He also refuses to acknowledge the right of the state to make him a party, by legislation and taxation, to the training of a large class of the future citizens, under a *regime* which he honestly believes to be adapted to make them both worse citizens and worse Christians.

We venture to hope that the distinctions pointed out in the foregoing remarks, and their fundamental relation to the whole argument, will without further enlargement be sufficiently obvious to any one who will take the trouble to consider them carefully. The fact is, as we understand it, that thoughtful Protestants are very far from being satisfied with a purely secular education, or regarding such an education as in any sense a complete or ideal one. They are fully persuaded that only as it is constantly accompanied and supplemented with religious training by parents and religious teachers can it be regarded as taking in the whole, or the highest part, of the child nature and faculties. But, agreeing heartily with the principle laid down and advocated by Mr. Ewart in his second pamphlet, viz., that "the state has nothing to do with religion," they draw from it a conclusion which is the direct opposite of that reached by Mr. Ewart. Instead of reasoning thus : "The state has nothing to do with religion, and cannot possibly decide what is true religion, and what is not, therefore it should enter into partnership with a professedly religious body, which claims to have the true religion, and put the public schools, to a large extent, into the hands of such a body;" they say: "The state has nothing to do with religion, therefore it should have nothing to do with the teaching of it, nor should it tax any class of citizens for the purpose of teaching any system of religion whatever, but content itself with leaving the whole subject to the voluntary efforts of the various religions bodies who have it in hand, merely protecting individual liberty of conscience." They see clearly that the primary responsibility for the education of children belongs not to the state but to the parents, and that the state's right to intervene is merely derived and inferential, arising out of its obligation to protect the state from the injurious effects of ignorance and to secure at least that minimum of intelligence in its citizens which is necessary to its self-preservation. They therefore regard the public school system as an expedient, the best practicable, for securing this minimum of universal intelligence. The secularization of the schools they regard as a compromise growing out of the necessities of the situation and the only means of securing to the individal freedom of conscience in matters of faith. At the same time they desire that the state should afford every reasonable facility for the teaching of religion by the various churches in connection with the schools though never as a part of the school machinery, or in any wise at the expense of the state which, it is agreed, cannot decide what is true religion and what is not. Religion, they hold, is in its very nature voluntary, and its fundamental principles are violated the moment the funds of the state, derived from compulsory taxation, are used in its support, whether those funds are contributed by Catholics or Protestants, or by those who are neither the one nor the other, but whose rights of citizenship are just as sacred as those of the most ponounced religionists.

And this reminds us of another assumption which is, we conceive, invalid and misleading, but is nevertheless vital to whatever force or plausibility there may be in much of Mr. Ewart's reasoning. That assumption is expressed in the following sentence:

> With the exception of the cities there are very few places in which the population is of a mixed character. In the districts in which the Catholics have schools, there are very few and sometimes no Protestants.

Granting that these statements are accurate at the present moment, have the "very few" Protestants no rights, because they are very few? Again, under the local management system which is happily characteristic of all our free school methods, a purely Catholic section would as a matter of course have the choice of their own teacher, and, while he should not be permitted to teach denominational tenets during school hours, or as a part of the school course, there could be little difficulty in arranging the matter of religious instruction in such a case. But the Manitoba Legislature is surely bound to legislate for the future, that great future to which we all look forward, when the country shall be the home of millions instead of the thousands who are now scattered over its vast and fertile expanses. It is not surely to be supposed that the North-West Provinces are to be settled on sectarian lines in that good time coming. Mr. Ewart would, unless we sadly misapprehend his views, be one of the first to deplore such a state of things, and to agree with us that it would be a strong condemnation of the separate school system should it tend to favour and perpetuate a division of the whole population on narrow creed lines.

Mr. Ewart's Letter to The Week, 15th April, 1892.

To the Editor of The Week:

Sir,—In the course of your courteous criticism of my recent pamphlets you object to my ascribing to Protestants less zeal for the combination of religious and secular education than I accord to Catholics. You say:

> The true Protestant certainly attaches no less value to religion as an indispensable factor in all education, every day in the week, than the most devout Roman Catholic. The difference is that he, as a citizen of the State, recognizes the rights of all other citizens, and declines to force the teaching of his own religious views upon them, or their children ; and, as both Christian and citizen, he denies that it is within either the power, or the duty, of the state to provide for genuine religious teaching. . . . The secularization of the schools they (thoughtful Protestants) regard as a compromise growing out of the necessities of the situation, and the only means of securing to the individual freedom of conscience in matters of faith.

My pamphlet dealt with the Manitoba aspect of the question. The distinction which I drew would, I admit, not hold in England. Perhaps it may not hold in Ontario, although my own opinion is that it would. That it exists in Manitoba there can be little question. Allow me to mention two out of many proofs.

1. From 1870 to 1890 our schools were divided into Protestant and Roman Catholic, each denomination having full control of its schools, and *carte blanche* to make them exactly as they wanted them. The Protestant Board of Education consisted of five clergymen and two laymen. One of its first acts was "to exclude all distinctive religious teachings from its schools," and to enjoin "the reading of the Holy Scriptures, and the prayers as published in the by-laws and regulations, at the opening and closing of the school." The secularization ("with a vestige"), you will observe, was not decreed out of

tender regard for Roman Catholics (for the schools were avowedly and by name Protestant, and Roman Catholics had no part or lot in them), but merely because the Protestants wanted to give their schools a secular character. Now, contrast the action of the Roman Catholic Board—but I need not tell you, sir, what *that* Board did.

2. Our School Act of 1890 abolished both Protestant and Catholic schools, and established Public schools. It provides that religious exercises may ("at the option of the school trustees of the district") be conducted "just before the closing hour in the afternoon," and enacts that "no religious exercises shall be allowed therein except as above provided." The Act took away, from both Protestants and Catholics, the ample powers which they had as to religious education under the previous statute. We may test opinion by asking, How was this legislative divorce between secular and religious education received by the two bodies? The Rev. Prof. Bryce in an affidavit tells us that "The Presbyterian Synod of Manitoba and the North-west Territories, which represents the largest religious body in Manitoba, passed, in May, 1890, a resolution *heartily approving* of the Public School Act of this year; and I believe it is approved of by the great majority of the Presbyterians in Manitoba." Contrast the action of the Roman Catholics—once more, sir, you need no information. The Protestants gave thanks for the final blow to all chance of religion in the schools, and for the effacement of their power to provide it. The Roman Catholics are on their way to the Privy Council to try and get relief.

3. Allow me to forestall your reply to these points, by the remark that your statement that Protestants regard a secular school system as an acceptable "compromise" (so I understand you), of itself establishes my point. In Roman Catholic view their can be no compromise in the matter. Secular schools violate the dogmatic, and historic, position of their Church. That Protestants will for the sake of convenience or economy agree to the secularization of the schools—that they will dispense with "an indispensable factor in all education," and that Roman Catholics will not, establishes the difference to which I referred.

Your criticism, moreover, is directed to a statement which, from your point of attack, is immaterial to the argument. I argued that Roman Catholics, as a matter of conscience (differing in this respect from Protestants), insisted "upon all education being permeated with religion," therefore, (other premisses now understood) they should be allowed to supply their children with that kind of education. You take issue upon the parenthesis, "differing in this respect from Protestants." My argument would have been as valid were the parenthesis left out, and if Catholics were represented by X. Let me show this clearly, and for that purpose assume that the true Protestant does, as you say, attach " no less value to religion as an indispensable factor, etc." Let me also assume your statement to be correct, that " the true Protestant . . . . . denies that it is within the power, or the duty of the state, to provide for genuine religious teaching." Protestant and Catholic are now agreed upon premisses, and may both be included under X. The "true Protestant" argument now runs this way: *The state ought to protect itself from vice by education. Religion is "an indispensable factor in all education, every day in the week." Therefore it is the duty of the state to educate, but* to have nothing to do with religion.* The true Protestant should observe that his conclusion "It is the duty of the state to educate," is contradicted the moment he asserts that it is *not* the duty of the state to teach "an indispensable factor in all education." It is as though he said: It is the duty of the state to build warships, but it is not the business of the state to furnish them with rudders. A rudderless warship, and an irreligious education are, to Roman Catholics, similar abominations—great capacities for evil.

The true Protestant clearly argues badly. I submit the alternative conclusion for his consideration: *The state ought to protect itself from vice by education. Religion is an "indispensable factor in all education every day in the week." Therefore it is the duty of the state in proceeding to protect itself, not to drop the indispensable, but to devise means by which it may be retained.* If means cannot be devised, then of course the indispensable must go, and education be truncated. But let us first be very sure that so fatal a step is absolutely necessary. Let us see.

The true Protestant makes his fundamental mistake when he skips from separation of church and state, to secularization of schools; and shuts out all other alternatives. He attributes to me the following: "The state has nothing to do with religion . . . . therefore it should enter into a partnership with a professedly religious body." Therefore it should do something else, I say.

As pointed out by John Stuart Mill there are two distinct methods by which the state can deal with education. It can establish schools of its own, or it can assist denominational or other schools. In the one case it undertakes the control of the schools and adopts a scheme of its own for their management—just as it establishes, owns, and manages, a navy. In the other case it observes merely the practical results of the management of schools by other bodies, and renders assistance according to such results. These are (1) state schools, and (2) state-aided schools. Both of these systems are now in force in England. The Province of Ontario acts, to-day, upon both principles with reference to charitable institutions.

Now it is very clear that there is no breach of the principle of the separation of church and state, when the city of Toronto subscribes to the maintenance of some Roman Catholic charity. Good secular work is being done and the city is glad to help, even if the institution has

---

* The words "to educate, but" were omitted originally, but were afterwards supplied.

a religious side to it. In the same way the principle is not violated in England where denominational schools are helped by public funds. Good work is being done, and as the state has no objection to religious education, there is no reason for refusing help, which would otherwise be granted, merely because religion is taught there. While the state will not assist in the propagation of religion, it will not refuse to recognize an institution because of its religion. In other words, the state will neither patronize, nor antagonize, religion.

The way is now clear for the statement that there is no infringement of the principle if the state should incorporate all those who think alike on educational matters, and, instead of giving them public money (which the Government would draw from the people), should provide machinery by which they can pay their own money directly to their own trustees. All the state does, in this case, is to erect a corporation, to which certain persons may pay their proportion of money necessary for education, if they think fit so to do.

You admit that parents are primarily responsible for the education of their children, "and that the state's right to intervene is merely derived and inferential, arising out of its obligation to protect the state from the injurious effects of ignorance," etc. State-aided education is, therefore, more nearly right than state education. In both cases public money is used, but in the former the primary right and responsibility of the parents is preserved, while in the latter all individual choice of method is annulled, and an "indispensable part" of education necessarily omitted. To put the matter syllogistically: *The state ought to protect itself from vice by education. Education can better be conducted by agencies other than the state, because of the latter's incapacity anent a certain indispensability, etc. Therefore, the state ought to assist other agencies, rather than itself take the management.*

Now, sir, let me point out that separate schools are more nearly allied to state-aided, than to state, schools. They are, in their essential characteristics, still less obnoxious to principle (if that were possible) than state-aided schools. For all that the state does is to organize Roman Catholics so that they may support themselves apart from the state. If their revenue be supplemented by a ratable contribution from the general fund, that is by no means a necessary part of the system. It might be an easily-answered argument for the stoppage of the supplement, but not for the abolition of the schools. It is clear, then, that we are not shut up to a choice between two alternatives (1) abandonment of separation between church and state, and (2) abandonment of an "indispensable part of education." There is a *modus vivendi* to be found in (*a*) state-aided education, or (*b*) separate schools with no state aid at all—only a charter.

In fact, the true Protestant is easily driven to admit that the question is merely one of money. He wants one set of schools because it is cheaper than a double set; and, for the sake of economy, he will forego religion in the schools. Roman Catholics maintain that the economy would be false, and the divorce disastrous to the eternal welfare of the children. I gave one answer to the economy argument, when I pointed out in my pamphlet that, at present, in Manitoba, the saving would be a bagatelle. But the best answer is not that, but this: that to Roman Catholics the matter is not one of money at all, but of conscience. In matters of conscience, Protestant denominations are wildly prodigal of their money; as witness the thousands of dollars which they annually spend in ungenerous competition with one another in every little village in Manitoba, and the North-west Territories. They have a perfect right, no doubt, so to compete, and to urge subscriptions for the ruinous contest upon grounds of conscience; but let them not say to Catholics that in a very much more important matter *their* consciences must be sacrificed to economy.

For summary, I ask you to reperuse the foregoing italicized sentences, and then consider the following: The state ought to protect itself from vice by education. The state ought not to interfere with religion. Yet religion is deemed by some "an indispensable factor in all education every day in the week." State schools have advantages over state-aided, or state-chartered, schools, except (principally) in the matter of this indispensability. Protestants are either (*a*) not impressed with the importance of this "indispensability," or (*b*) are willing to waive it. Catholics make its retention a matter of conscience. For Protestants, therefore, state schools, and for Roman Catholics state-aided, or state-chartered, schools should be prescribed. If Protestants are impressed, etc., and are not willing to waive, then they also are entitled to separate schools.

JOHN S. EWART.

ARTICLE IN "THE WEEK," 15TH APRIL, 1892.

All logical argument should be based on clear definitions. Probably Mr. Ewart may not be to blame for having failed to understand some of the terms used in our remarks on the Manitoba school question, in the sense in which they were intended, but it must be evident to the careful reader that, if he had so understood them, a large part of his rejoinder in another column would not have been written in its present form. For instance, Mr. Ewart devotes a considerable part of his article to an attempt to show that our statement that the true Protestant attaches no less importance to religion as an indispensable factor in all education than the Roman Catholic, is not correct; at least, so far as Manitoba is concerned. Now, in the first place, what is meant by *education?* Mr. Ewart's whole argument rests apparently on the assumption that it means simply and only the training which is, or ought to be, given to children in the public school. We regard the part of education that is, or that can be, imparted in the public school as but a fragmentary part of the education of the child. He agrees with us that the parent, not the state, is primarily responsible for the education of the child. But his whole argument rests upon the assumption that this work of education, as a whole, is to be handed over to the state and done in the public school. We, on the other hand, maintain, as we hoped we had made clear, that the state's right to intervene in the matter at all is merely derived and inferential, and that it extends only so far as may be necessary to secure that minimum of intelligence which will fit the man or the woman for the discharge of the ordinary duties of citizenship. Hence, when we said that the true Protestant, no less than the true Catholic, regards religion as an indispensable factor of all education, nothing was farther from our thoughts than the notion which Mr. Ewart seems to work from, that the public school is the sole educational agency. We regard it as but one, and by no means the most important one, of a variety of agencies which are, or ought to be, constantly, or simultaneously, at work in the educational process. The purely intellectual and moral elements of this training may be relegated (in part) to the public school. Other and higher elements of it the public school is, from its very nature as the creature of the state, unable to provide. It by no means follows that these elements are not to be supplied by their own proper agencies, *e.g.*, the church, the Sunday school, above all the powerful and perpetual influence of parents, and the sacred associations of the home circle. If it be objected that the latter are too often defective, or wholly wanting, we can only reply: "More's the pity." But the public school cannot be, and ought not to be, relied on to supply the lack. It can be supplied only by the zeal and energy of the agencies which are distinctively religious. When we denied that it is within "either the *power* or the duty" of the state to provide for genuine religious teaching, we should perhaps have stayed to explain our meaning. By so doing we might have prevented Mr. Ewart from overlooking the word "power" in the construction of his syllogism. That word was of primary importance, for it is evident that what the state cannot, in the nature of the case, do, that it cannot be its duty to do. What we meant to insist on as the true Protestant view is this: Religion is a thing not of the intellect, but of the heart. In other words, it is spiritual in its nature, and can be understood and discerned only by the spiritually minded. Hence, it can be efficiently taught only by teachers who are spiritually qualified. But the state is not necessarily religious. The Government which constitutes its executive may be infidel or agnostic, or even atheistic. Hence it cannot be trusted with the examination of teachers to see whether they are religiously qualified. It will be seen, then, that the fault which vitiates Mr. Ewart's first syllogism is the ambiguity of its middle term, *education*. In the first premiss *education* means, and can only mean, that modicum of intellectual training which can be imparted in the public school, whereas in the second premiss it must mean the complete round of training and influence which mould the whole nature—intellectual, moral and spiritual.

In the second place, we must point out very briefly another faulty assumption which quite invalidates Mr. Ewart's argument to show that Protestants in Manitoba do not attach the same importance to religious education as do Roman Catholics. This assumption is that the two-fold division, "Protestant and Roman Catholic," exhausts the citizenship of the province. But Protestants find themselves bound by their own cherished principle of liberty of conscience to have regard constantly to the rights of various classes of citizens who are neither Protestants nor Catholics. There are always a considerable number in every community who do not wish their children to be taught the creeds of either Protestants or Catholics. Some of them belong to no religious sect. Others object on principle to having their children drilled in any dogmatic system. Yet Protestants recognize that the rights of citizenship of these men are just as sacred as those of any other class of taxpayers. Another distinction of still greater importance, in this connection, is the outcome of the principle of religious liberty, which is dear to the hearts of all true Protestants. As a result of the operation of this principle, Protestants are divided into numerous sections among themselves, each holding its own peculiar views of religious truth, and differing from others on minor points of doctrinal belief. From these two sources, their regard for the rights of non-believers, and their differences of opinion among themselves, as well as from their broader objections to the teachings of Catholicism, representing as it does the principle of authority, as opposed to liberty in religion, also from their utter unwillingness to permit the secular authority to meddle officially with the sacred doctrines of Christianity, and the no less sacred rights of conscience, it is surely easy to see why the various Protestant bodies should reach the conclusion that religious teaching in state schools is as impracticable in fact as it is objectionable in theory, and so to acquit them of the charge of being indifferent to religious teaching itself, for which they make other provision.

Admitting, for argument's sake, the force of the objections to religious teaching in state schools, as involving the principle of a union of church and state, Mr. Ewart goes on to point out what he deems a way of escape from this difficulty, without the sacrifice of the religious teaching in the schools. He would substitute for the state school, the state-aided or the state-organized school. The objections to both these alternatives are to our thinking so many and serious, that we are at a loss to know how to deal with his subject in the small space still at our disposal. As an illustration of the principle involved in the state-aided school, Mr. Ewart instances the case in which the City of Toronto subscribes to the maintenance of some Roman Catholic charity, and says that it is very clear that there is no breach of the principle of separation of church and state in such an arrangement. We suppose he will think us hopelessly cantankerous when we say that, on the contrary, we think it a distinct violation of that principle. In the same way we hold that the principle is violated in England, where denominational schools are helped by public funds. On the religious side, we maintain that the Christian religion is a system of voluntaryism in its very essence, and that one of its fundamental principles is violated whenever a professedly Christian body accepts funds derived by compulsory taxation, for the carrying on of its work of any kind. From the political side we maintain that the system is wrong in principle, because the funds collected by the state are trust funds, and the Government and Parliament, which are the trustees of these funds, have no right to appropriate them to any institution which is not under direct Government inspection. Here we note another confusing ambiguity which lurks in the use of the word "religion." Would the Catholics be satisfied with any religious teaching that could possibly be acceptable to Protestants? If not, it is not religious teaching, but Roman Catholic teaching for which they are contending. It is well known that doctrines which the Roman Catholic holds to be of the very essence of religion, the Protestant regards as the most deadly error, and *vice-versa*. What more irrational than for the same Government with the one hand to help spread the disease, and with the other supply the antidote? What more unjust than for it to use the taxes paid by the Catholic to aid in the propagation of the doctrines which the good Catholic detests, and the opposite? What more clear than that the only proper and logical attitude for the Government of a free country in relation to the sects is that of strict neutrality? But if not state-aided schools, why not state-organized schools? Why not find a *modus vivendi* in "separate schools with no state aid at all—only a charter?" To prevent misapprehension let us say, just here, that we hold firmly to the right of any body of people, Catholic or Protestant, or neither, to unite and organize for the establishment and support of schools for the education of their children, on any plan, and according to any system, which they deem best, so long as the intellectual education provided is sufficiently thorough to meet the reasonable requirements of the state in regard to citizenship. It would be, in our opinion, an outrage to forbid the Catholics from continuing their separate schools for the education of their own children, and, so far as we are aware, no such outrage has ever been proposed in Manitoba. The main question, then, is as to what is meant by state organization—the charter—under the proposed system? Why should the aid of the state be needed? If merely to confer corporate powers, there could be no objection. But if to enable compulsion to be used to make any one contribute to, and patronize, a denominational school against his will, simply because he might happen to be recognized as a member of that denomination, we should demur. This suggests other serious objections. Suppose that the different denominations were able and willing to support their respective separate schools, what would be done with the scattered remnants of population, those who would regard it as an infringment upon their rights of conscience to compel them to choose between the denominational schools? If all citizens were either Catholics or Protestants, and the Protestants were as homogeneous in their religious views as the Catholics, the question would be greatly simplified. Even then, however, there would arise the serious question whether the state should have nothing to do with preparing its future citizens for citizenship. On the whole, is it not pretty clear that the fairest settlement of the difficulty is secular teaching by the state, and religious teaching by the parents and the churches?

Article in "The Week," 22nd April, 1892.

We received from Mr. Ewart, too late for its intended use, a note supplying a few words which had been accidentally omitted from his letter on the Manitoba School Question, which appeared and on which we commented last week. As Mr. Ewart deems the omitted words of special importance to his argument, we repeat the sentence and context with these words supplied:—

> The argument now runs this way: The state ought to protect itself from vice by education. Religion is "an indispensable factor in all education every day in the week." Therefore it is the duty of the state to educate; but to have nothing to do with religion! The true Protestant should observe that his conclusion, "it is the duty of the state to educate" is contradicted the moment he asserts that it is not the duty of the state to teach "an indispensable factor in all education."

The correction, it will be observed, does not affect our position in the slightest degree; because, as we have before seen, there is no contradiction whatever between the Protestant's conclusion that " it is the duty of the state to educate," and his assertion that "it is not the duty of the state to teach an indispensable factor in all education" —meaning religion. The fatal fault in Mr. Ewart's argument is his failure to observe that in the first proposition the Protestant, whose views we attempted to interpret, uses the term "educate" only in a very restricted sense—as was, we think, clear from the whole tenor of our reasoning— to denote merely such elementary and rudimentary mental training as is deemed indispensable to intelligent citizenship. In the logical terminology, of which Mr Ewart seems fond, his syllogism is made worthless by the vice of an "ambiguous middle term." To suppose us to assent to the statement, "It is the duty of the state to educate," using the word "educate" to include the whole training of the child, mental, moral and religious, is to credit us with giving away our case, with a simplicity so transparent that it would hardly be worth the while of a clever logician like our correspondent to expose it.

Mr. Ewart's Letter to "The Week," 29th April, 1892.

To the Editor of The Week:

Sir,—It would not be proper for me again to intrude upon your columns any lengthened discussion. Permit me, however, to note, with pleasure, the very close approximation to which the discussion has brought us. We agree:

1. That the state ought to protect itself from vice by education (or a modicum thereof).

2. Catholics may "unite and organize for the establishment and support of schools for the education of their children, on any plan, and according to any system, which they deem best, so long as the intellectual education provided is sufficiently thorough to meet the reasonable requirements of the state in regard to citizenship."

3. "There could be no objection" "to confer corporate powers" upon them, to enable them so "to unite and organize."

4. But these powers should not "enable compulsion to be used to make any one contribute to, and patronize, a denominational school against his will."

5. The state may properly raise money by taxation for the purposes of education.

6. There is nothing "more unjust than for it to use the taxes paid by the Catholic to aid the propagation of the doctrines which the good Catholic detests" (rightly or wrongly is immaterial).

7. Or, by parity of reasoning (let me add, without agreement possibly), to use it in diffusing a purely secular education "which the good Catholic detests" (rightly or wrongly again immaterial; but that he is right, a large number of Protestant ministers would warmly testify. Possibly even you, sir, would baulk at the French notion of a purely secular education).

8. And what more just (can we not agree?) that Catholics (united and organized by the state for the purpose of education) should be permitted to pay their own taxes, if they desire to do so, to their own schools, instead of having them applied to the erection of "rudderless warships" which they detest.

You have agreed to proposition three and four. If we add to these, proposition eight (almost self-evident, I think) we have the separate school system in Ontario; for there, as you are aware, it is purely optional with a Catholic whether he pays his taxes to the Catholic schools or to the public schools. There is no "compulsion." If it be said that the Catholic schools receive a ratable share of other moneys, again I answer that that is not "a necessary part of the system. It might be an easily-answered argument for the stoppage of the supplement, but not for the abolition of the schools."

JOHN S. EWART.

(The foregoing letter was mailed before Mr. Ewart had received the issue of the *Week* of 22nd April. After reading the article in that issue he forwarded an addenda to the above letter as follows. It reached Toronto too late for publication).

"Allow me one word of direct reply, necessary perhaps for the cursory reader. In your issue of the 22nd April you reconcile the statements. "It is the duty of the state to *educate*; but to have nothing to do with religion," which "is an indispensable factor in all *education* every day in the week," by explaining that the word "educate" is used "in a very restricted sense . . . to denote merely such elementary and rudimentary mental training as is, etc." I so understood you. But this in no way removes the contradiction. Re-state the proposition and see: "It is the duty of the state to provide *some* education, but to have nothing to do with religion which is an indispensable factor in *all* education." I think that you overlooked the effect of your universal "all"; nor can you now restrict that word, for you first used the expression as equivalent, or at least not in contrast, to my assertion, that a true Roman Catholic "insists upon *all* education being *permeated* with religion." Your reply was, "The true Protestant certainly attaches no less value to religion as an indispensable factor in *all* education, every day in the week, than the most devout Roman Catholic."

Article in The Week, 29th April, 1892.

While we are glad to find ourselves at one with our correspondent, Mr. Ewart, on several points in regard to the school question we have been discussing, we are sorry to find that, in order to guard against being supposed to give consent, by silence, to propositions from which we emphatically dissent, and which seem to us to involve educational and political principles of the very first importance, we are obliged to recur to the subject. In so doing we shall merely point out, as briefly as we may be able, the points of difference which we deem of fundamental importance. To Mr. Ewart's first six propositions we take no exception. The assumed "parity of reasoning" in the seventh, we are quite unable to concede. The things compared—religious "doctrines" and "secular education"—are utterly disparate, for the purposes of this argument. With the one, as we have shown, the state has no right to interfere in any way whatever; the other, as a matter of self-protection and national well-being it must of necessity include within its domain. Hence, "while nothing could be more unjust than for it to use the taxes paid by the Catholics to aid in the propagation of the *doctrines* which the good Catholic detests," the same element of injustice is not at all present, so far as we can see, when the state uses those taxes for the purpose of imparting the "purely secular education" which we are agreed it is the province and the duty of the state to secure amongst all classes of its citizens. As this secular education is a necessary part of education, it seems a little absurd to speak of the Catholic as detesting it. If it be said that the emphasis is on the "*purely*," the reply is easy. The education need not be *purely* secular, because the good Catholic parent is at liberty to mix as much religion with it as he pleases. Hence, when we have eliminated the fallacy that lurks in the word "purely," the alleged injustice which would certainly be present if the state school prevented the Catholic parent, or guardian, or priest, from infusing as much religion as he chooses into the educational process, as it goes on from day to day, vanishes. We may just observe, further, that the mere fact that a Catholic, or any other citizen, detests a certain thing, does not of itself prove that the thing is wrong or unjust. That must be demonstrated on other grounds. Many citizens, both Catholic and Protestant, it is to be feared, detest paying their fair share of the necessary taxes, but that does not make it unjust for the state to collect those taxes.

Two points more and we have done with the Manitoba School question for the present. From Mr. Ewart's eighth proposition we are forced to dissent squarely. First, there is a broad and fundamental difference between our admission that corporate powers may be conferred upon Catholic (or any other) citizens to enable them to unite and organize for voluntary educational work, and the proposition with which our correspondent asks us to agree. The parenthetical clause which he has introduced, "united and organized by the state for the purposes of education," introduces the very principle against which we have been protesting from the first. The state has, we hold, nothing to do with uniting and organizing Catholics or Protestants for educational or any other purposes. The state has to do only with citizens as *citizens*. To organize one particular sect for educational purposes, and to pledge all its resources and all the machinery of organized society for the carrying out of those purposes, a principal part of which is the teaching of the doctrines and ritual of that denomination, would be to violate some of the most fundamental principles of politics. In the second place, to so organize the members of a religious sect, with the understanding, which the proposition in question implies, that the members of that sect are to be exempt from the payment of the taxes necessary for the maintenance of the public schools, which are admitted to be necessary for the safety and well-being of the state, would be to add wrong to wrong. It will not do to say that the state may proceed in the same way with all other denominations, for the result would still be that a large residuum of the future citizens would be unprovided for, and these of the very classes whose presence, in every community, makes the state educational system a necessity.

CHAPTER XIV.

THE MANITOBA PUBLIC SCHOOL LAW.*

By D'Alton McCarthy, Q.C., M.P.

Public interest is centred more on the fate of the School Law of Manitoba, and on the novel, and unexampled, proceedings that are now pending before the Privy Council at Ottawa, with a view, if it be possible, to find a reasonable pretext to overturn the decision of the Judicial Committee of the Privy Council, which affirmed that the Act was constitutional, than perhaps on any other matter now engaging attention—the necessity of tariff amendment possibly only accepted.

The proceedings referred to are, in themselves, and quite irrespective of the deep interest which, for one cause or another, is felt by a great majority of Canadians in the fate of the measure, sufficient to excite attention, and even to create alarm. For here we have an Act of a Provincial Legislature, which has been passed with the approval of a great majority of the people interested—the inhabitants of Manitoba—after it had run the gauntlet of the law courts of the Dominion, and of the highest legal tribunal of the Empire, assailed by a procedure unknown to the law, and before unheard of. This extraordinary attack is made before a body composed of politicians—the Dominion Cabinet—who, whatever be their qualifications in other respects, are not, it is safe to say, conspicuous for that impartiality, and freedom from bias, respecting a matter of great political importance, which we are accustomed to associate as an indispensable attribute of those who wear the ermine, and administer justice in the name of the Sovereign.

It is not proposed to discuss the merits or the demerits of the Public School Act of the Prairie Province, as to which the minds of most thinking people of the Dominion are already made up. But rather is it intended to direct attention to the last function which the Privy Council of Canada has assumed the right to take part in—to examine by what authority a new, and hitherto unknown, legal tribunal has unexpectedly manifested itself—and to consider, with all the gravity and earnestness that such an enquiry demands, whether the rôle, that the Privy Council is now engaged in playing, is permitted by the Manitoba Constitution, the British North America Act, or by any other law known to the British constitutional system.

---

* Reprinted from The Canadian Magazine, March, 1893.

It will be remembered that the legality, or constitutionality, of the Act was impugned on this ground, that although, generally speaking, the Legislature of the Province is endowed with power "exclusively" to "make laws in relation to education," it had violated the limitation imposed on its general authority in that by the Public School Act the rights or privileges with respect to denominational schools which the Roman Catholics "had by practice" (it was not contended that any class of persons had any right or privilege " by law ") in the Province at the time of the Union, had been prejudicially affected. After protracted litigation in which, in the name of one Barrett, the Dominion, on behalf of the Roman Catholic minority of the Province, claimed that the Provincial law was *ultra vires*—this proceeding having in the courts of the Province terminated adversely to that contention, to be decided in the Supreme Court of Canada in the opposite way— was finally solved, so far as the power of the Legislature is concerned, by the judgment pronounced on the appeal to the Judicial Committee in July last, by Lord Macnaghton. This distinguished jurist on behalf of the Council, expressed not only the decision that the Public School Act was within the power of the Legislature to enact, but went on, having been invited thereto by the line of argument adopted by the counsel on behalf of the Dominion, to express the opinion of the Committee,

That if the views of the Respondents (the Roman Catholic minority as represented by the Dominion) were to prevail, it would be extremely difficult for the Provincial Legislature, which has been entrusted with the exclusive power of making laws relating to education, to provide for the educational wants of the more sparsely inhabited districts of a country almost as large as Great Britain, and that the powers of the Legislature, which on the face of the Act appear so large, would be limited to the useful, but somewhat humble office, of making regulations for the sanitary condition of school-houses, imposing rates for the support of denominational schools, enforcing the compulsory attendance of scholars, and matters of that sort.

This authoritative judgment ought, one would have thought, as indeed most Canadians did think, to have ended the controversy that had now raged, exciting much embittered feeling in the Province and great interest throughout the Dominion, for a period of nearly two years, in which the somewhat unfortunate, not to say unseemly, exhibition was presented of the Dominion Government assailing the constitutionality of a provincial Act, as to which the Government, as such, had no ground of complaint.

But it seems that the end was not yet; for, unhappily for the peace of the Dominion, Sir John Thompson made a report to the Council, which was approved, ostensibly to show why the Public School Act should not be vetoed by the Governor-General, but as some supposed to postpone for a season the unpleasant duty of denying the petition of the Roman Catholic Episcopacy of the Dominion of Canada (including the Cardinal, and Bishop Cameron of Antigonish), who prayed

His Excellency in Council to afford remedy to the provincial legislation
 . . and that in the most efficacious way.

In this report the Minister of Justice said, amongst other things, that

it became apparent at the outset that these questions, namely, whether the School Act did prejudicially affect any right or privilege which the Roman Catholic had by law or practice at the Union, required the decision of the judicial tribunal, more especially as an investigation of facts was necessary to their determination;

And went on to say,

If the legal controversy should result in the decision of the Court of Queen's Bench (which had been in favor of the Province) being sustained, the time will come for your Excellency to consider the petitions which have been presented by and on behalf of the Roman Catholics of Manitoba for redress under sub-sections 2 and 3 of section 22 of the Manitoba Act, etc., etc.

The decision of the Queen's Bench of the Province has been upheld, and the event, therefore, has happened, which, as Sir John Thompson advised His Excellency, would require that the petitions which had been presented should be "considered;" and the Minister further explained his meaning by adding that

Those sub-sections contain in effect the provisions which have been made as to all the provinces, and are obviously those under which the Constitution intended that the Government of the Dominion should prevail, if it should at any time become necessary that the Federal powers should be resorted to for the protection of a Protestant or Roman Catholic minority, against any act or decision of the province or of any provincial authority affecting any right or privilege of any such minority in relation to education.

The parties interested in having the provincial legislation annulled were not slow to take advantage of the loop-hole which the Minister of Justice had suggested, based, it must be said, on a construction of the Manitoba Act unique and unprecedented; for to no one before had it ever occured in relation to the kindred subject of the New Brunswick School Law, on the analogous legislation which was in force respecting the four old provinces, that the question involved in the consideration of the policy of the School Law of a province was subject to review by or before the Dominion Cabinet. Accordingly petitions were presented, emanating from a body or "organization," as the report of the sub-committee styles it, called "The National Congress" ("National," it is presumed, as representing the French nationality sentiment), and from the Archbishop of St. Boniface, complaining of the two Acts of the province respecting education, passed in 1890, the constitutionality of which had been upheld; and both petitions prayed for redress under sub-sections 2 and 3 of section 22 of the Manitoba Act to the Governor-General in Council.

So far, it will be observed, the only law under which redress was thought of, or the authority of which was invoked, was the Manitoba Act, which contains in itself a complete code respecting education, differing in many respects from the cognate provisions of the British North America Act, which, accordingly, have always been thought to be inapplicable to the Province of Manitoba.

But in the month of November last, a further and supplemental petition was presented, emanating from the same "national congress" whose president, it seems, is the Mayor of St. Boniface, and the Archbishop of the same place, and repeating the charges made in the preceding memorials, they claim that the Acts in question violate the provisions of the British North America Act as well as the Manitoba Act, in this, that the system of separate schools which had been established in the first session of its Legislature, had given rights to the Roman Catholics which the province could not subsequently disregard.

The difference between the enactment as to the provincial legislative powers between the Act confederating the four original provinces, and the Act constituting the Province of Manitoba, which, of course, is a Canadian Act, consists in this, that in the former it is provided that not only when there is a system of separate schools at the time of the union, but also where one " is thereafter established by the legislature of the province, that an appeal shall lie " from an act or decision of any provincial authority affecting any such right to the Governor-General-in-Council. There is no such provision in the Manitoba Act, and it is hardly open to serious question that the subsection (3) of section 93 of the British North America Act, in which the provision is found, does not apply to Manitoba, which, as has already been stated, has a set of clauses on the subject of education specifically providing for the new province.

In this paper it is not proposed to "consider" the questions which have been argued, firstly, before the Sub-Committee of the Privy Council, and which resulted in the report given to the public on the 5th January last in the chief Government organ; and which were again re-stated and re-enforced *ex-parte* on behalf of the "National Congress" and the Archbishop of St. Boniface, on the 22nd January, before the Privy Council (all the members being present), but not, be it observed, before "the Governor-General-in-Council." The Government of Manitoba, who, it is said, had been notified of the proceedings, declined to appear and repudiated the jurisdiction of this new tribunal. Much may have to be said on this subject, but for the present it is to the pretence that has been set up by the Government of Sir John Thompson that in this matter the Government are to act judicially, not politically, that needs the careful attention of the Canadian public.

That there may be no mistake on this head, it is proper to quote the report of the sub-Committee, which has been approved by Council, and on which the subsequent proceedings have been based.

The application comes before Your Excellency (says the report) in a manner differing from other applications which are ordinarily made under the constitution to Your Excellency in Council. In the opinion of the sub-Committee the application is not to be dealt with at present as a matter of political character or involving political action on the part of Your Excellency's advisers. It is to be dealt with by Your Excellency in Council regardless of the personal views which Your Excellency's advisers may hold with regard to denominational schools, and without the political action of any of the members of Your Excellency's council being considered as pledged by the fact of the appeal being entertained and heard. If the contention of the petitioners be correct that such an appeal can be entertained, the enquiry will be rather of a judicial than of a political character. The sub-Committee have so treated it in hearing counsel, and in permitting their only meeting to be open to the public.

There is no mistaking this language; no misinterpreting its meaning. The Government are declining the duty of advising His Excellency, who is the Executive under our system of government, as to whether he should or should not interfere with the Manitoba School Act. It is

not to be dealt with at present as a matter of political character or involving political action on the part of Your Excellency's advisers

is the express language of this report. On the contrary it is to be an enquiry which

will be rather of a judicial than of a political character.

This is a departure so new in our constitutional proceedings that it has hardly yet been fully appreciated. That, so far, if not designed, it has served a useful "political" purpose, although the enquiry is to be judicial cannot be gainsayed. For whenever the awkward Manitoba School question came up it was quietly laid at rest by the apparently unassailable statement given by the Minister of the Crown, who up to this time was always supposed to be a responsible Minister, bound to justify every act, nay, every word officially uttered by the Governor-General, that he had no opinion on the subject, or, if he had, it would be improper for him to give utterance to it. For was he not one of the Council, if not of the sub-committee who was to determine whether the Act should be interfered with—whether a remedial order should be made directing the Province of Manitoba to undo its work on the subject of education, and was he not acting "judicially" and not in a "political" capacity as Minister?

And so at the nomination at the bye-election in Soulanges where the Hon. Mr. Ouimet graphically pictured his unhappy position in the face of an excited electorate as that of one "walking on razors," he sheltered himself under the sacred character which he filled as that of a judge who was denied the privilege of speaking of a matter that was *sub judice*. And when the new Minister of the Interior went back to his constituents for re-election and some ill-informed elector, who had been nurtured in the spirit of the British constitutional system, and in the belief that for every act of the Government the Ministers were responsible to Parliament and the constituencies, innocently asked the Manitoba representative in the Cabinet, whether he could be relied on to stand by the rights of his province, he was dumbfounded—it is doubtful whether he has yet recoverd from his astonishment—when he was told that on this subject the Minister not only had not, but could not properly have, an opinion. For was not he the Minister to hear the question of the "appeal" argued as one of the sub-Committee and afterwards as one of the Council! And when at the dinner given in Toronto by the Board of Trade, at which the Premier himself referred to the subject, his language was as follows:—

For the Government the guide shall be, as far as I am able to judge, the constitution of this country by which we propose to be guided and which we propose to obey from beginning to end."

It is evident, as has already been remarked, that this doctrine whether so designed or not, was worthy of the most crafty of political experts. It would indeed reflect no discredit on a Richelieu or a Machiavelli and it revives the best days of the Schoolmen. For it enabled the Minister of Public Works to perform the somewhat hazardous feat of "walking on razors" without injury; and the Minister of the Interior to bamboozle the honest yeoman of Selkirk; and it afforded the Premier the opportunity of figuring in the rôle of all others the most congenial, that of an oracle imbued with mysterious power, controlled and guided by the overruling principles of justice and law, and undisturbed by considerations of policy, or unaffected by motives of expediency which might perchance sway a more ordinary mortal. It is "by the constitution," as the enlightened jurists of the Dominion Cabinet, who up to the moment that they assumed the judicial garb, had been actively promoting the cause on behalf of the petitioners, may interpret it, that the fate of the Manitoba School Law is to depend. If it was not profane it would not be inappropriate that divine interposition should be invoked on behalf of the province!

It may not unreasonably be asked, for no grounds for the course being adopted have been given, on what pretext is this doctrine of irresponsibility of the advisers of the Crown set up? It is not easy to answer that inquiry, and it is, perhaps, well that it should be left to the Minister and to those, if any there be in this era of constitutional government who are willing to defend him, to state their argument. To the writer, it seems absolutely clear, admitting of no doubt, that "an appeal to the Governor-in-Council" is a right to ask the intervention of the Government of the Dominion to be exercised by the Government, as all other acts of administration and questions of policy are determined, as political Acts, in the sense that the Cabinet is responsible to Parliament, and the country, for them—and equally clear does it seem that, if the "appeal" was to be dealt with as a question of legal right, and not as a matter of political discretion, it would not have been to a body, of which it is not too much to say that partizanship, not impartiality, is the very essence of its existence.

It is not denied that in the determination of this, as indeed of almost every question which comes before the Government for decision, the consideration of legal questions may be involved. The veto power involves the legal question of the constitutionality of every Provincial Act. The right to exempt vessels that have passed through the canals from tolls requires that the Cabinet should consider and determine the meaning of the Washington Treaty, which as an international obligation, is a law overriding all municipal law. And so with almost every matter that comes up for determination by the committee known as the Dominion Cabinet or Council.

That it is not a trifling, technical, or practically unimportant matter but one of the most vital moment, if our system of responsible Government is to be maintained, hardly needs demonstration. For if Sir John Thompson's view is correct, that the Manitoba question is to be considered judicially, then, no matter what conclusion the Government adopt, there is complete freedom from responsibility. The Ministers cannot be called to account in Parliament, even though the Order-in-council as a remedial measure should direct the Legislature of the province to repeal its School Acts of 1890 ; for a Judge or judicial tribunal is not answerable for his or its bad law. It is only when a Judge acts corruptly or dishonestly that his conduct can be called in question. It would be grossly unfair and unjust to blame the Cabinet for their legal conclusions arrived at regardless of the personal views which they "notwithstanding that they are his Excellency's advisers, may hold with regard to denominational schools." And so the well-settled practice and theory of responsible Government is overturned. Let there be no evasion, no hairsplitting in this all important matter on which depends in no small degree the peace and welfare of the Dominion. Manitoba has had scant courtesy and but little consideration at the hands of the Government of Canada. Her railway legislation was vetoed so persistently that her people were driven to the verge of rebellion. These acts, if unwise and harsh, were at least within the lines of the constitution. But the attack now launched against her exclusive right to manage her educational system is fraught with perilous consequences to the Dominion ; and for the initial steps that the Government at Ottawa have taken to accomplish that end it should be held to strict account, or Parliament will lamentably fail in its duty ; and the pretence that the Cabinet, acts as a judicial tribunal, and not as political advisers of the Crown, should meet with the contempt and condemnation it invites at the hands of the Representatives of the people.

CHAPTER XV.

ISMS IN THE SCHOOLS.*

By John S. Ewart, Q.C.

"What a melancholy notion is that which has to represent all men, in all countries and times, except our own, as having spent their life in blind condemnable error—mere lost Pagans, Scandinavians, Mahometans—only that *we* might have the true ultimate knowledge! All generations of men were lost and wrong, only that this present little section of a generation might be saved and right! They all marched forward there, all generations since the beginning of the world, like the Russian soldiers into the ditch of Schweidnitz fort, only to fill up the ditch with their dead bodies, that we might march over and take the place. It is an incredible hypothesis. Such incredible hypothesis we have seen maintained with fierce emphasis, and this or the other poor individual man, with his sect of individual men, marching as over the dead bodies of all men, towards sure victory; but when he, too, with his hypothesis and ultimate infallible *credo*, sank into the ditch and became a dead body, what was to be said? Withal, it is an important fact in the nature of man, that he tends to reckon his own insight as final, and goes upon it as such." So said Thomas Carlyle (The Hero as Priest), and mournfully added: "He will always do it, I suppose, in one or the other way."

And yet one would think that by this time Cromwell's adjuration addressed to the General Assembly of the Kirk of Scotland:

I beseech you, in the bowels of Christ, think it *possible* you may be mistaken,

would in some small measure be commencing to take effect, even upon Scotchmen. Surely the scantiest information as to the intellectual and moral development of the human race, would teach any one, that not the blockheads only among our ancestors, but the wise heads as well, have been hopelessly — I had almost said stupidly — wrong upon countless matters that appear to us to be as simple as the addition of a couple of units. But no; so far Carlyle's prophecy, "He will *always* do it," bids fair to realize itself.

---

* Reprinted from The Canadian Magazine, July, 1893.

And the reason is not far to seek. Toleration is based upon culture (of which there is but scant crop), and especially upon those parts of it included under (1) wide reading, that you may know that the road to your own opinion has been over many a nobler thinker now stark in the Schweidnitz ditch; (2) experience, that you may have seen your own most cherished opinions go to the ditch ahead of you ("The latter part of a wise man's life is taken up in curing the follies, prejudices and false opinions he had contracted in the former," said Swift); and (3) a certain sympathetic and imaginative power, that you may patiently investigate the foundations and strength of opposing opinion, and be able to appreciate its arguments, not from your own point of view, but from that of your opponents. You must come to the question as an enquirer—not with heady confidence, arrogantly asserting infallibility and completed investigation; but, on the contrary, with open mind ready and willing to re-examine your best beloved beliefs in the light of that which may be urged against them—a very rare frame of mind. If the question be one upon which you have no very fixed ideas, the possibilities are that your mind will receive its first (and last) impression from the first person you meet, whether nurse or philosopher. But if it be a question of politics or religion, and you have arrived at the age of—say puberty—what prospect is there for the clearest truth, as against the stupidest falsehood which may have theretofore, in some way or other, got into your head?

I am not blaming you, although for like offence you are constantly turning up your intellectual nose at other people. I am not even saying that you, in your individual list of beliefs, have subscribed to a single false one. All that I am intending is to "beseech you, in the bowels of Christ, think it *possible* that you may be mistaken"—in some small, but specified, one of these, beliefs, if you cannot admit as to two of them; it will do you good as a commencement. You can look back over the little history you know, and grant that had other people doubted in any smallest measure their inerrancy, oceans of blood, and infinitudes of misery, would have been spared; but for yourself you see no lesson there, for were they not all wrong, and is it not clear that you are right? Ah! there's the rub, *you* are right—be it a "melancholy notion" or not, "all generations of men *were* lost and wrong, only that your little section of a generation might be saved and right." You and *your* "ultimate infallible *credo* are *not* bound for the ditch. I pray you, do try and remember that all these poor Schweidnitz fellows had likewise, every one of them, seen a clear route across the Pagan and Mahometan stupidities, but nevertheless were plainly, as we now see it, every one of them, ticketed for the ditch. Aye, and did veritably go there, they and their hypotheses, and are now plainly *not* right. And when you come to think of it, why should you be infallible, and all the ditch occupants, and perhaps a large majority of those still outside of it, indubitably wrong? Tell me that you have studied more deeply, more diligently, and with greater ability than they, and I shall accept your answer. Tell me merely that you "know" that you are right, and I shall merely translate your "know" into "my father told me," and wonder that you did not know enough to do that for yourself.

Will you let me tell you something? Here is a fundamental and, you think, easily solvable question, viz., that relating to toleration of contrary opinion, religious or other. Let me shortly review it for you.

Plato* prescribed thus for unbelievers:

> Let those who have been made what they are only from want of understanding, and not from malice or an evil nature, be placed by the judge in the house of reformation, and ordered to suffer imprisonment during a period of not less than five years. And in the meantime let them have no intercourse with the other citizens, except with members of the nocturnal council, and with them let them converse touching the improvement of their souls' health. And when the time of their imprisonment has expired, if any of them be of sound mind, let him be restored to sane company, but if not, and if he be condemned a second time, let him be punished with death.

Plato was wrong.

Pagan Emperors (knowing that *they* were right) persecuted and put to death thousands of Christians, and Christians did the same for Pagans in proportion to their power. *Pagans and Christians were wrong.*

Roman Catholics (knowing that *they* were right) persecuted and put to death thousands of Protestants; and Protestants did the same thing for Catholics in proportion to their power. Said Canon Farrar: †

> The idea of man's universal rights, of universal freedom and liberty of conscience, was alien to the views of the whole ancient world. Indeed, it is of quite modern introduction. It was not known even in Christendom, not even in the Protestant part of it, till the seventeenth century.

Catholics and Protestants, including Calvin, Knox, etc., etc., were wrong.

Hobbes ‡ in 1658 said:

> Christians, or men of what religion soever, if they tolerate not their king, whatsoever law he maketh, though it be concerning religion, do violate their faith, contrary to the divine law, both natural and positive; nor is there any judge of heresy among subjects, but their own civil sovereign. For heresy is nothing else but a private opinion obstinately maintained, contrary to the opinion which the public person—that is to say, the representant of the commonwealth—hath commended to be taught. By which it is manifest that

---

* Laws, X., 909; Jowett's Translation, IV., 421.
† History of Free Thought, Note 15.
‡ Leviathan, cap. 42.

an opinion publicly appointed to be taught cannot be heresy ; nor the sovereign princes that authorize them, heretics. For heretics are none but private men that stubbornly defend some doctrine prohibited by their lawful sovereign.

Which heretics he counselled, could they not comply with the king's requirement, to go off courageously "to Christ by martyrdom," and leave the land in peace. *Hobbes was wrong.*

John Locke gained for himself much renown by his noble plea for toleration, and was, we think, much in advance of the day when he wrote (1689); but he makes this qualification :*

> Lastly, those are not to be tolerated who deny the being of a God. Promises, covenants and oaths which are the bonds of human society can have no hold upon an atheist. The taking away of God, though but even in thought, dissolves all. Besides, also, those that by their atheism undermine and destroy all religion, can have no pretence of religion whereupon to challenge the privilege of a toleration.

Locke was wrong.

Bishop Warburton,† in 1736, insists in the strongest terms upon the natural right of every man to worship God according to his conscience, and upon the criminality of every attempt on the part of the state to interfere with his religion :

> With religious errors, as such, the state has no concern.

And it may never restrain a religion except when it produces grave "civil mischiefs." In asserting, however, that :

> Religion, or the care of the soul, is not within the province of the magistrate, and that consequently matters of doctrine and opinion are without his jurisdiction, this must always be understood, with the exception of the three fundamental principles of natural religion—the being of God, His providence over human affairs, and the natural, essential difference of moral good and evil. These doctrines it is directly his office to cherish, protect and propagate, and all oppugners of them it is as much his right and duty to restrain, as any the most flagrant offenders against public peace.

And the reason of this exception, he says, is obvious :

> The magistrate concerns himself with the maintenance of these three fundamental articles, not as they promote our future happiness, but our present. . . . They are the very foundation and bond of civil policy. Without them oaths and covenants and all the ties of moral obligation upon which society is founded are dissolved.

Warburton was wrong.

Rousseau, in 1761,‡ drew up a civil profession of faiths and prescribed that :

> If any one declines to accept them, he ought to be exiled, not for being impious, but for being unsociable, incapable of sincere attachment to the laws, or of sacrificing his life to his duty. If any one, after publicly recognizing

---

* First letter on Toleration, p. 31.
† Alliance of Church and State.
‡ Contrat Social iv., viii., 203.

these dogmas, carried himself as if he did not believe them, then let him be punished by death, for he has committed the worst of crimes—he has lied before the laws.
Rousseau was wrong.

Blackstone, the great English jurist, in his commentaries (1765) wrote :

> Doubtless the preservation of Christianity as a national religion is, abstracted from its intrinsic truth, of the utmost consequence to the civil state, which a single instance will sufficiently demonstrate. The belief in a future state of rewards and punishments, the entertaining just ideas of the moral attributes of the Supreme Being, and a firm persuasion that He superintends and will finally compensate every action in human life (all which are clearly revealed in the doctrines and forcibly inculcated in the precepts of our Saviour Christ), these are the grand foundations of all judicial oaths which call God to witness the truth of those facts which perhaps may be only known to Him and the party attesting. All moral evidence, therefore, all confidence in human veracity, must be weakened by irreligion and overborne by infidelity. Wherefore, all affront to Christianity or endeavors to depreciate its efficacy, are deserving of human punishment.

Blackstone was wrong.

Burke, in 1773, in a speech in the House of Commons, alluding to the argument that if non-conformity were tolerated, atheism would gain protection under pretence of it, said :

> If this danger is to be apprehended, if you are really fearful that Christianity will indirectly suffer from this liberty, you have my free consent: go directly and by the straight way and not by a circuit ; point your arms against these men who do the mischief you fear promoting ; point your own arms against men . . . who by attacking even the possibility of all revelation, arraign all the dispensations of Providence to man. These are the wicked Dissenters you ought to fear ; these are the people against whom you ought to aim the shaft of the law ; these are the men to whom, arrayed in all the terrors of Government, I would say : You shall not degrade us into brutes. These men—these factious men, as the honorable gentleman properly called them—are the just object of vengeance, not the conscientious Dissenter. . . . . . Against these I would have the laws rise in all their majesty of terrors to fulminate such vain and impious wretches, and to awe them into impotence by the only dread they can fear or believe. The most horrid and cruel blow that can be offered to civil society is through atheism. Do not promote diversity : when you have it bear it : have as many sorts of religions as you find in your country ; there is a reasonable worship in them all. The others—the infidels or outlaws of the Constitution, not of this country, but of the human race—they are never, never to be supported, never to be tolerated. Under the systematic attacks of these people, I see some of the props of good Government already begin to fail—I see the propagated principles which will not leave to religion even a toleration. . . . . Those who hold revelation give double assurance to their country. Even the man who does not hold revelation, yet who wishes that it were proved to him, who observes a pious silence with regard to it, such a man, though not a Christian, is governed by religious principle. Let him be tolerated in this country. Let it be but a serious religion, natural or revealed—take what you can get—cherish, blow up the slightest spark. . . . By this proceeding you form an alliance, offensive or defensive, against those great ministers of darkness in the world who are endeavoring to shake all the works of God, established in

order and beauty. Perhaps I am carried too far, but it is in the road which the honorable gentleman had led me. The honorable gentleman would have us fight this confederacy of the powers of darkness with the single arm of the Church of England. Strong as we are, we are not yet equal to this. The cause of the Church of England is included in that of religion, not that of religion in the Church of England.

Burke was wrong.

Paley writing in 1785* perceived

No reason why men of different religious persuasions may not sit upon the same bench, or fight in the same ranks, as well as men of various or opposite opinions upon any controverted topic of natural philosophy, history or ethics. Every species of intolerance which enjoins suppression and silence, and every species of persecution which enforces such injunctions, is adverse to the progress of truth ; forasmuch as it causes that to be fixed by one set of men, at one time, which is much better, and with much more probability of success, left to the independent and progressive inquiry of separate individuals. Truth results from discussion and from controversy ; is investigated by the labors and researches of private persons. Whatever, therefore, prohibits these, obstructs that industry and that liberty which it is the common interest of mankind to promote. In religion, as in other subjects, truth, if left to itself, will almost always obtain the ascendency.

But after so much good sense he adds :

Under the idea of religious toleration, I include the toleration of all books of serious augmentation ; but I deem it no infringement of religious liberty to restrain the circulation of ridicule, invective and mockery upon religious subjects ; because this species of writing applies only to the passions, weakens the judgment, and contaminates the imagination of its readers ; has no tendency whatever to assist either the investigation or the impression of truth ; on the contrary, whilst it stays not to distinguish between the authority of different religions, it destroys alike the influence of all.

Paley was wrong. He underrated, or rather misrated altogether, the function of ridicule in argument.

This is somewhat of a formidable list of names to collect together for the mere purpose of condemning their opinions without a word of argument. Plato, typical of every body down to the seventeenth century (Pagans, Protestants and Catholics), Hobbes, Locke, Warburton, Rousseau (Voltaire may be added), Blackstone, Burke, Paley—all more or less wrong, and you and I right? Yes, you say, most certainly we are—and from Chelsea we may still hear reverberating, "He will always do it, I suppose."

And we, the infallibles, have our opinions, too, upon the question of free trade *versus* protection, no doubt ; although perhaps we are old enough to have changed them, at the same time that our leaders did. Prior to 1876 (say) we were all free traders, or at least revenue-tariff men ; about that time, perhaps, we became eager protectionists, and so voted in 1878 ; and we could then have demonstrated to any one not absolutely imbecile that there was no

---

* Principles of Moral and Political Philosophy, Bk. VI., Cap. X.

doubt in the world that we were right—could we not distinguish between successful free trade in England, and triumphant protection in the United States? But now, oh! now, we, and thousands such as we, having lost our prophet, clamorously acclaim a new found apostle who promises to lead us out of the Egyptian night in which we have been groping, and show us our land flowing with milk and honey. Stop a moment here. Have you ever contemptuously and in real earnest called yourself a fool, for having believed otherwise than you now do, on this or any other subject? If so, perhaps, you had ground for your charge (although not for your lack of politeness); and possibly you may not have yet much improved in wisdom! (This is a consideration which should give you a little pause before throwing stones at others.) On the other hand, if you have never so characterized yourself, should you not treat with the same leniency and respect those who continue to hold the opinions which you have abandoned. There is a possibility that they have been always right. There is no such possibility for you! Your insight into your own mistakes, as well as into those of others, you reckon as final, and you go upon it as such!—" He will always do it, I suppose, in one or the other way."

It is worth while paying attention to the way in which you came by some of your opinions. Looking about you, you seem to observe that as a rule the son inherits the opinions of his father, in much the same fashion as he does his real estate. In fact, family opinions seem frequently to be appurtenant to the family possession; as the lawyer would say, they run with the land. Lord A's estate produces oak trees, and liberal politics; while Lord B's produces beech trees, and tory politics. Neither of the noble Lords had anything more to do with the formation of their opinions, than with the growth of their trees—both came to them ready made. And now when they assert that trees and opinions are clearly their own, I agree; and in each case for exactly the same reason—because they quite lawfully inherited both. This is all very trite, no doubt, but what, perhaps, is not so very trite, is that it applies to yourself, and that you do not think that it does. (I am taking one chance out of a thousand.) You see that it applies to everybody else: but *everybody else sees that it applies to you*. If you *do* hold the opinions of your father, may it not be because his trees were oaks?, and that your boasted insight is limited to the ascertainment of what kind of ideas you were born with?

Your opinion then (be it live oak, or dead basswood, merely) is that Plato, and the rest, were indubitably wrong. Not stupid, you say, but under the influence of superstition, or other properly discarded rag-tag: dominated to some extent by their uncultivated environment, grovelling in the darkness out of which we have arisen to such effulgent light. Yes, my friend, without having read a word of these men, you condem them; but what are you going to say about all those of your contemporaries who disagree with you—effulgent light notwithstanding; people who believe that all society is hooked and buttoned together by religion, and that the button-loppers must be stopped that society may not return to original nudity and barbarism. I do not wish to argue these points with you, I merely want to ask you, what do you say about all these contemporaries? That you are right, and they are wrong, and that you can prove it? That may be so, but they tell me precisely the same thing, namely, that they are right and you are wrong, and that it is the easiest thing in the world to demonstrate it.

Now, no one objects to your holding your opinions, as well as your trees; to the advocacy of your opinions, and to the supplanting of all other trees with oaks, if you can convince the owners of them that the thing ought to be done. The point I want to come at is this, that your opinions are not entitled to one whit greater deference or respect (even should they be concurred in by vast majorities) than are the opinions of others. Frankly, and unreservedly, will you go with me that far? You believe that all opinions not harmful to society should be tolerated. A great many other people say, "yes, that is true, but atheistical opinions *are* harmful and should therefore not be tolerated." You reply that "atheistical opinions are not harmful." This is not a question of principle, but a question of fact—Are atheistical opinions harmful to society?—and it is a fact that we cannot agree about; several centuries of endeavoring to do so having proved that matter to us. What then is to be done? Perhaps we can get some help by a technical statement of the argument:— Opinions harmful to society ought to be suppressed : some people (A) believe atheistical opinions to be harmful; while the others (B) believe that they are not; therefore the some people (A) ought to have their way, and such opinions ought to be suppressed. You see clearly that this conclusion is wrong; but how does it help you to yours; If the conclusion is not right that the some people (A) must have their way, and the opinions be suppressed; neither is the other conclusion right, that the others (B) must have their way and the opinions be tolerated. If we cannot decide whether the opinions are harmful or innocent, (A) has as much right to have his way as (B), has he not? Let me suggest a solution, for there is no *impasse* here. (A) wants the opinions of (B) suppressed; he has no right to interfere with other people's opinions, unless they are harmful to society; on him therefore lies the *onus* of proof that the opinions that he seeks to suppress, are harmful. If he cannot prove this (and in the supposed case he cannot) nothing is done; and the decision is not that (B) is right, but that (A) has not made a case for interference with him. The normal condition is liberty. Let him who desires to circumscribe it prove his right. If he cannot, then he has no title to interfere.

But why elaborate all this? No one now-a-days thinks of interfering with opinions. Think you so, my friend? So far I have been endeavouring to get you to agree with me upon general principles, (before proceeding to apply them), and I fancy that I have found little difficulty; but now we are going to separate. *You* see very little or no intolerance in the world. On the contrary, I see as much as ever there was, and more, for the population is rapidly increasing. I do not mean that we are burning or jailing one another just now—that was the *form* merely which intolerance in rougher times assumed. But I do say that the incapacity to appreciate, and sympathetically understand, an opinion contrary to our own, is as rare to-day as ever in the world before. I know that education is more widespread, but in my opinion intolerence *commences* with knowledge (as disease with life), and succumbs to nothing but much culture, which is far from being widespread; and the cocks are as sure now as they ever were. The " important fact in the nature of man, that he tends to reckon his own insight as final, and goes upon it as such," has, by many centuries of culture, to be eradicted out of human nature, before its offspring, intolerance and persecution, will leave the world in peace. No doubt asperities have been rubbed down, and the more dreaded penalties for non-conformity to majority-opinion probably for ever ended; but the old intolerant spirit is still alive, manifesting itself, and dominating as far it as can, in strict conformity with the softened manners of the times. Principal Cave (I think it was) said that:

> It should be made an unpleasant thing for a man to call himself an infidel.

And he is but frankly stating the tactics of modern inquisitors. With social penalties, if not with hanging; with sarcasm and contempt, if not with thumb-screw and boots, the bigot still insists upon conformity to *his* plans and specifications; and, to the best of his ability, limits and controls the liberty and opinions of others. Cocksure and its brood " with fierce emphasis " are still vigorously dragooning the world.

My purpose in this article, however, is not to call attention to this pigmy war, which must be left to burn itself out (after various centuries more have passed), but to enter a *caveat* against its incursions into a new realm, against the irruption of intolerance in our public schools. Men seeing that it is becoming more and more difficult to force their opinions upon adults, are now turning their attention to the children, where their conquest will be easy if their access be permitted. I want to see impregnable walls opposed to the incursion of all proselytizers into the schools.

And, as a basis for my argument, I have been endeavoring to win assent to these few propositions: (1) That human thought is, even at the best of it, upon social and religious questions, far from being infallible; (2) that other people of equal intelligence, who honestly differ with us, are as likely to be right as we are; (3) that religious and irreligious opinion is in the category of the debatable (many on *both* sides say it is not, which to my mind proves that it is); (4) that the true policy with reference to all such questions is that of perfect liberty, for the *onus* of proving the harmfulness of opposing opinion cannot be discharged. Now let me apply these principles to the schools.

Perhaps you, reader, have been urging that certain things (apart from mere secular education) should or should not, be taught in the schools, because, as you say, these things are right or are wrong, although other people do not agree in your opinion of them. Perhaps you are an Imperial Federationist, and want to instil Imperial ideas in the minds of the young. Mr. Parkin has written a book for use in the schools, emphasizing his hobby. You agree with him and want his book introduced into all the schools. In other words, you want to insist that the children of people who do not agree with you are to imbibe your opinions, and not those of their parents. You would send these children home to tell their parents that they are acting dishonorably in advocating a rupture of the British connections, and that (as Principal Grant has it) the suggestion of union with the United States " should crimson the faces of people who do not pretend to be fishy-blooded "—that is, the faces of their parents. I know that you are, no doubt, right, so do not tell me that ; but again I would remind you that men whose opinions are entitled to as much weight as yours do not think so, and I beseech you " to think it possible you may be mistaken." I ask for liberty.

Or, perhaps, you believe in militarism, and the inculcation of a warlike spirit, and you insist upon flags and drills and painted muskets, so that the fighting propensities (you call them the capacities for defence) may be developed. Other good people abhor the notion of war, and dread the effect upon their boys of these appeals to their combativeness. You would have the boys tell their peace-loving fathers that they are old women, and that a fighter is the highest type of the English gentleman. You are right, of course, and they wrong ; but again I plead for liberty.

Or, perhaps, you believe that education is a vicious thing, unaccompanied by religion, and that the State is turning out " clever scoundrels " instead of worthy citizens. You insist upon religious instruction in all the schools. You quote all our old authorities, a great many of our new ones, and piles of most convincing statistics, to prove that society is held together by morality, and that there can be no morality without religion ; and, so far from being shocked with the idea of setting child against parent, you would pray that "it might be the means under Providence, of," etc., etc. Beyond peradventure, your " little section of a generation " has arrived at the " ultimate infallible *credo*," but, once more, let me remind you that many people, your equals in intelligence, believe that the religion you want taught is mere superstition and nonsense, which should be educated out of the parents, and not into the children. Once more, I say, let there be liberty.

Perchance Sabbatarianism is your particular hobby, and you believe that a nation which "desecrates the Sabbath" will be cursed of God. You probably, therefore, want the commandments, and particularly the fourth, learned by heart by every Canadian child. It is not enough for you to teach your own children so, but you insist upon the children of people, who think your Sabbatarianism Puritan fudge, to be taught that their parents misbehave themselves shockingly on Sunday. I repeat, let us have liberty.

Or is the abolition of alcoholism your particular ambition? Then you desire that the deplorable effects of fermented liquors should be impressed upon the rising generation—the body (God's temple) should be kept pure from the degrading thing; nine-tenths of the vice, sin, and shame are its offspring, etc., etc. All, beyond doubt as well founded as are the arguments to support all the other isms of which you make so little; but, for the last time, I tell you that thousands of excellent people believe you to be a mere crazy bigot, and would much rather have your children taught to think so, than that theirs should be trained to think like you. There must be liberty.

And so I would have no isms in the schools at all? you ask—no Imperial Federation, no Militarism, no Pietism, no Sabbatarianism, no Anti-Alcoholism? Quite the contrary, my friend; I would have all these, and every other ism, of such like, you can think of, in the schools; but upon this one condition, that the parents of all the children should be willing to have them there. In the name of liberty, I would say to the parents, certainly you have a right to teach, or have taught to your children anything you like, so long as you can agree about it. I would not ask that a whole province should be unanimous before Sabbatarianism could be taught in a single county; nor that a whole county should be made unanimous before militarism should be taught in one of its school districts; nor even that a whole school district should be unanimous before Imperialism should be taught in one of its schools. What does the principle of liberty require? This and nothing more, that parents should not be required to subscribe to the school rates, and at the same time have their children taught some ism that they abhor; and, on the other hand, that where the parents of all the children in any school desire that an ism should be taught, taught it ought to be. And I shall add, that when I speak of unanimity I mean practical unanimity, and not such as would make it necessary to include all mere eccentric or isolated opinion, of every ordinary or extraordinary sort. We can never expect to have theoretical perfection in the application of even undoubted doctrines to all possible conditions and contingencies.

Let me gather up some conclusions. Education can be conceived as something entirely apart from all isms. Nevertheless in the community are many people who desire to have particular isms taught in the schools. Liberty requires that children should not be taught isms to which their parents are opposed. But at the same time liberty does not require that children should be allowed to grow up entirely illiterate. Liberty further requires that where the parents of the children of any one school desire that a particular ism should be taught, taught it ought to be. And it further requires that in arranging the schools, reasonable facilities ought, if possible, to be given for the combination of such children in separate schools. It would be the antipode of liberty that such combination should be prevented in cases in which it did not materially interfere with the efficiency of other schools.

Let me put a concrete case. In the Province of Ontario there is a large number of Roman Catholics who believe that their children would be very improperly educated were they sent to secular schools or even to schools which Protestants would approve of. In that case, what does the principle of liberty require? Merely this, that opportunities should be given for the combination of Roman Catholics in certain of the schools, if that can be done without disturbing unduly the efficiency of the other schools. They desire that an ism should be taught to their children. By all means let it be so, if it costs nothing, or very little, to other people. Liberty to them, and all others, should be accorded even at some expense to the community, for one of the objects of our institutions is to afford as much individual liberty as possible. The opportunities they desire may, without loss to the community, be given to them in two sets of cases: (1) where the population is dense, and yet mixed, (in these cases there will be room for two sets of schools); (2) in districts where the population is sparse, but entirely Roman Catholic. Against the propriety of granting facilities for separate schools in these cases, there can be nothing said without intolerance, and the breach of our most cherished principles of liberty.

One word of application to the Manitoba schools. The Rev. Dr. Bryce, one of the bitterest opponents of the separate schools, has recently stated as follows:

> Out of 719 school districts in Manitoba, when the Act of 1890 was passed, 91 were Catholic. Of these *all but a very small percentage are in localities almost entirely French*.

I may add that of the "very small percentage" there were only four school districts in which the population, although mixed, was not large enough to support a school of each kind. Our principle of liberty, applied to Manitoba therefore, requires that in all but four out of the 91 schools the Catholics ought to be allowed to have their way, and to teach their religion to their children if they wish, provided only that the just requirements of the State with reference to secular learning are observed. Acting upon the very contrary doctrine, namely, that of intolerance, consciously or unconsciously having in view the hindrance of the teaching of the Catholic religion as something depraved, Manitoba has said to a large section of her people, unless you undertake to stop teaching your own religion, to your own children, in schools to which no one goes except those of your own faith, we will not permit you to organize yourselves together for the instruction of those in whose education the whole community has a decided interest. We would rather see them illiterate, than Catholic; but we hope to avoid illiteracy by driving them into adoption of secular schools, under stress of financial difficulties with which we shall surround them.

And so we have, even in the last decade of the 19th century, the spirst of intolerance as rampant and vigorous as ever; although with this difference principally, that whereas in the past the churches have had their innings, and the unbelievers have had to do much active fielding, the parsons are now out, and are finding it tolerably difficult to keep within limits the scoring (they are receiving); for all of which, in my humble judgment, the churches have themselves to thank. Love your enemies was always their doctrine, but never their practice. And now their day has come, and while the Tudors would not have allowed any one to teach unless under license from the Bishop, modern regulations require the Bishop himself to have his certificate, and charge him straightly not to say a word concerning that which he believes to be the essence of all education. I do not mean to imply that unbelievers have now a monopoly of intolerance. What I would rather say is that, in my opinion, the *most* intolerant people of the day are the sceptics (I speak, of course, of the class); that it is they (not merely those so avowed, but that very much larger class that is practically unbelieving, although still pronouncing the shibboleths) that are the most determined in their hostility to the Catholic religion being taught in the Catholic schools. Large numbers of believing Protestants, no doubt, agree with them, and the rancour of many individuals among these cannot be exceeded; but very many of this class would be glad to accord liberty to the Catholics could they but get a little of it themselves. That they cannot do so is due, I believe, to those who deem religion not to be of the highest importance—that is, that scepticism avowed and unavowed (perhaps repudiated, but nevertheless dominating), is now at the wicket. I know that sceptics believe themselves to be the most tolerant of people, but I am convinced that my estimate of them is correct. (Rousseau required all his citizens to be tolerant, having first directed to be exiled, or executed, all who would not subscribe and live up to *his* profession of faith). Burke, a hundred years ago, spoke of atheists as holding

those principles which will not leave to religion even a toleration.

And Priestly* a few years earlier wrote:

> The most unrelenting persecution is to be apprehended not from bigots, but from infidels. A bigot who is so from a principle of conscience may possibly be moved by a regard to the conscience of others; but a man who thinks that conscience ought always to be sacrificed to political views has no principle on which an argument in favor of toleration can lay hold.

To the writers of those days I shall add one of the most brilliant of the present—John Morley,† himself by many thought to be a mere secularist, because free from the current dogmatic religion:

> That brings us to the root of the matter, the serious side of a revolution that in its social consequence is so unspeakably ignoble. This root of the matter is the slow transformation now at work of the whole spiritual basis of thought. Every age is in some sort an age of transition, but our own is characteristically and cardinally an epoch of transition in the very foundations of belief and conduct. The old hopes have grown pale; the old fears dim; strong sanctions have become weak, and once vivid faiths very numb. Religion, whatever destinies may be in store for it, is, at least for the present, hardly any longer an organic power. It is not that supreme, penetrating, controlling, decisive part of a man's life, which it has been and will be again. . . . The native hue of spiritual resolution is sicklied o'er with the pale cast of distracted, wavering, confused thought. The souls of men have become void. *Into the void have entered in triumph the seven devils of secularity.*

And so secularism must have its day, and show what of weal or woe there is in it. It may be the "ultimate infallible *credo;*" but it, too, most probably will sink into the ditch and become a dead body, and another warning for all later cock-sure philosophers. Upon this it is not necessary that an opinion should be offered by one whose humble belief is that

> Our little systems have their day;
> They have their day, and cease to be,

and that for the most part we are but children crying in the night, "and with no language but a cry." Let us, I say, while our particular little system is disappearing, have peace; let us have sympathy and tolerance, the one for the other; and whether these or not, at the least let us have liberty.

---

* Essay on the First Principles of Government, 290.
† On Compromise, 136.

CHAPTER XVI.

THE MANITOBA SCHOOL QUESTION.*

By George Bryce, LL.D., Winnipeg.

Mr. John S. Ewart, of Winnipeg, wrote in the July number of the *Canadian Magazine* a readable and erudite article entitled "Isms in the Schools," in which, though the field of treatment was much wider, yet our schools were plainly the objective point.

Mr. Ewart discusses at some length the subject of toleration and writes many melancholy extracts embodying the intolerance of our forefathers. These citations from the writings of the great, and may we not say the good, of the past, would make us pity the race, did not Mr. Ewart embrace himself and all of us with the rest, and describe us with a touch of raillery as "we, the infallibles."

We may well admire his adroit and good-humored use of the *bon mot* of Oliver Cromwell to the Scottish General Assembly:

> I beseech you in the bowels of Christ, think it possible you may be mistaken.

No doubt Mr. Ewart regards the writer, whom he calls "one of the bitterest enemies of the separate schools," as the direct lineal ecclesiastical descendant of the Scottish Assembly. It must be confessed that those descended from the race to which Mr. Ewart and the writer belong have a great deal to fight against. The "perfervidum ingenium" of which we have heard so much as a Scottish characteristic, overcomes the best of us. We must all plead guilty to a charge made by a brilliant litterateur against the Scottish people, that "their obstinacy is truly sublime." Indeed we can all heartily join in the prayer of that fellow countryman who pleaded for heavenly direction, saying:

> "Lord, thou knowest gif I dinna gae richt, I'll gang far wrang."

So Mr. Ewart's five columns of extracts ranging from Plato to Paley, each one dismissed with just a spice of dogmatism,—"Warburton was wrong," "Burke was wrong," and the like—lead us to conclude that Mr. Ewart's own doctrine of toleration needs some examination.

---

* Reprinted from the Canadian Magazine, September, 1893.

Carlyle, a favorite of Mr. Ewart, suggested in one of his lectures that toleration may be abused. He says:

> Well, surely it is good that each of us be as tolerant as possible. Yet, at bottom, after all the talk there is and has been about it, what is tolerance? Tolerance has to tolerate the unessential, and to see well what that is. Tolerance has to be noble, measured, just in its very wrath when it can tolerate no longer. But, on the whole, we are not altogether here to tolerate? We are here to resist, to control, and vanquish withal. We do not tolerate Falsehoods, Thieveries, Iniquities, when they fasten on us; we say to them, Thou art false; thou art not tolerable! We are to extinguish falsehoods and to put an end to them, in some wise way.

Nor has Carlyle, in the trio—Falsehoods, Thieveries, Iniquities—exhausted the intolerable things. We do no tolerate injustice, disloyalty, anarchic tendencies, or official stupidity, against which it has been said "even the gods fight in vain." We say to them "Get thee behind me; thou art false; thou art not tolerable." What a genuine ring there is about the words of the sage of Chelsea! There is a false—hate it, exclude it, destroy it. There is a right—a true—search for it, and treasure it up when you find it. It is hard to find, as all truth is; but it exists; it is worth the toil, and sweat, and tears, and blood, of the search.

Contrast with this Mr. Ewart's doctrine. *My right is your wrong; my wrong is your right. One for me is as good as the other for you.* There is no fixed right. There is no hope of reaching a common standard.

Surely this is what Mr. Ewart means, for he says (page 362):

> If we cannot decide (and Mr. Ewart says we cannot decide) whether the opinions are harmful or innocent, A has as much right to have his way as B, has he not?

Or again (page 361):

> Your opinions are not entitled to one whit greater deference or respect than are the opinions of others.

Plainly Mr. Ewart believes there is no common standard of opinion; that there can be no consensus of right; that there can be no invariable moral principle in man which can serve as a basis of agreement, and hence of truth.

That being the case, then each must be allowed to believe, and act, as he likes. One man's opinion may be harmful to society, but the man says it isn't so. His opinion is as good as mine. He must have liberty. Society is thus debarred from interference with him. Absolute, unrestrained liberty to do as he may choose must be given him. To the mind of the writer, these are the elementary principles of anarchy.

In making this statement, the writer is not condemning Mr. Ewart, who is a prominent and useful member of our Winnipeg community, but simply stating the inevitable drift of the opinions advanced by Mr. Ewart, for he says :

> Religious and irreligious opinion is in the category of the debatable ; the true policy with reference to all such questions is perfect liberty.

Or again :

> In the name of liberty, I would say to the parents, certainly, you have a right to teach, or have taught, to your children, anything you like, so long as you can agree about it.

Now it is the contention of the writer, in opposition to these views :

1. That *the state has a right to form and enforce an opinion of its own at variance with the opinions of many of its subjects*, or, in other words, where it sees cause to disregard the "perfect liberty" claimed by Mr. Ewart. A few instances may suffice. The state may rightly insist on the education of all the children in it, whether the parents approve or disapprove. Ignorance is a public danger : the prejudice of a parent in favor of illiteracy may not be permitted. Mr. Ewart is compelled to admit this, when he says :

> But at the same time liberty does not require that children should be allowed to grow up entirely illiterate ;

Though he had just stated that :

> Liberty requires that children should not be taught isms to which their parents are opposed,

knowing perfectly well that one of the commonest isms or prejudices, many people have is resistance to the education of their children. The state may compel *vaccination*, although, as every one knows, a good many of the inhabitants of the Province of Quebec are are as much opposed, in the very presence of smallpox, to the vaccination of their families, as they are to their education. The state in time of epidemic may rightly dismiss the schools, and prevent people from meeting for public worship, if the public health would thereby be endangered. Every one knows the great powers of *expropriation* vested in the state by which the rights of the individual may be trespassed upon, although in every rightly constituted state the individual is entitled to compensation. It is surely useless to show further how Mr. Ewart's doctrine of "*perfect liberty,*" unwarily advanced by him, *would render the existence of the state impossible.*

2. The writer further contends that *the state, being founded on justice, may not give special privileges to any class of its subjects.*

Lieber says :

> Everything in the state must be founded on justice, and justice rests on generality and equality. The state, therefore, has no right to promote the private interests of one, and not of the other.

This is a generally admitted principle. What does Mr. Ewart propose ? He proposes that the people of Manitoba should have their public schools, and that one denomination should be singled out and be allowed to teach their "ism" in certain schools to be controlled by them. He was most strenuous, when pleading the Roman Catholic position before the courts, in insisting that Episcopalians and Presbyterians had no rights in the same way. Though they had schools in the Red River settlement, yet Mr. Ewart contended that their sectarian wishes might be disregarded, and that they had no rights except as bulked together with half a dozen other sects as "Protestants." Is that justice?

Further, the state has now said there shall be public schools for all classes of the people in Manitoba. Its exact words are:

The public schools shall be entirely non-sectarian.

No one maintains that the ordinary subjects of education are not within the scope of the action of the state. They are subjects taught by the Roman Catholics everywhere, as well as by others. Nobody proposes that the Roman Catholics shall "have their children taught some ism that they abhor." Since the Roman Catholic people are, "all, but a very small percentage, in localities almost entirely French," they have local control of their schools. Is there the slightest ground for Mr. Ewart's unwarrantable statement that, acting from intolerance,

Manitoba has, consciously or unconsciously, in view the hindrance of the teaching of the Catholic religion as something depraved?

Manitoba has simply declared, as the Privy Council has decided she had a right to do, that the public schools shall be non-sectarian; and the Manitoba educational authorities are doing their best justly and temperately to carry out the law.

But the mild, gentle-faced tolerance that Mr. Ewart so adroitly pleads for, is not the reality for which he is arguing. He knows perfectly well that the school which he regards as the creation of so many parents wishing their "ism" taught "so long as they can agree about it," is not the reality. Mr. Ewart's theoretical school involves an element just as objectionable to the Roman Catholic Church as the public schools contain. The Roman Catholic objection to the public schools is that they are not under the control of the Church. It is the question of authority that is at issue. See how ruthlessly the bishops in Quebec crushed out the aspirations of Mr. Masson and his associates! Read the assertion of the position of the Church in the pastoral of the Roman Catholic bishops of the United States, and see its arrogant claim of control. To have recognition by the state of the teachers which its religious orders provide, and to decide what text-books shall be used in the schools are most strenuously insisted on. Under the late separate school law in Manitoba no text-book could be used in the Roman Catholic schools without the approval of the "competent religious authority."

Mr. Ewart's decentralizing, and ultra-democratic, suggestions for overcoming the difficulty will be met with the same disfavor as the Public Schools Act of 1890. To have a portion of the schools of Manitoba, say one-eighth, with the relative proportion probably decreasing, organized separately under the control of the authorities of a special church; to have that church dictating the character of the teaching, certificating teachers, and fixing its *imprimatur* on the school and its work, is contradictory to the fundamental idea involved in a state, is an "imperium in imperio," which a free people may justly unite in addressing with Carlyle's words: "Thou art not tolerable."

3. The writer contends that *religion is outside of state interference, unless religion invade the state's domain.*

Render to Cæsar the things that are Cæsar's, and to God the things that are God's,"

is more than ever coming to be recognized by large numbers of Christians, and by those outside of Christianity as well, as the true principle. The declaration of Jesus Christ,

My kingdom is not of this world,

is best interpreted by the statement that the sphere of the Church, of which Christ is the king and head, is outside that of the state. The school of thought in which Mr. Ewart, and the writer, were brought up in Toronto taught this so certainly, and the concensus of opinion of the vast majority of people in Canada and the United States is so strongly in favor of it, that possibly it is hardly worth while to argue it further.

The limitation, however, is somewhat necessary, that *the state may interfere in the religious* sphere. The case of Mormonism is one to the point. There a so-called religious doctrine is regarded by the state as destructive of social order and is so repressed. Certain churches regard marriage as a religious contract; the state, for cause, dissolves the marriage thus formed, by granting a divorce. Religious bodies, which in their worship destroy the peace of the Sabbath and interfere with public convenience, are rightly checked by the state.

But on the whole, the trend of modern thought is to allow as great liberty as possible to religious opinion. This is willingly allowed where Mr. Ewart's "perfect liberty" cannot be permitted. Probably most would say that should Roman Catholics, or others, desire to educate their children in private schools, at their own expense, so long as illiteracy does not result, it would be well to allow it. But where this is permitted, for Roman Catholics then to put in the plea of exemption from the public school taxes is plainly unjust; for it would violate the condition of equality on which the state is founded, were this allowed. Many Protestants prefer to educate their children at private schools and denominational seminaries. They never dream of asking exemption from the public school taxes. No one rushes to their aid to denounce the state as persecuting them.

And here, too, comes in the opportunity for granting a large amount of liberty to those who desire special "isms" taught their children, and who are willing to pay for it. If some parents wish their children brought up imbued with the principles of "Imperial Federation and Militarism," private enterprise provides such schools, and we might name them, to which they may be sent. The state may deem it wise to shut its eyes to this so long as illiteracy is avoided. Should others desire their children to be immersed in the doctrines of "Pietism, Sabbatarianism and Anti-Alcoholism," for them, too, private, or church, enterprise will supply schools, such as we might name, and the state may shut its eyes again so long as general education is not neglected. So with schools to educate the young in Conservatism or Dogmatism, in Anglicanism or Agnosticism. One may express doubt as to the wisdom of such a course on the part of parents; but they may enjoy the luxury, by paying for it.

When, however, such an one approaches the state to demand exemption from paying his public school taxes, the Privy Council, the people of Manitoba, and, we venture to think, common sense unite in saying: "The public schools are for all; they may be used by all; thou art asking an advantage over thy fellow subjects: thy claim is not tolerable."

Nor does our advocacy of the principle of the separation of church and state justify Mr. Ewart's dithyrambics at the close of his article, where he says: "And so secularism must have its day, and show what of weal or woe there is in it. It may be the 'ultimate infallible credo'; but it, too, most probably will sink into the ditch and become a dead body, and a warning for all later cock-sure philosophers."

The public schools of Manitoba are supported by the vast majority of the religious people of Manitoba. And in Manitoba the religious education of the children is not neglected. The Church, the Sunday School, and the family circle, are all agencies for cultivating the religious life of the young. The public schools of Manitoba are essentially the same as the public schools of Ontario. In Ontario the second and third generations of the population have grown up under this system.

The writer has seen many countries of the world, but can say with firmest belief that nowhere will be found a more intelligent, sober, and religious people than the people of Ontario. There are probably fewer secularists or infidels in Ontario than in any population of its numbers in the world. As the writer has said elsewhere, if there be a defect either in Ontario or Manitoba, it is because the Church has not done its work thoroughly; it is not the fault of the public school.

In conclusion, the writer is of opinion that the people of Manitoba have followed a wiser, and more patriotic, course than that suggested by Mr. Ewart, with his lax and unphilosophic plan of so-called toleration. The problem facing Manitoba was unique. The province was made up of people of many nations. Its speech is polyglot, with the majority English-speaking; it has eight or ten thousand Icelanders; it has fifteen thousand German-speaking Mennonites; it has some ten or twelve thousand French-speaking half-breeds and Quebecers; it has considerable numbers of Polish Jews; it has many Hungarians and Finlanders; it has Gaelic-speaking Crofter settlements. The Icelanders petitioned the educational board, of which the writer is a member, for liberty to have the Lutherans prepare their candidates for confirmation in the schools: the Mennonites with singular tenacity have demanded separate religious schools: the French had their Catholic schools, and their spirit may be seen when their late superintendent, Senator Bernier, refused to consent to a Protestant being a member of a French-Canadian society: many of the other foreigners are absolutely careless about education.

What could patriotic Manitobans do? They were faced with the prospect of whole masses of the population growing up illiterate. The Mennonites, who came from Russia, are more ignorant to-day as a people than when they came from Russia eighteen years ago. Yes, British Manitoba has been a better foster-mother of ignorance than half-civilized Russia had been.

The only hope for the province was to fall back on the essential rights of the province, and provide one public school for every locality, and have a vigorous effort made to rear up a homogeneous Canadian people.

It has required nerve on the part of the people to do this, but the first steps have been taken, and in the mind of most there is the conviction that the battle has been won.

And yet the people of Manitoba are not intolerant. They are, as Mr. Ewart knows, a generous people. Last year the general election in Manitoba turned on this question. There was no abuse of Catholics, or Mennonites, or foreigners. There has not been the slightest animosity manifested. Violence was unknown in the campaign, or at the polls. There was simply the conviction that public schools are a great necessity for the province; that they are the only fair system yet devised for meeting prevailing ignorance; and that in order to make us a united people, a patriotic love of our province demands this expedient.

Our French-Canadian and Mennonite fellow-countrymen are coming to see this. Among both of these classes the public schools are spreading. The Department of Education and advisory board are both in a thoroughly conciliatory mood, and earnestly desire every locality to avail itself of government co-operation and the government grant. So mote it be!

CHAPTER XVII.

STATE EDUCATION AND "ISMS."[*]

By W. D. Le Sueur.

Professor Bryce has done well in replying from his own point of view to the "readable and erudite article," as he styles it, of Mr. Ewart, entitled "'Isms' in the Schools," which appeared in the July number of this magazine. Seldom, in my opinion, has a more erroneous position been taken up (on the subject of public education) than that invented for himself by Mr. Ewart, and were it not that the question at issue is one which calls a great deal of passion into play, the common sense of the community might safely be left to do justice to that gentleman's paradoxes. As it is, it hardly seems to me superfluous, even after what Professor Bryce has written, to attempt a further brief exposure of the fallacies which Mr. Ewart has offered as his contribution to the Manitoba School Question.

The first part of the article is that which has won commendation for it as erudite, and consists of a passably long array of instances in which various authorities, of more or less weight in the intellectual world, had held and expressed erroneous views on a certain subject—to wit, toleration. After citing their several opinions, the writer asserts that Plato was wrong, that Pagan emperors and Christian ecclesiastics were wrong, that Hobbes and Locke and Warburton were wrong, that Rousseau and Blackstone and Burke were wrong, that Paley was wrong; and then, turning round on the reader, asks him whether, like a kind good man, he will not admit that *he* also may be wrong. It seems to me that most of us would have been prepared to make the admission without the pressure of such a preamble; nor do I see how the preamble facilitates the admission in any degree, unless the catalogue of errors is intended to suggest that nothing but error is possible for mankind; in which case the admission demanded should have been not that we *may* be wrong, but that we *must* be wrong. It would have been just as easy, we may assume, for Mr. Ewart to have given us a list of right opinions held by Plato, Hobbes and the rest, and then, following a parallel course, he might have looked pleadingly into our eyes, and asked us to admit that perhaps we too may be in the right. Why, indeed, we should be asked to affiliate our opinions

[*] Reprinted from *The Canadian Magazine*, October, 1893.

upon all the errors of the past ages, rather than on the true conclusions arrived at, is not very apparent. As the case stands, we admit frankly, fully, and beyond recall, that we may be in error—that we may be just as wrong in our day, as Plato ever was in his, or Burke in his, but we go no further. If we are asked whether, because we admit our fallibility, we are going to shun the responsibility of putting any of our opinions into practice, we answer decidedly "No." Better some line of action than none; the business of the world must be carried on.

Mr. Ewart reminds us that opinions are often inherited. So they are, and an inherited opinion let me add, is better than no opinion. There never was a time in the history of the world in which men carried about with them only such opinions as they had made for themselves by observation, experience and reasoning; and if the future is destined to bring such a condition of things it will probably be a very distant future indeed. But what are we going to do about it? The only thing to do is to use all the means in our power to vanquish prejudice in ourselves and others, and to perfect both our own knowledge and the general intelligence of the community, and then go ahead with some definite line of action.

The conclusion which Mr. Ewart draws from his preamble is one for which few of his readers not previously acquainted with his views can have been prepared. It may be expressed thus: Seeing that Plato and Locke and Burke and Paley all fell into more or less serious error, and that, like those illustrious men, we are all liable to blunder, it would be advisable to dispense with any general and uniform system of education, and let each local group throughout the country wield the taxing power conferred by the school law, for any purpose that may seem good to a decisive majority of them. The only proviso he throws in is that children must not "be allowed to grow up entirely illiterate." *Hoc salvo* he would have "every ism you can think of" taught in the schools provided that "the parents of the children should be willing to have them there." In stipulating thus for local unanimity he means, as he explains, "practical unanimity—not such as would make it necessary to include all mere eccentric or isolated opinion, of every ordinary or extroardinary sort."

Well, now let us get back to the fundamental theory of public school education. Imagine that in a given community there is no system of state education, and that the disadvantages of such a condition of things are making themselves painfully felt. It is proposed to establish public schools and to support them by taxation. What all are agreed upon is that the children of the country should have better means of acquiring the elements of education as ordinarily understood. One would suppose, therefore, that there would be no difficulty in arranging a system of education to meet this special object; nor would there be, if certain sections or elements of the population did not seek to take advantage of the new machinery for purposes entirely different from those primarily in view. But all at once come demands which virtually imply the capturing of the machinery of education, for the advancement of various interests, with which education, in the general sense, has nothing to do. All the "isms" clamor at once for recognition, and it becomes quite evident that education is going to be made a cloak under which a great many different secondary projects are going to seek sustentation and advancement. Upon reading, writing, arithmetic and geography, etc., as elements of education *all* are agreed; in regard to other matters there is no general agreement. Mr. Ewart's advice to the community under the circumstances is: "Well, start the taxing machinery anyway, and go and fight it out in your several localities. Choose your 'isms' by a majority vote, and let those who want education 'straight' and who cannot get it in the local schools, do the best they can. They may be very sensible people in their way, more sensible, perhaps, than those who go in for the 'isms,' but if they are a minority they must suffer." That this is really Mr. Ewart's view there is no possibility of doubting. He speaks of "practical unanimity," but he must and does know perfectly well that if the legitimacy of "isms," as he understands the expression, is once recognized, no "practical unanimity" would be required for their introduction into a school. What power does he look to to check a school district which, dispensing with "practical unanimity," wants to introduce some fad into the school by a majority vote? If there is a power that should, and could, interfere in such a case might not that power equally pronounce a fad a fad, and forbid its introduction altogether?

But it is not for the fads or the "isms," as he himself calls them, that the writer in question is arguing. He has constructed an argument which requires him to champion the fads, but they are not his chief care. His chief care is the claim of an influential section of the community to use the public school system for the furtherance of the power and influence of their church. Plato was wrong and Hobbes was wrong and so were Blackstone and Burke, *ergo*, the Roman Catholics may possibly, or quite probably, be right in demanding that the taxing power should be given to them for a purpose altogether apart from education in the commonly understood sense of the word. It is hard to see why the argument should take this exact shape. Why might not Mr. Ewart's allocution, with its erudite preamble, have been addressed to the Roman Catholics, inviting them to recognize that, whereas the mighty dead had erred, *they* might be in error also? Alas, that would not have worked; for, while there is no difficulty in getting an admission of fallibility from *nous autres*, fallibility is precisely what the opposite side will not acknowledge.

Supposing now that on that simple ground we were to withdraw our acknowledgment of fallibility, saying to those who demand the taxing power for ecclesiastical purposes: "You are infallible, you say, or infallibly directed, which comes to the same thing. Well, we are going to be infallible too, *pro hac vice*. We don't believe in our infallibility one bit, but we can't afford not to be infallible when you are." I fail to see wherein it would be in the least unjust or unreasonable if the opponents of the Catholic claims took up this position, but fortunately there is no need for them to do so. It is sufficient to take their stand on the broad ground that the power of the state should not be used to advance religious opinions peculiar to one section of the population.

We may be met here by the argument that the power claimed is a limited power, that taxes are only to be taken from those who are willing to pay them and have them applied in the specific manner proposed. To this the reply is, that though the scope of the power is limited, the power itself is the power that belongs to the state as a whole, while the purpose to which it is to be applied is not one in which the state as a whole has any interest. Let us get back to the question. Is, or is not, ignorance in relation to the ordinary branches of secular knowledge an evil, which the power of the state should be used to combat? Upon this point I am myself a bit of a heretic, not believing as devoutly in the need for state interference as is the almost universal fashion to-day. But that is neither here nor there; the verdict of the country on the point is a powerful, and practically unanimous, affirmative. Catholics as well as Protestants say: "Yes, the power of the state is required for that purpose." The state may therefore be said to get a mandate to establish secular schools. Does the state get any similar mandate to teach theology in the schools, or to place the schools in the hands of those who will teach theology? Most unquestionably it does not. It gets from a part of the community a demand to have their own theology taught in the schools; but the answer to that, and a sufficient answer as it seems to me, is that there is no *national demand* for the teaching of theology, nor is there any one theology that could be taught, and that, therefore, so far as the state schools are concerned, theology shall not be taught in them, nor any "ism" not approved by the people at large. How impossible it would be to obtain the passage of any general law specifically providing for the teaching of different kinds of theology in different sections of the country it is needless to point out; but if so, why should that be done *indirectly* which could not be done directly—which would not even be proposed, or hinted at, as a desirable policy? Surely the state has a right to say: "Teach all the theology you like, and all the 'isms' you have a fancy for, but do not ask that the schools which have been established for the great national purpose of teaching branches of knowledge, which *all* agree are not only useful but necessary, shall be made subservient to the propagation of your peculiar ideas in these matters.

This seems to be the proper place to remark that Mr. Ewart's idea of handing over local minorities to local majorities without any check from the general law of the land would, if carried into effect, simply mean political disintegration, and local tyranny of the most odious kind. A recent writer, Mr. Wordsworth Donisthorpe, has treated this subject of local legislation very instructively :

"If local authorities," he says, "are to be permitted to legislate independently, it is clear we are brought back to the original position of local anarchy."*

Under such a condition of things the individual citizen' instead of enjoying the full measure of rights which his position as a free member of the whole community, whether province or nation, entitles him to, has these rights cut and trimmed according to the good pleasure of his neighbors. He wants his children taught to read, write and cipher ; but his neighbors say that his children shall not be taught these things unless he is willing to have them indoctrinated at the same time in some "ism" or fad. Mr. Donisthorpe neatly exposes the fallacy of those who hold that local majorities ought to rule in matters of this kind.

The right of a majority in a locality, he observes, is not based on the superior force of the majority in that locality, but on the superior force of the effective majority in the country of which it is a part, which force is *delegated* to the numerical majority or other portion of the inhabitants of the said district. . . . Thus the local majority has no more right to act on its own initiative than the local minority, or than the policeman who carries out the will of the state.

Should the state think fit, he adds, to enact that the will of a majority in a given district shall *in all things* prevail,

the process, to whatever extent it is carried, is one of political disintegration.

It is also a process fatal to any broad conception, or full enjoyment, of individual liberty. Imagine for one moment, if we can, a country given over to "isms" or fads, not held as matters of private speculation or individual practice, but enforced by multitudinous local laws ! Mr. Ewart invokes a reign of "isms" in the name of liberty ; he should have done it in the name of tyranny. Liberty consists in being as little governed as possible, and in having the largest possible scope left for private initiative ; whereas the policy suggested implies an intolerable quantity of government, to a mere pennyworth of individual freedom. Liberty consists not in the power to make other persons do your will, but in being able to prevent other people imposing their will on you. When Mr. Ewart pleads, therefore, for power to local majorities to introduce any variations they like into public school education he is pleading for tyranny, not for liberty. The minorities in the case supposed are

---
* Individualism ; A System of Politics." Page 25.

not seeking to impose their will on the majorities, because *what the minorities want the majorities want also*, nor is the majority in the country at large agreed upon anything else than just what the local minorities are conceived as wanting—the simple elements of secular education. The local minorities, therefore, those who do not want the fads, stand—as Mr. Ewart places the case before us—for liberty, and the local majorities (supposing them to want the fads) for tyranny.

The public school system, we cannot too frequently remind ourselves, derives its authority from an assumed national admission that popular education should be the care of the state. It is possible that if the Government of Manitoba stands firm in not consenting to have theology mixed up with state education, a portion of the community may withdraw their assent from the proposition and say: "No; education, we now find, is not a matter with which the state should meddle, because it cannot be satisfactorily given under state auspices—at least, not to *our* satisfaction. We therefore no longer join in the demand for state education." What course should the state take in such a contingency? My own opinion, in which I know many who will have followed me thus far with approval will not concur, is that in such a case those who withdrew their adhesion to the demand for state education, if at all a considerable body, should be allowed to count themselves out, and should be both exempted from taxation for school purposes, and excluded from the benefits accruing therefrom. School laws are passed because the people demand them, and a legislature has no warrant for passing them, apart from a popular demand. If, then, the demand ceases throughout a large section of the community, should schools, and taxation for schools, still be forced on that section? I cannot see that they should. At least, the only case in which they should would, in my humble opinion, be when the resulting ignorance—if ignorance resulted in the section concerned—became a clear and specific source of danger to the rest of the community. It would not be right, however, to presume that ignorance would result, nor should any rash theorizing be indulged in as to the effects of an ignorance not yet a developed fact. I plead for liberty, not the liberty to seek out "isms," and get them imposed by rough-shod majorities upon prostrate minorities, for I am too much impressed by Mr. Ewart's preamble for that; but I plead for liberty in the sense of the lightest, and simplest, and least intrusive, form of government, consistent with social order, and the largest possible exemption for all of us from legalized fads and "isms" and theologies. We can make or choose all these things for ourselves, and enjoy them privately to the top of our bent; but why in the name of common sense and common justice should we seek to impose them by force upon others?

CHAPTER XVIII.

THE MANITOBA SCHOOL QUESTION.*

By JOHN S. EWART, Q.C.

In the July number of the *Canadian Magazine*, I pleaded for liberty of thought and opinion. As one argument, I suggested that possibly even the cockiest bigot might be wrong; and I mentioned a few out of the millions of opinions that had already gone to the ditch. Might his not go too?

I beseech you in the bowels of Christ, think it *possible* you may be mistaken.

After seven pages, I summarized the proposition, to which I had "been endeavoring to win assent," as follows:

(1) That human thought is, even the best of it, upon social and religious questions far from infallible; (2) That other people of equal intelligence, who honestly differ with us, are as likely to be right as we are; (3) That religious and irreligious opinion is in the category of the debatable . . .; (4) That the true policy, with reference to all *such* questions, is that of perfect liberty; for the *onus* of proving the harmfulness of opposing opinion cannot be discharged.

Then follow four pages wherein I applied these principles to the schools.

The Rev. Dr. Bryce in the September number, makes reply, and that in the very simplest manner possible. He puts into my pages opinions, and contentions, that are not there, and, so far as I am aware, I never entertained; and then, without much effort, victoriously confutes them. He might have spared himself the confutation, for the poor, miserable things, with all possible shifts, straddles, and devices, could never have stood upright, even if left alone. The worthy Doctor would have accomplished all his purpose had he contented himself with saying, in a single sentence, "Mr. Ewart's whole article is a foolish defence of the geocentric theory." My discomfiture would thus have been sufficiently apparent to all men, without wasting pages to disprove the antiquated absurdity.

Not that Dr. Bryce had the slightest intention of misrepresenting me. He is merely a singularly good example of that "incapacity to appreciate, and sympathetically understand, an opinion contrary to his own," to which I referred in July. Instead of either understanding

---

* Reprinted from the Canadian Magazine, January, 1892.

my argument, or telling me that it was something "no fellow could understand," he flings a heap of wretched inanities at me, saying : "Your opinion is that

my right is your wrong ; my wrong is your right. One for me is as good as the other for you. *There is no fixed right.* There is no hope of reaching a common standard . . . Plainly Mr. Ewart believes there is no common standard of opinion ; that *there can be no consensus of right* ; that there can be no invariable principle in man which can serve as a basis of agreement, and hence of truth. That being the case, then each must be allowed to believe, and *act*, as he likes. Absolute, unrestrained liberty *to do* as he may choose must be given him.

He might just as well have added :

And Mr. Ewart believes that alligators are Divine emanations, and ought to be protected with forty-five per cent.

He seems to say :—

"As for you,
Say what you can, my false o'erweighs your true."

In order to justify his ascription to me of these absurdities, Dr. Bryce quotes four passages from my article. They are as follows (numbered and italicised) :—

FIRST PASSAGE.—"*If we cannot decide (and Mr. Ewart says we cannot decide) whether the opinions are harmful or innocent, A has as much right to have his way as B, has he not ?*" What opinions was I alluding to ? Whether alligators are emanations or not ? Whether A. is to have "absolute and unrestrained liberty to *do* as he may choose," or not ? No neither of them ; but whether atheistical opinions are so certainly harmful to society as to warrant the state in suppressing them. That is what I said could not be decided. Was I not right?

SECOND PASSAGE :—"*Your opinions are not entitled to one whit greater deference or respect than are the opinions of others.*" If Dr. Bryce refuses to admit "that other people of equal intelligence, who honestly differ with him, are as likely to be right as he is," then in all politeness, I shall make an exception in his favor. With this qualification, I believe the statement to be perfectly accurate. Nevertheless I will reverse it entirely, if he wishes, and say that every person's opinions *are* entitled to "greater deference and respect than are the opinions of others." But it must be understood that the change was made to oblige Dr. Bryce. Plato, more modest than the Doctor, would have said :*

To be absolutely sure of the truth of matters concerning which there are many opinions is an attribute of the gods, not given to man, stranger ; but I shall be very happy to tell you what I *think.*

---

* Laws, Bk. I.; Jowett's Trans. IV., 172.

THIRD PASSAGE :—"*Religious and irreligious opinion is in the category of the debatable; the true policy with reference to all such questions is perfect liberty.*" With the same understanding I will reverse this, too; I shall say: Religious questions are *not* "in the category of the debatable;" that from the time of Elijah and the Prophets of Baal, down to the time of Prof. Briggs and Prof. Campbell, they never have been debated. I shall further say that "the true policy with reference to all such questions is" *not* that of liberty at all, perfect or otherwise; but that of the Doctor's Confession of Faith in the words following:

> The civil magistrate . . . hath authority, and it is his duty, to take order that unity and peace be preserved in the church; that the truth of God be kept pure and entire; that all blasphemies and heresies be suppressed; all corruptions and abuses in worship and discipline prevented, or reformed; and all the ordinances of God duly settled, administered, and observed. For the better effecting thereof, he hath power to call synods, to be present at them, and to provide that whatsoever is transacted in them be according to the mind of God.

It must, however, again be most distinctly understood that the change was made to oblige Dr. Bryce. (I find myself still muttering something like "*E pur si muove.*")

FOURTH PASSAGE :—"*In the name of liberty, I would say to the parents: Certainly you have the right to teach, or have taught, to your children anything you like, so long as you can agree about it.*" Robbed of all its own context, and surrounded with a totally different one, this sentence might be taken to mean that I thought that parents were acting quite properly, did they teach their children "falsehoods, thieveries, iniquities, injustice, disloyalty, anarchic tendencies." With its own context it is plainly limited to Imperial Federationism, Militarism, Pietism, Sabbatarianism, Anti-alcoholism, and every other ism "*of such like* you can think of."

These are the four quotations to prove that one of my principles must be that

> absolute unrestrained liberty to *do* as he may choose must be given him.

Of course they are laughably worthless for that purpose; but they serve excellently another (probably not intended), namely, to show with what extroardinary fitness the Doctor selected, for his opening page, the words:

> "Lord, thou knowest gif I dinna gae richt, I'll gang far wrang."

In future he can apostrophise all Canada as well.

But he goes much further "wrang" than this. Having tripped up quite successfully the rickety Aunt Sallys, that the first passing butterfly would have tumbled over, he proceeds to enunciate three propositions which he says are "in opposition to these views." Three propositions—every one of them as certain, as well known, and as broad-based as Ararat, Blanc or his own Nevis! Three propositions —and not one of them in opposition to anything, so far as my views are concerned. On the contrary, while the first of them is as irrelevant as would be any proposition in Euclid, the other two are among the foundations of my July argument. These are the three (numbered consecutively and italicised):

I. *That the State has a right to form, and enforce, an opinion, at variance with the opinions of many of its subjects.*

Why this platitude, rather than any other—"Some things are good to eat," for example—I cannot imagine. "The State has a perfect right to form and enforce an opinion" *upon some matters* "at variance with the opinions of many of its subjects," is, surely, what the Doctor intends. He does not mean that the State ought to form, and enforce, an opinion upon *all* matters—upon the literary value of the Psalms, upon the use of meat on fast-days, upon attendance at church, etc. He does not advocate (probably) the return to Acts of Conformity, and Test Acts. His proposition, if intended to be universal, is unquestionably wrong. If intended to be limited, it is perfectly correct, but at the same time perfectly worthless; for there always remains to be proved that the matter under discussion is one of those upon which the State may form and enforce an opinion. "Far wrang!"

II. *The writer further contends that the State, being founded on justice, may not give special privileges to any class of its subjects.*

Most certainly, Doctor; that is what I was hitting at, and you were objecting to, when I said: "A. has as much right to have his way as B., has he not?" "Your opinions are not entitled to one whit greater deference or respect than are the opinions of others;" and "The true policy with reference to all such questions is perfect liberty." A few pages ago you said that "these are the elementary principles of anarchy." What do you think of them now? "No special privileges to any class of its subjects,"—let us adhere to that, for it is good.

And it is not in the least opposed to my views, as the Doctor seems to think. He says:

What does Mr. Ewart propose? He proposes that the people of Manitoba should have their public schools, and that one denomination should be singled out, and be allowed to teach their "isms," in certain schools, to be controlled by them.

To which I can only reply that I never proposed any such thing, or anything having the faintest resemblance to it; and that the whole drift of my article is entirely opposed to any such notion, and directly contrary to any such contention. "Far wrang!" "Far wrang!"

The Doctor tries in another way to make it appear that my purpose is as he alleges. He says that I

was most strenuous, when pleading the Roman Catholic position before the courts, in insisting that Episcopalians and Presbyterians had no rights in the same way.

Which is to say, that because I argued as to the meaning of certain words, in a certain statute, therefore my contention must be that that statute, with that certain meaning, upon abstract principles is just and good. Far, "far wrang" again! A lawyer might argue as to the meaning of one of Dr. Bryce's sermons surely, without being compelled to justify it? But the Doctor is wrong, not only in his logic, but in his facts. I did not so argue, for I was not even engaged in the case in which the question was debated. Once more "far wrang!"

Why does not the Doctor tell me that my real object is to destroy all belief in an isosceles triangle? And why, at all events, does he not doggedly adhere to that method of arguing, rather, at all events, than change to another very much worse? For, on the whole, I would much rather be told that I had said something that I did not, than have it alleged that the "mild, gentle-faced tolerance that Mr. Ewart pleads for, is not the reality for which he is arguing." This means, either that I am endeavoring to mislead, or that I do not know what I am arguing for—sufficiently uncomfortable horns both of them. I take some comfort, however, in the fact that it is the "far wrang" professor that so charges me, and the chances are infinity to one that he is "far wrang" again.

But what is this dreadful, or evasive, "reality, for which" I am arguing—this thing too horrible to mention, or too elusive for common apprehension? Veritably this: a desire to place the schools "under the control of the church"—that is, under the same kind of control as is the college in which Dr. Bryce has spent the best part of his life, as a most worthy and estimable professor! He sees nothing improper in *his* school being governed by a church, but deems the design of a similar government for other schools, a purpose altogether too heinous for public acknowledgment. Were he the professor of "far wrang" (and I do not think he ever did lecture on exegesis), he could not go much further "wrang" than this, surely? He may endeavor to distinguish. He will say that his school is sustained by private subscription. The distinction does not appeal to me as having much validity. Some of my income goes directly to the support of his school, and some of it indirectly (through the tax-collector), to the support of the other schools. To me, it is either well, or ill, that all these schools should be under church government—well or ill, that is, for the pupils. Whence come the salaries, can, by no means, affect the benefit or disadvantage to the children. He may urge, too, that theology is taught in his college, and that there is, therefore, for it, a necessity for church-government. But I do not refer to the theological department of his college, which, in numerical proportion, is but an adjunct of it; but to the larger body of the institution, the part in which the Doctor himself labors so successfully—to the ordinary every-day school for general education. Is church government for such schools well, or ill, Doctor? You spend a little of your time arguing for the suppression of them, because:

(1) The only hope for the province was to * * have a vigorous effort made to raise up a homogeneous Canadian people.

And

(2) In order to make us a united people, a patriotic love of our province demands this expedient.

And you employ the main energies of your life in working in, and seeking support for, a particular school of that very class. I know that you can distinguish again, and that your church is always right, and the others always wrong; so do not tell me that. But, "I beseech you, in the bowels of Christ, think it possible that you may be" gone "far wrang!"

I say that this, the second of the Doctor's propositions, is not only not opposed to my views, but that it is one of the foundations of my July argument; and I further say that it is entirely opposed to the action of the Manitoba Government.

Let us suppose that there are in a community three classes of persons, each with desires and ideas in reference to education. There are (A) those who desire it to be purely secular; (B) those who desire to have a certain spice, or flavor, of religion in it; and (C) those who desire to have it distinctly religious—history taught as in the Old Testament (God acting all the time), and not as in Gibbon (chance and circumstances at play). And now, Doctor, what I want to know is: How, upon the "no special privilege" plan, you pick out B, and determine that *he* must have his way? This is what Manitoba did. Do you say that B is in the majority? Very well, then, we must amend our principle, and say "that th state may not give special privileges to any class of its subjects, *except the majority*. Is it right now? If you think so, take it down to Quebec, set it to work, and watch it a little while. You will change your mind!

III. The last of the broad-based propositions (said to be opposed to my contentions), for which the Rev. Doctor contends is,

That religion is outside of state interference, unless religion invade the state's domain.

But this is *not* opposed to my contentions. On the contrary it is one of them, and the one to which I constantly make appeal as against the action of the Manitoba Legislature. What did that Legislature do? There were two sets of schools in existence—in one was a little religion suitable to Protestants, and in the other a little more religion suitable to Catholics. Under such circumstances, if the Doctor desires to know "What could patriotic Manitobans do!" I can have no objection to say, that if in the name of patriotism (or of all biology), they felt bound to abolish the one set of schools, and to strengthen the other, they could not have hit upon a more stupid reason for their action than that "religion [*all* religion that is] is outside of state interference." Any first-come law of dynamics (the science which treats of the action of *force*), would have been much more appropriate. Surely, far, "far wrang!"

For religion has not been removed from the schools. Episcopalian and Presbyterian Synods thank God annually that it is still there; while Roman Catholics bemoan its character. At present religion is taught, but taught perfunctorily, indirectly, circuitously, and as though people were ashamed of it. This may be taught, and that may not. The Bible may be read, but it must be read "without note or comment." The meaning of words, probably, cannot be given; the local customs, or notions, must not be referred to; the connection with the previous chapter must not be pointed out. Christ's life is to be read in this foolish fashion, and in detached snatches, with a minimum of ten verses at a time; but no one must say a word to help the children to understand, or appreciate it. All which, to my mind, is worse than making a fetish of the Bible; it is making a bore and an annoyance of it. Why does not some educationist propose that history or philosophy be taught in the same way? There must be no note or comment on the Bible; but, on the other hand, some of the means to be employed for "instruction in moral principles," are "stories, memory-gems . . . didactic talks, teaching the Ten Commandments, etc." Should the professor again write upon the school question, I beg of him to tell us: (1) Whether, working under these prescriptions, religion is, or is not, taught in the schools; (2) whether religion ought to be taught in the schools; (3) if yea, how it comes that his maxim, "that religion is outside of state interference," leads to state-directed religion in state schools. And let me anticipate one of his replies: "Yes, there is religion in the schools, but it is purely of a non-sectarian character." I shall still (1) ask him to apply his maxim, or to submit to its amendment, so that it shall read "Religion, *other than non-sectarian religion*, is outside of state interference;" but further (2) I shall beg him to remember (as said D'Israeli) that "a non-sectarian religion is a new religion." "Non-sectarian," is it? Look at the "Form of Prayer," and tell me if any Jew or Unitarian would join in it. Read at one sitting a Presbyterian and a Roman Catholic catechism, and see what they would respectively make of "teaching the Ten Commandments." Will Dr. Bryce say that he would consent to Roman Catholics, in their way, "teaching the Ten Commandments" to Protestant children? Of course he will not, but he thinks it quite right in the name of "patriotism," and of "homogeneity," and of "a united people," to require Roman Catholic children to take their ideas from Protestant teachers. As he says, "a patriotic love of our province demands this expedient." "Far wrang!" "Far wrang!" Toujours perdrix!

One more effort to make myself understood. In my July article, quoting from Dr. Bryce, I said that of the Catholic school districts:

All but a very small percentage are in localities almost entirely French.

And I added:

Manitoba has said to a large section of her people: Unless you undertake to stop teaching your own religion, to your own children, in schools to which no one goes except those of your own faith, we will not permit you to organize yourselves together for the instruction of those in whose education the whole community has a decided interest.

This is too true to be denied, and the Doctor does not deny it. He contents himself with denying the motive which actuated it. Let the motive go; there is the fearful fact. Catholics *are* thrown upon voluntary effort and subscription, *unless they will abandon that which is to them a sacred duty.* If this be not intolerance and persecution, then the world never saw those horrid monsters and never will see them.

Dr. Bryce helps me splendidly here:

Probably most would say that should Roman Catholics or others desire to educate their children in private schools, at their own expense, so long as illiteracy does not result, it would be well to allow it.

There are three conditions: (1) "Private schools"; (2) "at their own expense," and (3) "so long as illiteracy does not result." The difference between private and public schools (apart from expense) is that in the latter there is public inspection and oversight, a common standard, control by the vote of the people. It could be no reason for *not* allowing Roman Catholics to educate their children that they were willing to permit public inspection and oversight, to adopt the common standard, and to substitute control by the people for control by the church. Upon the contrary, this would evidently remove an objection quite formidable to many minds, and make Manitobans all the more willing one would think, to allow the Roman Catholics to proceed in their own way. Shall we, therefore, rub out the first condition? By so doing we shall also dispose of the third, shall we not? Where are we now? We have Catholics in public schools, under public regulation, governed by the people, working up to a common standard. Well, then, the only condition left is —" at their own expense," and they (*mirabile dictu*) unanimously reply, "Why, certainly! We do not want a sixpence of anybody's money but our own." What do they propose? Merely this (they are not beggars, although most of them are poor), that they should be allowed to organize *themselves* for the purpose of taxing *themselves* to raise money for *their own* schools.

Take an example. In the district of X there is an exclusively Roman Catholic population. Up to 1890 there was a state school there. To-day there is none. This is what is known as providing "one public school for each locality.") The people, therefore, pay no taxes for school purposes at all. They contribute voluntarily, but not in a sufficiently systematic way, for the purpose of providing private education for their children. They want power to tax themselves, in order better to support their schools—schools which shall have all the qualities of public schools. And Manitobans ("as Mr. Ewart knows, a generous people") reply: "Certainly you may do so, but upon one condition. You must promise to read the Bible 'without note or comment' of any kind, and either refrain from teaching religion altogether, or else adopt and teach this emasculated thing called 'non-sectarian religion.' This is our ultimatum. Accept, or go and be hanged—you and your children." "A patriotic love of our province demands this expedient," coolly adds Dr. Bryce, seated comfortably in his study—and continues to act on the exact contrary of "this expedient."

In addition to the right to tax themselves, and as something which Manitobans may or may not, according to their sense of justice (no one asks for generosity), withhold, the Catholics further propose this: Out of public funds there is paid to each school a certain sum in aid of the amount raised by taxation. These public funds belong to the people, Protestants and Roman Catholics alike, and "the State, being founded on justice, may not give special privileges to any class of its subjects." The people of district X say: Give us our share. We will conform to all your secular requirements, to inspections, to regulations, to standards; "religion is outside of State interference;" leave it, therefore, outside of your regulations. Pay us our share, if in every respect we do the proper and efficient work of a secular school. And "generous" Manitobans reply: No; your school may be the best in the Province, but you will not get a cent if you comment on the Bible. When we said that "religion was outside of State interference," we meant that the State could quite properly interfere with the teaching of religion, and that, by one of the most drastic of penalties, namely, the threatened illiteracy of your children; it could with the most perfect justice, indeed in the exercise of much generosity, prevent Catholics teaching Catholic children the Catholic religion in the only way in which Catholics believe it can effectively be done.

Let us dissect a little this seemingly simple proposition, "Religion is outside of state interference," and let us distinguish, because in *not* understanding it, simple as it is, lie many difficulties for many people. Guizot says* church and state have maintained four forms of relations to one another:— (1) "The state is subordinate to the church;" (2) "It is not the state which is in the church, but the church which is in the state;" (3) "The church ought to be independent, unrestricted in the state; the state has nothing to do with her; the temporal power ought to take no cognizance of religious creeds;" (4) "The church and the state are distinct societies, it is true, but they are at the same time close neighbors, and are nearly interested in one another; let them live separate, but not estranged; let them keep up an alliance on certain conditions, each living to itself, but each making sacrifices for the other; in case of need each lending the other its support."

Many people apprehend clearly enough the two first situations, but the last are usually jargogled together. And yet what a wide difference between them. Under the one principle, a man-of-war goes to sea, and many of her crew go to their graves beneath the water, without the services or offices of a clergyman. Under the other, the state recognizes the *fact* of religion (although refusing to say anything as to its truth), and, among each ship's officers, places one of the spirituality. The state in this case has regard to the wants of the crew. Even as provision is made for food and raiment as wants, so provision is made for *de facto* spiritual wants. It may be considered by many to be a very foolish thing to wish to have a clergyman with you on a battle-ship; even as others think it very absurd to want "baccy" or grog. But the state recognizes the *existence* of these wants (not their wisdom), and *refuses* the men neither the one nor the other. Again, under the one principle, the name of God, and everything which could suggest the fact of religion, is excluded from the schools. While under the other, the state takes cognizance of the existence of religion; and the wants of the parents respecting it are, so far as practicable, recognized and acceded to. The distinction is now, I think, sufficiently clear. Which of them is correct? To my mind, he who is actuated by the true spirit of liberty will undoubtedly choose the latter.

With this understanding, let us return to Dr. Bryce's proposition, "Religion is outside of state interference." By this is properly meant that, revolving as they do in different orbits, they ought not to collide with, or clash, or oppose one another. It does not mean that one can deny the existence of the other, or act as though it did not exist, or invade the territory of the other, saying, "Make way, for we must not collide." It means, so far as the state's action is concerned, that the *fact* that religion exists must be recognized; and that in so far as its orderly observance and propagation are concerned, it is "outside of state interference." Dr. Bryce himself concedes that "on the

---

* Civilization in France, Lect. 3, Vol. I, p. 317, and see Lect. 12, Vol. II, p. 27.

whole the trend of modern thought is to allow as great liberty as possible to religious opinion."

Let us go back to District X. Prior to 1890, the school there was under state control and governance; the people taxed themselves to support the school; and according to the secular work accomplished, they obtained the same assistance from public funds that other schools received. In addition to secular instruction, the children were taught the way of salvation, as believed by the parents of every child in the school. The state, true to principle, interposed no obstacle. It allowed as "great liberty as possible." It did not interfere. It did not oppose. It did not object. Then Manitobans ("as Mr. Ewart knows, a generous people") informed these poor parishioners, that unless they would cease telling the children about Jesus, they would be deprived of their organization, they would lose their share of the public moneys, and might get along as best, (or as worst) they could. Since then the Government (the people have not yet approved the step) has had the astounding hardihood to send agents to these poor people to sympathize with them, and to urge them to forego their conscientious convictions, in order that they may have the pecuniary advantages of which, for their religion's sake, they were deprived. Than this history records nothing more intolerant, and, but that it is done without proper reflection, more base. I use the word deliberately. These people have been taught to believe, and do most thoroughly believe, that it is their duty to provide a certain kind of education for their children. It is not proposed to remove this belief by argument. It is proposed to tempt these people with money to act contrary to their belief. If the word "base" is not too strong to apply to the Judas who exchanges conscience for mere cash does not the tempter who, to accomplish a base betrayal, appeals to the basest of motives, also richly merit the same word.

And is it not in the last degree extraordinary, that of all principles, social or scientific, mundane or divine, or other whatsoever, the one which most strongly and clearly condemns such gross interference with religious liberty—*Religion is outside of State interference*—is the very principle selected by Dr. Bryce to support it? We must leave him, venturing and proffering this suggestion, namely, that if, at any time, he does

heartily join in the prayer of that fellow-countryman, who pleaded for heavenly direction, saying, "Lord, gif I dinna gae richt, Thou knowest I'll gang far wrang,"

the proper hymn for the occasion would be, in my humble opinion, "For those at sea"—far, far at sea. Failing relief by this method, I am afraid nothing remains but the traditional surgical operation.

Si quid per jocum dixi, nolito in serium convertere; for

> Though they may gang a kennin wrang,
> To step aside is human.

The few passages of my July article which escaped misconstruction at the hands of Dr. Bryce, have, at those of Mr. Le Sueur, shared the general fate. This latter gentleman seems to think that one of my contentions was, that because opinion might be erroneous, therefore we ought to

shun the responsibility of putting any of our opinions into practice.

This is not my "therefore," nor the proper "therefore;" but this rather: that as our opinions *may* be erroneous, we ought not *unnecessarily* to ride rough-shod over the opinions of others—that while acting upon our opinions, we should proceed, not as if they were certain to be right, but *as if, possibly, they might be wrong*; and that, therefore, if in our economy, scope can be left, or made, for the free play of contrary opinion, left or made it ought to be. A general may be of the opinion that the enemy is 40,000 strong. He ought to act upon that opinion; but he would be a fool if he made no provision for a sudden reversal of his idea.

Suppose that the city of London determined to establish a number of public hospitals, and that there came to be determined the question of the system of medicine to be adopted. Alderman A proposes the allopathic system (which he *knows* to be the best), and has the majority on his side. Alderman B, who is an homœopathist, urges that many of the people are of his way of thinking; that, possibly, the majority may be wrong; and that both kinds of hospitals ought to be established, so that the people of both opinions may be accommodated. Alderman A says: "Certainly not. The majority must act upon its opinion, and not be deterred by the fact that they may be entirely wrong. If homœopathists want special treatment they can have it at their own expense, and at other places." In such case, Alderman B, in my opinion, is, most undoubtedly, right. A is wrong, because he acts upon his opinion as though it were the "ultimate infallible *credo*."

Is my meaning now clear? This imagined case may be made further useful. Allopathic hospitals may be taken to represent Protestant schools, and homœopathic hospitals, Catholic schools. In such case Alderman C proposes that, inasmuch as the people are not agreed upon the question of medicine, there should not be any practice at all of a sectarian character, in the hospitals. "We are all agreed," he says, "upon surgical matters; we are all agreed that nursing and low diet are beneficial in fever cases; there is much about which there is unanimity. There is a national mandate thus far. Let us, then, have non-sectarian hospitals, and if any patient wants more than that, let him pay for it out of his own pocket." Then, quoting Mr. Le Sueur, he adds: "Do not ask that the hospitals, which *all* agree are not only useful, but necessary, shall be made subservient to the propagation of your peculiar ideas in these matters." Manitoba has established non-sectarian hospitals (as she chooses to call them), and many of the people will make no use of them. Could not Alderman B have given them a better idea ?

Mr. Le Sueur gives me credit, also for the

> idea of handing over local minorities to local majorities, without any check from the general law of the land.

My article was, as I understand it, one long argument *against* this idea— *against* the exercise of the power of majorities ; and I am indebted to my critic for the great support which he gives me. The single sentence in my article which has led Mr. Le Sueur astray refers to *unanimities*, and not to majorities and minorities at all. "Practical unanimity," or the disregard of merely "eccentric, or isolated opinion," I, for one, can by no means translate into a "majority vote." And if I am asked, "What power does he look to, to check a school-district which, dispensing with practical unanimity, wants to introduce some fad into the school by a majority vote?" the answer is very simple : I look to the "check from the general law of the land," which my critic makes me say that I do not look to. I must have some little license to speak for myself.

Passing from these misconceptions, Mr. Le Sueur says that

> the State may, therefore, be said to get a mandate to establish secular schools. Does the state get any similar mandate to teach theology in the schools.

I beg to recommend these sentences to Dr. Bryce, and to Manitobans in general. There is more point in them, I venture to say, than will be admitted ; for they avoid the inconsistency of arguing from the principle of entire separation of Church and State to the practice of teaching some certain limited religion in the schools, and the exclusion of a few degrees more of it. But Mr. Le Sueur is speaking beside the facts. If there was any mandate about which Manitobans were more emphatic than another, it was that the schools should *not* be secular. For the rest, the mandate of the majority was to continue non-sectarian schools, and the mandate of the minority to re-establish the old system. Mr. Le Sueur's argument, leading, as it does, to secular schools, therefore, may for present purposes be disregarded. The subject is interesting, but purely academic, so far as the pending controversy is concerned.

I have to thank Mr. Le Sueur for another sentence :

> Liberty consists in being as little governed as possible, and in having the largest possible scope left for private initiative.

Apply this to district X and some scores of other districts in Manitoba. In them, the Catholics, if "governed as little as possible," will be required to keep their schools up to certain secular standards ; and will not be forbidden (for it is unnecessary) to comment on the Bible-reading of the day, if unanimously they desire to do so. Am I not right? Is it in the name of liberty, or of tyranny, that all such comment, when unanimously desired, is by law stringently prohibited? Is this imposing the will of other people upon them, or is it freedom to act as they like?

Mr. Le Sueur is more successful, if I may be allowed to say so, when he advocates the rights of the Catholics to "be allowed to count themselves out," as he expresses it. Suppose this was done, and that the Catholics of district X applied for a chrter under which they could organize themselves for the support of education. This would not, surely, be refused them, so long as every other good purpose is being aided in similar fashion. The charter having been granted, suppose that the Catholics in district X all became members of the Association, and agreed to pay certain rates per annum into the exchequer, and to charge their properties with the amounts. Mr. Le Sueur would, I think, see nothing wrong in all this. How far would he then be away from the separate school system? He will say that the arrangements would be purely voluntary. He is aware that in Ontario every Catholic must support the public schools unless he *voluntarily* supports some separate school. Make the law the same in Manitoba, and give each school district a separate charter, or provide for all by one general law as you wish. That difference, if insisted upon, would not cause much grumbling or discontent. Mr. Le Sueur is, I think, more with me than with Dr. Bryce to whom, nevertheless, he says, "well done."

CHAPTER XIX.

EXTRACT FROM AN ADDRESS BY

MR. JOSEPH MARTIN, M.P.

(*Before the Liberal Club, Winnipeg, 20th Feb. 1894.*)

The next question was how far should the government go in the matter of education? And here he would like to turn aside for a minute to speak on the existence of separate schools. They were aware that a considerable section of the community were not in favor of the government undertaking the education of their children, and were of opinion that secular and religious training should be given in the same school. He regretted that the carrying out of the principles in which he believed should have met with such bitter opposition, but his attitude was due to deep conviction of the rights of the case, and to no personal issue. He denied the right of the state to deal with the question of religion. It must be decided by the individual. It was agreed that a state church in Canada was an impossible thing. Then if that were clearly followed up it would appear that any interference by the state with the question of religion would not be in accordance with the principles of our constitution. Roman Catholics said that the proposed legislation in favor of separate schools was a violation of their constitutional rights, but the courts had disproved this assertion, and for his part he believed that the Roman Catholics would be found willing to submit to the law of the land, even when contrary to their personal opinions. He was himself not satisfied with the school act, and had never been so. He had made a strong effort to have the public schools, controlled by the Government, really made national schools, with religion obliterated. And he was now more convinced than ever that that was the only school which could be justified as constitutional. They said that the state had no right to interfere with the different denominations, but had the right to interfere in the matter of religion ; but he contended that they could not do the one without the other. It had been urged by satisfied supporters of the Act that none could complain of the devotional element introduced, as it was of the broadest nature, but they found that the Roman Catholics had the very greatest objections to this provision of the Act, and he was dissatisfied himself, and was glad many Protestants shared his objections. It had been said, that in the event of his opinions being adopted our public schools would be Godless schools ;

but by many staunch supporters of the school Act it had been privately admitted to him that the religious exercises practised in the schools at that time were without value. But as a matter of sentiment, they added,—Oh, as a matter of sentiment, perhaps—but he could not understand such an argument. Of what value was the form if no good resulted; and of how much harm was it productive if it acted as a stirrer up of strife? The Roman Catholics had honestly stated that in their belief the two forms of education should go together. The Protestants admitted, on the other hand, that it was impossible to have religious training in schools, and only asked that it be recognized, insisting, however, on imposing their views on others in that respect, Rather than that small amount of religious training should be done away with in the schools, the Protestants said they would prefer the old state of affairs. He would leave it to his audience to determine which was the more honest stand of the two.

CHAPTER XX.

EXTRACT FROM SPEECH OF

HON. MR. LAURIER.

(*Winnipeg, 3rd Sept., 1894.*)

I am a firm believer in Provincial rights. In the Dominion House of Commons I have stood up for the authority of the Provinces. When I took up the petition of my fellow-religionists of Manitoba, complaining of the legislation of the Government of Manitoba, I asked myself, What is the complaint? I took the petition of the late Archbishop Taché, a man who, I believe, was revered in this Province by friend and foe. I took up the petition of the Archbishop and those who signed it with him, and the complaint which was made was that the Government of Manitoba—I speak here in the presence of the members of the Government—had adopted legislation which, instead of imposing Public Schools upon the minority, imposed upon them Protestant schools, and that they were bound to send their children to Protestant schools. On the other hand, the Government of Manitoba denied the statement in toto. They did not admit that the legislation had that effect. They did not admit that the legislation was to have the effect of sending Roman Catholic children to Protestant schools. I said to the Government, Here is a simple question of fact. You have to determine whether the statements are true or not; but instead of doing that, they went on appealing to the courts and evading the question. I did more. I said then—I say it here now—if the complaint of the Catholics were true, that Catholic children had been forced to attend Protestant schools—if that were true, it would be such an outrage upon the rights of conscience that no community would permit it. I said upon the floor of the House of Commons:— "Prove to me that the complaint of the Roman Catholic minority is true, that their rights are outraged to this extent, that, instead of sending their children to schools where there is no religious teaching, they are forced to send their children to schools where there is religious teaching, not their own, and I will be prepared to go before the people of Manitoba and tell them that such legislation should not stand. I have nothing else to say in Winnipeg than what I have said on the floor of Parliament, in Quebec and elsewhere.

CHAPTER XXI.

EXTRACT FROM A SPEECH BY
MR. DALTON McCARTHY.

(Creemore, 24 July, 1894.)

He gave an explanation of his statement about which the Conservative press has been making a clamor, that he would rather have Separate Schools than secular schools. A secular school system was one from which the word of God was excluded. This was a Christian country, and it would be a scandal, he said, if there was no opportunity given to have the religion common to the whole people taught in the schools. Although there were some people in this country who did not believe in any religion, their number was small, and it would be a terrible hardship to the people generally if the word of God were the only book excluded from the schools. Surely, he said, there were in the Bible chapters on which all could agree and which would not promote sectarianism. But he was not meaning to dictate to the 66,000 people of the Northwest. He would let them do as they think best, and make the choice they see fit, whether it be Separate, or secular schools, or the Ontario system of Public Schools.

PART III.

THE MANITOBA ACT
AS A TREATY.

PROTESTANT PROMISES.

BY

JOHN S. EWART.

CHAPTER I.

INTRODUCTORY.

When it is urged on behalf of the Roman Catholic minority, that the Manitoba Act was the result of negotiation and treaty, between the Red River settlers, and the Dominion Government, it is sometimes answered with contemptuous, but ignorant sneer, that "the Red River settlers" were nothing more than "a few Red River priests, and half-breeds"; and sometimes with lofty patriotism, that "Her Majesty did not barter terms with rebels." It is the object of the succeeding pages to prove:—

1. That the provisions of the Manitoba Act were the result of negotiation and treaty.

2. That the Imperial Government refused to sanction resort to military measures, to force "the sovereignty of Canada on the population of Red River, should they refuse to admit it"; and agreed to it only "provided reasonable terms are granted to the Red River settlers."

3. That the Dominion Government sent, to the settlers, commissioners, who invited them to send delegates to Ottawa.

4. That delegates were sent to Ottawa in pursuance of the Government's request.

5. That "the Red River settlers" who sent the delegates, were not "a few Red River priests and half-breeds"; but on the contrary, that prior to the departure of the delegates, and as a result of three general elections held in the settlement within a period of four months (Nov. 1869; Jan. 1870; and Feb. 1870, a Provincial Assembly and Government had been set up, established, and concurred in by the almost unanimous vote of the freely chosen representatives of the settlers.

6. That protracted negotiations took place daily at Ottawa, between the delegates and a Committee of the Dominion Government, lasting from the 23rd April, to 2nd May; and that on this latter date an understanding was arrived at, and the Manitoba Act introduced into the House of Commons. It was passed 12th May.

7. That the delegates forthwith returned to Red River, carrying with them the Act, which was accepted by the Legislative Assembly by unanimous resolution, amidst enthusiastic cheering :—

"That the Legislative Assembly of this country do now, in the name of the people, accept the Manitoba Act, and decide on entering the Dominion of Canada, on the terms proposed in the Confederation Act."

8. That while the establishment of self-government, without the sanction of Her Majesty, was undoubtedly illegal, yet that the whole movement found its sufficient causes (1) in the attempt to transfer the people of Red River, and their territory, to the Dominion of Canada "like so many head of cattle" (in Col. Wolsely's phrase), without a word of communication with the settlers upon the subject, without a hint as to the form of government to be imposed upon them, without a suggestion as to policy with reference to the ownership of lands, and without the slightest evidence of good-will; (2) in the "anticipation by the Canadian Government of the transfer," by undertaking "certain operations in respect to land," thus "giving occasion to an outbreak of violence;" (3) in the overbearing and insulting conduct of representives and agents of the Dominion Government, and in their open threats, and endeavors to possess themselves of lands claimed by the Metis; (4) in the utterly illegal, and criminally reckless, efforts on the part of agents of the Dominion Government, and others, to establish authority over the settlers; and (5) in the turbulence, and absurd agitation and resistance, of the Canadian party, after the great majority of the settlers had concurred in the necessity for the establishment of a Provincial Government, and after every part of the settlement had elected representatives in its Assembly.

9. That there was no rebellion against Her Majesty, or the Sovereignty of the Empire; that there was a well-regulated defence against unauthorized agents of the Dominion Government—for Canada had no jurisdiction in the settlement until after "the troubles" were all over; that the only object of the Metis was to obtain assurances as to the form of government proposed, as to their titles to lands, and other matters, about which it was reasonable that their rights, interests, and desires, should have been consulted.

10. That the object of the Metis was attained, and large and important benefits procured by their action.

11. That, upon the whole, the conduct of the Metis throughout the movement was characterized not only by great moderation and self-control, but by a regard for legal forms, and constitutional action, which, remembering the character and education of the people, must be regarded as striking and surprising.

12. And that the passage by the Manitoba legislature of the school Acts was a violation of faith pledged to Catholics, upon at least three several occasions :—

(1) It was a violation of the spirit and true intent of the Manitoba Act—of a treaty entered into under the direction, and with the sanction and approval of the Imperial Government.

(2) It was a violation of pledges made to the Catholics in 1876, when the Catholic members of the Manitoba Legislative Assembly agreed to the abolition of the Provincial Senate, and thus to the abolition of the strongest guarantee for the maintenance of minority rights.

(3) It was a violation (most flagrant, and heartless) of the pledges made in 1888, on behalf of the Liberal party in Manitoba, at the election (St. Francois Xavier) which enabled it to defeat the Harrison Government, and thus paved the way for its own accession to office.

As the pages which follow are in some sense an argument (although it is hoped a perfectly fair one) the writer has italicized words in many of the quotations to which he desires to call attention, and thus in many cases saved the repetition of language, with obvious remarks as to its relevancy. This has been done so frequently that it is better to guard the reader in the Introduction, rather than by repeated foot-notes.

CHAPTER II.

THE RED RIVER SETTLERS.

The 15th day of July, *1870* (note it well), is the date upon which the North Western Territory was admitted into, and became part of the Dominion of Canada; and consequently the date at which all claim to jurisdiction, on the part of the Hudson's Bay Company came to end. For some years prior to that date, however, the Company had with increasing difficulty, maintained its authority; and in the previous November (1869), that authority had been completely superseded by the promoters of the Provisional Government. In truth, the power of the Company to establish courts of law, and to punish criminals, was never well-settled or acknowledged. During long years, when the only white people were either associated with the Company, or were at all events not antagonistic to it, there was little disposition to question the despotic power which its officers asserted. But the advent of "Canadians" bent upon competition with the Company, and of a "Canadian party," at once put in question the legality and authority of its proceedings; and the Company, feeling its position to be far from secure, first parleyed with those who treated its process with contempt, and finally submitted to such humiliating compromises as it could secure. One historian* puts it thus:

"So long as the people of the country were in a state of peace, order and contentment, it was neither a hard, nor an expensive undertaking to frame and carry out the few laws necessary for their guidance; but when unprincipled men put them at defiance, and preached to the otherwise quiet settlers that they were abused people, then the Hudson's Bay Company found that it required both money and force to carry out the laws."

The population of the Red River settlement in 1870 was composed of about 2,000 whites, 5,000 English half-breeds, and 5,000 French half-breeds or Metis.† There was a cross-division into three parties, viz.: the English, the French, and the Canadians.

"THE FRENCH HALF-BREED, called also Metis, and formerly Bois-Brulé, is an athletic, rather good-looking, lively, excitable, easy-going being. Fond of a fast pony, fond of merry-making, free-hearted, open-handed, yet indolent and improvident, he is a marked feature of border life. Being excitable, he can be roused to acts of revenge, of bravery, and daring ....The Metis, if a friend, is true, and cannot in too many ways oblige you....Louis Riel was undoubtedly the embodiment of the spirit of unrest and insubordination in his race. Tribes and peoples do at times find their personification in one of their num-

---

* Mr. Begg. † See Dominion Census, 1871.

her. Ambitious, vain, capable of inspiring confidence in the breasts of the ignorant, yet violent, vacillating and vindictive ; the rebel chieftain has died, etc.*"

ENGLISH HALF-BREEDS. "As different as is the patient roadster from the wild mustang, is the English-speaking half-breed from the Metis."†

THE CANADIANS. "Unfortunately for Canada, the very men who maligned and defied the law of the land, styled themselves the Canadian party in Red River, and their principal cry seemed to be the superiority of Canadians generally over the Red River settlers. 'You will see what Canada will do when she takes hold of the country,' was a common observation."‡

Numerically the Canadians were insignificant, but, in point of education, ability, energy, and progressiveness, they were an extremely important factor in the settlement. They saw clearly enough that both "patient roadster," and "wild mustang," would have to give way before Canadians ; and they seem to have been at no pains to conceal their views, and their contempt for the old-fashioned methods of Company rule. In 1868 the Canadian Government sent Messrs. Snow & Mair into the settlement to commence some roadmaking. This was nearly two years prior to Canada having any jurisdiction there. Naturally enough, but quite indiscreetly, they became associated with the Canadian party; and the boastings of these latter thus seemed to receive official confirmation.

"Coupled with this, Mr. Mair made himself particularly busy in speaking and writing in favour of the principles of the party. Instead of confining himself to his government duties, he employed a portion of his time in preaching a doctrine sufficient of itself to cause distrust in the minds of the Red River people as to the intentions of the Canadian Government."§

---

* "The Old Settlers of Red River." By Rev. Dr. Bryce.
† Ibid   ‡ Begg's History, 21.   § Begg's History, 21.

CHAPTER III.

CAUSES OF THE OUTBREAK—"PROCEED WITH THE SURVEYS."

Here then, we have all the materials necessary for an explosion. "Patient roadster" and "wild mustang," divided by disposition, by race, and by religion, yet united in interest, about to be driven out of their old-fashioned methods by these new people, who hold the methods of both in contempt. Roadster and mustang, alike, want to know what is going to be done, and especially why *anything* is being done, prior to the transfer of the territory to Canada. Roadster and mustang are given to understand that they are to have nothing to say upon the subject. Roadster and mustang wanting to know who is to rule them, and with what kind of bridles and bits? Roadster and mustang objecting that their drivers have not yet bought them, or got title to them? What nonsense! Nonsense, perhaps, but roadster and mustang can kick, one patiently, the other somewhat wildly; and kick they do, five men being killed in the sequence of it, as will hereafter be related.

Does the above fairly indicate the causes of the outbreak? It does. The proof is overwhelming.

Until the 15th July, 1870, the Canadian Government had no more right to exercise jurisdiction at Red River than had the President of the United States. Let this clearly be borne in mind—there could by no possibility be a rebellion against Canada prior to July, 1870. There might be an invasion by Canada, and an usurpation by it of power; but the Tasmanian Government could have acted in the same way, and with the same right, and, probably, have met with the same resistance! Canada was, no doubt, in treaty for the acquisition of the territory, but she had not got it, and every act of her government, in anticipation of the grant, was entirely illegal.

Notwithstanding this fact (well-known, and admitted, as it was), the government sent Col. Dennis, with a body of surveyors, into the settlement, for the purpose of laying off in lots the land which the settlers had so long peaceably occupied. As the survey progressed some of the "Canadian party" laid claim to such parts as pleased them, and took possession of them by ploughing furrows, or by driving in stakes carrying their names.

"Wild mustang" is unable to watch all this with that perfect equanimity, and stoical indifference, which a philosopher, in the most advanced stages, might be expected to exhibit. On the contrary he grows fretful, apprehensive, indignant, angry ; and Col. Dennis, on the 21st August, 1869, reported to Ottawa as follows :—

"I find that a considerable degree of irritation exists among the native population in view of surveys and settlements being made without the Indian title having been first extinguished. . . . In connection therewith, *I would reiterate* to you my conviction, as expressed while at Ottawa, that no time should be lost. The necessity for prompt action is more apparent to me now than it seemed even then . . . In the meantime, the French half-breeds, who constitute about one-fourth or one-fifth (say 3,000) souls, of the settlement, are likely to prove a turbulent element. This class has gone so far as to threaten violence should surveys be attempted to be made."

Afterwards, on the 28th August, 1869, Col. Dennis reported :—

"I have *again* to remark the uneasy feeling which exists in the half-breed and Indian element, with regard to what they conceive to be *premature action* taken by the Government, in proceeding to effect a survey of the lands, without having extinguished the Indian title, and I beg permission to reiterate the conviction expressed on a former occasion, that *this must be the first question of importance dealt with* by the Government."

But this was not the first question dealt with. . It was not dealt with at all, until everything Col. Dennis easily enough foresaw, had happened. "Dealt with"! it was dealt with in this fashion :—

"OTTAWA, Oct. 4, 1869.

"SIR,—I have the honor to inform you that the Government, upon the recommendation of the Minister of Public Works, has approved of the system proposed by you, in your report dated the 28th August last, for the survey and sub-division of townships in the North-West Territories. *You are, therefore, authorized to proceed with the surveys on the plan proposed.*

I have the honor to be, sir,
Your obedient servant,

J. STOUGHTON DENNIS, P.L.S.,   F. BRAUN,
    Red River Settlement.   *Secretary.*

"Proceed with the surveys"! Col. Dennis and the settlers say, "Settle these title matters as 'the first question of importance'." *After* the difficulties had seriously commenced, the Canadian Government sent delegates to pacify the settlers, and to assure them of reasonable terms. But prior to the outbreak the word is one of lofty and contemptuous command—"Proceed with the surveys."

And "proceed with the surveys" they did, but with no great success. "Patient roadster" becomes restive, and "wild mustang" raises his heels :—

"No arms were seen with the party, but by standing on the surveyor's chain and using threats of violence, if the survey was persisted in, it became evident that to go on with the surveys would probably have led to a serious collision."[*]

---

[*] Schedule to letter—Hon. W. McDougall to Secy. State, 31st Oct., 1869.

And thus the heels have been raised, but, as yet, not to strike—merely to be shown, and then put down again, firmly, on the chains: —"These chains have no right here; take them off, and yourselves too!" Col. Dennis has no alternative; "proceed with the surveys" has become impossible, and so gathering up the chains he makes his way south to the boundary, there to report to Mr. McDougall, and receive further impossible orders. As he journeys let us peruse the testimony of some of the historians, and others, as to the causes of the outbreak.

REV. DR. BRYCE'S TESTIMONY.

The Rev. Dr. Bryce, whose writings show little sympathy with those who were trying to get terms from their proposed new masters, testifies as follows : *

> "Suffice it to say that the hasty action of the Canadian Government in sending roadmakers and surveyors to the North-west, before the transfer had been made, the unwise conduct of a number of these forerunners, and the natural fear of the Red River people that their interests would be neglected, *account for the rising.* To these must be added the restless character of the French half-breeds, who, as hunters and traders, were accustomed to the use of fire-arms, had a hereditary bent to insubordination, and were led by a few daring leaders."

MR. BEGG'S TESTIMONY.

Mr. Begg's "History of the Red River Troubles" is by far the most complete account obtainable of the events it deals with. Mr. Begg resided at Fort Garry throughout the whole period, and kept a carefully compiled diary, not only of events, but of the rumors and anticipations of the days as they passed. His story has therefore much interest. At page 24, he says:—

> "Soon after Col. Dennis had commenced his surveying operations throughout the settlement, these same men began to lay claim to all the most valuable spots of land not actually belonging to the settlers. The plan adopted was as follows:—When a lot was chosen by an individual, he proceeded to cut a furrow round it with a plough, and then drive stakes with his name marked upon them into the ground here and there. This was considered sufficient to give the claimant a right to the land; and in this way hundreds of acres were taken possession of, for the purpose of speculation. It seemed, as soon as there appeared a certainty that the Hon. Wm. McDougall was to be Governor, that the men, who professed to be his friends in Red River, made it a point to secure as much of the country to themselves as possible. It is notorious that the principal one in this movement, the leader of the so-called Canadian party, staked off sufficient land (had he gained possession of it) to make him one of the largest landed proprietors in the Dominion. *Can it be wondered at if the people looked with dismay at this wholesale usurpation of the soil? Is it surprising if they foresaw the predictions of the very men who acted as usurpers as likely to come true, namely, that the natives were to be swamped by the incoming strangers.*"

---

* "The Provisional Governments in Manitoba," p. 3.

Mr. McTavish's Testimony.

Mr. McTavish, who was Governor of the Hudson's Bay Company at Fort Garry, in a letter to Mr. McDougall, at Pembina, (9th November, 1869) thus delicately says the same thing:—

"It is unquestionable that the preservation of the public peace is the paramount duty of every government; but while in ordinary circumstances it might be reasonable enough to cast upon us the exclusive responsibility of preserving the public peace, it may perhaps at the same time admit of doubt whether some degree of responsibility did not also rest upon others in a case of so exceptional a character as this—a case in which not merely a whole country is transferred, but also in a certain sense a whole people, or where at least the political condition of the people undergoes such a great change; *and it may moreover be a question whether, on the part of the Dominion, the preliminary arrangements for introducing that change have proceeded upon such a just and accurate appreciation of the country, and the peculiar feelings and habits of its people,* as on such an occasion was desirable, if not absolutely essential, and whether the complications by which we are now surrounded may not, to a great extent, be owing to that circumstance."

The Bishop of Rupert's Land's Testimony.

The Anglican Bishop of Rupert's Land, on the 6th December, 1869, wrote as follows to Col. Dennis, who was then engaged in levying troops to attack Riel:—

"Further, it would be well not to act till you ascertain clearly the mind of the Canadian Ministry and people on the way of settling this affair, and I think something is due to the people from Governor McDougall. *I for one am at this moment perfectly ignorant of any detail of the character or policy of this Government.* Personally, I do not care for this. I am not only fervently loyal to the Queen, but I have unquestioning confidence in the management of Canada. I know all will be right; still there is not less a great want, *a very conciliatory attitude is what is wanted from Governor McDougall, and a plain setting forth of how the Government is to be conducted*, meeting, as far as possible, any of the wishes expressed by the disaffected persons, and perhaps referring others to Canada, but promising a generous consideration of the whole grievance."

Col. Dennis's Testimony.

Col. Dennis was (later on) Mr. McDougall's Lieutenant, and as Conservator of the Peace empowered by him to make war on the settlers. His testimony will not probably be biased in their favor. Before a House of Commons Committee he swore as follows:—

"I have little doubt that *the primary causes of the outbreak were an unsettled feeling in the minds of the people as to the form of government that was likely to be established, and a general fear and anxiety that their interests might be sacrificed,* inasmuch as there had been no previous communication with them, with a view to ascertaining the exact political situation—and forming a system of government appropriate to the country. The French half-breeds were evidently jealous of the action of the Hudson's Bay Co. with regard to the transfer of the territory unless they shared in the payment. This feeling was participated in to a certain extent by the other classes of the inhabitants, namely, the English half-breeds and the Canadian settlers. Before I reached the territory I was told that there was an uneasy feeling."

Lord Dufferin's Testimony.

Lord Dufferin in a despatch of 10th December, 1875, said:

"Your Lordship is so well acquainted with the history of the troubles *which were occasioned by the somewhat precipitate attempts made in the year 1869 to incorporate the present Province of Manitoba with the Dominion, before the conditions of the proposed union had been explained to its inhabitants,* that, etc."—

Mr. George Stewart's Testimony.

Mr. Geo. Stewart, Jr., the historian of the "Administration of the Earl of Dufferin," writes as follows (pp. 381-6):—

"Early in the year 1869 surveying parties proceeded to Fort Garry, with the intention of laying out portions of the country in townships and lots. *The overbearing conduct of some of these persons, and the injudicious speeches and movements of the others, very speedily provoked the hostility, and aroused the fears of the settlers,* mostly men of crass ignorance and narrow prejudices, who saw in the action of the surveyors an interference with their proprietary rights. Nor was any effort made to disabuse their minds of these fears. A contrary line of conduct, either through malice or ignorance, was followed, and this and other causes aroused the squatters to feelings inimical to Canada, and bitterly hostile to the Government."

"Rumors of all kinds prevailed. It was said that the plots of ground, where some of them had dwelt and reared families for fifty years, would be torn from their possession by the Government of Canada, and themselves cast adrift; their rights to the soil would be invaded, their houses taken from them, enormous taxes would be levied, and the most absolute tyranny forced upon them. They would be bought and sold like slaves. With these views firmly established in the very hearts of the populace *we cannot wonder at the popularity of the movement which was created to resist to the death what some called Canadian coercion. Our only astonishment is, all things considered, that there was not more blood spilled, and more cruelties practised than there were.*"

"The mad freaks of Colonel Dennis and Captain Cameron did not a little to increase the hostility of the forces of Riel, and Mr. Macdougall's presence on the border was *a constant menace to the rebels, who, with wonderful forbearance, committed scarcely any violence to him or his immediate staff.*"

Major Boulton's Testimony.

Major Boulton was not only a participant (upon the Canadian side) in the events, but was for a time one of Riel's prisoners. His history of the "rebellion" is nevertheless wonderfully fair. He tells us (Reminiscences of the North-West Rebellion, pp. 61, 75, 52, 58):—

"There did not seem to be any disposition on his (Riel's) part, or that of his people, to oppose the cession of the country to Canada; but the opposition he offered seemed to be confined to the entrance of the Governor, or the establishment of the authority of Canada, *until certain rights, which he, and his supporters claimed to be their privilege, and to have been granted them as inhabitants of the country, had been conceded.*"

"As Canadians on the spot, we beheld with pleasure the advent of the Lieutenant-Governor, and were disposed to judge severely all who were not inclined to view the coming of the Queen's representative in the same light. In this we represented the ambition and hopes of Canada, in having so magnificent a domain added to her boundaries, the value of which, being resident in the country, we thoroughly appreciated. *We could not enter into the feelings of those who were about to be subjected to a new order of things, the effect of which, no one, at this time, could know.*"

"This was followed by a surveying party, under Colonel Dennis, to run the meridian lines and lay the foundation of the future surveys of the territory, upon the American principle of square blocks, containing six hundred and forty acres each, with a road allowance around the four sides. *This proceeding created a feeling of hostility among the population, which had not been consulted, and were not cognizant of any policy propounded, or that might be pursued towards them, in regard to their holdings.*"

"Some of the party were struck with the beauty of the country in the neighborhood, and determined upon taking up land. *Then and there they staked it out for future occupation.* This gave rise to jealousy on the part of the half-breeds in the neighborhood, who watched their proceedings; and Riel, as it turned out, followed us down to ascertain what our movements were likely to be."

TESTIMONY OF MESSRS. BUCKINGHAM AND ROSS.

In their "Life of Alexander McKenzie," Messrs. Buckingham and Ross write:

"When it became known to the settlers at Fort Garry and other points in the Territories that the Dominion Government was to assume the control of their affairs, they became greatly alarmed—perhaps without sufficient reason, although *had the government exercised proper forethought, it is quite clear the alarm of the inhabitants would not have assumed the aggressive form which it did.* They felt that to send up a ready-made government to take charge of their affairs was a poor compliment to their intelligence. Many of them, half-breeds as they were, were well educated and had accumulated considerable property during their residence in the country. They had been contented and prosperous under the Hudson's Bay rule, and they felt that their transfer to another power, without consultation, was treating them somewhat cavalierly. Besides, rumors, no doubt false, with regard to Mr. McDougall's treatment of the Indians, while Commissioner of Public Lands, were promulgated for the purpose of arousing the hostility of the half-breeds. And so, personal opposition to their future ruler was added to their aversion to the methods by which it was proposed to govern them.

"Colonel Dennis, who had been sent up in advance of Mr. Macdougall to survey the country, was also regarded with suspicion. The settlers could not understand what the surveying of their lands by a band of officers meant, if they had no sinister object in view, as they believed that their farms were already sufficiently well defined for their own purposes. To add to their alarms, Mr. Howe's visit, as Secretary of State, was inopportune. Instead of pouring oil upon the troubled waters, and reassuring the discontented that due consideration would be given to all their complaints, he connived at their threatened opposition to Mr. McDougall, should he presume to enter the country as Lieutenant-Governor, and in this way, perhaps, inadvertently strengthened their determination to offer resistance to his authority."

Col. Wolsley's testimony.

Col. Wolsley, as is well known, led the expedition which was sent from Ontario to Red River in 1870. After his return he wrote an article in Blackwood * from which the following extract is made :

" We are warned by a French proverb that the first step in all transactions is a most important one ; and that taken by the Dominion Government towards establishing their authority was no exception to the rule. Their first direct step was to send forward surveyors to plot out the country into townships ; and *this was the actual circumstance that gave rise to the first overt act of rebellion* on the part of the French people there. The men employed on the service, as well as their assistants and followers, were all either from England or Ontario. Around these surveyors, as round a centre, were collected a small band of Canadians, who had followed in their wake, hoping to obtain large grants of land and make fortunes when the new Government was established.

The people of the country were thoroughly discontented at the cavalier way in which they had been treated, as their will had never been consulted by any of the three parties who had arranged the terms of transfer. A feeling of irritation was abroad, which the bearing of the surveyors, and other Canadians, towards them served to increase beyond measure. Many of the latter began to stake out farms for themselves, which they openly declared they meant to claim as soon as the new Governor had arrived.

The Hudson Bay officials residing in the territory were loud-spoken in denouncing the bargain entered into by their Directors in London ; they said it injured them materially, without providing any compensation for the loss they were about to sustain ; that they, the working bees of the hive, were to receive nothing, whilst the drones of stockholders in England were to get all the honey in the shape of the £300,000.

The English speaking farmers, although thoroughly loyal, and anxious for annexation to Canada, so as to be delivered from what many called the "thraldom of the Hudson Bay Company," regarded the terms of the transfer in no favorable light.

They thought that they *should have been consulted ;* and the injudicious silence of the Canadian Ministry with reference to the form of Government to be established, caused many divisions amongst this party. Although they would have scorned to take part in any actual resistance against the new order of things, yet they were by no means sorry to see the Ottawa Ministry in difficulties. They considered themselves slighted, and were sulky in consequence. They had no intention of giving themselves any trouble to aid a Government that had *not only failed to consult, or to consider, their interests, but had ignored their existence altogether.*

With the exception, therefore, of the small handful of Canadian adventurers already alluded to, no one residing in the settlement in 1869 was pleased with the arrangement, and many were loud-spoken in denouncing it. Where such active elements of discontent existed, it may easily be imagined how simple it was to fan the smouldering embers into a flame of active rebellion.

. . . Unfortunately the arrangement entered into had an air of purchase about it, and a cry resounded throughout the Northwest that its inhabitants were being bought and sold like so many cattle. With such a text the most commonplace of democrats could preach for hours ; and poor indeed must have been their clap-trap eloquence if an ignorant and impressionable people such as those at Red River had not been aroused by it.

The surveyors were at work all through the autumn of 1869, and in prosecuting their operations frequently ran *chain-lines across the farms of men*

---

* December, 1870, p. 206, ff.

whose language they could not speak, and with whom they had no feelings in common. A report soon got abroad that the Canadian Govenment intended possessing themselves of all the land, for the purpose of alloting it amongst the host of emigrants who, rumor said, were to follow the establishment of the new order of things. A large proportion of farmers could produce no title-deeds to the lands they claimed; many could not even assert what is generally recognized as the outward visible symbol of possession in such matters—namely, the fact of their being fenced in . . .

No attempt was made by the Ottawa Government to conciliate their newly acquired subjects. The Governor appointed by the Hudson Bay Company who was to exercise authority until Mr. McDougall reached Fort Garry, was never even communicated with. One would have thought that common civility, if not political tact, would have caused the Ottawa Ministry to have informed him in writing of Mr. McDougall's appointment, and of the date at which his arrival might be expected; the old Governor's co-operation and assistance in establishing the new order of things might, with advantage, have been solicited at the same time. *No explanations were made as to what was to be the policy of Canada in its dealings with Rupert's Land.* In fact the people of that country were so thoroughly ignored, they were easily led to believe that their material interests would be so also, in favor of the emigrants that rumor, and the Canadian surveyors, said might shortly be expected to arrive at Red River."

Captain Huysche's Testimony.

Captain Huysche accompanied the expedition to Red River, and testifies as follows : *

"In these negotiations between the Hudson's Bay Company and the Imperial and Dominion Governments, *it does not appear that the feelings of the little colony at Red River were taken into account at all.* The French Emperor had not then set the world the example of a plebiscite vote; the concurrence of the people so vitally interested does not appear to have been asked, nor was any guarantee that their rights and privileges should be respected held out as an inducement to the settlers to acquiesce quietly in the new order of things. Though there can be no doubt that they would have been fairly and justly treated by Canada, yet *it cannot be a wonder to any impartial person* that they did not take quite the same view of the matter, but objected to be transformed from a crown colony to a "colony of a colony," and handed over to the Dominion, bon gré mal gré, *like so many head of cattle.*

During the summer of 1869, a surveying party under a Colonel Dennis, of volunteer fame, had been engaged surveying the country, and dividing it into townships, etc., for future allotment by the Canadian Government. The proceedings of this party had given great offence to the French half-breeds. The unsettled state of the land tenure, as regards the half-breeds and Indians, not unnaturally excited apprehensions in their minds that their lands would be taken from them and given to the Canadian immigrants, and *the injudicious conduct of some of the members of the surveying party, who put up claims, here and there, to tracts of land that they happened to take a fancy to, did not tend to allay these angry feelings.* The irritation raised by these causes operating together on the uneducated French half-breeds culminated on 10th October, 1869, in open opposition to the surveying party: a band of some eighteen men, headed by a man named Louis Riel, stopped one of Colonel Dennis's surveying parties and compelled them to discontinue their operations. . . .

---

* "The Red River Expedition" p. 3 ff.

On 24th November,* Riel, with an armed party, took possession of Fort Garry, ostensibly to prevent its falling into the hands of Mr. McDougall, but in reality to obtain funds and provisions for carrying out his plans of making himself sole ruler of the country. Governor McTavish had twelve hours' notice of the intended occupation of the fort, but took no measures to prevent it. And here I must observe, that the uniform success of the insurgents in all their plans points undoubtedly, not only to advice and assistance from their own clergy (which is too notorious to need any argument), but also to sympathy, if not collusion, on the part of some of the Hudson's Bay Company's officials at Fort Garry. It is impossible to acquit the latter of all blame. Their utter inertness, and *laissez aller* policy, cannot be explained away by the illness of the Governor. He had the advice of a council, composed of many of the leading residents, to whom the prevalant feeling of discontent must have been well known, but yet nothing was done to check the rising spirit of rebellion, which soon passed beyond the control of its originators. Nothing could have been easier than to have prevented Riel's occupation of the fort by simply shutting the gates and refusing to let him in. Without the fort and its stores of money, arms, and ammunition, and provisions, the *émeute* must have fallen to the ground of itself, and have collapsed for want of the necessaries of life. The only rational inference can be, that *the Company's officials at Fort Garry were secretly pleased to find that Canada was not going to have such an easy time of it as she expected*; and loth to lose the government of the country themselves, they looked on with indifference at the troubles which welcomed their successors."

THE BRITISH GOVERNMENT'S TESTIMONY.

Canada was to pay £300,000 to the Hudson's Bay Company for a release of its rights to the territories, and had, in the first instance, agreed to make the payment on the 1st December, 1869. The Canadian Government claimed, however, that peaceable possession should be given, and objected to pay until this could be accomplished. Recriminations ensued between the Company and the Government as to which of them was responsible for the outbreak. *Neither of them claimed that the settlers were the real offenders—each blamed the other.* In a despatch from Earl Granville to the Governor-General (30th November, 1866), the Company's position is thus stated:—

"This being the state of the case, the Canadian Government, *in anticipation of the transfer*, now agreed on by all parties, *undertook certain operations in respect of land*, subject in the first instance to a faint protest from the Company, and directed the future Lieutenant-Governor to enter the territory. The result, unfortunately, has not met the expectations of the Colonial Government. Mr. McDougall was met, it appears, by armed resistance, and the disturbances *caused by his presence* seem to have resulted in the plunder of the Company's stores and the occupation of Fort Garry by the insurgent portion of the population. But *the Canadian Government having, by this measure, given occasion to an outbreak of violence* in a territory which they have engaged to take over, now appear to claim the right of postponing indefinitely the completion of their engagements to the Company."

---

*This should be 2nd Nov.

THE CANADIAN GOVERNMENT'S TESTIMONY.

The Canadian Government, on its part, retorted upon the Company by an Order-in-Council (16th December, 1869), as follows:—

"That there would be an armed resistance by the inhabitants to the transfer was, it is to be presumed, unexpected by all parties; it certainly was so by the Canadian Government. In this regard *the Company cannot be acquitted of all blame.* They had an old and fully organized Government in the country, to which the people appeared to render ready obedience. Their Governor was advised by a Council, in which some of the leading residents had seats. They had every means of information as to the state of feeling existing in the country. They knew, or ought to have known, the light in which the proposed negotiations were viewed by the people under their rule. If they were aware of the feeling of discontent, they ought frankly to have stated it to the Imperial and Canadian Governments. If they were ignorant of the discontent, the responsibility of such wilful blindness on the part of their officers must rest upon them. For more than a year these negotiations have been actively proceeded with, and *it was the duty of the Company to have prepared the people under its rule for the change;* and have explained the precautions taken to protect the interests of the inhabitants, and to have removed any misapprehensions that may have existed among them. *It appears that no steps of any kind, in that direction, were taken. The people have been led to suppose that they have been sold to Canada, with an utter disregard of their rights and position.* . . . The resistance of these misguided people is evidently *not against the sovereignty of Her Majesty, or the government of the Hudson's Bay Company, but to the assumption of the Government of Canada.* They profess themselves satisfied to remain as they are, and that if the present system of government were allowed to continue they would at once disperse to their homes.

"It is obvious, then, that the wisest course to pursue is, for the present, to continue the authority of the Company, which the insurgents appear to respect, while steps are being taken to remove the misapprehensions which exist, and to reconcile the people to the change. *Any hasty attempt by the Canadian Government to force their rule upon the insurgents would probably result in an armed resistance and bloodshed.*"

It required no seer so to prophesy, and no great statesman so to divine. But, unfortunately, while resort to force was deprecated, and postponement of change of government arranged, at Ottawa, Mr. McDougall proceeded to act as though the change had already been accomplished, as though he were already Governor, as though force were the only course in honor open to him; and this, as was probable, resulted "in armed resistance and bloodshed."

CHAPTER IV.

THE HON. W. MACDOUGALL, AT PEMBINA.

The Hon. W. McDougall was the Minister of Public Works, upon whose recommendation (as we have seen) Colonel Dennis was "authorized to proceed with the surveys." It had been determined that after the transfer of the territories to Canada he should be the Lieutenant-Governor, and should frame and administer the laws for the prairie land. In anticipation of the transfer he had been directed to proceed to the settlement in order to make investigations and preliminary arrangements. He arrived at Pembina on the 30th October, 1869, on the American side of the international boundary, and about 60 miles south of Fort Garry, where Col. Dennis, unable to "proceed with the surveys," joined him on the 1st November.

By this time "standing on the chain" has developed into a determination on the part of the French, to prevent, by force, if necessary, the entrance of Mr. McDougall into the settlement; and the "wild mustangs" have thrown up a barricade across the road, with intent to defend it until assurances and information are obtained. The "patient roadsters," meanwhile, have expressed themselves in this way :—

"We feel confidence in the future administration of the government of this country under Canadian rule. At the same time, *we have not been consulted in any way* as a people, in entering the Dominion. The character of the new government has been settled in Canada *without our being consulted*. We are prepared to accept it respectfully, to obey the laws, and to become good subjects; but when you present to us the issue of a conflict with the French party, with whom we have hitherto lived in friendship, backed up as they would be by the Roman Catholic Church, which appears probable by the course at present being taken by the priests—in which conflict it is almost certain the aid of the Indians would be invoked and perhaps obtained by that party—we feel disinclined to enter upon it."*

Everything, therefore, now depends upon tact and diplomacy. Taking possession of the territory illegally, and without deigning information as to intentions—"proceed with the surveys," has produced armed resistance by the French, and stolid indifference on the part of the English. A change of attitude may still avert all violence. What will Mr. McDougall do? In his despatch to the Secretary of State (31st Oct., 1870) he says :—

"This morning I determined to send Mr. Provencher . . . . to Fort Garry, if permitted to go so far, with a verbal message to Governor McTavish announc-

---

* Dennis Report, 27th Oct., 1869.

ing my arrival within his jurisdiction, and claiming his protection for myself and party. Mr. Provencher was instructed to ascertain from the insurgents, by friendly conference, if possible, their object, and the extent of the force at their command. He was instructed to assure them of the determination of the Government to deal quietly with all classes, and to respect existing rights without reference to race or religion. But he was to explain to them that *until the new government was organized, and so long as they remained with arms in their hands, no official communication could be had with them by me or any one on my behalf.*"

Two days afterwards Mr. Provencher returned, and reported to Mr. McDougall that he had not been permitted to proceed further than the Sale River, where he had talked with the leaders of the men :—

"I was surprised to hear that they did not know anything about what had been done either in the Canadian or Imperial Parliament relating to the North-West Territory. They only knew that Canada had paid to the H. B. Co. £300,000 for their rights in that country.

"*The general complaint of these men*, as far as I could ascertain, was *that they had not been consulted on the new political changes about to take place.* They said they tolerated the government of the Company from the mere fact of its existence, and because in reality the charges where so light that they had no reason to ask for a change, though for many years they had agitated the question of electing their representatives in the Council of Assiniboia, and now they were resolved to take advantage of the recent changes to realize that desire. They said moreover that *they had been greatly abused by a few people, looked upon as representing the views of the Canadian government*, and that they had been led to fear that great danger would arise to them from the establishment of the new contemplated government. Under these circumstances they decided to prevent at once any possibility of establishing that new form of government by not allowing the newly-appointed governor to come into the country. At about 4 o'clock, p.m., I was introduced to the President of the so-called Special Committee of the half-breeds, who began by asking me in what capacity I was there. I explained what was your mission and my own, when he told me that as the newly-appointed chief of the half-breeds he could not acknowledge the validity of any of the proceedings of the Canadian Government towards them, nor our appointment; nevertheless if the Canadian Government was willing to do it, *they were ready to open negotiations with them, or with any person vested with full powers, in view of settling the terms of their coming into the Dominion of Canada.*"*

During the rest of November Mr. McDougall remained at Pembina. He expected that the territory would be united to Canada on the 1st of December, when his authority would commence, and he could "proceed with the surveys," by force, if necessary. Meanwhile he did various other things. He appealed to Mr. McTavish, the governor of the Hudson's Bay Company, to issue a proclamation (which was done on the 16th November); he intimated to one who "would report my remarks as he passed through the rebel camp" that

"I had been sent as a civil governor, and was prepared to treat all classes and parties in the most friendly and impartial manner ; but *if they preferred a military regime and martial law, they were taking the proper course to secure it.*"†

---

* Report of Mr. Provencher, 3rd Nov., 1869.

† Mr. MacDougall's letter to Secretary of State, 5th Nov., 1869.

he enabled the "loyal" party to contradict false reports as to Canadian intentions, but "*avoided direct communication with unofficial persons*" * ; and for the rest was engaged in making "efforts to *arouse the loyal people* of the settlement for a fight." †

One can hardly think that this was the best method of dealing with people whose general complaint was (as reported both by Col. Dennis, and Mr. Provencher), "that they had not been consulted on the new political changes about to take place"; more particularly when those persons had come to

"understand, perfectly, that I (Mr. MacDougall) have no legal authority to act, or to command obedience, till the Queen's proclamation is issued." ‡

He himself, it seems, was, in reality, a mere "unofficial person."

While he is thus waiting, and preparing, for the 1st of December, when he hopes to become "official," and to have forces enrolled sufficient to "proceed with the surveys," meanwhile refusing all "communication with unofficial persons," let us return to Red River, and recount the events of the month.

---

* Mr. MacDougall's letter to Secretary of State, 20th Nov., 1869.
† Mr. MacDougall's letter to Secretary of State, 2nd Dec., 1869.
‡ Mr. MacDougall's letter to the Secretary of State, 14th Nov., 1869.

CHAPTER V.

NOVEMBER AND EARLY DECEMBER AT RED RIVER.

While Mr. McDougall awaits the 1st of December, when he expects to be Lieutenant Governor, the settlers are not inactive. Their grievances are already partly known to us. Up to the present their actions have not only been natural, but perfectly reasonable. And if it be said that Mr. McDougall, as a British subject, had as much right to come into the territories, as they had to be there—that they were acting illegally in opposing his entrance; it may fairly be replied that their opposition was not to a British subject, but to a person claiming to represent, with power, a colony that had no greater jurisdiction in the territory than had South Australia. It may be justly added, too, that their act was not the first that was illegal. Who can answer Earl Granville's indictment of the Canadian Government, that it had "given occasion to an outbreak of violence," by undertaking "certain operations in respect of land," "in anticipation of the transfer" of the territory to Canada? The outbreak was a vigorous protest against these "certain operations in respect of land," which to the settlers bore such sinister aspect.

And the opposition was not of such wild character as one would have expected from unbridled "mustangs." On the contrary they surrounded their proceedings with much regard to legal form, and constitutional usage. Indeed, nothing is more forcibly impressed upon the student of this period than the strong parallelism between its events and those of the American revolution, in regard to the display of legal ability, the observance of legal forms, and the gradual increase of resistance, well-proportioned to the more strenuous efforts to enforce sovereignty.

Council of Assiniboia. Prior to the period at which we have now arrived, the government of the territory, within a radius of 50 miles from Fort Garry, had been carried on by the "Council of Assiniboia," members of which were nominated by the Hudson's Bay Company. It is very difficult to ascertain whether the Company, and this Council, were in reality in sympathy with Riel or not. Mr. McDougall writing from Larose's farm on 7th Nov., 1869, enclosed a communication which he had received from friends at Fort Garry, in which it is said that "The Hudson's Bay Company are evidently with the rebels, and their present role is to prevent your having any official intercourse with them. It is said the rebels will support the government of the Hudson's Bay Company as it exists." Mr. McDougall, himself, came to hold that opinion; and Captain Huyshe (page 8) also believed it. On the other hand an address to Mr. McDougall by the Council (19 Oct., 1869) tends strongly the other way. The impression left upon the mind of the present writer, after a perusal of all papers accessible to him, is that while officially the Council protested against all resistance to Mr. McDougall, and while, officially, Governor McTavish issued a proclamation denouncing those engaged in it, yet that privately the Governor, and many of the Council, were not sorry that an attempt was being made to extract information as to the future government of the territory; and that all, without exception, were convinced that the Canadian Government had brought the trouble upon itself.

On the 25th October, 1869, the Council held a meeting. The following is an extract from the minutes:—

"The Council unanimously expressed their reprobation of the outrageous proceedings referred to by the President, but feeling strongly impressed with the idea that the parties concerned in them must be acting in utter forgetfulness, or even perhaps ignorance, of the highly criminal character of their actions and of the very serious consequences they involved, it was thought that by calm reasoning and advice they might be induced to abandon their dangerous schemes before they had irretrievably committed themselves. With this object in view, therefore, Mr. Riel and Mr. Bruce, who were known to hold leading positions in the party opposed to Mr. McDougall, had been invited to be present at the meeting of the Council, and on being questioned by the Council as to the motives and intentions of the party they represented, Mr. Riel, who alone addressed the Council on the occasion, substantially said, in the course of a long, and somewhat irregular, discussion, that *his party were perfectly satisfied with the present Government and wanted no other; that they objected to any Government coming from Canada without their being consulted* in the matter; that they would never admit any Governor, no matter by whom he might be appointed, if not by the Hudson's Bay Company, *unless delegates were previously sent with whom they might negotiate* as to the terms and conditions under which they would acknowledge him; that they were uneducated, and only half civilized, and felt that if a large immigration were to take place they would probably be crowded out of a country which they claimed as their own; that they knew they were in a sense poor and insignificant, but that it was just because they were aware of this that they felt so much at being treated as if they were even more insignificant that they in reality were; that their existence, or at least their wishes, had been entirely ignored; that if Mr. McDougall were once here most probably the English-speaking population would allow him to be installed in office as Governor, and then he would be our "Master," or King, as he says, and that therefore they intended to send him back; that they consider that they are acting not only for their own good, but for the good of the whole settlement; *that they did not feel that they were breaking any law, but were simply acting in defence of their own liberty*; that they did not anticipate any opposition from their English-speaking fellow-countrymen, and only wished them to join, and aid in securing their common rights; that they might be opposed by some Canadian party in the country, but for that they were quite prepared; and that they were determined to prevent Mr. McDougall from coming into the settlements at all hazards.

2nd, November 1869. If the opposition to Mr. McDougall was to be effective, Riel saw that the possession of Fort Garry was all essential. He had no antipathy to, or fear of, the Company; but a far less able man would have at once comprehended the disadvantages of his position, were the "Canadian party" once installed within the fortifications. The steps he took are related in Mr. McTavish's letter to Mr. McDougall (Nov. 9th, 1869):—

"The occurrence to which I have alluded in the preceding paragraph as being serious is this, that on the afternoon of Tuesday, the 2nd inst, a number of these daring people suddenly, and without the least intimation of their intention to make such a move, took possession of the gates of Fort Garry, where they placed themselves inside and outside the gates to the number, in all, of about 120, and where, night and day, they have constantly kept a pretty strong armed guard. On being asked what they meant by such a movement upon the fort, they said their object was to protect it. Protect it from what? they were asked. Their answer was, From danger. Against what danger? they were asked. To this question they replied that they would not now specify the danger, but that they would do so hereafter, and obstinately took up the position they have since kept, in spite of all our protests and remonstrances at such a bold and high-handed proceeding. On coming into the fort they earnestly disclaimed all intention of injuring either person or property within it—and it must be allowed that in that respect they have kept their word."

Mr. McTavish added

"with a feeling of inexpressible regret, that to the Council and myself it appears that *your early return to Canada, is not only essential for the peace of the country, but also advisable in the interest of the establishment in the future of the Canadian Government.*"

It is very easy to be wise after the event—to realize that Mr. McDougall did wrong in remaining at Pembina after having received this letter. Had he returned at once, (he did so six weeks after), it is almost certain that there would have been nothing further to relate. In justice to Mr. McDougall, however, it must be said that he had some reason for suspecting the good faith of the suggestions made to him by Mr. McTavish. He was informed by the Canadian officials that, were he to show his authority the, "rebellion" would dissolve into nothing before the most trifling display of force. That this information was absurdly erroneous was no fault of Mr. McDougall's. All that can be fairly charged to him is that reports of enthusiastic military men, with their contempt for half-breed methods, were not sufficiently discounted. The Dominion Government at Ottawa (as has already appeared), saw clearly enough, *before* the event, that "any attempt by the Canadian Government to force their rule upon the insurgents would probably result in armed resistance and bloodshed." The Governor of the Hudson's Bay Company, at Winnipeg, *foresaw* the same result. Mr. McDougall, at Pembina, misled by Col. Dennis, and others, saw nothing but a few simpletons who would properly retire before imposing grandeur as soon as displayed.

Riel's reason for taking possession of Fort Garry is given by himself in his letter to Lieutenant-Governor Morris (3rd Jan., 1873 :)

"On the following day, he (Mr. McDougall) entered the Province, and proceeded towards Fort Garry, with a view of taking up his residence at the seat of government. The self-styled soldiers then took up a very threatening attitude amongst us. They talked of taking Fort Garry. The knowledge of this scheme, which we were afraid would be carried out, suggested to us the idea of seizing the Fort; and we endeavored to keep Mr. McDougall at a distance in order that his party, which were so hostile to our interests, might not, under such circumstances, get possession of the government of our native country."

6th November, 1869. Thus far the French had proceeded without the concurrence, but also without the opposition, of the English; Riel now bent his energies upon enlisting these latter upon his side, and to arouse them to action in defence of their own interests. With this object the following public notice was issued:

" PUBLIC NOTICE TO THE INHABITANTS OF RUPERT'S LAND.

"The President and representatives of the French-speaking population of Rupert's Land in Council (the invaders of our rights being now expelled), already aware of your sympathy, do extend the hand of friendship to you, our friendly fellow-inhabitants; and in doing so, invite you to send 12 representatives from the following places, viz:

St. John's	1	St. Margaret's	1
Headingly	1	St. James'	1
St. Mary's	1	Kildonan	1
St. Paul's	1	St. Andrew's	1
St. Clement's	1	St. Peter's	1
Town of Winnipeg	2		

in order to form one body with the above Council, consisting of 12 members, to consider the present political state of the country, and to adopt such measures as may be deemed best for the future welfare of the same.

A meeting of the above Council will be held in the Court House at Fort Garry, on Tuesday, the 16th day of November, at which the invited representatives will attend.

By order of the President,

WINNIPEG, Nov. 6th, 1869.　　　　　　　　LOUIS RIEL, Secretary.

Elections were held in pursuance of this request, and the following English representatives were sent to the Council.

Town of Winnipeg	{ Henry McKenney. { H. F. O'Lone.
Kildonan	James Ross.
St. John's	Maurice Lowman.
St. Paul's	Dr. Bird.
St. Andrew's	Donald Gunn.
St. Clements	Thomas Bunn.
St. Peter's	Henry Prince.
St. James'	Robert Tait.
Headingly	William Tait.
St. Anne's	George Gunn.
Portage-la-Prairie	John Garrioch.

It would have been difficult to have secured twelve men better entitled, or qualified, to represent these districts—two of them, at least, were then members of the Council of Assiniboia. The Council of November (let it so be called), sat on the 16th, 17th, 22nd, 23rd and 24th of November.

"The proceedings resulted in the French members declaring their intention to form a Provisional Government *for the purpose of treating with Canada for the future government of the country*, and at the same time they asked their English brethren to join them. As the English delegates were not prepared to act in this emergency, without first consulting the people whom they represented, it was decided that the convention should be adjourned till Wednesday, the 1st December."*

1st December, 1869. Meetings for discusssion of this proposal having being held in the constituencies (those in Winnipeg, where the Canadian party was strongest, being fully as lively as those of late years), the English delegates met on the 1st December for separate conference.

At 6 o'clock, p.m., of the same day the French and English delegates met together, when the former presented a Bill of Rights for discussion. The Bill, and the action upon it appear in an enclosure sent with a report made by Mr. McDougall to the Secretary of State, dated December 16th, 1869:—

"LIST OF RIGHTS.

1. That the people have the right to elect their own Legislature.
2. That the Legislature have power to pass all laws local to the territory over the veto of the Executive by a two-thirds vote.
3. That no Act of the Dominion Parliament (local to the Territory) be binding on the people until sanctioned by the Legislature of the Territory.
4. That all sheriffs, magistrates, constables, school commissioners, etc., etc., be elected by the people.
5. A free homestead and pre-emption land law.
6. That a portion of the public lands be appropriated to the benefit of schools, the building of bridges, roads, and public buildings.
7. That it be guaranteed to connect Winnipeg by rail with the nearest line of railroad within a term of five years; the land grant to be subject to the Local Legislature.
8. That for a term of four years, all military, civil, and municipal expenses be paid out of the Dominion funds.
9. That the military be composed of the inhabitants now existing in the Territory.
10. That the English and French languages be common in the Legislature and Courts; and all Public Documents and Acts of Legislature be published in both languages.
11. That the judge of the Supreme Court speak the English and French languages.

---

*Begg's' History, p. 97.

12. That treaties be concluded and ratified between the Dominion Government and the several tribes of Indians in the Territory, to ensure peace on the frontier.

13. That we have a fair and full representation in the Canadian Parliament.

14. That all privileges, customs and usages existing at the time of transfer be respected.

"All the above articles have been severally discussed, and adopted by the French and English representatives, *without a dissenting voice*, as the conditions upon which the people of Rupert's Land enter into Confederation. The French representatives then proposed, in order to secure the above rights, that a delegation be appointed, and sent to Pembina to see Mr. McDougall, and ask him if he could guarantee these rights by virtue of his commission, and if he *could do so, that then the French people would join, to a man, to escort Mr. McDougall to his government seat*. But on the contrary, if Mr. McDougall could not guarantee such rights, that the delegates request him to remain where he is, or return till the rights be guaranteed by Act of Canadian Parliament.

"The English representatives refused to appoint delegates to go to Pembina to consult with Mr. McDougall, stating they had no authority to do so from their constituents, upon which the Council dissolved.

"The meeting at which the above resolutions were adopted, was held at Fort Garry, on Wednesday, December 1st, 1869.

One cannot help regretting this refusal on the part of the English to send delegates to Mr. McDougall. As a basis of negotiation the list of rights cannot be thought to be unreasonable. At all events the English believed it to be fair and proper. Why did they not send delegates to present it? The present writer is disposed to think that the real, and only, difference between the English and French, at this period, was that the latter were determined to negotiate first and be governed afterwards; whereas the former were willing to reverse the order. The English, therefore, while willing to present the List of Rights, were not willing to refuse Mr. McDougall's entry into the settlement pending discussion of it. The result, as will appear hereafter, justified the French view, that better terms would be obtained by adopting their methods, rather than taking what would, without pessure, have been conceded.

The events of November and early December, at Red River, maybe summed up in this:—Riel and his friends had formed themselves into a Provisional Government; they had by a display of force compelled Mr. McDougall to leave the territory and denied him re-entry; they had taken possession of Fort Garry, the principal and strongest fort in the settlement; a Council of 24 persons freely elected by the different parishes had been formed; this Council had met and consulted, had adjourned in order to obtain the views of the constituents, had met again and agreed upon a list of rights, but had disagreed upon the policy of resistance pending the discussion of these rights. On the other hand the Canadian party was only less openly active because of the restraint put upon them by Mr. McDougall. As yet Canada had no jurisdiction, and Mr. McDougall no more legal authority than

Riel. He would not therefore sanction the belligerent proceedings proposed to him by the more impetuous of the Canadians. He appears however to have quite approved the military preparations which were being made in anticipation of the great 1st of December, when the mantle of authority was expected to fall upon him. Organization of companies, and the drilling of them; formation of a "committee of public safety"; negotiations for the assistance of the Indians; threats of an Indian uprising, etc., were the engagements and business this month of November—this weary wait for the 1st of December. And Riel, it is supposed, ought to have refrained from all preparations upon his side; should have left Fort Garry to be seized by his opponents (as, after the 1st December, they seized the other Hudson's Bay Fort); should have mildly waited to be captured and shot!

Let it be frankly admitted (but upon both sides) that in the eye of the law all this was irregular and illegal; but let it be also acknowledged that "the Canadian Government" first gave the "occasion to an outbreak of violence" by "certain operations in respect to land"; that Riel, withstanding these operations, endeavored to justify, as well as fortify, himself by obtaining the sanction of Councillors elected by the people; and that if he seized Fort Garry, it was to prevent it falling into the hands of his enemies--it was a strategic measure, necessarily incident to the general design, namely, that the settlers must be consulted before their political *status* is changed.

This further must be observed—and it is a remark which will apply to the events related, as well as to those to come—that the severity of Riel's actions increased in direct proportion to the opposition which was offered to him by the Canadian party. The French settlers were determined upon negotiation first, and government afterwards; the English settlers thought this reasonable, but were not willing to fight for it; the Canadian party were determined to fight *agai st* it by "hasty attempt . . . to force their rule upon the insurgents," with the result of "armed resistance, and bloodshed."

We are now far enough advanced in the recital of the events to say that the Canadian party (and not Riel) was the cause of all the difficulty at Red River.

In the Canadian party must be included Col. Dennis and his body of surveyors, and also Mr. McDougall and his *entourage*. Mr. McDougall's blameworthiness (apart from his direction to "proceed with the surveys,") was principally in that he allowed himself to be misled as to the state of feeling in the settlement; in his refusal to communicate directly with any "unofficial persons"; and, finally, in that he illegally directed Col. Dennis to levy war upon the people. Upon the others of the Canadian party lies heavy responsibility. Some of them, in times but recently passed, had shown the example of opposition to, and defiance of, the Hudson's Bay Company. By their unconcealed contempt for the Metis, and by "certain operations in land," they had plainly pointed to themselves as the superior successors, not to say masters, of the "illiterate half-breeds." When the French demanded negotiation prior to new government, it was not the English settler, but the Canadian party that placed itself in opposition, and stirred up, to the best of its power, race and religious antipathy. While the Council of Assiniboia was counselling Mr. McDougall to return to Canada as a step "not only essential for the peace of the country, but also advisable in the interest of the establishment, in the future, of the Government of Canada," * it was the Canadian party that not only urged him to the contrary course, but offered, upon their own responsibility, to institute armed opposition to Riel.

* See page 331.

CHAPTER VI.

MR. McDOUGALL STILL AT PEMBINA.

The great 1st of December is approaching, and we must return to Mr. McDougall. What he did, and why he did it, he shall himself narrate (Report to Secretary of State):—

"Sir, I have the honor to report that I am still at Pembina in the territory of the United States . . . , and unable, in consequence of the continued occupation of the road by armed men to proceed to Fort Garry.

"I have further to report that *I have not received any instruction for my guidance* on and after the day of the transfer of the territory to Canada, nor any notice of the Order-in-Council, which has no doubt been passed to effect it.

"In these circumstances I am compelled to act upon the general powers and directions of my commission, and of the Acts of Parliament, Canadian and Imperial, which seem to bear upon the case.

"I have accordingly prepared a proclamation to be issued on the 1st day of December, reciting so much of the several Acts of Parliament as seemed necessary to disclose the requisite authority, and stating, by way of recital, the fact of surrender by the Hudson's Bay Company, acceptance by Her Majesty, and transfer to Canada, from and after the 1st December, A. D., 1869. *Those facts I gather from the newspapers, from a private letter* to me of the Deputy Governor of the company, and my own knowledge before I left Ottawa, that the 1st of December had been agreed upon as the date of the transfer."

This was Mr. McDougall's great mistake. He had much reason for knowing, before he left Ottawa that it was the intention to issue the Queen's proclamation on the 1st of December; but he could not, and did not know, whether or not that intention had been changed. Unfortunately for him it had been changed, and all his actions based upon his idea that he was now governor were wholly illegal.

Mr. McDougall issued three documents. The first was a proclamation in the name of the Queen, which, after reciting that Her Majesty had "declared that Rupert's Land, and the North-Western Territory, shall from the first day of December, 1869, be admitted into and become part of the Dominion of Canada," proceeded:

"Now know ye, that we have seen fit by our Royal Letters Patent . . . to appoint the Hon. William McDougall . . . on, from, and after the day to be named by us . . . to wit, on, from and after the 1st day of December, 1869, to be, during our pleasure, the Lieutenant Governor of the North-West Territories."

This document he, and his secretary signed, and issued in the name of the Queen, having no more right so to do than they had to proclaim him Czar of Russia. Lord Granville said of it (26th Jan. 1870):

"The proclamation recited that Her Majesty has transferred Rupert's Land to Canada, which has not been done; assumed the authority of Lieutenant-

Governor, which did not legally belong to him; and purported to extinguish the powers belonging to Mr. McTavish, who is in fact the only legal Governor of the Territory."

The second document issued by Mr. McDougall, after declaring the admission into Canada, and that he had been appointed Lieutenant-Governor proceeded as follows:

"I do hereby require, and command, that all and singular the public officers and functionaries, holding office in Rupert's Land, and the North Western Territory, at the time of their admission into the Union as aforesaid, *excepting the public officer or functionary at the head of administration of affairs*, do continue in the execution of their several and respective offices, duties, plans and employments until otherwise ordered by me," etc.

The third document was of more formidable character. The powers granted by it to Col. Dennis are worth transcribing in full.

"Know that reposing trust and confidence in your courage, loyalty, fidelity, discretion and ability, and under and in virtue of the authority in me vested, I have nominated and appointed, and by these presents do nominate and appoint you, the said John Stoughton Dennis to be *my Lieutenant, and a Conservator of the Peace*, in and for the North-West Territories; and do hereby authorize and empower you, as such, to raise, arm, equip, and provide, a sufficient force to *attack, arrest, disarm, or disperse, the said armed men*, so unlawfully assembled, and disturbing the public peace; and for that purpose, and with the force aforesaid, *to assault, fire upon, pull down, or break into any fort, house, stronghold, or other place*, in which the said armed men are to be found. And I hereby authorize you, as such Lieutenant and Conservator of the Peace, to hire, purchase, *impress, and take all necessary clothing, arms, ammunition, and supplies, and all cattle, horses, waggons, sleighs, or other vehicles which may be required* for the use of the force to be raised as aforesaid. And I further authorize you to appoint as many officers and deputies under you; and to give them such orders and instructions, from time to time, as may be found necessary for the due performance of the service herein required of you, reporting to me the said appointments, and orders, as you shall find opportunity for confirmation or otherwise.

"And I hereby give you full power and authority to call upon all magistrates, and peace officers, to aid and assist you, and to order all, or any, of the inhabitants of the said North-West Territories, in the name of Her Majesty the Queen, to support and assist you in protecting the lives and property of Her Majesty's loyal subjects, and in preserving the public peace; and for that purpose to seize, disperse, or overcome by force, the said armed men, and all others, who may be found aiding or abetting them in their unlawful acts.

"And the said persons so called upon, in Her Majesty's name, are hereby ordered, and enjoined, at their peril, to obey your orders and directions in that behalf; and this shall be sufficient warrant for what you, or they, do in the premises, so long as this commission remains in force.

"Given under my hand, and *seal at arms*, at Red River, in the said Territories, the first day of December, in the year of our Lord one thousand eight hundred and sixty-nine, and in the thirty-third year of Her Majesty's reign.

WILLIAM McDOUGALL,

" By command J. A. N. PROVENCHER, *Secretary.*

CHAPTER VII.

"CALL TO ARMS," AND WHAT CAME OF IT.

Col. Dennis, armed with this awe-inspiring parchment, proceeded in dashing military fashion. What he did, and how much he accomplished, he shall himself in part relate. Having made inquiries from a few persons, he tells us that :

"*1st Dec.*—I concluded it to be my duty, under my commission, to make the call, satisfied that there was every prospect that it would be generally responded to.

"Under the conviction that the insurgents would seize upon the stone fort, so soon as my arrival in the settlement, and the nature of my orders, became known, I proceeded on to that point, arriving about 6 o'clock, p.m ...Reported my arrival, and occupation, of the stone fort to Governor McTavish, mentioning the object of such occupation, and enclosing him also a copy of my commission."

This strikes one as a proceeding somewhat similar to that of Riel in possessing himself of Fort Garry ; and it seems to show that Riel was not far wrong in thinking that if he acted illegally in manning Fort Garry, he was only anticipating by a few days the Canadian party.

"*2nd Dec.*—Assembled Chief Prince's men in the fort to-day. The proclamation was read and explained by....to the men in Indian....They all seemed loyally disposed, cheering heartily for the Queen, and those of them who had guns firing them off with evident enthusiasm.

"*4th Dec.*—Received a note from Dr. Schultz this morning, in which he states that a number of the enrolled Canadians, and others, collected at his house last evening, were present at his request, anticipating a possible attack upon his property and the government provisions in his charge ; that in the course of the night bodies of men of the French party repeatedly made their appearance around the outside of his house and premises, evidently inviting attack from the party inside ; that they repeatedly adjourned for liquor to O'Lone's saloon ; that they were harangued by Riel ; finally that they came to the front of the house, went through various manœuvres, detaching parties to the rear, etc.; and then went off to the fort, leaving the doctor and his party between one and two o'clock, a.m., unmolested. From the occurrences of last night it is evident to me that a very critical condition of affairs exists at Winnipeg. A single shot, which may be fired by either party, would precipitate possibly deplorable results. As yet the force I am organizing is not, nor will it be probably in a condition to justify a collision for ten or twelve days. I shall, therefore, *give orders to the Canadians to withdraw from Winnipeg*, and with that view have written an order, a copy of which is marked A.1."

Excellent advice this, but the Canadians were in no humour to give place to mere Metis ; so they disregarded the order to withdraw, with the result which we shall see.

"*5th Dec.*—Mr. Snow very desirous to have the Canadians allowed to remain in Winnipeg to guard government provisions, etc. *I told him that whoever stayed there after the orders that I had given, assumed the responsibility* ;.

that as representing the government, I did not desire a guard continued on the provisions at the risk of its causing a collision at the present time."

On the 6th Dec. Col. Dennis issued a general "call to arms," which, after reciting his commission as "my lieutenant, and a conservator of the peace," proceeded as follows:—

"By virtue of the above commission from the Lieutenant-Governor, I now hereby call on, and order, all loyal men in the North-West Territories, to assist me by every means in their power, to carry out the same, and thereby restore public peace and order, and uphold the supremacy of the Queen, in this part of Her Majesty's Dominion. Given under my hand at the Stone Fort, Lower Settlement, this 6th day of December, A.D., 1869.

J. S. DENNIS,
Lieutenant-Colonel."

On the same day a further order was sent to "the enrolled Canadians at Winnipeg," in which Col. Dennis said:—

"I cannot be a party to precipitating such an event just at the present time, *and must therefore reiterate my orders of the 4th inst.*, to the enrolled Canadians, *to leave the town*, and establish themselves at Kildonan school-house," etc.

All this organizing, drilling, proclaiming, haranguing of Indians, and calling to arms, had its quite natural, but (strange to say) to the Canadians, wholly unexpected, effect upon Riel. Until this time Dr. Schultz, and the other Canadians who resided at Winnipeg, within gunshot of Fort Garry, had taken part in the public meetings, and exercised openly their influence against Riel. Col. Dennis seized the Lower Fort on the 1st December; assembled the Indians there on the 2nd; issued his "call to arms" on the 6th. Riel responded by paying Dr. Schultz's house an unfriendly visit on the night of the 2nd; a still more unfriendly one on the night of the 3rd; and by establishing a state of siege a few days afterwards. Col. Dennis continues:—

"*7th Dec.*—She brought a verbal message from Dr. Schultz to me . . . that some forty Canadians were in a state of siege in his house; that they could not go out either to get food or water, and begged for help. *This, it is clear, would not have occurred, had my previous orders, repeatedly given, for the Canadians to leave the town, been obeyed.* . . . Thinking however of the moral effect on the object I had in view, should the Canadians be captured, it seemed a duty to relieve them, if possible, and believing, as Mrs. Black said, the French in the town were not more than fifty in number, that *on the mere appearance* of a considerable body of men coming from the Lower Fort, the French guard would fall back on Fort Garry, and so leave time for the besieged party to come out and return with us, and that the relief could be effected in this way, without necessarily having had a collision, I determined on that course.

"I found, however, that the requisite force would not be forthcoming. Indeed, there appeared to be *an entire absence of the ardor* which existed previously . . . and it became evident that the project for the relief of the Canadians must fall to the ground."

Desiring to investigate how it was that the settlers thus refused to go to the relief of the Canadians, Col. Dennis called a meeting of "the leading men in the Scotch settlement":—

"*7th Dec.*—I speedily became satisfied that the only condition on which the Scotch people would now arm and drill would be to act strictly on the defensive.

Indeed, I was informed that a public meeting held in the vicinity, had just broken up, at which delegates were appointed to visit me at the Stone Fort, without delay, to request that aggressive measures might for the present be abandoned. . . . Taken altogether, it appears to me probable that *the resort to arms, to put down the French party at the present time, must be given up.* I shall not, however, discontinue the drill going on in the several parishes, believing that such will not be without good moral effect on probable negotiations."

Two days afterwards Col. Dennis wrote to Mr. McDougall, saying:—

"You may rely upon it, these people are fully in possession for the winter, and say themselves that with the promises they have of Fenian and Fillibusterers' support, they will be able to hold the country. *I should not be surprised but they may get many people here to join them too.* I think they would do anything, many of them, rather than offend the French now, as (they say) *they are per "list of rights" that the French ask nothing very unreasonable.*"

Col. Dennis' "call to arms" was issued on the 6th December.

"On the 7th of December Riel harangued his men in front of Dr. Schultz's house, and in the course of his speech he produced a copy of Col. Dennis' commission, which he read aloud, and then, throwing it on the ground, he trampled it under his feet."

Before night Dr. Shultz and his Canadians (forty-five in all) had surrendered, and been marched off to Fort Garry. "The moral effect" of organizing, and drilling, seems to have been really more immediate than Col. Dennis anticipated. In fact he sadly mistook not only the number, but the kind, of men he had to deal with; he succeeded, not in frightening them, by "mere appearance," as he had hoped, but only in goading them on to severer action.

On the 6th December Col. Dennis issued his "call to arms." On the 7th he called a public meeting to ascertain the feeling of the people! On the 9th, after his actions, and the stubbornness of the Canadians, had resulted in the imprisonment of forty-five persons, he issued the following:—

"LOWER FORT GARRY,
Red River Settlement, Dec. 9th, 1869.

"*To all whom it may concern:—*

"By certain printed papers of late put in circulation by the French party, communication with the Lieutenant-Governor is indicated, with a view to laying before him alleged rights on the part of those now in arms. I think that course very desirable, and that it would lead to good results. Under the belief that the French party are sincere in their desire for peace, and feeling that to abandon for the present the call on the loyal to arms, would, in view of such communication, relieve the situation from much embarrassment, and so contribute to bring about peace, and save the country from what will otherwise end in universal ruin and devastation, *I now call on, and order, the loyal party in the North-West Territory to cease from further action* under the appeal to arms made by me, and I call on the French party to satisfy the people of their sincerity in wishing for a peaceful ending of all these troubles, by *sending a deputation to the Lieutenant-Governor* at Pembina, without unnecessary delay.

"Given under my hand at the Lower Fort Garry, this 9th day of December, 1869.

J. S. DENNIS.

Insincerity, imbecility and stupidity mark every word of this document. Not one week ago the French had desired to send delegates from the Provisional Council to Mr. McDougall, but " the English representatives refused to appoint delegates, . . . stating they had no authority to do so from their constituents." Mr. McDougall, moreover, had steadfastly refused to hold communication with " unofficial persons," as Col. Dennis must have well known. Col. Dennis now pretends to believe that " the French party are sincere in their desire for peace," yet he held a commission to make war upon them, and had been acting up to it, as best he could!

Col. Dennis underrated entirely the intelligence of the French, when he announced, as the reason for his abandonment of the "call to arms," the "printed papers of late put in circulation by the French party." Every one knew that the true, and only, reason that led him to disband his army was his ignominious failure.

And now, having issued his "call to arms," stirred up people in all the parishes, harangued and excited the Indians, hurried hither and thither, crying first " To arms, to arms!" and a week after " Cease from further action," the Colonel hurries back, once more, to Mr. McDougall, (disguised as a squaw), this time to report that he can make no better progress under the direction to " levy war " than under the old " proceed with the surveys," and leaving behind him forty-five Canadians in gaol, and the whole country in wild ferment of excitement. On the 15th December, just seventeen days after he left Pembina, he returned, having accomplished this much.

It is fitting here to quote a few words from a despatch written by the Secretary of State for Canada, to Mr. McDougall (24th December, 1869) anent Col. Dennis' report of his own proceedings :—

> "Had the inhabitants of Rupert's Land, on the breaking out of the disturbances, risen and put an end to them, or had Governor McTavish organized a force to occupy his forts and maintain his authority, all would have been well, and Riel and his men would have been responsible for any bloodshed or property destroyed. But, *Col. Dennis, with no legal authority, proceeds to sieze the fort, not in possession of the insurgents, but of the Hudson's Bay Company, and to garrison it with a mixed force of whites and Indians, and proposes to give battle to the insurgents,* should a junction be formed with some forces which he has ordered to be drilled on the Assiniboine. He appears never to have thought that the moment war commenced, all the white inhabitants would be at the mercy of the Indians, by whom they are largely outnumbered, and divided as they would be, might be easily overpowered.
>
> "It is impossible to read the Colonel's account of his attempt to persuade Judge Black to aid him in proclaiming martial law, without strong feelings of regret that you should have been represented in the settlement by *a person of so little discretion.* It is no wonder that Judge Black was "frightened" at the proposal, as he must have known that *Col. Dennis would have to answer at the bar of justice, for every life lost, by such an assumption of authority,*" etc.

Rather lucky for Col. Dennis, it would seem, that his " call to arms " fell so flat !

CHAPTER VIII.

MR. McDOUGALL STILL AT PEMBINA.

Col. Dennis returned to Pembina, as we have said, on the 15th December, with the doleful news of the frightful mess into which he had precipitated affairs. Mr. McDougall had heard it before (namely, on the 11th Dec.) and had wondered what he should now do—still outside, as he was, of the promised land, and still calling himself its *Governor.* He had "thus far avoided direct communication with unofficial persons,"—even while unofficial himself—which, as we have seen, was much to be regretted. He was now, he thought, Lieutenant-Governor, and Riel had become something worse than a mere "unofficial person,"—a person in arms, namely, against constituted authority. The disparity was wider than ever. What could be done? This :—

"PEMBINA, December 13th, 1869.

" *To Louis Riel, Esq. :*

Sir,—I hear from the Hudson's Bay Bay Post that you are expected to arrive there from Fort Garry to-night. I send this note to inform you that *I am anxious to have a conversation with you,* before answering despatches which I have recently received from the Dominion Government.

" I have not yet had any communication from you, or from any one else on behalf of the French half-breeds, who have prevented me from proceeding to Fort Garry, stating their complaints or wishes in reference to the new government.

" As the representative of the sovereign, to whom you, and they, owe, and, as I am told, *do not wish to deny, allegiance,* it is proper that some such communication should reach me. It will be a great misfortune to us all, I think, if I am obliged to return to Canada, and hand over the powers of government here to a military ruler. This will be the inevitable result unless we find some solution of the present difficulty very soon.

" I have full powers from the government, as well as the strongest desire personally, to meet all just claims of every class and section of the people. Why should you not come to me and discuss the matter ?

" *I beg you to believe that what has occurred will not affect my mind against you,* or those for whom you may be authorized to speak.

" The interview proposed must be without the knowledge or privity of certain American citizens who pretend to be *en rapport* with you.

" I trust to your honour on this point.
Very faithfully yours,
WILLIAM McDOUGALL.

Four days afterwards, without having received reply from Riel, without knowing whether the letter had reached its destination, Mr.

McDougall commenced his return journey to Canada (taking with him Col. Dennis, and, it is presumed, the "Seal-at-arms"), thus tardily following the advice of Governor McTavish, and the Council of Assiniboia, but having, by the delay, aroused bitter enmities, and fierce passions, which were not to be allayed without bloodshed. Prior to leaving he had the humiliation of having to acknowledge to Governor McTavish (16 Dec.) that his assumption of the position of Lieutenant-Governor, and all his other official acts, were possibly illegal:

"If, in consequence of the action of the Dominion Government, the surrender and transfer of the country did not take place on the first of December, as previously agreed upon, then *you* are the Chief Executive Officer as before, and responsible for the preservation of peace, and the enforcement of the law".

And so Mr. McDougall turns his back upon Governor McTavish and the Red River people, leaving them to fight it out, or settle it, as best they can. Could he but have taken some of the Canadians with him all would have been well; but with them still in the territory, their pride, temporarily, in their pockets, and some of their pockets temporarily, in gaol—the elements of further trouble were not wanting.

Before parting with Mr. McDougall it will be well to quote from the despatch to him of the Canadian Secretary of State (24 Dec. 1869):

"SIR,—Your despatch, dated Pembina, 2nd December, and its enclosures A. & B. reached this office on the 18th inst., and were promptly laid before the Governor-General and Council.

"As it would appear, from these documents, that *you have used the Queen's name without Her authority, attributed to Her Majesty acts which she has not yet performed, and organized an armed force within the Territory of the Hudson's Bay Company without warrant or instruction*, I am commanded to assure you that the grave occurrences which you report have occasioned here great anxiety.

"The exertion of military force against the misguided people now in arms, even if under the sanction of law, was not to be hastily risked, considering the fearful consequences which might ensue were the Indians—many of them but recently in contact with the white inhabitants of the neighboring states—drawn into the conflict. But, *as the organization and use of such a force by you, was, under the circumstances entirely illegal*, the Governor-General and Council cannot disguise from you the weight of responsibility you have incurred."

Mr. Begg has the following with reference to Mr. McDougall's departure:

"About the time of Mr. McDougall's departure from Pembina it became generally known throughout the settlement that the proclamation which he had issued as coming from the Queen was a false one, and it was strange to perceive the complete revulsion of feeling that took place among the settlers generally. If there was one thing more than another that assisted to strengthen the hands of Riel it was that. People who professed to be supporters of the incoming government at once cooled in their ardor, and this led the way, more than anything else, to place Riel in the position which he afterwards held."

CHAPTER IX.

CANADIAN COMMISSIONERS—DELEGATES TO OTTAWA—PROVISIONAL GOVERNMENT.

Canada had now to retrace her steps. Her representatives had endeavoured by force, and (as it appeared to the settlers) by fraud, to impose a new government upon a people who had long occupied the country. Force and fraud had alike failed, and the position of Riel had thereby been immeasurably strengthened. Few of the settlers now questioned the wisdom of his policy of negotiation prior to government. He had become a statesman and a hero. Under these circumstances Canada might have adopted the methods usual to the stronger—methods generally condoned by what is called (absurdly enough) national honor and prestige—that is to say, she might have treated the settlers as mere Chinese or Afghans, awarding them contempt for complaint, and bayonets for answers to "lists of rights." Canada, however, pursued a much more honorable course. Acknowledging openly to the settlers that her officials had acted wrongly, she sent to them three representatives (and afterwards a fourth) to quiet their apprehensions, to explain her policy, and to win them over to her side.

And the men were well chosen. They were the Very Rev. Grand Vicar Thibault, Col. de Salaberry, and Mr. Donald A. Smith. The instructions of the two former bear date the 4th Dec., 1869, and entrust to them " the delicate task of representing the *views and policy* of this government to the people of the Hudson's Bay Territory," and continue thus :—

" I think it unnecessary to make more than a passing reference to the *acts of folly and indiscretion* attributed to persons who have assumed to represent the Dominion and to speak in its name, but who have acted on their own responsibility, and without the knowledge or the sanction of this government."

The instructions of Mr. Donald A. Smith (10th Dec., 1869) direct him to act as a

" special commissioner to inquire into and report . . . on the cause of the discontent and dissatisfaction at the proposed changes, which now exist there ; also to explain to the inhabitants *the principles upon which the Government of Canada intend to govern the country, and remove any misapprehension which may exist on the subject.*"

The sincerity and loyalty of the Metis will be tested by their reception of such delegates as these. To Mr. McDougall, who came refusing all communication with " unofficial persons," the Metis refused entrance into the settlement. How will they receive negotiators? They have always professed to be anxious to discuss first, and be governed afterwards.

Vicar-General Thibault arrived at Fort Garry on the 26th December, having left Col. de Salaberry at Pembina. His report has the following:—

"I at once informed the President that I was sent by the Canadian Government, with Col. de Salaberry, and that I wished to know at once whether that hon. gentleman would be permitted to enter Red River. After some moments' reflection, and in view of the assurance that I gave him, that his integrity might be relied on, I was told that he would be sent for, and that he might enter as soon as possible; and, accordingly, on the 6th of January, I had the pleasure of welcoming my companion."

Concerning Mr. Smith's arrival Mr. Begg has the following:—

"On the 27th of December, Donald A. Smith in company with Mr. Hardisty, of the Hudson's Bay Company service, arrived at Fort Garry, and were met at the gate by Riel, who demanded to see their papers before he would admit them. Mr. Smith, having left his principal papers at Pembina, showed those he had in his possession, which were found to have little, if any, connection with the affairs of the country, and, on declaring that these were the only documents he had with him, he was admitted into the Fort. It was not until sometime afterwards that it became known that Mr. Smith was a commissioner from Canada, although Riel had some idea that he knew more than he would disclose, and therefore kept a strict watch over his movements, and would not allow him outside the Fort walls."[*]

In his report the Grand Vicar further says: —

"We immediately communicated our instructions to the President and his Council, and they were taken into consideration.

"Some days afterwards, we were invited to appear before the Council, and the President then said that he was sorry to see that our papers gave us no authority to treat with them, but that they would, at the same time, be very glad to hear us, trusting that we had only good news to tell them.

"'Since you have kindly done us the honor of hearing us,' said we to them, 'we will commence by telling you that we are in truth the bearers of good news; and we are enabled to assure you that the instructions of the government, who have sent us to you, are altogether those of peace and good-will. It desires to respect your persons, and your rights, to labour for the improvement of your country by making a road in order to communicate more easily with Canada,' etc.

"*It acknowledges that it has been deceived in the choice of those employés whose foolish conduct may possibly have compromised it in the territory; but it strongly condemns the arbitrary acts of those particular employés who have so shamefully abused its confidence.*

"At the close of the conference, which lasted some hours, during which we were listened to with much attention and respect, we ventured to take upon ourselves to propose a delegation, as being the surest means of arriving most speedily at a conclusion satisfactory to both parties. Then the President, after thanking us very courteously, without indeed giving us any official assurance, gave us reason to hope that we might arrive at a satisfactory settlement, telling us he would look into the matter with his Council, which seemed sufficient for us at the moment, and that he would give us an answer later. What contrib-

---

[*] Begg's History, 201, 2.

uted not a little to inspire us with hope was a few words which the President whispered to Colonel De Salaberry as he was leaving the hall. Colonel, said he, don't be in a hurry to leave, it is probable I may entrust you with a commission, which cannot but be agreeable to you."

Riel was evidently very distrustful of Mr. Smith. While the other delegates were allowed full liberty, Mr. Smith seems to have been kept under strict surveillance. The difference in tone between the reports of the Grand Vicar and Mr. Smith, shows clearly the reason for the difference in treatment. Mr. Smith was in keen sympathy with the Canadians, and did not dissemble his antagonism to Riel; while the Grand Vicar's rôle was that of the placating negotiator. Mr. Smith's first interview with Riel was quite enough to put a less able man on his guard against him. Mr. Smith in his report (12th April, 1870) described it in this way :

"The gate of the Fort we found open, but guarded by several armed men, who, on my desiring to be shown to Governor McTavish's house, requested me to wait till they could communicate with their chief. In a short time Mr. Louis Riel appeared. I announced my name; he said he had heard of my arrival at l'embina, and was about to send off a party to bring me in. I then accompanied him to a room occupied by ten or a dozen men, whom he introduced to me as members of the '' Provisional Government." He requested to know the purport of my visit; to which I replied in substance, that I was connected with the Hudson Bay Company, but also held a commission from the Canadian Government to the people of Red River, and would be prepared to produce my credentials as soon as they, *the people*, were willing to receive me. I was then asked to take an oath not to attempt to leave the Fort that night, nor to upset their government legally established. This request I peremptorily refused to comply with; but said that being very tired, I had no desire to go outside the gate that night; and promised to take *no immediate steps forcibly to upset the so-called " Provisional Government," legal or illegal, as it might be, without first announcing my intention to do so.* Mr. Riel taking exception to the word illegal, while I insisted on retaining it, Mr. O'Donoghue, to get over the difficulty remarked, 'That is as he' (meaning myself) 'understands it ;' to which I rejoined, 'Precisely so.'"

This is very dignified—very much after Mr. McDougall's fashion of refusing to communicate with " unofficial persons," and meanwhile threatening great things. He says in effect :—

I hold a commission to the *people* of Red River, and I will produce it " so soon as they, *the people*, are willing to receive me "; and I will take " no immediate steps forcibly to upset the so-called Provisional Government . . . *without first announcing my intention to do so.*" Why could not Mr. Smith have said, plainly, " I am here ' to remove any misapprehensions which may exist . . . and to report on the best mode of quieting, and removing, such discontents and dissatisfactions '.* My errand is entirely peaceful, and I have no authority to appeal to force. What are your grievances ?" Here he was in the

---

*See his Commission, p 347. It is not intended to assert that Mr. Smith's conduct of the negotiations was unwise. Mr. Begg, a competent authority, is of opinion that the mission was characterized by much skill. That Mr. Smith's treatment by Riel was the natural outcome of the attitude he assumed, is the the point attempted in the text.

very presence of the discontented and dissatisfied, and to them he hints of force instead of investigation ; he will appeal to "the people," and not bother with the disaffected ; and yet he was sent to call, not the righteous, but the sinners, to repentance. One can hardly wonder that he was treated as though he meant what he said.

Nevertheless, he had his way, and a mass-meeting of the settlers was called for, and held on, the 19th January (hereafter referred to as the Mass-meeting).

"So many were present that the assembly had to be held in the open air, and this when the thermometer stood at about 20 degrees below zero. The meeting lasted some five hours.

"On motion of President Riel, seconded by Pierre Lavellier, Mr. Thomas Bunn was called to the chair.

"Mr. Riel was elected interpreter, and on the motion of Mr. Angus McKay, seconded by Mr. O'Donoghue, Judge Black was appointed secretary to the meeting."*

Mr. Donald A. Smith then read, and explained to the meeting, his commission. *The New Nation* gives the following account of what followed :—

"Business being resumed, Mr. Riel, seconded by Mr. Bannatyne, moved that twenty representatives shall be appointed by the English population of Red River to meet twenty other representatives of the French population, on Tuesday, the 25th inst., at noon, in the Court House, *with the object of considering the subject of Mr. Smith's commission, and to decide what would be best for the welfare of the country.*—Carried.

"On a motion of Judge Black, seconded by Mr. O'Donoghue, it was resolved that a committee consisting of Thomas Bunn, Rev. J. Black, the Bishop of Rupert's Land, John Sutherland and John Fraser be appointed to meet and apportion the English representatives for the different parishes in the settlement, and to determine the mode of election. Committee to meet tomorrow at noon at the Bishop's.

"BISHOP MACHRAY was sure that every one would heartily respond to the kind feeling expressed, and do what was possible to promote union and concord. (Loud cheers). The rights of all present were the same, and on all reasonable propositions there could not be very much difference of opinion. (Cheers). For his part he had the greatest hope that their coming together on that occasion, and their gathering next week as proposed, would lead to a happy settlement of public affairs. (Cheers). And therefore he hoped that we would be as united in future as we had been in the past. (Loud and repeated cheers.)

"MR. RIEL then addressed the meeting as follows :—Before the assembly breaks up I cannot but express my feelings, however briefly. I came here with fear. We are not yet enemies, (loud cheers) but we came near being so. As soon as we understood each other we joined in demanding what our English fellow subjects in common with us believe to be our just rights. (Loud cheers). I am not afraid to say our rights, for we all have rights. (Renewed cheers). We claim no half rights, mind you, but all the rights we are entitled to. Those rights will be set forth by our representatives, and what is more, gentlemen, we will get them. (Loud cheers).

"The meeting then adjourned."

Forty representatives having been elected in accordance with the foregoing resolutions, they met for business on the 26th January.

---
*Begg's History, 242.

Lord Dufferin says of this convention (Despatch 10th Dec., 1875) that it

"was composed of a number of French and English delegates, *fairly elected from the population at large; that persons of very great respectability were members of it, and took part in its proceedings.*"

On the motion of Riel, Judge Black was appointed chairman, and Mr. Caldwell and Mr. Schmidt secretaries. The Council of Forty (as we may style it) remained in session until the 11th day of February. Its proceedings (reported at great length in *The New Nation*) were conducted in usual parliamentary style; and the debates will not suffer by comparison with those of later provincial assemblies. Mr. Smith at the opening of the proceedings made an address, in good taste, after which a committee of six was appointed to draft a new "List of Rights." This list was debated, clause by clause; the discussion extending from the 29th January to the 3rd of February. On the 8th of February Mr. Smith again appeared before the Council, and Riel pressed him

"to give a guarantee that the list of rights, or even a part thereof, would be granted by Canada, which, however, that gentleman did not feel sufficiently authorized to do. The result of this was that the list of rights was reviewed clause by clause by Mr. Smith, and his opinions taken upon the several articles contained in it, so far as the probability of their being granted by Canada was concerned."*

About the same time two of the Canadian commissioners invited the Council to send delegates to Canada with power to negotiate. *The New Nation* has the following account of the invitation as made to the Council:—

"FATHER THIBAULT—We were trusted by the Canadian Government to a certain extent (cheers); and as such we counselled this course—a course which we were sure would be good if the people of the country could adopt it, viz.:— to send a delegation to the Canadian Government in order to treat with the Canadian Parliament. This delegation should be invested with the necessary power to negotiate for what the nation wants (cheers). I must say, of course, that this is more advice than anything else. But at the same time I am certain that the delegation would be well received by the Canadian Government.

"MR. SMITH—This being the case, and looking at the suggestion put forward by the Very Rev. the Grand Vicar, with reference to a delegation from this country to Canada, I have now on the part of the Dominion Government, and as authorized by them, to invite a delegation of the residents of Red River to meet, and confer with, them at Ottawa (cheers). A delegation of two or more of the residents of Red River, as they may think best: the delegation to confer with the Government and Legislature, and explain the wants and wishes of the Red River people, as well as to discuss and arrange for the representation of the country in Parliament (cheers)."

Thereupon it was moved by Mr. Ross, seconded by Mr. Riel, and carried unanimously:—

"That inasmuch as the Canadian Commissioners invited delegates from this country to Canada, to confer with the Canadian Government as to the affairs of

---

*Begg's History, 267.

this country, and as a cordial reception has been promised to said delegates : Be it therefore resolved that the invitation be accepted, and that the same be signified to the Commissioners."

On the 8th and 9th of February, according to *The New Nation*, speeches, of which the following are extracts, were delivered :—

"MR. RIEL—But there has been a spirit of moderation and friendship under all this earnest working to secure the rights of the people. One of these days, then, manifestly, we have to form a government in order to secure the safety of life and property, and establish a feeling of security in men's minds, and remove a feeling of apprehension which it is not desirable should continue for a moment

"MR. ROSS—The tone and sense of Mr. Riel's speech this morning, the spirit it breathed, and the object at which it was aimed, were such as to command our approbation. We can no longer waive this question (cheers). We are not in a satisfactory position in this settlement at present. We feel that we are met here to take such steps as may be best for the future welfare of the country. We must deal with this question of government. I hold it to be our duty before we separate to come to some basis of a government in which we can work on a common cause - the good of the whole country (cheers). The fact is, we have no option in the matter. We must restore order, peace, and quietness to the settlement.

"MR. SUTHERLAND—I would like to say that we did not take any active part in the proceedings alluded to, because we did not see our way clearly. Many of our people to-day say that they did not consider these proceedings at all necessary. The greater part of the list of rights which has been drawn up we expect to get at all events. The commission given to Mr. McDougall includes in the main your bill of rights ; and on these grounds we did not consider it neccessary to join in the former proceedings. *But at present we occupy a different position, and are willing to form a government for the sake of harmony and good will. We are willing to go as far as we can with our friends on the other side, and form a government.* Another point is, that it is generally felt that by joining the Provisional Government, our people incurred too much responsibility, and threw away a certain portion of loyalty. We are all British subjects, and the general inquiry among our people was how far it would be right and proper for us to join a Provisional Government unless we have legal authority for so doing, and where can we get that authority.... In order to clear away my own doubts I went with Mr. Fraser to see Gov. McTavish, I asked his opinion as to the advisability of forming a Provisional Government. *He replied, " Form a government for God's sake, and restore peace and order in the settlement"* (cheers).

"MR. ROSS—The greatest difficulty the English people had to come into a union with their French brethren was the legality of the Government. We did not like to go outside of the law, lest it might involve us in responsibilities which we did not like to incur. *The difficulty is, I conceive, now done away with.* The man in this county who has, if anybody has, legal authority— authority from England, has told us plainly that for his part we are at perfect liberty to go forward and form any government we think best for the welfare of the country. (Cheers).

"MR. FRASER, seconded by Mr. D. Gunn, moved that the committee previously appointed to draw up the list of rights, be reappointed *to discuss and decide on the basis of details of the Provisional Government, which we have agreed is to be formed for Rupert's Land and the North-West Territories,—* Carried, with the substitution of Mr. O'Donoghue for Mr. Schmidt, who was absent.

The following is the report of the committee :—

"1. That the Council consist of twenty-four members; twelve for the English and twelve for the French-speaking population.

"2. Each side shall decide as to the appointment of its own members of Council.

"3. That Mr. Jas. Ross be Judge of the Supreme Court.

"4. That all Justices of the Peace, Petty Magistrates, Constables, etc., retain their places, with the exception of Mr. Dease, J.P., whose place shall be taken by Herbert Laronce.

"5. That Henry McKenney be Sheriff as before.

"6. That Dr. Bird be Coroner as before.

"7. That the General Council be held at the same times and places as formerly; and that the Petty Court be held in five districts (naming them).

"8. That Mr. Bannatyne be continued postmaster.

"9. That John Sutherland and Roger Goulet be Collectors of customs.

"10. That the President of the Provisional Government be not one of the twenty-four members.

"11. A two-thirds vote to over-ride the acts of the President of the Provisional Government.

"12. That Mr. Thomas Bunn be Secretary to the Provisional Government and Mr. Louis Schmidt, Under-Secretary.

"13. That Mr. W. B. O'Donoghue be Treasurer.

After some discussion the report was adopted and Riel elected President of the Provisional Government " without a dissenting voice" —the chairman (Judge Black), Mr. Boyd, and Mr. Cummings, not voting.

The President then nominated as delegates to Canada, the Rev. Mr. Richot, Judge Black, and Alfred H. Scott (one of the members for Winnipeg); and a general election was directed to be held for the formation of an Assembly composed of 24 representatives from every portion of the colony.

"It was now near midnight, and as soon as the decision of the convention was known the guns of Fort Garry thundered out the news, which was answered by a few parties in the town in the shape of bonfires and fireworks— the latter, curious to say, were those intended for the celebration of Mr. McDougall's entrance into Red River; and it may therefore be imagined that the individuals who made use of them on the occasion we have been describing were very well pleased with the results of the convention. Governor McTavish, Dr. Cowan and Mr. Bannatyne were released that same night, and a promise was given that the rest of the political prisoners would be set at liberty soon afterwards." *

With reference to the abdication of Governor McTavish, Lord Dufferin reported (Despatch 10 Dec., 1875):

"On the other hand, it is to be noted that when the proposal to constitute a Provisional Government was mooted in the convention, a certain portion of the English deputies declined to take part in the proceedings, until they had ascertained whether or no, Governor McTavish, the legal ruler of the territory, still considered himself vested with authority. A deputation accordingly was appointed to wait upon him in his sick chamber, for this gentleman had unfortunately during many previous weeks been suffering from the mortal disease of which

---

* Begg, 272.

he soon after died. In reply to their enquiries Governor McTavish told them that *he considered his jurisdiction had been abolished by the proclamation of Mr. McDougall, that he was a "dead man," and that they had therefore, better construct a government of their own to maintain the peace of the country.* Returning to their colleagues, the deputation announced to the convention what Governor McTavish had said, and as a result, Riel and his colleagues were nominated to their respective offices."

Here at last we have a somewhat broad basis for a Provisional Government :—

1. Commissioners are sent from Canada to the settlers.

2. These Commissioners call a Mass-meeting.

3. The Mass-meeting directs elections to be held for the selection of forty representatives " with the object of considering the subject of Mr. Smith's commission, and to decide what would be best for the welfare of the country."

4. Elections are held and good men appointed.

5. This Council of Forty agrees to send delegates, with a list of rights to Canada, and meanwhile to form a Provisional Government.

6. The Hudson's Bay Company was the only authority claiming any jurisdiction which could be displaced by the Provisional Government, and it, through its Governor, had intimated that " we are at perfect liberty to go forward, and form any government we think best for the welfare of the country."

CHAPTER X.

THE PORTAGE ESCAPADE.

The Canadians were far from pleased at the turn events had taken. A Provisional Government was the very thing that all along they had fought most strenuously against; and a Provisional Government with Riel (a Metis) at its head, although agreed to by representatives of all the people, was more than they intended to put up with.

Riel was elected on the 10th, and the Council of Forty finished its labors on the 11th day of February.

"On the forenoon of the 14th February it became known in Fort Garry that a party of Canadians and others from Portage la Prairie had arrived at Headingly, on their way to this place, with the avowed object of liberating the prisoners *and overthrowing the French party.*

"Simultaneously with this movement a general rising took place in the lower part of the settlement, in the parishes of St. Andrews and St. Clements, from which a multitude of several hundred men came to Frog Plain, where they were joined by the party of more than 100 men from the Portage.

"The party from the lower settlement was led by Dr. Schultz, and on their arrival at Frog Plain they billeted themselves in the Scotch church at that place. They sent a message to Fort Garry demanding the liberation of the prisoners, which had been promised by Riel on the formation of the Provisional Government, but had only been partially fulfilled. The French party had collected to the number of about 700 men, and were prepared to defend the fort."*

The opinion of Mr. Donald A. Smith as to this foolish escapade is worth transcribing :—

"Had these men, properly armed and organized, been prepared to support the well-affected French party, when the latter took action about the middle of January, or even in the beginning of February, during the sitting of the Convention, order might have been restored, and the transfer to Canada provided for, without the necessity for firing a single shot ; but now *the rising was not only rash, but purposeless, as, without its interrention, the prisoners would unquestionably have been released.* . . . My sympathies were, in a great measure, with the Portage men, whom I believed to have been actuated by the best of motives ; but under the circumstances it was not difficult to foresee that the issue could not be otherwise than disastrous to their cause. The attempt was, therefore, greatly to be deplored, as it resulted in placing the whole settlement at the feet of Riel. *The great majority of the settlers, English and Scotch, discountenanced the movement and complained bitterly of those who had set it on foot.*"†

Major Boulton was in command of the Portage men. His opinion of the affair is important‡ :—

"Our sources of information were meagre, as all mail communication was stopped, and we knew nothing about the action of the convention, nor did we

---

*Extract from letter, Governor McTavish to H. B. Co., 6th April, 1870.
†Mr. Smith's report, 12th April, 1870.
‡Reminiscences, pp. 100-107.

know what was going on at the Fort. Some of the people had friends among the prisoners, and were anxious about their safety. Rumors came from time to time that they were suffering from close confinement and were ill-treated. Attempts had been made on one or two occasions to organize a party to secure their release, which I discouraged, *knowing that Commissioners had been appointed by the Canadian Government on a mission of peace. My orders from Colonel Dennis, moreover, were to do my utmost to keep things quiet.* . . .

"As it was known that I had previously discouraged such attempts, the meetings for the purpose of organization were held secretly, and information withheld from me. But when I discovered that that they were determined to go, I felt it my duty to accompany them, and endeavor to keep them to the legitimate object for which they had been organized. . . .

"We took our departure, lightly armed, many of the men having *only oak clubs.* . . .

"This trying march of sixty miles, *without transport, and without provisions,* the boldness of the undertaking will be seen to be great. . . .

"Some of the settlers, seeing us arrive at Kildonan, were alarmed at the sudden turn affairs had taken. The action of the convention, they expected, was *about to bring a peaceful solution of the difficulties,* which they had hoped would be realized, but *the appearance of another armed force on the scene cast all their hopes to the wind.*"

Major Boulton gives it as his opinion that the release of Riel's prisoners was a consequence of the Portage rising. This is a mistake. Mr. Donald A. Smith, residing, as he was, at Winnipeg, had much better opportunity for judgment, and he, as we have seen, says:

"Without its intervention the prisoners would undoubtedly have been released."*

Major Boulton admits too that :—

"Before leaving Portage la Prairie, we had, of course, no knowledge of the arrangements that had been made between the commissioners, and Riel, and the population, a few days before."†

Mr. Begg relates the events with close circumstantiality. From his account, all the prisoners were released on the evening of the 15th February, while Norquay (Major Boulton's messenger) did not reach Riel until the morning of the 16th! The Council of Forty had separated only on the 11th. Some of the prisoners were released almost at once, and all the others by the evening of the 15th. The delay was caused by the disinclination on the part of some of the prisoners to take the oath not to take up arms against the Provisional Government. When Norquay arrived at Fort Garry, Riel was able to reply :—

"FORT GARRY, Feb. 16th, 1870.

"FELLOW COUNTRYMEN,—Mr. Norquay came this morning with a message, and even he has been delayed. He will reach you time enough to tell you that for my part I understand that war, horrible civil war, is the destruction of this country ; and Schultz will laugh at us if, after all, he escapes. We are ready to meet any party, but peace, our British rights, we want before all. Gentlemen, *the prisoners are out—they have sworn to keep the peace.* We have

---

*See p. 335.   † Reminiscences, p. 105.

taken the responsibility of our past act. Mr. William McTavish has asked you, for the sake of God, to form and complete the Provisional Government. Your representatives have joined us on that ground. Who will now come and destroy Red River Settlement. LOUIS RIEL."

Mr. Hill * agrees with Mr. Begg :—

"On the assembling of the people at Kildonan, a meeting was held, and Tom Norquay appointed to proceed to Fort Garry, and demand the release of the prisoners. By the time, however, that Tom had reached the Fort, the desired end had been accomplished."

Notwithstanding that the "great majority" of the settlers disapproved the movement ; that it "cast all their hopes to the winds"; that it rendered impossible "a peaceful solution of the difficulties"; and that the people, by their representatives, had unanimously established a Provisional Government, the Portage men arrogated to themselves, without the least pretence of authority, the right, not merely to protest against such a Government, but to make war upon it, and to arrest, and detain as prisoners, those whom they deemed to be its partizans. Among the prisoners was a half-breed named Parisien. The unfortunate circumstances relating to this incident are thus recounted by Mr. Begg† :—

"The chances for peace now appeared to be good, when the next morning information was received that changed, for a time, the whole aspect of affairs—namely, that young Sutherland had been shot by Parisien, who, having succeeded in escaping from his guard, and meeting his victim riding along the river on the ice, fired at him, wounding him in the wrist. Young Sutherland then partly fell from his horse, when Parisien again fired at him, this time inflicting a mortal wound. The object of the murderer must either have been to obtain the horse to facilitate his escape, or else he must have been actuated by a dread that Sutherland intended to intercept him ; whereas the young man was merely riding down to the English camp, to see what was going on, he never having mixed himself up in any way in the rising on either side. The avengers, however, were soon on the track of the murderer, for hardly had he fired at young Sutherland the second time, and before he could capture the horse, his pursuers from the English camp were close upon him. Parisien, on seeing this, darted into the woods, but was soon afterwards overtaken, and in the struggle that ensued, he received injuries from which he died some days afterwards."

Major Boulton says that, "His feet were tied together with a sash, and he was being dragged along the ice by another sash which was tied around his neck."‡

For over three months Riel had maintained himself as President of the Provisional Government without shedding a drop of blood. He had met Col. Dennis' "call-to-arms" firmly and courageously, but with moderation and forbearance ; and had so far won the confidence of the English settlers that, at last, they had agreed to join in the project of self-government. This is the moment selected by the Portage men for an attempt which was not only fruitless, but had been almost entirely innocuous were it not for the Parisien incident. Blood had

---

* History of Manitoba, 286. †History, p. 284-5. ‡Reminiscences, p 103.

now been shed, and for it the Portage men were directly reponsible. If it be said that had there been no Riel, there had been no Portage men, it is not difficult to reply that had there been no McDougall, and no Dennis, and no Canadian party, there had been no Riel.

The opinion of the "great majority" soon made itself felt. Col. Dennis had issued his "call-to-arms" on the 6th December, and had withdrawn it on the 9th. The Portage men joined with the lower settlement party on the 14th February, and on the 16th they had determined to disperse to their homes. But meanwhile the Metis had been thoroughly aroused, seven hundred of them had been brought together, and the excitement of threatened war, and the death of Parisien, with its savage accompaniments, had set wildly flowing the hot "mustang" blood. English and French had but a few days ago met in friendly convention, and now by the foolishness of a few of the "members of Col. Dennis' surveying party who had been left behind by the conservator, when he started back with Mr. McDougall for Canada,"* all the good that had been accomplished by conciliation was roughly undone.

Col. Dennis by his "call-to-arms," his musterings and haranguings and organizings had consigned 45 persons to imprisonment at Fort Garry. The only result of the Portage escapade was to send 48 more to the keeping, this time, of men who felt that vengeance was now more in order than further forbearance. The last of the first party of prisoners had been released on the 15th February, in a spirit of friendship and union. On the 17th, amid anger and hate, the Portage party came to occupy their places.

Riel, with some show of reason, now regarded himself as the head of a duly organized government. In point of law, the Queen's sanction not having been obtained, the proceedings were technically irregular; but this does not seem to have occurred to any of the representatives at the Council of Forty, whether English or French. The Provisional Government, too, whether legal or illegal was the *only* authority in the settlement. The government of the Hudson's Bay Company was too weak to preserve order even prior to the advent of Col. Dennis; its authority had now been completely ended, and superseded, by the assent of its governor, and the action of the people.

What government, moreover, it may well be asked, did the Portage men propose to set up, that would have had better right to acknowledgment? Were we to regard Riel's government as that of mere usurpers, its opponents could claim no higher *status* than that of those they attacked. They, at all events, had not even the semblance of authority, or warrant, either from the Queen, or from the people.

It must be remembered, too, that the now established government was, and was acknowledged to be, merely provisional—organized for the purpose of negotiating for, and obtaining, information, and

---

* Begg 283.

assurances as to the new forms about to be imposed upon them, and to preserve order in the meantime. It must also be remembered that, so far, no force not necessary for the accomplishment of these objects had been resorted to. That Riel was always polite and considerate; that the personification of a race of "wild mustangs" was always self-controlled, and deferential, is not pretended; but that moderation, wisdom, and self-control, were displayed, in marked degree,* is strongly evidenced by the fact that throughout all the stormy and exciting incidents hitherto related, not a drop of blood had been spilled for which Riel was responsible— hundreds of Metis, armed and eager to fight with Canadians whom they hated, for the contempt shown them, and not a bullet has yet searched its billet!

That Riel—now President by the voice of the people—was greatly angered, and much inflamed, by the Portage episode; and that he regarded it not only as an attack upon the Government set up by the people, but also as an absurd and criminal breach of the peace, requiring, in the interest of the community, to be put down with strong hand, are abundantly apparent. In the heat of the moment four of the new batch of prisoners (their leader, Major Boulton, and three others) were condemned to be shot. Almost immediately afterwards the three were pardoned, but it was not without much entreaty that the Major's life was given him. Mr. Donald A. Smith, who was one of the interceders, thus relates the events:—

"Riel was obdurate and said that the English settlers and Canadians, but more especially the latter, had laughed at and despised the French half-breeds, believing that they would not dare to take the life of anyone; and that, under these circumstances, *it would be impossible to have peace and established order in the country*; an example must, therefore, be made, and he had firmly resolved that Boulton's execution should be carried out, bitterly as he had deplored the necessity for doing so. I reasoned with him long and earnestly, until at length, about ten o'clock, he yielded; and addressing me, apparently with much feeling, said, "Hitherto I have been deaf to all entreaties, and in now granting you this man's life," or words to that effect, "may I ask you a favor?" "Anything," I replied, "that in honor I can do." He continued, "*Canada has disunited us, will you use your influence to re-unite us? You can do this, and without this it must be war, bloody, civil war!*" I answered that, as I had said on first coming to the country, I would now repeat, that, "I would give my whole heart to effect a peaceable union of the country with Canada." "*We want only our just rights as British subjects*," he said, "*and we want the English to join us simply to obtain these.*" "Then," I remarked, "I shall at once see them, and induce them to go on with the election of delegates for that purpose;" and he replied, "If you can do this, war will be avoided; not only the lives, but the liberty of all the prisoners will be secured, for on your success depend the lives of all the Canadians in the country." He immediately proceeded to the prison and intimated to Archdeacon McLean that he had been induced by me to spare Captain Boulton's life, and had further promised to me that immediately on the meeting of the Council shortly to be elected, the whole of the prisoners would be released, requesting the Archdeacon, at the same time, to explain these circumstances to Captain Boulton and the other prisoners."

---

* See letter Arch. Taché to Secretary of State, 11th March, 1870.

CHAPTER XI.

THE PRISONERS.—THOMAS SCOTT.

It will be remembered that on the 7th December, 45 Canadians had been taken from Dr. Schultz's house, as a reply to Col. Dennis' "call-to-arms," and confined as prisoners in Fort Garry. The guard kept upon them was not sufficient to prevent the escape of some of them, and others, as cause for apprehension disappeared, were released. On the 2nd January, Nimmons escaped. On the 3rd, 6 or 7 were released.* On the 9th, "a number of the prisoners escaped through a window of the court house."† "It was at this time also that Mr. Thos. Scott escaped."‡ "On Sunday, 23rd January, Dr. Schultz succeeded in making the escape from prison."§ The Council of Forty closed with the establishment of a Provisional Government, and the election of Riel as its President, on the 10th of February. On the 12th, Riel liberated 16 prisoners.‖ Shortly afterwards "all the prisoners, except 24 were released; those remaining having, from some misunderstanding, refused to sign or take the oath not to take up arms against the Provisional Government." ** Finally on the 15th February, all the prisoners were induced to sign a paper agreeing to keep the peace and all were released. ††

To this extent Riel must be held accountable, that he arrested and locked up, those whom he thought to be dangerous to the success of his movement; but *per contra*, this must be credited to him, that he interfered with no others; and that he released those arrested as he became assured of their neutrality. The majority of the prisoners seem to have steadfastly refused to give any such assurance until after the Council of Forty had unanimously agreed upon the establishment of a Provisional Government, and that Riel should be President of it. This was, as we have seen, on the 10th of February. The union of the English and French, thus accomplished, and the general acknowledgment of the new government, removed the scruples of the prisoners, and opened an easy way to accommodation and release. On the 15th they signed, and were released. On the 17th, as we have seen, 48 of the Portage men came to fill the vacant cells.

Thomas Scott was a Canadian and one of the most active against Riel. He had come up with Mr. Snow's surveying party, and must have been of turbulent and quarrelsome disposition, for when Mr. Snow declined to pay him certain sums which he demanded, he with

---

* Begg 207. † Ib. 215. ‡ Ib. § Ib., 246. ‖ Ib., 276. ** Ib., 277. †† Ib., 284.

a few others, dragged their chief to a river and there as Mr. Snow states "he was forced under threats and grievous bodily harm to pay to Scott and others of the working party, the sums opposite their respective names." He had had some quarrel with Riel, and there existed private enmity between the men.*

Scott was among those who had assembled at Dr. Schultz's house about the time of Col. Dennis' "call-to-arms," and was arrested about the same time as the Schultz party of 45 was imprisoned (7th Dec.). He escaped about the middle of January, and early in February joined the Portage party with a view of attacking the French, and shortly afterwards he made a descent upon a house where he thought Riel was, with a view of arresting him.† Scott was one of the 48 taken prisoners by Riel—the only result of the Portage escapade. There he seems to have conducted himself in turbulent, swaggering fashion, for which on the 1st of March, he was placed in irons. Even here his tongue was uncontrollable, and at length he succeeded in inflaming his keepers to such an extent that a short session of an irregular court martial condemned him to be shot. The court appears to have been little more, if anything, than a pretence. Scott's fate was evidently fixed in advance—he was not even present at his own trial. Great efforts were made by his friends to save his life, but this time Riel was thoroughly enraged, and proved completely inexorable. The poor fellow was shot (4th March).

This was Riel's great mistake. To him it may have appeared an imperious and unfortunate necessity of peace, but it cannot so appear to one now calmly studying the events of the time. The Canadians had evidently made their last attempt at resistance. Riel had the "great majority" of both English and French on his side, and had merely to continue in the constitutional methods voted by the Council to attain all that he could properly desire. One cannot read the able despatch to Earl Carnarvon by Lord Dufferin (10th Dec., 1875) and not agree with the conclusion "that all the special pleading in the world will not prove the killing of Scott to be anything else than cruel, wicked and unnecessary crime." At the same time it is not fair to lay this crime at the door of the French as a party. Mr. Begg (who was on the spot) says :

"The feeling of horror at the deed was as strong amongst a large portion of the French as it was with the English; and it must not be thought that it was the desire of the French people that Scott should suffer, for such was not the case."‡

A memorandum of the acting Canadian Minister of Justice at the time has some pertinent remarks :

"No one, outside of the circle of the difficulties existing for some time in the Red River Settlement, can come to any other conclusion than that the shooting of Scott, without speaking of the illegality, was, to say the least of it,

---

* Hill's History of Man, 293.   † Boulton's Reminiscenses, 105.   ‡ History, p. 303.

an act of excessive abuse of power, and of cruel brutality ; but to well appreciate the character of the deed, one must, as it were, transport oneself into the midst of the excited community, at the time the deed was perpetrated, and must consider well the habits, and current of thought, of that community, and also consider well the links in the chain of illegal events which unfortunately took place for several months before the perpetration of the deed.

"To begin · First, there is no doubt that there was a strong feeling of antagonism—unanimously, almost, it may be said—in the half-breeds, of all races and religions, against the introduction of Canadian authority into the settlement ; but *at no time before or after the trouble did those feelings exist against the sovereign power of the Queen, nor even against the political rule of the Hudson's Bay Company*, which, though weak, was considered as benevolent and patriarchal, and to some extent was popular.

"It is beyond doubt that the few who were opposed to the growing rule of the Hudson's Bay Company before the disturbances, were mostly *settlers from Canada, who seem to have directed their energy in opposing the Hudson's Bay Company's government ;* and who advocated it being replaced by the Canadian authorities. These few Canadians, by their opposition, and their policy against the Hudson's Bay Company, rendered themselves most objectionable, and to some extent detestable to the half-breeds of all origins and creeds, almost unanimously, who had been brought up to like and respect the patriarchal rule of the Hudson's Bay Company.

"The unauthorized Major Boulton movement placed the community of settlers of all creeds and races, and Riel in particular, in a very difficult position. That additional movement *of a nature of warlike invasion* in the Red River settlement, must have increased, in an immense degree, the violence of feelings of the majority of the community, and of Riel himself as a matter of course.

"Riel and his co-associates in their *extreme desire to protect the community of Red River against the further invasion of their territory*, by the unauthorized movements of the Canadians, must, very likely, have become excited to madness, and under their over-excited feelings, come to the conclusion that some of the so-called Canadian invaders should perish as an example of warning to any temerarious invader, according to their own appreciation.

"Riel must have been under the delusive conviction, that, in ordering the shooting of Scott he was *saving the community from future danger of invasion*, and was meeting the feelings of the majority of the community."

It is fair, also, to allow Riel to speak for himself. From a communication addressed by him and Lepine to Lieut. Governor Morris, (3rd January, 1873) the following extract is made :—

"The Indians of the entire country—those below Fort de Pierre and those at the Portage, who were apparently the most excited—seemed ready to threaten the country with one of their attacks. Even the prisoners who were kept at Fort Garry, having had wind of these plottings outside, and being encouraged by them, were hurried on to acts of violence. Many of them, notably Mr. McLeod and T. Scott, beat their prison gates and insulted, and went so far as to strike their guards, inviting their fellow-prisoners also to insult them.

"Seeing then that a punishment, long deserved and terrible, could alone restrain these excited men, and finding ourselves compelled to avert evils with which we were threatened by the inhabitants of the Portage conspiring with the Indians—in a word, *to secure the triumph of peace and order, which it was our duty to establish* throughout the settlement, we had recourse to the full authority of government.

"Consider the circumstances; let the motives be weighed; if there was a single act of severity, one must not lose sight of *the long course of moderate conduct which gives us the right to say that during our troubles of 1869-70, we sought to disarm, rather than fight, the lawless strangers who were making war against us.*

"We succeeded in establishing quiet. We availed ourselves of it to hurry the departure of our delegates, who repaired at once to Ottawa."

As for the rest of the Portage prisoners, one-half of them were released on the 15th of March, being the day on which the Council of the new Provisional Government commenced its proceedings, and the remainder were discharged shortly afterwards. Riel still dreaded, it seems, a revival of the Portage affair, and had deemed it prudent to keep in confinement, for a time, those who had been most prominent in the previous effort.*

---

*Begg, 319.

CHAPTER XII.

THE LEGISLATIVE ASSEMBLY.

The election of members of the Council of the Provisional Government (or Legislative Assembly, as it was afterwards called) were held on the 26th February. This was the third set of elections that had been held. The first (as may be remembered) was held about the middle of November, 1869, when twenty-four members were elected as a Council (the Council of November), "to consider the present political state of the country, and to adopt such measures as may be deemed best for the future welfare of the same." The second was held in pursuance of the resolution passed at the mass-meeting, when forty representatives were chosen (the Council of Forty), "with the object of considering the subject of Mr. Smith's commission, and to decide what would be best for the welfare of the country." Those forty representatives had resolved to establish a Provisional Government, consisting of a president and a council of twenty-four members, and had directed elections for membership of this Council. These last elections having now taken place, the Assembly met for the despatch of business on the 9th of March.

Amongst a mass of other business, resolutions were passed as follows :—

"That notwithstanding the insults and sufferings borne by the people of the Northwest heretofore—which sufferings they still endure—*the loyalty of the people of the Northwest towards the Crown of England remains the same*, provided the rights, properties, usages, and customs of the people be respected, and we feel assured that as British subjects such rights, properties, usages and customs will undoubtedly be respected.

"That the Constitution of the Provisional Government for Rupert's Land and the Northwest Territories be now drawn up—that a committee be appointed to draft the same and submit it for the approbation of the Legislative Assembly, and that said committee be composed of French representatives ; The Hon. the President, and Hon. Messrs. Lepine, O'Donoghue, and Bruce ; English representatives, Hon. Messrs. Tait, Bird, Bunn, and Jas. Ross, Esq., Chief Justice.

The following is the preamble and the principal clause of the constitution as adopted :

"That we the people of Assiniboia, *without disregard to the Crown of England, under whose authority we live*, have deemed it necessary for the protection of life and property, and the securing of those rights and privileges which we are entitled to enjoy as *British subjects*, and which rights and privileges we have seen in danger, to form a Provisional Government, which is the only acting authority in this country and we do hereby ordain and establish the following constitution.

"That all legislative authority be vested in a President and Legislative Assembly composed of the members elected by the people, and that at any future time another House, called a Senate, shall be established when deemed necessary by the Legislature."

The business of the Assembly terminated on the 26th March, according to the report in the *New Nation*, as follows:—

"The President then addressed the House, announcing that the business of the session was over, and urging strongly on the members the duty of doing all in their power *to promote a spirit of conciliation among the people.*"

Some prejudiced persons will read these pages, and continue to assert that the actors, in the events related, " were nothing more than a few Red River priests, and French half-breeds." That the assertion may be made more difficult, the names of some of the English-speaking representatives in the Assembly are here given :— A. G. B. Bannatyne, W. Fraser, Thos. Bunn, Geo. Gunn, John Norquay, E. Hayes, A. H. Scott, Dr. Bird, Wm. Tait, etc. Any one at all acquainted with the settlers of 1870, will at once recognize that some of the most prominent of the English-speaking section of them were among the members of the Assembly. If this be not enough, it may be added, that both in the Council of Forty, and in the Legislative Assembly, the English, and not the French, took the leading part in the debates, and work of the session. For example, it was Mr. Sutherland (now Senator) and Mr. Fraser, both English, who formed the deputation to Governor McTavish, for the purpose of consulting him, as to the propriety of forming a Provisional Government (page 350). It was on motion of Mr. Fraser, seconded by Mr. Gunn, both English, that a committee was appointed, to decide " on the basis of details of the Provisional Government, which we have agreed is to be formed " (page 350). It was Mr. Scott, seconded by Mr. McKay, both English, who moved the resolution affirming loyalty to the Crown, " notwithstanding the insults, and sufferings, borne by the people of the North-west heretofore—which sufferings they still endure " (page 362). It was upon motion of Mr. Bunn, seconded by Mr. Bannatyne, both English, that it was resolved, "That the Constitution of Provisional Government for Rupert's Land, and the North-west Territories, be now drawn up." And, finally, the the resolution declaring that the people of Assiniboia " have deemed it necessary, for the protection of life and property . . . to form a Provisional Government" (page 362), was moved by Dr. Bird, seconded, only, by Riel.

CHAPTER XIII.

THE RED RIVER DELEGATES, THE LIST OF RIGHTS AND THE MANITOBA ACT.

It may be remembered that the Canadian commissioners, invited the Council of Forty to send delegates to Ottawa "to confer with the Government and Legislature, and explain the wants and wishes of the Red River people, as well as to discuss and arrange for the representation of the country in Parliament;"* that this invitation had been accepted by the Council; that three delegates had been nominated, viz., the Rev. Mr. Richot, His Honor Judge Black, and Mr. Alfred H. Scott; and that a list of rights had been settled and approved by the Council.

It had been understood that these delegates should leave for Ottawa immediately after the Council adjourned (10th Feb., 1870). The Portage escapade effectually prevented this, by precipitating a state of war, and thus not only interposing reasons personal to the delegates for remaining at their homes, but, by destroying the unanimity of their mandate, rendering their mission less representative. Nothing (curiously enough) seems to have been said about the non-departure of the delegates during the session of the Legislative Assembly which lasted from the 9th to the 26th of March. On the 23rd of this month, the executive sent the delegates off upon their mission. By this time over two months had elapsed since the Council of Forty had prepared its List of Rights. Since then a regular constitution had been formed, elections held, and a settled form of government brought into existence. Much discussion, too, had taken place in the House, and opinion had, probably, in this way become much more matured. Be this as it may, certain it is that the delegates did not carry with them the "List of Rights" framed by the Council of Forty in February, but that the executive of the Provisional Government drew out another list, and that it was this new list which the delegates carried with them to Ottawa.

Controversy has arisen as to the exact form of this new list. The difference between the asserted lists may best be seen by placing them in parallel columns:—

No. 3.	No. 4.
1. That the territories heretofore known as Rupert's Land and	1. That the territory of the North-West enter into the Con-

---

* See page 349.

[364]

North-West shall not enter into the Confederation, except as a province, to be styled and known as the Province of Assiniboia, and with all the rights and privileges common to the different Provinces of the Dominion.

2. That we have two representatives in the Senate, and four in the House of Commons of Canada, until such time as an increase of population entitles the province to a greater representation.

3. That the Province of Assiniboia shall not be held liable at any time, for any portion of the public debt of the Dominion contracted before the date the said province shall have entered the Confederation, unless the said province shall have first received from the Dominion the full amount for which the said province is to be held liable.

4. That the sum of $80,000 be paid annually by the Dominion Government to the Legislature of the province.

5. That all properties, rights and privileges enjoyed by the people of this province up to the date of our entering into the Confederation be respected, and that the arrangement and confirmation of all customs, usages and privileges be left exclusively to the Local Legislature.

federation of the Dominion of Canada as a province, with all the privileges common with all the different Provinces in the Dominion.

That this province be governed:
1. By a Lieut.-Governor, appointed by the Governor-General of Canada.
2. By a Senate.
3. By a Legislature chosen by the people with a responsible Ministry.

2. That, until such time as the increase of population in this country entitles us to a greater number, we have two representatives in the Senate, and four in the House of Commons of Canada.

3. That in entering the Confederation, the Province of the North-West be completely free from the public debt of Canada; and if called upon to assume a part of the said debt of Canada, that it be only after having received from Canada the same amount for which the said Province of the North-West should be held responsible.

4. That the annual sum of $80,000 be allotted by the Dominion of Canada to the Legislature of the Provinces of the North-West.

5. That all properties, rights and privileges enjoyed by us up to this day be respected, and that the recognition and settlement of customs, usages and privileges be left exclusively to the decision of the Local Legislature.

6. That during the term of five years the Province of Assiniboia shall not be subject to any direct taxation, except such as might be imposed by the Local Legislature for municipal or local purposes.

7. That a sum equal to eighty cents per head of the population of this province be paid annually by the Canadian Government to the Local Legislature of the said province, until such time as the said population shall have increased to 600,000.

8. That the Local Legislature shall have the right to determine the qualifications of members to represent this province in the Parliament of Canada, and in the Local Legislature.

9. That in this province, with the exception of uncivilized and unsettled Indians, every male native citizen who has attained the age of twenty-one years; and every foreigner being a British subject, who has attained the same, and who has resided three years in the Province, and is a householder; and every foreigner, other than a British subject, who has resided here during the same period, being a householder, and having taken the oath of allegiance shall be entitled to vote at the election of members for the Local Legislature and for the Canadian Parliament. It being understood that this article be subject to amendment exclusively by the Local Legislature.

10. That the bargain of the Hudson's Bay Company in respect to the transfer of the government

6. That this country be submitted to no direct taxation except such as may be imposed by the Local Legislature for municipal or other local purposes.

7. That the schools be separate, and that the public money for schools be distributed among the different religious denominations in proportion to their respective population according to the system of the Province of Quebec.

8. That the determination of the qualifications of members for the Parliament of the Province, or for the Parliament of Canada be left to the Local Legislature.

9. That in this province, with the exception of the Indians who are neither civilized, nor settled, every man having attained the age of twenty-one years, and every foreigner being a British subject, after having resided three years in this country, and being possessed of a house, be entitled to vote at the elections for the members of the Local Legislature, and of the Canadian Parliament, and that every foreigner other than a British subject, having resided here during the same period, and being proprietor of a house, be likewise entitled to vote on condition of taking the oath of allegiance.

10. That the bargain of the **Hudson's Bay** Company with respect to the transfer of govern-

of this country to the Dominion of Canada be annulled so far as it interferes with the people of Assiniboia, and so far as it would affect our future relations with Canada.

11. That the Local Legislature of the Province of Assiniboia shall have full control over all the public lands of the province, and the right to annul all acts or arrangements made or entered into with reference to the public lands of Rupert's Land and the North-West, now called the Province of Assiniboia.

12. That the Government of Canada appoint a commission of engineers to explore the various districts of the Province of Assiniboia, and to lay before the Local Legislature a report of the mineral wealth of the province within five years from the date of entering into confederation.

13. That treaties be concluded between Canada and the different Indian tribes of the Province of Assiniboia, by and with the advice and co-operation of the Local Legislature of this province

14. That an uninterrupted steam communication from Lake Superior to Fort Garry be guaranteed to be completed within the space of five years.

15. That all public buildings, bridges, roads, and other public works, be at the cost of the Dominion Treasury.

16. That the English and French languages be common in

ment of this country to the Dominion of Canada, never have in any case an effect prejudicial to the rights of the North-West.

11. That the Local Legislature of this province have full control over all the lands of the North-West.

12. That a commission of engineers, appointed by Canada, explore the various districts of the North-West, and lay before the Local Legislature, within the space of five years, a report of the minerals of the country.

13. That treaties be concluded between Canada and the different Indian tribes of the North-West, at the request and with the co-operation of the Local Legislature.

14. That an uninterrupted steam communication from Lake Superior to Fort Garry be guaranteed to be completed within the space of five years, as well as the construction of a railroad connecting the American railway, as soon as the latter reaches the international boundary.

15. That all public buildings and constructions be at the cost of the Canadian exchequer.

16. That both the English and French languages be common in

the Legislature, and in the courts, and that all public documents, as well as all Acts of the Legislature, be published in both languages.

17. That whereas the French and English-speaking people of Assiniboia are so equally divided in numbers, yet so united in their interests, and so connected by commerce, family connections, and other political and social relations, that it has happily been found impossible to bring them into hostile collision, although repeated attempts have been made by designing strangers, for reasons known to themselves, to bring about so ruinous and disastrous an event.

And whereas, after all the trouble and apparent dissensions of the past, the result of misunderstanding among themselves, they have, as soon as the evil agencies referred to above were removed, become as united and friendly as ever; therefore, as a means to strengthen this union and friendly feeling among all classes, we deem it expedient and advisable;

That the Lieutenant-Governor, who may be appointed for the Province of Assiniboia, should be familiar with both the English and French languages.

18. That the Judge of the Superior Court speak the English and French languages.

19. That all debts contracted by the Provisional Government of the Territory of the North-West, now called Assiniboia, in consequence of the illegal and inconsiderate measures adopted by

the Legislature, and in the courts; and that all public documents, as well as the Acts of the Legislature, be published in both languages.

17. That the Lieutenant-Governor to be appointed for the Province of the North-West be familiar with both the English and French languages.

18. That the Judge of the Supreme Court speak the English and French languages.

19. *The same.*

Canadian officials to bring about a civil war in our midst, be paid out of the Dominion Treasury, and that none of the members of the Provisional Government, or any of those acting under them, be in any way held liable, or responsible, with regard to the movement, or any of the actions which led to the present negotiations.

20. That in view of the present exceptional position of Assiniboia, duties upon goods imported into the province shall, except in the case of spirituous liquors, continue as at present for at least three years from the date of our entering the confederation, and for such further time as may elapse until there be uninterrupted railroad communication between Winnipeg and St. Paul, and also steam communication between Winnipeg and Lake Superior.

20. *The same.*

These lists may be referred to hereafter as lists Nos. 3 and 4, in order to distinguish them from the list (p. 333) prepared in December by the first Council (list No. 1); and the list (p. 349) formulated by the Council of Forty in February (list No. 2).

Attention is called to paragraph 7 in list No. 4:—"That the schools be separate." There is no reference to schools in list No. 3. Hence the dispute. Did, or did not, the Provisional Government demand that the schools should be separate? On the one hand is produced what is said to be "the official copy, found in the papers of Thomas Bunn (now deceased) secretary of Riel's Government." This is identical with list No. 3. Mr. Begg in his history gives this list No. 3 as the true one, and accompanies it with a copy of the instructions given to the delegates. That such a list is among Mr. Bunn's papers is sufficient to show that it had actual existence It is no evidence, of course, that it was not superseded (as already two others had been superseded); and Mr. Begg, although careful and trustworthy, may have been misled through not having heard of a subsequent list.

The best, and only direct, evidence that has been adduced upon the subject, is the sworn testimony of the Rev. Mr. Ritchot (himself one of the delegates), who was called as a witness when Lepine was being tried for the murder of Scott (1874), and when no one could have had any object in misstating the facts. At that trial Mr. Ritchot produced list No. 4, and swore that it was the list given to him as a delegate.

Other evidence, and of very strong character, may be added :— After much consultation between Sir John A. Macdonald and Sir George Cartier, on the one hand, and the Rev. Mr. Ritchot and Judge Black on the other, a draft Bill was submitted to the delegates as that which the Government was prepared to concede. The Rev. Mr. Ritchot made observations in writing upon all the clauses in the draft and sent them to the Ministers. Section 19 of the draft dealt with the schools, and the following are the observations made upon it by Mr. Ritchot :—

"Cette clause étant la même que celle de l'Acte de l'Amerique Britannique du Nord, confére, je l'interprette ainsi, comme principe fondamental, le privilège des écoles séparées dans toute la plenitude et, en cela, est comformé à l'article 7 de nos instructions."

(This clause being the same as the British North America Act, confers, so I interpret it, as fundamental principle, the privilege of separate schools to the fullest extent, and in that is *in conformity with article 7 of our instructions*.)

Internal evidence, too, is not wanting in support of Mr. Ritchot's statement. Paragraph 1 of list No. 4 demands a Senate for the new province, and a Senate was granted, although the expense of it was much objected to. List No. 3 says nothing about a Senate. Again, list No. 4 (paragraph 7) demands "that the schools be separate," and clauses were inserted to that end in the Manitoba Act. List No. 3 says nothing about schools. It would be strange if both these points could have got, by chance, into the Manitoba Act—an Act which, as we shall soon see, was the result of elaborate negotiations with the delegates. It may be added that list No. 3 asks that the province shall be "styled and known as the Province of Assiniboia." List No. 4 suggests no name. It is inconceivable that the Dominion should have deliberately refused to adopt the name "Assiniboia," had it been asked, for the Dominion has since then called a large part of the territories by that very name.

Comparison of the lists will show that No. 3 was probably the draft, and No. 4 the finally revised form of the list of rights. Observe that while No. 4 often adopts the language of No. 3, it varies from it, not only in the important respects already referred to, but frequently in mere verbal expression. Judge Fournier, of the Supreme Court, in his recent judgment adopts No. 4 as the true list (see p. 82).

There can be no doubt that it was a list of the Provisional Government, and not that of the Council of Forty (No. 2), that formed the basis of negotiation. The radical difference between these lists lies in this, that the list of the Council of Forty is based upon the settlement becoming a territory, under governmental control from Ottawa; whereas the first article of the other lists (whether No. 3, or No. 4) requires that the settlement should at once become a province, with local government as such. And this was accorded, although much against the Canadian Government's desire.

Enough has been said about these different Lists of Rights. The importance of the controversy is not, to the mind of the present writer, very great. The underlying point has usually been taken to be this: If the settlers asked for separate schools, then the Manitoba Act in granting them may be regarded, in some aspects, as a treaty; but if the settlers did not ask for them, then the appearance of treaty is taken away. But this is not a fair way of looking at the matter, nor is the conclusion justified. The delegates asked for several things which by the Manitoba Act were not accorded. Suppose then that separate schools and other things, not demanded, were, nevertheless, made part of the Act; the effect of this, so far as the settlers are concerned, is that the offer of the settlers (taking the offer as a whole) is rejected by Canada, and Canada by her Manitoba Act, makes a counter proposition, which counter proposition is accepted by the settlers. Let it be remembered that when the Manitoba Act was passed, the territory had not yet become Canadian, and that Canada was under Imperial direction to negotiate with, and, if possible, to satisfy the settlers. Troops were not to be used unless "reasonable terms are granted to the Red River settlers." Whether, therefore, the settlers asked for separate schools, or the idea came from Canada, makes no difference as to the result. In either case the Manitoba Act was a treaty.

Clearing our sight of all technicalities, it is not difficult, however, to see where the idea of separate schools came from. Whether List No. 4 is authentic or not, it is clear that it was the one used by the Rev. Mr. Ritchot; that it was that gentleman who took the leading part in the negotiations; and that the idea of separate schools came from clause seven of that list No. 4. Canada *thought*, at all events, that separate schools had been demanded; acceded to that demand; and the Provincial Assembly agreed to it, as shall presently appear.

The delegates had no sooner arrived in Ontario that two of them were arrested as accessories to the murder of Thomas Scott. It would appear as though nothing was to be left undone, that stupidity could devise, to incense once more the settlers of Red River. The delegates were in Canada on the express invitation of the Government, and their coming had been eagerly looked forward to, both by the Imperial and Canadian authorities. And yet, without the slightest evidence, Canadians—(showing much more of the "wild mustang" than did the French at Red River)—were found excited and foolish enough to arrest a priest and a respectable citizen of Winnipeg, neither of whom had anything to do with Scott's death. This was the result :—

"Mr. Lees, after the opening of the court, informed his Lordship, that he had had a conversation with the witnesses intended to have been called, and with the private prosecutor. *He was satisfied that the evidence he could produce would not justify a committal.* As neither the Crown nor the private prosecutor could produce any further evidence on the charge, he begged to withdraw it."

The Governor-General in a despatch to Earl Granville (21st April) says with reference to the arrest of the delegates :—

"Nothing could well have been more untoward than this turn of affairs. In addition to the feelings to which it may give rise within the limits of the Dominion, it cannot fail to arouse anger, and possibly the desire for retaliating measures, in the minds of Riel and his followers when the news reaches Fort Garry. It has prevented me seeing the delegates, and delayed the opening of negotiations. The Ministers join with me in deploring the event, but are unable to prevent a private individual, over whom they have no control, from availing himself at his discretion of the ordinary forms and process of law."

No retaliating measures at Red River ensued.

It has been said that the arrival of the delegates had been eagerly looked forward to, by both the Imperial and Canadian authorities. Prior to their arrival, numerous telegrams had passed between the two governments, with reference to the organization of a military expedition, and the Imperial Government had declined to assent to the use of force, until reasonable terms of settlement had been granted. On the 5th of March Earl Granville telegraphed :—

"Her Majesty's Government will give proposed military assistance, *provided reasonable terms are granted* to the Red River settlers."

And on the 22nd March a despatch from the Under-Secretary of the colonies directs that

"troops should not be employed *in forcing the sovereignty of Canada* on the population of Red River, should they refuse to admit it."

On the 17th March Earl Granville cabled :—

"Let me know by telegram when you know delegates have started from Fort Garry."

On the 4th April the Governor-General telegraphed :—

"They say the delegates are coming."

And on the 7th as follows :—

"Last of the delegates is expected at St. Paul on Thursday, the 11th ; the others arrived there to-day, and may reach Ottawa on Saturday, the 9th."

On the 9th Earl Granville cabled

"Let me know as soon as you can by telegram result of negotiations with Red River delegates."

On the 23rd of April, Earl Granville thus informed the Governor-General:

"Canadian Government to accept decision of Her Majesty's Government on all portions of the settlers' 'bill of rights.'"

The negotiations with the delegates were carried on by Sir John A. Macdonald and Sir Geo. E. Cartier, who had been appointed by the government to be a committee for that purpose.

The interviews extended from the 23rd April to the 2nd of May, conferences taking place on the 23rd, 25th, 26th, 27th, 28th, 29th and 30th April, and the 2nd of May. On the 3rd of May, the Governor-General was able to cable:

"Negotiations with the delegates closed satisfactorily."

To this Earl Granville replied (18th May):

"I take this opportunity of expressing the satisfaction with which I have learned from your telegram of the 3rd inst., that the Canadian Government and the delegates have come to an understanding *as to the terms on which the settlements on the Red River should be admitted into the union.*"

These papers should be sufficient to show that negotiations were carried on with the delegates as delegates; but it may not be uninteresting to quote the commission which the delegates carried with them and the official acknowledgment of their position.

"*To the Rev. N. J. Richot, Ptr., etc.:*

"SIR,—The President of the Provisional Government of Assiniboia in Council, by these presents grants authority and commission to you, the Rev. N. J. Richot, jointly with John Black, Esquire, and the Honorable A. Scott, to the end that you betake yourselves to Ottawa, Canada; and that when there you should lay before the Canadian Parliament the list entrusted to your keeping with these presents, which list contains the *conditions and propositions under which the people of Assiniboia would consent to enter Confederation* with the other Provinces of Canada.

"Signed this 22nd March, 1871. By Order,

THOMAS BUNN,
Secretary of State.

OTTAWA, April 26th, 1870.

"GENTLEMEN,—I have to acknowledge the receipt of your letter stating that as delegates from the Northwest to the Government of the Dominion of Canada, you are desirous of having an early audience with the government, and am to inform you in reply that the Hon. Sir John A. Macdonald and Sir Geo. E. Cartier have been authorized by the government to confer with you on the subject of your mission, and will be ready to receive you at eleven o'clock.

"I have the honor to be, gentlemen,

Your most humble servant,

"To the Rev. N. J. Richot, Ptr. JOSEPH HOWE.
" J. Black, Esq.
" Alfred Scott, Esq.

If it be thought material to determine whether the delegates were received officially as delegates from the Provisional Government, or merely as delegates of the people, the present writer has no hesitation in saying, that the evidence corroborates the sworn statement of Sir John A. Macdonald (before the Common's Committee, May, 1874):

"Judge Black took me aside and stated that they had received and brought with them an authority from Riel, as Chief of the Provisional Government, to act on behalf of that Provisional Government, and also a certain claim, or Bill of Rights, prepared by that government. He asked me what was to be done with the authority, and the Bill of Rights. I told him they had better not be produced, as the Governor-General could not recognize the legal existence of the Provisional Government, and would not treat with them as such. *I stated however, that the claims asserted in the last mentioned " Bill of Rights" could be pressed by the delegates, and would be considered on their merits.*"

At the same time there can be no doubt that in every unofficial way, the Assembly set up by the settlers for their self-government was sufficiently recognized. Sir John A. Macdonald's letter of instructions to Archbishop Taché (who was sent by the Government as a peace-maker to Red River) is evidence of almost official recognition:

"Will you be kind enough to make full explanation to *the Council.*"

We have seen that on the 3rd of May the Governor-General cabled that the negotiations with the delegates had been closed satisfactorily. On the 2nd of May Sir John A. Macdonald introduced into the House of Commons the result of the agreement come to, in the form of a Bill, which ten days later became the Manitoba Act. There was a short discussion on the clauses relating to education—detailed in Hansard (1870, p. 1546) as follows:—

"Mr. OLIVER moved in amendment that the education clause be struck out.

"Hon. Mr. CHAUVEAU hoped that the amendment would not be carried. It was desirable to protect the minority in Manitoba from the great evil of religious dissension on education. There could be no better model to follow in that case than the Union Act which gave full protection to minorities. It was impossible to say who would form a majority there, Protestants or Catholics. If the population were to come from over the seas then the Protestants would be in the majority. If, as had been asserted, Manitoba was to be a French preserve, then the Catholics would be a majority. He did not care which, because he desired only to see the new province freed from discussions which had done so much injury in the old provinces of Canada. They presented a problem to the whole world, and the question was, could two Christian bodies almost equally balanced be held together under the British Constitution. He believed that problem could be worked out successfully.

"Hon. Mr. McDOUGALL, said the effect of the clause if not struck out, would be to fix laws which the Local Legislature could not alter in future, and that it would be better to leave the matter to local authorities to decide as in the other provinces. *He quite agreed with his hon. friend in giving the same powers to this province as the others* and it was for that reason that he desired to strike out the clause.

"Hon. Mr. McKENZIE was prepared to leave the matter to be settled exclusively by the Local Legislature. *The B.N.A. Act gave all the protection necessary for minorities,* and local authorities understood their own local wants better than the general legislature. It was his earnest desire to avoid introducing into the new province those detrimental discussions which had operated so unhappily on their own country, and therefore hoped that the amendment would be carried.

"After a long discussion a division was taken on the amendment, which was lost by 34 yeas to 81 nays."

It is quite apparent from this discussion that the only difference of opinion was as to whether Manitoba was to be in the same position (as to its powers in reference to education) as were the other provinces, or was to occupy a *better* position. The effect of the amendment if carried would have been that the provisions of the Confederation Act (p. 1) would have applied to the new province. It was the design of the bill as drawn, and as carried, to make the position of the future religious minority *stronger* than under the Confederation Act. The judgments of the courts of law as they now stand interpret the Manitoba Act as placing the minority in the province in a very much *worse* position than it would be in any of the other provinces.

CHAPTER XIV.

RED RIVER DURING ABSENCE OF DELEGATES.

During the absence of the delegates (24th March to 17th June) peace and happiness reigned at Red River. The Canadians, convinced at last of their helplessness, if not of their foolishness, enjoyed the liberty which, notwithstanding their turbulence, was accorded to them. The last of the prisoners **was released** about the 22nd of March.*

On the 2nd of April, an agreement **was** arrived at between the Hudson's Bay Company and the Provisional Government, and on the 8th, **the keys** of **the several warehouses were** returned to **Governor** McTavish.

On the 7th April the following proclamation was issued : †

"GOVERNMENT HOUSE,
Fort Garry, April 7th, 1870.
"*To the Inhabitants of the North and of the North-West Territories:*

"FELLOW COUNTRYMEN,—You are aware, doubtless, both of the series of events which have taken place at Red River, and become accomplished facts, and of the causes which have brought them about.

"You know how **we stopped, and conducted back** to the frontier, a Governor, **whom** Canada,—an **English colony like** ourselves—ignoring our aspirations **and our** existence **as a people, forgetting** the rights of nations, and our rights, *as British subjects*, **sought to impose upon us,** without consulting **or** even **notifying us.**

"You know also that **having been** abandoned **by our** own government, which had **sold its** title to **this country**, we saw the necessity of meeting in council, and recognizing the **authority of** a Provisional Government, which was proclaimed **on** the 8th December, **1869.**

"After many difficulties raised against it by the partisans of Canada and the Hudson's Bay Company, this Provisional Government is to-day master of the situation—because the whole people **of the** colony have felt the necessity **of union** and concord; because we have **always** *professed our nationality as British subjects*; **and** because our **army, though** small, has always sufficed to **hold high the noble** standard of liberty **and of country.**

"Not only has the Provisional Government **succeeded** in restoring order **and pacifying the country, but it has inaugurated** very advantageous negotiations **with the Canadian Government, and with the** Hudson's Bay Company. **You will be duly informed of the results of these** negotiations.

"People of the North and of the North-West! You have not been strangers either to the cause for which we have fought, or to our affections. Distance, not indifference, has separated us.

"Your brethren at Red River, in working out the mission which God assigned them, feel that they are not acting for themselves alone; and that, if

---
* Evidence of Mr. Bunn before Commons Committee.   † Begg 377.

their position has given them the glory of triumph, the victory will be valued only in so far as you share their joy and their liberty. The winning of their rights will possess value in their eyes, only if you claim those rights with them.

"We possess to-day, without partition, almost the half of a continent. The expulsion and annihilation of the invaders has rendered our land natal to its children. Scattered throughout this vast and rich country, but united to a man,—what matters distance to us, since we are all brethren, and are acting for the common good?

"Recognized by all classes of the people, the Government reposes upon the good will and union of the inhabitants.

"Its duty, in officially informing you of the political changes effected among us, is to reassure you for the future. Its hope is that the people of the North will show themselves worthy of their brethren in Red River.

"Still the Government fears that, from a misapprehension of its views, the people of the North and of the North-West, influenced by evil-intentioned strangers, may commit excesses fitted to compromise the public safety.

"Hence it is that the President of the Provisional Government deems it his duty to urge upon all those who desire the public good, and the prosperity of the country, to make the fact known and understood, by all those half-breeds or Indians who might wish to take advantage of the so-called time of disorder, to foment trouble, that the true state of public affairs is order and peace.

"The government, established on justice and reason, will never permit disorder, and those who are guilty of it shall not go unpunished. It must not be that a few mischievous individuals should compromise the interests of the whole people.

"People of the North and of the Northwest! This message is a message of peace. War has long enough threatened the colony. Long enough have we been in arms to protect the country and restore order, disturbed by evil-doers and scoundrels.

"Our country, so happily surrounded by providence with natural and almost insuperable barriers, invites us to write

"After the crisis through which we have passed, all feel more than ever, that they seek the same interests,—that they aspire to the same rights,—that they are members of the same family.

"We hope that you will also feel the need of rallying round the Provisional Government to support and sustain it in its work.

"By order of the President,
"LOUIS SCHMIDT,
"*Asst. Secretary of State.*"

On the 9th April the following further proclamation was issued :—

"*To the People of the North-West:*

"Let the Assembly of twenty-eight representatives which met on the 9th March be dear to the people of Red River. That assembly has shewn itself worthy of great confidence. It has worked in union. The members devoted themselves to the public interests and yielded only to sentiments of good will, duty and generosity. Thanks to that noble conduct, public authority is now strong. That strength will be employed to sustain and protect the people of the country. To-day the government pardons all those whom political differences had led astray only for a time. Amnesty will be generously accorded to all those who will submit to the government, who will discountenance and inform against dangerous gatherings. From this day forth the public highways are open. The Hudson's Bay Company can now resume business. Themselves contributing to the public good, they circulate their money as of old. They pledge themselves to that, of course. The attention of the government is also directed very specially to the northern part of the country in order that trade there may not receive any serious check, and peace in the Indian districts may thereby be all the more securely maintained. The disastrous war which at one time threatened us has left among us fears and various deplorable results. But let the people feel reassured. Elevated by the grace of Providence and the sufferings of my fellow-citizens to the highest position in the government of my country, I proclaim that peace reigns in our midst this day. The government will take every precaution to prevent this peace from being disturbed. While internally all is thus returning to order, externally also matters are looking favorable. Canada invites the Red River people to an amicable arrangement. She offers to guarantee us our rights, and to give us a place in the Confederation equal to that of any other province. Identified with the Provisional Government, our national will, based upon justice, shall be respected. Happy country to have escaped many misfortunes that were prepared for her. In seeing her children on the point of a war, she recollects the old friendship that used to bind them, and by the ties of the same patriotism she has re-united them again, for the sake of preserving their lives, their liberties, and their happiness. Let us remain united, and we shall be happy. With strength of unity we shall retain prosperity. O, my fellow-countrymen, without distinction of language or without distinction of creed—keep my words in your hearts. If ever the time should unhappily come when another division should take place amongst us, such as foreigners heretofore sought to create, that will be the signal for all the disasters which we have had the happiness to avoid. In order to prevent similar calamities, the government will treat with all the severity of the law those who will dare again to compromise the public security. It is ready to act against the disorder of parties as well as against that of individuals. But let us hope rather that extreme measures will be unknown and that the lessons of the past will guide us in the future.

"LOUIS RIEL.

"Government House, Fort Garry, April 9, 1870."

From the 26th April to the 9th May the Legislative Assembly was again in session. The laws which it enacted cover twenty-five pages of Mr. Begg's book, and include such subjects as the administration of justice, custom's duties, intestate estates, postal arrangements, setting out fires, animals at large, liquor traffic, roads, etc., etc.

The following are extracts from the report of the proceedings in *The New Nation*. The first of them is given as showing Riel's attitude at that time, and the second (Mr. McKay's speech) because it helps to a solution of the question of the form of the "List of Rights," which the Red River delegates carried with them to Ottawa.

"THE PRESIDENT in opening the proceedings addressed the House in French and subsequently in English. He said : It is a matter of sincere congratulation, gentlemen, that we have been enabled to meet here at this time under a condition of public affairs on which we may congratulate ourselves (hear, hear and cheers). You have each been, in your several parishes, among your people, and have been able to join in congratulations that you have had the happiness, some of you, to avoid the misfortune which, at one time, threatened all (hear, hear). But this is past; and none are, I am sure, sorry that they have heard the last of it (cheers). Our business now is to act—to show the people that we deserve their confidence by securing to them what they desire and expect of us (cheers).

"Hon. Mr. McKay—But at the same time I have observed in the other reports which have reached us that some importance is attached to one idea, namely, that the people here are divided, and that the conditions on which we were to receive Canada had been changed before they left here, with the Commissioners. *It is true that there has been a change, but it is I think one for the better,* as the terms proposed in the long run could more easily be assented to, than those agreed on in the convention. Some changes were found to be necessary by the executive, and they had to be quickly decided upon, as the Commissioners were expected in Canada, and the people here were anxious to see them starting to Ottawa. Hence the manner of making the alterations. But I would like to place them before the House so that hon. members might judge for themselves. Hon. Mr. Bunn, the Secretary, was with us while the alterations were being made, and so limited was our time for the work that we had to work day and night in order to finish and enable the Commissioners to start at the time they did. The Commissioners, of course, had certain powers in regard to these demands, but before anything was finally settled they were instructed that the approval of the Legislative Assembly of this country was necessary,—so that while complying with circumstances, we had at the same time a saving clause that the ratification of the action of our Commissioners depended altogether on the will of the Legislature of this country (cheers). To-morrow, if it is the wish of the House, I will place on the table the List of Rights as given the Commissioners printed in English and French.

"The President then (9th May) closed the session and intimated that in the event of anything official coming from the Commissioners in Canada he might call a special session of the Legislature."

" The 24th May, Queen's Birthday, was celebrated in good style; people assembled in parties all over the settlement to enjoy themselves —horse-racing was the principal feature of the day—but, altogether, so much good feeling existed between all classes, that one could only wonder at the change from a few weeks previous."*

---

*Begg, 377.

CHAPTER XV.

RETURN OF ONE OF THE DELEGATES.

The Rev. Mr. Ritchot reached Fort Garry on the 17th June, and on the 24th a special session of the Legislative Assembly was held to hear his report. He had brought with him a copy of the Manitoba Act, which he explained at length to the members. The following extracts from *The New Nation* detail the proceedings which ensued :

"HON. MR. BUNN—I have much pleasure in proposing a vote of thanks to Rev. Mr. Ritchot. We must all feel indebted to that gentleman and his co-delegates for the successful manner in which their work was performed, for the risk incurred, and the time, trouble, and expense taken in its accomplishment (cheers). In the first motion placed before our Parliament at its first session, I took the liberty of expressing our confidence that England would attend to the wants of our people as soon as they were made known; and she has done so (cheers). From the report brought by Rev. Mr. Ritchot, it will be found that that confidence was not misplaced, but that England is Old England still (loud cheers). I have much pleasure in proposing a vote of thanks to our delegate Mr. Ricthot. Hon. Mr. Bannatyne seconded the motion.

"REV. MR. RITCHOT—For myself I have expressed about the same thing to the Governor-General and Sir Clinton Murdock. I told them that the people had expelled Mr. McDougall, but were sure that as soon as England knew their causes of discontent she would be willing to satisfy them (cheers).

"HON. MR. SCHMIDT heartily endorsed the vote of thanks to Rev. Mr. Ritchot. The resolution passed amid loud cheers.

"THE PRESIDENT—We have seen the Manitoba Act—have heard the report of our delegation—and now we have to proceed to something else. Is it the intention of the House to pronounce on the Manitoba Act?

"H N. MR. SCHMIDT—I would move that the Legislative Assembly of this country do now, in the name of the people, accept the Manitoba Act and decide on entering the Dominion of Canada on the terms proposed in the Confederation Act (cheers).

"HON. MR. POITRAS seconded the motion, which was put and carried, the members cheering enthusiastically.

"HON. MR. SCHMIDT—I will now make another motion consequent on the former ones. I propose that we welcome the new governor on his arrival (cheers). The motion passed unanimously.

"THE PRESIDENT—We must not expect to exhaust the subject. If we have the happiness soon to meet the new Lieutenant-Governor, we will have time and opportunity enough to express our feelings. For the present let me say only one thing—I congratulate the people of the North-West on the happy issue of their undertakings (cheers). I congratulate them on their moderation and firmness of purpose, and I congratulate them on having trust enough in the Crown of England to believe that ultimately they would obtain their rights (cheers). *I must, too, congratulate the country, on passing from under this Provisional rule to one of a more permanent and satisfactory character.* From all that can be learned, also, there is great room for congratulation in the selection of the Lieutenant-Governor which has been made. For myself, it will be my duty and pleasure more than any other, to bid the new Governor welcome on his arrival (loud cheers). I would like to be the first to pay him the respect due to his position as representative of the Crown (cheers). Something yet remains to be done. Many people are yet anxious and doubtful. Let us still pursue the work in which we were lately engaged—the cultivation of peace and friendship, and doing what can be done to convince these people that we have never designed to wrong them (cheers); but that what has been done was as much in their interest as our own (hear)."

The Rev. Mr. Ritchot then spoke as follows:—*

"As delegate, you will understand, of course, that my position was a very difficult one. The Manitoba Bill passed; but you will observe it differed from our Bill of Rights, and, as delegates, we could not say if the people of the North-West could accept it. Hence, though fully alive to the fact that we had many friends in Canada—in the Legislature as well as out of it,—we could not express to them our sense of gratitude. The only thing we could do was to thank them for their sympathy. But now that our work, and that of the Canadian Parliament has been ratified by this House, my desire is, first, to thank the people of this country for the noble stand they have taken on this question. I have to thank the Canadian Ministry—particularly Sir John A. Macdonald and Sir George Cartier—for the liberal Bill framed by them, with the assistance of the delegation. I have to thank the Dominion House of Commons and Parliament generally, for while 120 voted with us, only eleven were found against us. I have to thank also the Queen of England, whose subject I have always been—whose subject I am to-day. But, above all, I have to express thanks and gratitude to a higher power than all others; I have to thank an over-ruling Providence for having been led through so many difficulties and dangers. Nor must we, at this time, think harshly of those who did not dare to come with us and demand rights; for it was a very risky and imprudent thing. That we succeeded is due to Providence. We have succeeded—but we have seen how difficult the task was. Why? Because we were divided. But now that we are united, we will be a strong people, and our little province will be the model province of Confederation. We will have an influx of strangers here. We want them, and will be glad to receive them. But let us be intelligent enough to distinguish between the good, and those who only came with selfish ends—to work against us. Let me add to what I have stated, in regard to the Manitoba Act, that, at first it was intended that Portage la Prairie should be left out of the province. This had been opposed by the delegates—those who worked for it were the enemies of the Portage—and as soon as Ministers understood the matter fully, they included that district in the Bill. I would, for my part, like it to be well understood that all I have done in the past has been done in good faith, and with a desire to serve the country. I have never tried to work against any part of the people. As one of the delegates, I brought the Bill to Canada, and on that Bill worked for the people of the country, as a whole, without distinction. I offer my sympathy to every denomination in the country, and will repeat that, if there were some among us who did not dare to oppose McDougall, they were, perhaps, right. While in Canada, let me say in closing, not only had we all the sympathy and attention we could have expected, but admiration was expressed for the stand taken by the people, who had, it was held, shown themselves to be a reflective, prudent people —wise to plan—resolute to act—so that, although jeopardized through dangers of the greatest magnitude, they passed almost unscathed through the crisis. It is easy to raise objections to the Manitoba Act, starting from an American point of view. I have heard many such objections. But these possess no weight with us.

"After the reverend gentleman had spoken as above, the assembly adjourned."

---

*Begg, 379.

CHAPTER XVI.

COL. WOLSELEY—OUTRAGES AGAINST THE METIS —FENIAN INVASION.

On the 24th of August, 1870, Col. Wolseley arrived at Fort Garry with the expeditionary force. No amnesty having been yet proclaimed, Riel crossed into the United States. He returned in March of the following year, and remained until February, 1872, when Sir John A. Macdonald gave him $1,000, and the Hudson's Bay Company gave him and Lepine £600 more, on condition that they would temporarily withdraw from Canada, where many people were " wishing to God they could catch them."

If during the many exciting months in which the " wild mustangs " conducted the affairs of government, dealing with plots, and risings, and "calls to arms"—if in the effort to enforce peace and quiet, Riel was responsible for the loss of one life (his opponents being accountable for two), the cultured from the east were now to show that under their rule, not many months, and not many weeks, were to pass without bloodshed—and bloodshed unretributed and unavenged.

On the 13th of September, Elzear Goulet (a Metis) was set upon, in Winnipeg, by a man who had been one of Riel's prisoners, and by some of Wolseley's volunteers. Goulet took refuge in the Red River, and in trying to escape by swimming to the other side, was struck by a pursuing missile, and was drowned.

"As no coroner had been appointed, Gov. Archibald ordered an investigation before two magistrates—Robert McBeth and Sam Hamelin—and H. G. McComville, a lawyer newly arrived from Montreal, was appointed to conduct the case. A verdict was returned that Goulet's death was caused by these three men, who belonged to the Canadian loyal party. It was felt, however, that to make an arrest in the excited state of the public feeling would have precipitated a conflict between the two nationalities and religions, far more disastrous than that of the preceding winter. It was, therefore, deemed expedient to defer action in the matter until popular feeling had quieted down.*"

Which is to say, that "popular feeling" would be less affected by the murder of a Metis by Canadians, than by the arrest of the murderers! Riel's rule was not very much below this standard of government! It is almost needless to add that the deferred time for prosecuting Goulet's murderers never arrived.

Nor was there in respect of this event any wild ebullition from Ontario: mass-meeting resolutions concerning the sanctity of

---

*Hill's History of Manitoba, 328.

British blood; rewards for captures; indignant denunciations of delinquent and dilatory magistrates, such as darkened the air when Scott was killed. The news went to Ontario as an ordinary "item," and was published (*The Daily Telegraph*) under the caption

"A MISCREANT DISPOSED OF."

Nevertheless it was to these very miscreants, that Canada, little more than a year afterwards, turned for help and protection, and turned not in vain. To-day they are rebels, banditti, robbers, miscreants; to-morrow they shake hands with the Lieutenant-Governor of the Province of Manitoba, and find their courage, loyalty and patriotism beyond adequate praise!

O'Donoghue had been one of Riel's supporters, and was either a fenian, or of fenian sympathies. Counting upon the divided character of the people, after the departure of Col. Wolseley, O'Donoghue organized an invasion from United States territory, with a view to plunder, if not to annexation. Lieut.-Governor Archibald at once bethought him of the "miscreants"—are they going to unite with the invaders?—and put himself in communication with some of them. There was, however, in his way, this very practical difficulty, that warrants of arrest for the leaders of these very men were in the hands of the local police! How could *they* be expected to appear at Fort Garry to defend it?—they might have to remain there to defend themselves! Under these circumstances, the Rev. Mr. Ritchot sent to the Lieut.-Governor a note, to which he received the following reply:

"Government House,
"October 5th, 1871.

"REVEREND SIR,—Your note has just reached me. You speak of the difficulties which might impede any action of Mr. Riel, in coming forward to use his influence with his fellow-citizens, to rally to the support of the province in the present emergency.

"Should Mr. Riel come forward, as suggested, he need be under no apprehension that his liberty shall be interfered with in any way, to use your own language, *pour la circonstance actuelle.*

"It is hardly necessary for me to add that the co-operation of the French half-breeds, and their leaders, in support of the Crown, under present circumstances, will be very welcome, and cannot be looked upon otherwise than as entitling them to most favorable consideration.

"Let me add that in giving you this assurance with promptitude, I feel myself entitled to be met in the same spirit.

"The sooner the French half-breeds assume the attitude in question, the more graceful will be their action, and the more favorable their influence.

"I have the honor to be Rev. Sir,   Yours truly,
"A. G. ARCHIBALD,
"*Lieut.-Governor.*

This letter having been communicated to Riel, Lepine and Parenteau—the leaders of the Metis—they joined in a note to the Lieut.-Governor, which elicited the following reply:

"Government House,
"Fort Garry, 8th October, 1871.

"GENTLEMEN,—I have it in command from His Excellency the Lieut.-Governor to acknowledge receipt of your note of this morning assuring His Excellency of the hearty response of the Metis to the appeal made to them in His Excellency's proclamation.

"You may say to the people, on whose behalf you write, that His Excellency is much gratified to receive the assurance which he anticipated in his communication with the Rev. Pere Ritchot, and which your letter conveys; and that he will take the earliest opportunity to transmit to His Excellency the Governor-General, the evidence of *the loyalty and good faith of the Metis* of Manitoba.

"His Excellency will be pleased to be furnished, as soon as possible, with a nominal list of the persons in each parish who desire to enroll for active service in the present emergency. His Excellency will rely upon their readiness to come forward the moment they receive notice.

"I have the honor to be, Gentlemen,
"To Messrs. L. Riel.   Your obedient servant,
         A. D. Lepine.   WM. O. BUCHANAN,
         Pierre Parenteau.   *Acting Private Secretary.*

The Lieut.-Governor afterwards described the position in a memorandum as follows:

"With some (I cannot say how many) of the volunteers who went up, a desire to avenge the murder of Scott was one of the inducements to enlist. Some of them openly stated that *they had taken a vow before leaving home to pay off all scores by shooting down any Frenchman* that was in any way connected with the event. The great bulk of the French population having been, one way or other, concerned in the troubles, the feeling gradually grew to be one of intense dislike towards the whole race, which was heartily reciprocated by the French.

"When the volunteers came to be disbanded, and were thus freed from all restraint, the hatred of the two classes exhibited itself more and more. Some of the immigrants from Ontario shared the feelings of the disbanded volunteers, and acted in concert with them. A body of French half-breeds had made a selection of a tract of land at Riviere aux Islets de Bois; some of them had made farms, or at all events enclosures, at that place. *There was abundance of land elsewhere equally good, but the new comers preferred this spot. They entered on that ground and staked it off, put up huts, and declared they would hold it against all comers.* To give character to their occupation, they discarded the name by which the river had been known, and called it the Boyne. Of course the half-breeds were enraged; they thought it bad enough to lose land they believed to be theirs, but in the new name they saw something worse —an insult to their religion. They seemed to think that property, race, and creed were all to be trodden under foot, unless they took care of themselves. They met in their parishes on the Assiniboine and Red River, and determined to march to the settlement and drive off the intruders. Fortunately I heard of their intentions.

"I sent some leading men among them, and warned them that if they lifted a hand or struck a blow, it was all over with them.

"The collision was arrested, but not without great risk. Had blood been shed on that occasion we should have had a civil war in which every French half-breed would have been an active participator; while from the English half-breeds, in accord on the question of property with the French, neutrality was the utmost that could have been counted on, and at this moment we had a garrison of only eighty men to defend all our military stores at Fort Garry, and to preserve the peace of half a continent besides.

"The danger was over for the moment, but the feelings of sullen discontent remained. This was in July. In October came the raid. *It was predicated on the discontent known to prevail among the French half-breeds.*

"The leader of the raid had been a member of the Provisional Government; the other members of that government were in the Province, outlawed for their offences, *abused by one press, and thrown over by the other,* and yet exercising a large influence among their own race and creed. *Under these circumstances, the chances were that the French would join the enemy.* I had a tough battle to fight.

"At last my remonstrances and persuasions began to take effect. The clergy assisted me in the movement. The colleagues of O'Donoghue in the Provisional Government, on whom he had counted, began to come out against him. *Riel went into the French settlements, and used his influence against O'Donoghue. These two men are said never to have been friendly.*

"O'Donoghue was always a Fenian, an annexationist; Riel was neither. His feelings were those of a Frenchman, and a Catholic. He could see a chance for his race and creed in the Dominion, where a large part of the population is French. The clergy who were of the same race naturally shared his feelings in this respect, and they felt more inclined to side with Riel, one of themselves, than with O'Donoghue, who differed from them in race, and as a Fenian, was not necessarily a good Catholic.

"With these influences operating on the French side, their sullenness and resentment were gradually overcome, and they were brought to take a stand in favor of the Crown."

Lord Dufferin (despatch 10th Dec., 1875) thus sums up these and some subsequent events :—

"It will be observed that the Lieutenant-Governor *reviewed the troops which had been collected under the command of Riel, Lepine, and their companions;* that he accepted their services; that he promised them at least a temporary immunity from molestation on account of the crime of which they were accused; *that he shook hands with them;* that he received a letter signed by them; and that, through his secretary, he addressed to them an official reply, *complimenting them on the loyalty* which they had shown, and the assistance which they had rendered. He further states that he has convinced himself—though Sir John Macdonald appears to have had misgivings on this point—that this exhibition of fidelity was genuine and *bona fide,* and that it largely contributed to the preservation of Her Majesty's Dominions from insult and invasion. In short, he is satisfied, to use his own language, that "*if the Dominion has, at this moment, a province to defend, and not one to conquer, they owe it to the policy of forbearance.* If I had driven the French half-breeds into the hands of the enemy, O'Donoghue would have been joined by all the population between the Assiniboine and the frontier, Fort Garry would have passed into the hands of an armed mob, and *the English settlers* to the north of the Assiniboine would have suffered horrors it makes me shudder to contemplate."

The Lieutenant-Governor afterwards in his evidence before a committee of the House of Commons testified as follows :—

"I believe that the action of the half-breeds, at the time of the Fenian raid was attributable to the negotiations with their leaders which I have described; and *if the half-breeds had taken a different course, I do not believe the province would now be in our possession."*

Canadian volunteers are lauded year by year, because when Fenians were on the frontier, they took their places in the ranks, and did their duty. Has ever anyone lauded the French half-breeds, because, forgetting the insults heaped upon them, forgetting their well-placed antipathy to many of the "new comers," they saved a province to the Dominion, and protected the English settlers from "horrors it makes me shudder to contemplate"? Scott has been wept and canonized; are the names, even, of Goulet, and of Parisien, known to those who speak of banditti and miscreants? On the whole, can one wonder that, as Lieutenant-Governor Archibald testified before the Common's committee:—

"It fact the whole of the French half-breeds, *and a majority of the English*, regarded the leaders in those disturbances as patriots and heroes; AND ANY GOVERNMENT WHICH SHOULD ATTEMPT TO TREAT THEM AS CRIMINALS WOULD BE OBLIGED VIRTUALLY TO DISREGARD THE PRINCIPLES OF RESPONSIBLE GOVERNMENT."

CHAPTER XVII.

"REBELLION," AND SUCCESS.

Nothing, it is said, justifies rebellion but success. Of the existence of a "rebellion" many people will remain well assured, notwithstanding all that has, and can be said. The foolish frenzy into which the Province of Ontario worked itself, while in absolute ignorance of all the facts, has left its drift of beliefs and prejudices, such as will require the lapse of another hundred years or so, wholly to remove. It might, by possibility, shorten the time a week or two, could the question be widely put, and fairly answered, Against whom was the rebellion?

THE REBELLION WAS NOT AGAINST HER MAJESTY THE QUEEN, OR BRITISH SOVEREIGNTY.

This much at all events is perfectly clear, and a short review will easily demonstrate it.

6th Nov., 1869. Riel's first published declaration calls upon the English-speaking settlers to elect 12 councillors,

"in order to form one body with the above council, . . . to consider the present political state of the country, and to adopt such measures as may be deemed best for the future welfare of the same" (p. 332).

24th Nov., 1869. The meetings of the Council

"resulted in the French members declaring their intention to form a Provisional Government, *for the purpose of treating with Canada for the future government of the country*" (p. 333).

2nd Dec. 1869. English and French at the Council agreed upon a List of Rights, and the French desired to send a deputation to Mr. McDougall to confer with him thereon (p. 334).

8th Dec., 1869. A proclamation is issued declaring,

"That we refuse to recognize the authority of Canada, which pretends to have a right to coerce us, and impose upon us a despotic form of government, still more contrary to our rights and interests as *British subjects*, than was that government to which we had subjected ourselves, through necessity, up to a recent date (p. 335) That meanwhile we hold ourselves in readiness to *enter into such negotiations with the Canadian Government* as may be favorable for the good government and prosperity of this people" (p. 336).

19 Jan., 1870. At the mass-meeting, Riel declared his position as an English subject.

8th Feb., 1870. The Council of Forty upon a motion *seconded by Riel*, determined to send delegates to confer with the Canadian Government as to the affairs of the country.

10 Feb., 1870. Riel declared to Mr. Donald A. Smith

" We want only our just rights *as British subjects.*"

March, 1870. The Legislative Assembly resolved,

"That notwithstanding the insults and sufferings borne by the people of the Northwest heretofore—which sufferings they still endure—*the loyalty of the people of the Northwest towards the Crown of England remains the same*, provided the rights, properties, usages and customs of the people be respected, and we feel assured that as British subjects such rights, properties, usages and customs will undoubtedly be respected."

7th April, 1870. A proclamation of the Provisional Government declared that,

" *We have always professed our nationality as British subjects.*" (p. 376.)

and gave as a reason for stopping Mr. McDougall, that he forgot

"the rights of nations and our rights *as British subjects.*" (p. 376.)

If doubt remain, read the proclamation of 9th April (p. 377); Riel's speech, 26th April, (p. 378); the account of the celebrations of the Queen's birthday (p. 379); the proceedings of the Legislative Assembly after the return of the delegates (p. 380); and finally remember the loyal assistance rendered by Riel and the Metis against the Fenians and filibusterers—"that if the half-breeds had taken a different course, I do not believe the province would now be in our possession."

If doubt still remain let the following authorities be cited:

Sir John A. Macdonald, before the Commons' Committee deposed as follows:

"The armed resistance was a very aggravated breach of the peace, but we were anxious to hold, and did hold, that under the circumstances of the case it did not amount to treason. We were informed that *the insurgents did not desire to throw off allegiance to the Queen, or sever their allegiance from the Empire*, but that their action was in the nature of an armed resistance to the entering into the country of an officer, or officers, sent by the Dominion Government."

Sir George Cartier, in a memorandum of 8th June, 1870, when acting as Minister of Justice, said:—

" First, there is no doubt that there was a strong feeling of antagonism, unanimously it may be said, in the half-breeds of all races and religions, against the introduction of Canadian authority into the settlement; but *at no time before, or during the troubles did those feelings exist against the sovereign power of the Queen, nor even against the political rule of the Hudson's Bay Co.*"

The Canadian Government, by an Order-in-Council (16th Dec., 1869) adopted a report of Sir John A. Macdonald, in which is found the following:—

"'The resistance of these misguided people is *evidently not against the sovereignty of Her Majesty, or the government of the Hudson's Bay Company* but to the assumption of the government by Canada. They profess themselves satisfied to remain as they are, and that if the present system of government were allowed to continue, they would at once disperse to their homes."

NOR WAS THE REBELLION AGAINST THE HUDSON'S BAY COMPANY.

The extracts above given are ample to prove this statement. Rebellion against, and defiance of, that company had been commenced and carried on somewhat successfully, before Riel's appearance, not by the half-breeds, but by the Canadian party; and that defiance and resistance had gone to the extent of the rescue by violence of those in gaol. If it be said that Riel seized one of the forts of the company, it may well be replied that if this, an incident of a struggle with Canadians, be rebellion against the company, then that the Canadians were also rebels against the company, for they, just as unceremoniously, seized another of the forts. The truth is that the company had received a mortal wound by the passing of the Confederation Act, and its *coup-de-grâce*, by the Act of the Dominion Parliament (1869), which in advance of the transfer made provision for the future government of the North-West. It was in its death-agonies when the Canadian surveyors commenced the operations, and was as little able, as, unfortunately, was its Governor (through illness) to take any part in the struggle between settler and Canadian. Both sides treated it as defunct.

Against whom then was the "rebellion"? A Minister of the Crown is said to have described it as a " rebellion against the Hon. Wm. McDougall." And if the word is to be retained, the present writer cannot suggest a better sentence in which to place it.

And what was the measure of success attained? for by that we are told we must to some extent judge it. To answer this question we must compare the position in which the half-breeds would have occupied had there been no resistance, with their position under the Manitoba Act—their position in two respects, first as to form of government, and second as to lands, language, education, etc.

As to form of government the answer is not difficult, for the Dominion Parliament had declared, prior to any outbreak, the manner in which it was intended to govern the territory.* A Lieutenant-Governor, and a Council of seven to fifteen persons, were to be appointed by the Government *at Ottawa*

" to make provision for the administration of Justice therein, and generally to make, ordain and establish all such laws, institutions and ordinances as may be necessary.

" The Lieutenant-Governor shall administer the government under instructions from time to time given him by Order-in-Council."

And the Council was to have such powers

" as may be from time to time conferred upon them by Order-in-Council."

---

*See the Statute, 32 and 33 Vic. c. 3.

In other words, a branch, or agency, of the Dominion Government was to be established at Winnipeg, while the head-office remained at Ottawa. And this policy the Dominion Government endeavored, through its delegates, to induce the settlers to accept.*

Under the Manitoba Act the settlement at once became *a Province*, with all the powers enjoyed by all the other Provinces; and with the same proportional representation in the Dominion Parliament. This is point number one gained by the "rebellion against the Hon. Mr. McDougall."

Although a very substantial point, it was not the principal one. The quarrel has been traced to "certain operations in land" of sinister aspect—the settlers particularly wanting to know what is to become of the land; what is the significance of all this surveying and staking out? This was the principal topic debated between the Dominion Government and the Red River delegates. Until then no policy had been adopted by the government, and is impossible to say what, had there been no resistance, the future policy might have been. All one can say is that the delegates obtained more than the government would for some time, during the negotiations, consent to give; and one may judge from that whether, without a lever, they would have succeeded so well. By the Manitoba Act (1) all grants of any estate made by the Hudson's Bay Company were to be confirmed by grant from the Crown in fee simple; (2) all titles by occupancy with the sanction of the company were to become estates in freehold; (3) all persons in peaceable possession were to have pre-emptive rights; (4) rights of common and of hay-cutting were to be adjusted; and (5) 1,400,000 acres were to be distributed among the children of the half-breeds! This is point number two gained by the "rebellion against the Honorable William McDougall."

Then there was the language question. English and French are equally divided, what language shall be officially used? Section 23 of the Manitoba Act provided in a manner quite satisfactory to a population equally divided, that both languages should be used—a provision which the English (in a spirit of "English fair play"), now that they are in a majority, have completely disregarded; and by statute, so far as they can, have repudiated. This was point number three gained by the "rebellion, etc."

And, lastly, there was the question of education, settled also to the satisfaction of an equally divided population—as it had been settled long before in Ontario and Quebec.

Settled? Everyone, at the time, thought that it was settled; but owing to some looseness in the drafting, the present position is as indicated in one of the best of the Toronto periodicals:

"That the constitution of the Province does not provide for the perpetuation of separate schools is now certain. *But it is scarcely less certain that it was*

---

*See Letter of Instructions, Hon. Mr. Howe to the Rev. Mr. Thibault, 4th Dec., 1869.

the intention of the original framers of that constitution to secure their perpetuation. Such being the case, it would seem at first thought that the provincial authorities should, as honorable men, be guided by the intention, rather than by the letter of that charter. But here a variety of considerations present themselves to modify or reverse these conclusions."

Among which are named (1) "The justice and the wisdom of the intention"; (2) That the expectation " that the new province would be peopled to a very great extent by members and adherents of the Roman Catholic Church has utterly failed of realization"; (3) and that there can be no rest until the intention is violated or set aside.

A solemn compact is made, and is to be violated, (1) because it was not a wise one to enter into; (2) because the party attacked is not so strong as it was thought it would be (in which case it would have looked after itself); and (3) because the stronger party is restless—public opinion, once more, become too sensitive! If Catholics so reasoned it would be denounced as "jesuitical casuistry;" and fathered upon their supposed principles that " there ought to be no faith kept with heretics"; that the " end justifies the means," etc.

But such bare-faced word-juggling is not a whit worse than the bare-faced repudiation of the acknowledged agreement, some of the incidents of which must now be related.

CHAPTER XVIII

PROTESTANT PROMISES.

Almost every step in the constitutional history of Canada has been accompanied by assurances given to Roman Catholics. (Protestants have also received assurances, but they are not detailed here.)

The capitulations of Quebec and Montreal provided (1759 and 1760)

"That the free exercise of the Catholic, Apostolic and Roman Religions shall be preserved."

The Treaty of Paris (1763), containing the cession of Canada from France to Great Britain, had the following :—

"His Britannic Majesty on his side agrees to grant the liberty of the Catholic religion to the inhabitants of Canada ; he will consequently give the most precise, and most effectual orders, that his new Roman Catholic subjects may profess the worship of their religion, according to the rites of the Romish Church, as far as the laws of Great Britain permit."

The Quebec Act (1774)—the first Imperial Statute as to the government of the colony, 14 George III., cap. 83, sec. 5, enacts that

". . . subjects may have, hold and enjoy the free exercise of the religion of the Church of Rome subject to the King's supremacy . . . and that the clergy of the said Church may hold, receive and enjoy their accustomed dues and rights, with respect to such persons only as shall profess the said religion."

The Constitutional Act (1791), 31 George III., cap. 31, sec. 42, provides that

"Whenever any Bill shall be passed containing any provisions which shall in any manner relate to, or affect the enjoyment or exercise of any form, or mode of religious worship ; or shall impose or create any penalties, burdens, disabilities or disqualifications in respect of the same ; or shall in any manner relate to, or affect the payment, recovery or enjoyment of any of the accustomed dues or rights," etc., then the Royal assent was not to be given until thirty days after the Bill should have been laid before the Imperial Parliament.

The Union Act (1840,) 3 and 4 Vic. cap. 35, contained the clause just quoted.

The Confederation Act (1867) has the provisions with reference to education already quoted (p. 1), and provisions for the official use of the French language.

The Manitoba Act, and its safeguarding clauses have already been referred to.

The assurances which rendered that Act possible, and acceptable, must now be collected. They are:—

1. In the instructions to Col. de Salaberry and the Rev. Mr. Thibault, Commissioners from the Canadian Government to the Red River Settlement, is the following:—

"You will not fail to direct the attention of the mixed society, inhabiting the cultivated borders of the Red River and Assiniboine, to the fact which comes within your daily knowledge and observation, and is patent to all the world, that in the four Provinces of this Dominion, men of all origins, creeds, and complexions, stand upon one broad footing of perfect equality in the eye of the government and the law; and that no administration could confront the enlightened public sentiment of this country, which attempted to act in the North-West, upon principles *more restricted and less liberal than those which are fairly established here.*"

2. In the letter of instructions to the other Canadian Commissioner (Mr. Donald A. Smith) from the Governor General there is the following:—

"The people may rely upon it that *respect and protection will be extended to the different religious denominations*; that titles . . . ; and that all the franchises which have existed, or which the people may prove themselves qualified to exercise, shall be duly continued or liberally conferred.

"In declaring the desire and determination of her Majesty's Cabinet, you may safely use the terms of the ancient formula, that '*right shall be done in all cases.*'"

3. In a letter written by the Governor-General to Mr. McTavish, then the Governor of the Hudson's Bay Company, about the same date (6th Dec., 1869) is this:

"And the inhabitants of Rupert's Land, of all classes and persuasions, may rest assured that Her Majesty's Government has no intention of interfering with or setting aside, or *allowing others to interfere with the religions, the rights, or the franchises hitherto enjoyed, or to which they may hereafter prove themselves equal.*"

4. About the same time (7th Dec. 1869) the Canadian Secretary of State wrote to Mr. McDougall:

"You will now be in a position to assure the residents of the Northwest Territories:

"1. That all *their civil and religious liberties will be sacredly respected.*

"7. That the country will be governed, as in the past, by British law, and *according to the spirit of British justice.*"

5. That these assurances might carry all the weight of Her Majesty's name, the Governor-General issued a proclamation (6 Dec., 1869) having the following:

"By Her Majesty's authority, I therefore assure you that, on the union with Canada, *all your civil and religious rights and privileges will be respected*, your properties secured to you, and that your country will be governed, as in the past, under British laws and in the spirit of British justice."

And the Governor intimates that there will always be a remedy in case of just complaint:

"Her Majesty commands me to state to you, that she will always be ready, through me, as her representative, to redress all well founded grievances ; and that she has instructed me to hear and consider any complaints that may be made, or desires that may be expressed to me, as Governor-General."

To all of these, some persons will answer, "Their religion has been respected; justice has been done; they have no well-founded grievance." But the assurances did not mean this: "Your religion will be respected in relation to education; your religion requires that your children's education should be accompanied by daily religious instruction; you will be permitted to indulge this fancy, but we will tax you for education of a very different character, on the ground that in our opinion it *is* a fancy, and that if you are foolish enough to insist upon it you must pay double. When we said that we would respect your religion, we did not say that we would not tax you on account of it!" Had this been thus plainly stated, does any one think that it would have gone very far towards the pacification of the Metis, or helped to pass the Manitoba Act?

The Manitoba Act (1870) contains in intention and spirit the promise of the Dominion of Canada that the religious minority is to be entitled to separate schools. This Act was, as we have seen, the embodiment of a solemn agreement, entered into under circumstances well-calculated to ensure its subsequent observation. But if it be permissible to urge for its breach that it is an old agreement, a foolish one, and moreover not binding unless the minority is strong enough to make it so, what can be said for the three following further assurances.

1. *Compact of 1876.* In a quite remarkable speech delivered by the Hon. Senator Bernier in the Senate (3rd and 4th April, 1894) occurs the following:

"During the administration of Mr. Mackenzie, the Local Government of Manitoba came to Ottawa for better financial terms. Mr. Mackenzie was not willing to help the province at the time, except on the condition that the province would abolish its Legislative Council, then a part of the legislative machinery. Our Manitoba pilgrims went back to Winnipeg and made the proposition to their colleagues. *The Legislative Council could not be abolished without the co-operation, and, in fact, the consent, of the Catholic representatives of the Province*, who felt at once that it was for them a serious action to take. *Their Legislative Council was considered as their safeguard against any future aggression upon their rights and privileges.* An appeal was made to their intelligence and patriotism. And at last, for the sake of the provincial interests at large, they did consent, and by their action assured the improvement of the financial condition of the province. As soon as the vote had been registered, a most interesting parliamentary scene took place. The generosity of our representatives on this occasion, the public spirit exhibited by them, and their expressed confidence in the loyalty of their English and Protestant countrymen had made a deep impression on the minds of their fellow representatives, and one of these immediately arose, and amidst the enthusiasm of the moment, and on behalf of the English and Protestant population, on behalf of the province, he eulogised the Catholic and French population, and pledged his people and province that the rights and privileges of the Catholics would never be interfered with, and for doing so he was cheerfully applauded by the whole House. That man was Mr. Luxton, who is still living, and was then a prominent member in the Legislature. He, at least, I must say, used his best efforts to have this pledge faithfully kept, and I am happy to send to him from my seat in Parliament the expression of the gratitude of the people whose rights he has so vigorously defended. But I am sorry to say that, unlike the people of Quebec under similar circumstances, our Province of Manitoba, as a whole, has failed to honor itself as did the old province on the banks of the St. Lawrence; and since 1890 we have been deprived, by the will of the Legislature, notwithstanding that solemn pledge, of our most cherished rights and privileges, our schools, and the official use of our language."

It may be as well to recall the language of some of the leading men who took part in the debate preceding the passing of the Bill to abolish the Provincial Senate :—

THE PREMIER (Mr. Davis)—" It may be said that the Council is a safeguard to the minority. *He could assure the minority that their rights would never be trampled upon in this province.* There would always be sufficient English speaking members in this House, who would insist on giving their French fellow subjects their rights, to protect them."

MR. NORQUAY (afterwards Premier)—" In 1870 when the Dominion Government invested the people of this province with the responsibility of self-government, they gave them a constitution, which, in their belief, would meet the demands of those who had offered opposition to the inauguration of Canadian authority in this province. . . . There was a certain class of people in this province, who in the belief that they would soon be in the minority required the protection of the Upper House. . . . No doubt the time will come when the privilege claimed by those speaking the French language will be waived, but he, for his part, would never like to see them deprived of the privilege of speaking their language on the floor of the House, and in the Courts of Justice; and also of being able to make themselves acquainted with the laws of the country by reading them in their own language if they cannot read them otherwise."

MR. LUXTON (then and still a very influential journalist)—" There were some questions of sentiment which lay close to the hearts of the French people, and he could assure them that the English speaking members would not ruthlessly deal with these, if the French representatives were sufficiently patriotic to support the measure before the House. *They would recognize their generosity and not forget it.*"

MR. FRANK CORNISH (then a prominent lawyer) " believed the old settlers and the French would make a common cause if their rights were infringed upon; and he could assure them that when the Canadian (that is the English speaking) party became the great majority *it would not be found oppressive.* . . ."

These assurances were accepted in the spirit in which they were given, and without the slightest suspicion that they were to be so soon violated. Mr. Royal, always a leader among the French Catholics, after referring to the power of disallowance, said :—

" But there was something else, for himself, which had not been guaranteed by any Act; he found it yesterday in the remarks of the Hon. Messrs. Davis and Norquay, in the applause given by Mr. Brown to the sentiments of Mr. Luxton, and in the expressions of Mr. Cornish."

Mr. McKay said—"He was very much pleased to hear the generous and just remarks of the Hon. Premier, the Hon. Prov. Secretary, and also that of the Hon. member for Rockwood, which gave the minoity in the House that confidence which the members of this House, and by their vote on this Bill would express, *the security they felt in the hands of that majority.*"

Will you walk into my parlor ?
Said the spider to the fly.

2. *Promises of Liberal Party in 1888.* In a speech delivered by Mr. James Fisher, M.P.P., (a life-long Liberal) in the Manitoba Legislature (2nd March, 1893) may be found the following :—

"I now desire to speak of a delicate matter, which may be somewhat distasteful to some who hear me, but I am bound to tell the truth, even if it may offend some. *I make the grave charge, that this school legislation was put upon the statute book of this province in defiance of the most solemn pledges of the Liberal party.* In January of 1888, an event occurred which brought the Liberals into power in this province. My hon. friend had for years been engaged in an effort to defeat the Norquay government, in which I helped them all in my power, because we felt that it would be to the advantage of the province to have a change. The crisis came when the St. Francois Xavier election took place at the time I have mentioned. Dr. Harrison was at the time Premier of the province, and he chose as his Provincial Secretary Mr. Joseph Burke, who, though he bears an Irish name, is really a French Canadian. He was living among his own people in the district of St. Francois Xavier, and had been elected as a member of the House in 1886 by acclamation. On accepting the office he went back for re-election. It was proposed that we should oppose him, though for myself I thought it was useless. Mr. F. H. Francis, an English-speaking Presbyterian, and a son-in-law of the late Rev. Dr. Black, the great pioneer Presbyterian missionary of this country, was asked to take the field against Mr. Burke in this French constituency. He could not possibly be elected, unless he got a large proportion of the votes of the French population. Without this, I say, his election was an absolute impossibility. Now, I state, on information and belief, that Mr. Francis, when consulted by leading members of the Liberal party, and asked to accept the nomination, said he would not accept unless empowered to give the electors a pledge that if the Liberals got into office they would not interfere with the institutions of the French, their language, or their school laws. I am informed that he was authorized to make that promise, that he went to the electors and gave them the pledge. I did not know that of my own knowledge, but I knew from the newspaper reports, and from information brought to the Winnipeg Liberals, that strong speeches were being made by Mr. Burke and his friends in the riding, calling upon half-breeds and French Canadians to vote against the Liberal candidate, on the ground that Liberals would likely pass laws interfering with their institutions. It was said, "Are you going to put into power people, who, when they get into office, will legislate away your schools and your language?" and the electors were appealed to oppose Mr. Francis for that reason. *This became practically the leading question of that campaign, and the contest was a crucial one.* Should the Liberals win, it was plain, in view of the losses sustained by the government, that they must resign. So that the success of the Liberal candidate meant that the party would at once attain power, while the election of Mr. Burke would almost certainly have ensured the continuance of the Liberals in opposition till this day. It became necessary for the party leaders, therefore, to meet this appeal to the religious and race feelings of the French and half-breed voters—the pledge given by Mr.

Francis appearing to be insufficient to satisfy them. Now, the Liberals had a defined platform, and their views were well understood. Personally, I knew well what our policy was. Perhaps no one, apart from Mr. Greenway and Mr. Martin, was in a better position to know fully our attitude on these questions. There was no doubt about that attitude. There is no doubt we were denouncing the abuses of the Norquay government with regard to the French printing, the l rge amount of money expended; and the Liberals were determined, if the party came into power, that they would do away with those abuses; but the idea of interfering with rights guaranteed, or supposed to have been guaranteed by the constitution, had never been suggested. On the contrary, it had frequently been pointed out on the public platform by Liberal leaders that the institutions were protected, and that our remedy was in correcting abuses and not in abolishing institutions. It was promised that the expenses arising from the use of the French language would be cut down and the grant for education increased. No one had ever asked or suggested that we should go a step further. When the question about the Liberal policy became so prominent and urgent in St. Francois Xavier, I was consulted, with others, about it, and Mr. Martin was asked to go out and assist the candidate. I was told that he went out and attended a meeting, and I was told of promises he had publicly made, which were, to my knowledge, in accord with what was intended he should make. I went with him myself to a second meeting. It was a large gathering, mainly composed of French and half-breed Catholics. The same charges were made by Burke as to what the Liberals would do if in office. The same appeals were made to his countrymen and co-religionists to defeat Mr. Francis for that reason. Mr. Martin, in a powerful speech, denounced the statements of Burke and his friends as false. *He told the meeting that it had never been the policy of Liberals to interfere with the language or institutions of the French Catholic population, and he appealed to them to trust the Liberals, and to support their candidate.* At that time I was president of the Provincial Association of Liberals, and Mr. Martin referred to my presence at the meeting, and said I could put him right if he was wrong. He went further, and not only said that Liberals had no idea of interfering with their institutions, but *he gave a positive pledge, in the name of the Liberal party, that they would not do so.* I have always thought that the movement to establish the present school law, abolishing all Catholic schools, against the strong protest of the minority, was, under the circumstances, and in the face of that promise, a gross wrong. Personally, I made no promise, I felt as much bound by the pledge given as if I had given it myself."

And the poor fly walked in.

3. *Further promises of the Liberal Party in 1888.*

By means of the assurances just referred to the liberal party carried the election in St. Francois Xavier, and as a consequence Mr. Greenway, the liberal leader, was called upon to form a government. To assist him in the work he personally called upon His Grace, the Archbishop of St. Boniface. His Grace being unwell, the interview was had with Vicar-General Allard. Mr. Greenway proceeded to assure the Archbishop (through the Vicar-General) that he was in entire sympathy with him upon the two questions of Catholic schools, and French language (as well as the maintenance of the French electoral divisions); that it would be the policy of his government to maintain them inviolate; and he requested that His Grace would name some one who would be acceptable to his people as a member of the Cabinet. The Vicar-General at a subsequent interview, informed Mr. Greenway that His Grace was extremely gratified with his protestations of good-will, and that he believed that Mr. Prendergast had the confidence of the people. Mr. Greenway gave the same assurances to the Liberal French members of the House, and as a result he met the elections with Mr. Prendergast as a colleague, and various French Catholic candidates as followers. After the election it was found that *he had thus secured, as supporters, five out of the six French members,* and a large majority in the House."

And the door closed on the poor fly.

Proof of these facts. Besides the evidence of Mr. Fisher, already quoted, there have been published the two following statutory declarations:

"MANITOBA, COUNTY OF SELKIRK, TO WIT:

"I, the Very Rev. Joachim Allard, O.M.I., of the town of St. Boniface, in the province of Manitoba, Vicar-general of the archdiocese of St. Boniface, do solemnly declare:

"I am now, and was during all the year of our Lord one thousand eight hundred and eighty-eight, the Vicar-general of the said archdiocese of St. Boniface, having my residence in the episcopal residence at St. Boniface.

"I distinctly remember that during the early part of the said year of our Lord, one thousand eight hundred and eighty-eight, the Hon. Thos. Greenway, with whom I was not then personally acquainted, called at said episcopal residence in St. Boniface in the company of Mr. W. F. Alloway, whom I personally knew, and the said Mr. Alloway then introduced the said Hon. Thos. Greenway to me, and the said Mr. Greenway then stated to me that he had called to see His Grace the Archbishop personally, touching a confidential matter. His Grace was then sick and confined to his bed, and I so informed the said Mr. Greenway and stated to him that, as the Vicar-general of His Grace, I could receive any confidential communications, and communicate the same to His Grace; and I then assured him that he could rely upon my discretion in any confidential communication that he wished to make, and that His Grace the Archbishop would also respect his confidence.

"The Hon. Mr. Greenway then stated to me that he had been called to form a new government in this province, and that he was desirous to strengthen it by taking into his cabinet one of the French members of the legislature, who would be agreeable to the Archbishop; whereupon I remarked that I did not think that His Grace would favor any French member joining the new administration unconditionally, and without any previous understanding as to certain questions of great importance to His Grace. Mr. Greenway replied that he had already talked the matter over with his friends, and that he (Mr. Greenway) was quite willing to guarantee, under his government, the maintenance of the then existing condition of matters with regard—

1. To separate Catholic schools.
2. To the official use of the French language.
3. To the French electoral divisions.

"I received the assurances of the said Hon. Thomas Greenway as above stated to me, and I promised him that I would convey the same to His Grace the

Archbishop, and I further told him that I believed his assurances so made would give great satisfaction to His Grace.

"The said Hon. Thomas Greenway then proposed to come again on the following day, to receive an answer as to the nomination of the French member of his cabinet; but I told him that I would not put him to that inconvenience, but that I would meet him in Winnipeg on the following day for that purpose; and it was then agreed between myself and him, that such meeting should take place on the following morning in Mr. Alloway's office, at the hour of nine o'clock. This finished the first interview I had with the said Hon. Thomas Greenway.

"During all the time that elapsed between the introduction of Mr. Greenway and the end of the said interview, as above set out, and his departure from said residence on that day, Mr. W. F. Alloway was personally present and heard all that took place between the said Hon. Thomas Greenway and myself as above stated by me. In pursuance of my promise, I, on the said day of the interview, visited His Grace the Archbishop in his bedroom and reported to him fully and faithfully what had taken place at said interview.

His Grace expressed his satisfaction, and instructed me to answer the Honorable Thomas Greenway that he would throw no obstacle in the way of his administration, and that I could say to him that His Grace would have no objection to Mr. Prendergast being taken into the new cabinet as a French representative, and His Grace particularly requested me to convey to Mr. Greenway the satisfaction given him by the assurance and promise made to me by the said Mr. Greenway.

"On the following morning, in pursuance of the appointment so made, I attended at the office of Mr. Alloway in Winnipeg, and then, again, met the said Hon. Thomas Greenway, and I then communicated to him the message of His Grace, so entrusted to me as above set out, and Mr. Greenway then expressed to me his personal gratification at the said message and attitude of His Grace, and he then assured me that faith would be kept by his government with His Grace; and, then again, and in specific terms, repeated to me the assurance that

First—The Catholic separate schools;
Secondly—The official use of French language;
Third—The number of French constituencies; would not be disturbed during his administration.

"I had promised not to violate the confidence of the Hon. Mr. Greenway by disclosing the particulars of said promises and assurances by the said Mr. Greenway on the floor of the legislature, notwithstanding that he had violated the terms of the same before that time, and but for such open denial by him of such promises, and his mistatements of what took place, I would not have felt at liberty to now disclose the same.

"Mr. W. F. Alloway was present at his office during the second interview with said Hon. Thomas Greenway, as above set out, and remained in the room where we where closeted during much of the time during which said second interview lasted.

"And I make this solemn declaration conscientiously believing the same to be true and by virtue of the Act respecting extra judicial oaths.

J. ALLARD,
O.M.I., V.C.

"Declared before me at the Town of St. Boniface in the County of Selkirk, this 1st day of April, A.D., 1892.

ALEX. HAGGART,
A Commissioner in B.R., etc.

"I, William Forbes Alloway, of the City of Winnipeg, in the County of Selkirk, banker, do solemnly declare that I have seen and read the statutory declaration of the very Rev. Vicar General Allard, made before Alex. Haggart, a Commissioner of the B. R., etc., on this first day of April, A.D. 1892, and I say that I was present as therein stated by him, and I did on said first occasion introduce the Hon. Thos. Greenway to the Vicar General, and I say that the account of said interview, as set out in said declaration of the Vicar General, is true in substance and in fact.

"I was present at the whole of the said interview and heard all that transpired between the Vicar General and said Thos. Greenway.

"I further say that I was present at my banking office on the following day when the Vicar General and the said Hon. Thos. Greenway met according to appointment made the day previous, and I heard most of the interview which took place between them on that second day, and I say that the promises and pledges as set out in the Vicar General's said statement were repeated in the said second interview, and the said Greenway then expressed himself as very much gratified with the attitude assumed by His Grace the Archbishop towards his Government, and expressed such satisfaction not only then, but in my presence afterwards.

"And I make this solemn declaration, conscientiously believing the same to be true, and by virtue of the Act respecting extra-judicial oaths.

W. F. ALLOWAY.

"Declared before me this 1st day of April, 1792, at the City of Winnipeg, in the County of Selkirk, aforesaid.

J. STEWART TUPPER,
A Commissioner in B.R., etc."

All Compacts Broken—The assurances just referred to were given by the liberal leaders in 1888, and thereby they gained office and a majority.

In 1890 the same men crushed their fly—they passed the School Acts!

And thus the humiliating history of Protestant promises ends :—

In 1867, to the Province of Quebec—Let us form a Confederation —a Dominion! Have no fear. The rights of minorities shall be always safeguarded and protected. Rupert's Land and the North-Western Territory, should they join, are to be admitted, "on such terms and conditions, in each case, as are in the addresses expressed, and as the Queen thinks fit to approve, *subject to the provisions of this Act*,"*—minorities there, too, shall be justly dealt with.

In 1870, to the French Metis—Lay down your arms; join the Canadian Confederation. Your religion, your rights, your privileges will all be respected. "Right shall be done."

In 1876, to the French members of the Manitoba Legislature— Give up the Legislative Council, which is useful only as a constitutional check. You have nothing to fear. Your rights will "never be trampled on." The majority will never "be found oppressive."

Should you concede, you may be sure the majority will recognize your "generosity and never forget it."

In 1888 to the Electors of St. Francois Xavier :—Elect the Liberal candidate. We have no idea of interfering with Catholic institutions. We give you a "positive pledge in the name of the Liberal party, that we will not do so."

In 1888 to the Archbishop of St. Boniface, and the French candidates :—We are "willing to guarantee under our government the maintenance of the three existing conditions with regard (1) to separate Catholic schools ; (2) to the official use of the French language ; (3) to the French electoral divisions."

Two short years after the last of these solemn pledges, they are all torn to shreds and cast to the winds !

<blockquote>
Yes, yes ; his faith attesting nations own,
'Tis Punic all, and to a proverb known,
</blockquote>

Memory has dimmed the fitness of the word "Punic" to express the lowest possible depth of treachery and perfidy. For an appropriate substitute Canadians need search neither ancient history, nor modern geography.

Sidney Smith in 1827 closed his celebrated essay on "Catholics" with words which, sage and true then, have special application now. They shall close this work also :

"To the No-Popery Fool.

" You are made use of by men who laugh at you, and despise you for your folly and ignorance* ; and who, the moment it suits their purpose, will consent to emancipation of the Catholics, and leave you to roar and bellow No-Popery ! to vacancy and the moon.

"To the No-Popery Rogue.

" A shameful and scandalous game, to sport with the serious interests of the country, in order to gain some increase of public power !

"To the Honest No-Popery People.

" We respect you very sincerely—but are astonished at your existence.

"To the Catholics.

" Wait. Do not add to your miseries by a mad and desperate rebellion. Persevere in civil exertions, and concede all you can concede. All great alterations in human affairs are produced by compromise."

---

*Ignorance of this, namely, relating to the Catholic priesthood :—"No other body of men have ever exhibited a more single-minded and unworldly zeal, refracted by no personal interests, sacrificing to duty the dearest of earthly objects, and confronting with undaunted heroism every form of hardship, of suffering, and of death."—Lecky's History of European Morals, II., 335.

www.ingramcontent.com/pod-product-compliance
Lightning Source LLC
Chambersburg PA
CBHW032145010526
44111CB00035B/1213